THINKING ABOUT PROPERTY

In this book Professor Garnsey explores ancient 'foundational' texts relating to property and their reception by later thinkers in their various contexts up to the early nineteenth century. The texts include Plato's vision of an ideal polity in the *Republic*, Jesus' teachings on renunciation and poverty, and Golden Age narratives and other evolutionary accounts of the transition of mankind from primeval communality to regimes of ownership. The issue of the legitimacy of private ownership exercises the minds of the major political thinkers as well as theologians and jurists throughout the ages. Among those whose ideas are woven into the discussion are Plato, Aristotle, Cicero, Jesus, Augustine, Thomas Aquinas, Bartolus, William of Ockham, Plethon of Mistra, Grotius, Pufendorf, Locke, Hume, Rousseau, Kant, Hegel and Proudhon. The book gives full consideration to the historical development of Rights Theory, with special reference to the right to property. It challenges the dominant historical paradigm that the ancient world made little or no contribution to Rights Theory. The book ends with a comparative study of the Declarations of Rights in the American and French Revolutions and seeks to explain, with reference to contemporary documents, why the French recognized an inalienable, human right to property whereas the Americans did not.

PETER GARNSEY is Director of Research in the Faculty of History at the University of Cambridge, having previously been Professor of the History of Classical Antiquity. His recent books include *Ideas of Slavery from Aristotle to Augustine* (1996), *Food and Society in Classical Antiquity* (1999), (with Caroline Humfress) *The Evolution of the Late Antique World* (2001) and (with Anthony Bowen) a translation, with introduction and notes, of Lactantius' *Divine Institutes* (2003).

IDEAS IN CONTEXT

Edited by
Quentin Skinner and James Tully

The books in this series will discuss the emergence of intellectual traditions and of related new disciplines. The procedures, aims and vocabularies that were generated will be set in the context of the alternatives available within the contemporary frameworks of ideas and institutions. Through detailed studies of the evolution of such traditions, and their modification by different audiences, it is hoped that a new picture will form of the development of ideas in their concrete contexts. By this means, artificial distinctions between the history of philosophy, of the various sciences, of society and politics, and of literature may be seen to dissolve.

The series is published with the support of the Exxon Foundation.

A list of books in the series will be found at the end of the volume.

THINKING ABOUT PROPERTY

From Antiquity to the Age of Revolution

PETER GARNSEY

University of Cambridge

CAMBRIDGE
UNIVERSITY PRESS

CAMBRIDGE UNIVERSITY PRESS
Cambridge, New York, Melbourne, Madrid, Cape Town, Singapore, São Paulo

Cambridge University Press
The Edinburgh Building, Cambridge CB2 8RU, UK

Published in the United States of America by Cambridge University Press, New York

www.cambridge.org
Information on this title: www.cambridge.org/9780521876773

First published 2007

Printed in the United Kingdom at the University Press, Cambridge

A catalogue record for this publication is available from the British Library

ISBN 978-0-521-87677-3 hardback
ISBN 978-0-521-70023-8 paperback

To

R. G.   R. G.   C. H.

Contents

Abbreviations	*page* viii	
Preface	ix	
Introduction	1	
1	Plato's 'communism', Aristotle's critique and Proclus' response	6
2	Plato's 'communism': from late antiquity via Islamic Spain to the Renaissance	31
3	Renunciation and communality: thinking through the primitive Church	59
4	The poverty of Christ: crises of asceticism from the Pelagians to the Franciscans	84
5	The state of nature and the origin of private property: Hesiod to William of Ockham	107
6	The state of nature and the origin of private property: Grotius to Hegel	136
7	Property as a legal right	177
8	Property as a human right	204
Conclusion	233	
Bibliography	238	
Index	262	

Abbreviations

AARC	*Atti dell' Accademia Romanistica Costantiniana*
AFLN	*Annali della Facoltà di Lettere e Filosofia di Napoli*
AJPh	*American Journal of Philology*
ANRW	*Aufstieg und Niedergang der römischen Welt*
CJ	*Codex Iustinianus*
CQ	*Classical Quarterly*
CSEL	*Corpus Scriptorum Ecclesiasticorum Latinorum*
CTh.	*Codex Theodosianus*
GCS	*Die griechischen christlichen Schriftsteller der ersten drei Jahrhunderte*
IJ	*Institutes of Justinian*
JbAC	*Jahrbuch für Antike und Christentum*
JRS	*Journal of Roman Studies*
JTS	*Journal of Theological Studies*
OSAP	*Oxford Studies in Ancient Philosophy*
PG	J. P. Migne, *Patrologiae cursus completus: Series Graeca*, Paris 1857–66
PL	J. P. Migne, *Patrologia Latina*, Paris 1841–55
REG	*Revue des études grecques*
RHD	*Revue Historique de Droit Français et Etranger*
RIDA	*Revue Internationale des Droits de l'Antiquité*
RISG	*Rivista Italiana per le Scienze Giuridiche*
SC	*Sources Chrétiennes*
SDHI	*Studia et Documenta Historiae et Iuris*
SP	*Studia Patristica*
St. Mon.	*Studia Monastica*
TAPA	*Transactions of the American Philological Association*
ZSS	*Zeitschrift der Savigny-Stiftung für Rechtsgeschichte*

Preface

This book has its origin in the Carlyle Lectures delivered at Oxford University in Hilary Term 2005. I would like to thank George Garnett and the other members of the Carlyle Committee for honouring me with their invitation to give the lectures, and the Warden and Fellows of All Souls College for extending to me their hospitality for the period concerned. I benefited greatly from discussing matters arising from the lectures with members of the audience during my time in Oxford. In composing a work of this kind, I have inevitably drawn on the learning of a large number of scholars who have written extensively and expertly in aspects of my subject. In addition, colleagues and friends have generously read my work or parts of it in draft and given me encouragement and advice. They include Margaret Atkins, Tim Blanning, Anthony Bowen, Peter Brown, Myles Burnyeat, Luigi Capogrossi Colognesi, Patricia Crone, John Crook, Michael Frede, Raymond Geuss, Richard Gordon, Verity Harte, Caroline Humfress, David Ibbetson, Melissa Lane, Geoffrey Lloyd, John Marenbon, Dieter Nörr, Michael O'Brien, Glenn Olsen, Christopher Rowland, Magnus Ryan, Malcolm Schofield, David Sedley, Quentin Skinner, Gareth Stedman Jones, John Thompson, Robert Tombs and Frank Walbank. I owe a special debt of gratitude to Raymond Geuss, Richard Gordon and Caroline Humfress for raising my sights and lifting my spirits. Niketas Siniossoglou has given me invaluable assistance in the closing stages. My family has been as usual tolerant, patient and supportive.

There were six lectures in the first instance. They have been expanded and two new chapters added (6 and 8). The book now consists of four pairs of chapters corresponding to four main themes. I hope that readers who were also members of the audience will agree that the changes form a natural and logical development of the original lectures.

Two days before I delivered my typescript to the Press the state of Virginia issued an apology for the enslavement of Africans and the exploitation of native Americans by the country's white settlers. It will be interesting to see whether this event, which might be expected to be replicated by some other American states, will revive interest in the significant decision of Thomas Jefferson, a slaveowner and landowner, not to include property among the inalienable and natural rights of man in his draft of the Declaration of Independence, which was later ratified by Congress in July 1776. The issue of the legitimacy of private property, its acquisition and its retention, which has troubled the human mind for over two millennia, has not gone away.

Introduction

The defence of private property has been a feature of philosophical, theological and legal discourse from antiquity to the present day. This book seeks to explore the ancient 'foundational' texts concerning ideas of property and their reception up to the early nineteenth century. I begin with Plato's thoughts on property in the *Republic* as expressed in his vision of the ideal polity, or Kallipolis. Other texts or foundation narratives include New Testament passages on the community of the first Christians at Jerusalem and the poverty of Christ and his apostles, and a collection of texts on primeval humanity drawn from a variety of literary works. But in addition to examining the various discussions relating to property and property regimes, I set out to challenge the dominant historical paradigm that the ancient world made little, or in some accounts no, contribution to Rights Theory, and in particular to the right to private property.

I am particularly interested in the confrontation that occurs in the works of philosophers, theologians and jurists, and other literary genres, between regimes of sharing of one sort or another and private property regimes, and I study the ways in which the themes of the origin of private property, and the transition to private property from primitive communality (as I call it), are handled by authors from antiquity to the Age of Revolution and the immediately following decades.

In contemplating this enterprise I have found reassuring and at the same time cautionary words in John Dunn's essay 'The History of Political Theory'.[1] He talks of four different kinds of questions 'that appropriately arise in attempts to understand the history of political theory'. The first two questions are: 'What did the author mean by his or her text?' and 'What does that text show us about the author's own society?' Question four is: 'What does the text in question mean for us, today?' It is question three

---

[1] Dunn (1996), ch. 2, at 24–5.

I

that especially interests me: 'What has this text meant to others, reading it then and subsequently, and why has it meant that and not something else?' Dunn explains:

Every great text (like any other human action) has an occasion – something which prompted it. But unlike most human actions, great texts also have a protracted and differentiated fate. That fate often stands (and indeed perhaps always stands) in a somewhat ironical relation to its author's original intentions. But its very scope and variety are themselves a tribute to the unsteady but urgent power of the text itself.

Dunn enthuses about this approach: 'The fate of great texts', he says, 'could be immensely fascinating, as well as exceptionally illuminating.' He goes on to issue the warning that such a project would be intimidating, because brutally labour-intensive.

Dunn's third question is effectively my question. It is of course essential that I study any given text itself, situate it within a contemporary context, and pay attention to the conditions (within the 'horizons of the possible') which framed its production. But I also want to see what happens to the ideas set out in the original texts as they come into the hands of other thinkers, and I want to follow those thinkers as they twist and turn them to suit their own interests. For we can be sure that the History of Ideas is not reducible to the study of supposedly fixed and unchanging concepts or ideas over time, shorn of the successive contexts in which they appear. In different periods, different perceptions produce more or less subtly different treatments of what is widely regarded as a central issue in social and moral life: property – its origins, legitimacy and status.

I take first Plato's concept of communality as set out in some detail in the *Republic* and more briefly in the *Timaeus*, *Critias* and *Laws*. I ask (in Chapters 1 and 2) how his ideas fared at the hands of selected succeeding thinkers: Aristotle, Proclus the late antique Neoplatonist, Averroes the Aristotelian commentator of Islamic Medieval Spain, and sundry Christian humanists of Platonic persuasion in the Quattrocento. I end my survey with two writers who drew inspiration from Plato, Gemistus Plethon of Mistra (first half of the fifteenth century) and Thomas More. How Plato's ideas 'fared' is an appropriate way to put it, as, beginning with Aristotle, commentators gave Platonic communality a meaning that Plato had not intended. The nature of the arrangements that Plato through Socrates imposes on the leadership of the city, that is, the Guards and Auxiliaries, has been misunderstood, so that what is in fact a regime of denial, both of private property and of individual family, has been read as a sharing of property and family. Such a regime, in the eyes of a number of modern commentators, is properly characterized as 'communistic', to my mind erroneously. What is more, Plato's prescriptions for the governing classes are generalized by later thinkers (with a few exceptions) to apply to the whole city.

In Chapter 3 I consider the nature of the first Christian community at Jerusalem as presented in Acts of the Apostles 2 and 4–5. The first Christians are said to have renounced private property and practised community of goods. These texts gave rise, in curious circumstances involving a deliberate misreading by Eusebius the ecclesiastical historian of an account of certain Jewish ascetic groups by the Hellenized Jew Philo, to a model or myth of the *ecclesia primitiva*. I trace through to the fourteenth century the rich and varied history of this model, as it was brought into service in the context of various reformist movements within the Church. It is a history which highlights Christianity's ambivalence between radical world-rejection and desire for this-worldly power.

In Chapter 4 I look sideways at another, analytically distinct, foundation narrative of New Testament origin, which I call the *vita apostolica*, this being shorthand for the story of Christ, his words and his lifestyle, and that of his apostles. I show how the texts which advocate the renunciation of property and the embracing of poverty proved inspiring but also controversial within Christianity; and further, how these same texts had an unexpected impact on the development of Rights Theory in the late Middle Ages, in the context of the Franciscan poverty dispute of the late thirteenth and early fourteenth centuries.

'By the law of nature everything was in common.' So Gratian wrote in his *Harmony of the Discordant Canons*, or *Decretum*, an authoritative and highly influential digest of Canon Law published in Bologna in around 1140. The principle enunciated by Gratian had its origin in the myth of the Golden Age, which can be traced back in literature to the Greek poet Hesiod of the eighth century BC. Thereafter it passed through different readings and interpretations at the hands of poets, philosophers and theologians of antiquity, the Middle Ages and beyond. Gratian presented the communal/private dichotomy in such a way as to raise very sharply the matter of the legitimacy of private property. He caused additional anxieties among canon lawyers and theologians by illustrating the above dictum with reference to both Plato's *Republic* and the Acts of the Apostles, and in such a way as to suggest that the regimes of communality set out therein were similar. In Chapters 5 and 6 I look at the ways in which the theme of communality is treated in discussions of the primitive or natural state of man, in classical pagan literature, in Christian writings of late antiquity and the Middle Ages, and in the works of philosophers and jurists in the seventeenth, eighteenth and early nineteenth centuries. I am particularly interested in the way the issue of the legitimacy of private ownership is handled in the context of discussions of first acquisition and the transition from the state of nature to civil society.

In Chapter 7 I consider a view that is widespread among modern historians of political thought and philosophers of law that the ancient world made no contribution to Rights Theory, in other words, that in this sphere at any rate there was an absence of foundation texts and authoritative authors coming through from antiquity. I argue that this view is mistaken. Focusing on the Roman juristic tradition as preserved in the emperor Justinian's sixth-century *Corpus* of Civil Law, but adducing additional evidence from other literature and from inscriptions, I show that the Romans had a very clear concept of positive legal rights, or rights that people can actually exercise as full members of a given society. In the Roman case these were rights held under the *ius civile*, Roman civil law, by Roman citizens *qua* citizens. Such rights included the right to own property according to Roman law. If my argument is correct, there are important consequences for the history of Rights Theory. Specifically, a reassessment is required of the precise contribution in the evolution of that theory, and of the right to property in particular, made by lawyers and philosophers operating in the Romanist tradition from medieval times to the Age of Revolution.

In Chapter 8 I sketch the history of natural or human rights, as distinct from the legal rights that were the subject of Chapter 7, from the twelfth century to the end of the eighteenth, with special reference to the natural right to property. In this case a formative stage in antiquity does appear to be lacking. I consider the hypothesis that slavery made it impossible, intellectually and in practice, for ancient societies to conceive of rights accruing to individuals as human beings, and more particularly human or natural rights to liberty and to property. Although ancient societies may not have had the concept of natural rights themselves, they did provide a platform upon which such a concept could be constructed in a favourable intellectual and cultural context. Such a context was provided by the rediscovery of Justinian's law books (around 1070) and Gratian's codification of canon law (around 1140), which coincided with a more general movement of cultural renaissance and renewal. The reception of natural law theory from antiquity – first systematized by the Stoics, subsequently transmitted to the Middle Ages in Christian dress – is particularly worthy of attention. It was from natural law theory that a fledgling natural rights theory was derived. The first natural right to see the light of day was the right to life, or self-preservation. In a brief case-study I show how this right emerged as a spin-off from the Christian doctrine of charity and then held its own as the primary natural right (and in the eyes of some thinkers, the only natural right) through to the eighteenth century. It did so rather at the expense of a natural right to property. Canonist lawyers fought hard for such a right, but at best secured for it the status of a natural but 'adventitious' or 'relative' right. And so it remained (at best) in the canonist tradition – whereas in the Romanist tradition, represented notably by the distinguished humanist jurist Donellus, an older con- temporary of Grotius, property remained a legal right. It was John Locke who put the right to property on a pedestal, entailed by the primary rights to life and liberty. In the Revolutionary Age the French accorded property the status of an inalienable right of man, the Americans did not. Politics played a crucial part in both decisions. But political philosophy also made a contribution. Jefferson was influenced by the natural law tradition which gave the status of a natural right but of a lower order. It was the French who proved themselves the true Lockeans.

CHAPTER I

Plato's 'communism', Aristotle's critique and Proclus' response

INTRODUCTION

Plato's ideal polity, or Kallipolis, is often characterized as a communistic society, in part or as a whole. Communism has been recently defined in this way:

[Communism is] the belief that society should be organized without private property, all productive property being held communally, publicly or in common. A communistic system is one based on a community of goods. It is generally presented as a positive alternative to competition, a system which is thought to divide people; communism is expected to draw people together and to create a community. In most cases the arguments for communism advocate replacing competition with cooperation either for its own sake or to provide a goal such as equality, or to free specific groups of people to serve a higher ideal such as the state or God.

The author proceeds to apply this (perfectly acceptable) definition to the ideal polity of the *Republic*: 'The idea of communism as collectively owned property first appears in classical Greece. Plato's *Republic* contains a notable defence.'[1]

This claim is mistaken. There is no collective or communal ownership of property in the ideal state of the *Republic*. Rather, Plato has Socrates prescribe for the political leadership and military (the Guards and Auxiliaries) an *absence* of property (coupled with a denial of individual families), or, to view it from a more positive angle, a community of use and a community of minds, involving the sharing of basic accommodation and subsistence, women and children, feelings and emotions. These arrangements coexist with, and are materially dependent upon, a private property regime enjoyed by a separate class of producers. No proprietor

---

[1] Sargent (1998).

6

can own very much, as there are to be no extremes of wealth and poverty in this community. I will call this polity Kallipolis A (or KA).[2]

But perhaps the ideal polity that is sketched out in the late (and unfinished) dialogue, the *Laws*, is more appropriately viewed as 'communistic'. At first sight it does look a more deserving candidate. As described, this time not by Socrates, but by an anonymous Athenian, it is characterized by the sharing of property and other possessions, along with wives and children *throughout the city*. I will call this polity Kallipolis B (or KB). KB actually figures relatively little in the very considerable literature on Plato's property arrangements, from his own time to the present day. From time to time the matter of its relation to the regime of the *Republic* has been raised; in fact the case that it represents a different and distinct regime from that of the *Republic* has been made again only recently.[3] The alternative, for which I will argue, is that it is more or less a restatement of the regime of the *Republic*. If this is right, then the property regime implied in KB will be no more communistic than that of Kallipolis A (KA).

After giving an airing (and no more) to KB, Plato confesses that it is for gods or sons of gods rather than humans, and moves on to the second-best city of the *Laws*, Magnesia. Magnesia, incidentally, is clearly not communistic, because Plato has given it a private property regime, albeit one in which control of property is not absolute. In this polity the 5,040 citizens or heads of families are allowed their own possessions as well as wives and children. Their property holdings are restricted in the cause of preventing extremes of poverty and wealth – an end shared with KA. Some land is held in common for the provision of public meals and religious sacrifices.

As I've said, the author of the dictionary definition is simply in error in saying that Plato sets out a defence for 'collectively owned property' in the *Republic*, with the implication that KA is such a regime. At least the mistake in this case can be picked up, because the author has stated what he takes communism to be. It is much more common for the term to be applied without an accompanying definition, and one is left to wonder whether it is being used strictly, to refer to communal ownership, or loosely, in some weaker sense. One suspects that for many, 'communist' or 'communistic' functions as a kind of umbrella term which can in principle be applied to a whole range of property regimes characterized by some sort of sharing or having in common, whether or not ownership of

---

[2] Plato calls his ideal state Kallipolis in *Rep.* 527c.   [3] Laks (2000); (2001); Bobonich (2002).

productive property is involved.[4] Such an all-encompassing definition of communism (whether stated or, more usually, implied) is unhelpful and misleading. There is a case for an all-inclusive and flexible term, but to use communism in this way is to court confusion. For want of a better term, I employ 'communality'.[5] Unlike communism, communality does not come already armed with a precise meaning. Nor, for that matter, again unlike communism, does it carry ideological baggage or historical specificity which can make its use problematic.[6] Whatever term is employed, it is crucial that its use should be accompanied by close analysis (preferably with a comparative dimension) of the nature of any particular property arrangements, and must not be taken as a substitute for such an analysis.[7]

If I appear insistent on the matter of terminological precision, it is because I have become aware that Plato's thoughts on property have suffered from misreading of various kinds over the centuries. The process predates the introduction of the word 'communism' in the nineteenth century. It begins with Aristotle, Plato's most distinguished pupil, according to whom Socrates in the *Republic* prescribed the sharing of property, women and children throughout Kallipolis. I devote the last part of this chapter and the whole of the next to following the destiny of Plato's thoughts on property as they were subjected to interpretation, simplification and manipulation at the hands of a chain of commentators from the fourth century BC to the fifteenth century AD, from Aristotle to Marsilio Ficino, the leading Platonist of the Italian Renaissance.[8]

---

[4] So Mayhew (1993b), 313, n. 3: 'When I speak of a city or class being communist, under communism, etc., I mean that at least in some area, in some way, the citizens share, own, or have something significant and typically private (namely women or property) in common.' Mayhew is exceptional in defining his terms.

[5] Burnyeat (1999) uses 'communality' for the arrangements for property and family in Kallipolis.

[6] I do not exclude the use of 'communism' with reference to periods (historical or imaginary) earlier than the nineteenth century, where communal ownership of property is involved. It is to be noted however that (to the best of my knowledge) Marx does not use the term communism when he talks of 'archaic' or tribal communal property regimes in which production and appropriation were collective, e.g. in his *Precapitalist Economic Formations*. On the concepts of positive and negative community as developed by Pufendorf in the seventeenth century for property arrangements in the state of nature, see Chapters 5 and 6 below. Whereas Hont and Ignatieff (2005) are rightly content to use this terminology, Waldron (1988) talks in terms of 'communism', 'primitive' or 'original', even in the case where this term might mean 'nothing more than an absence of private property rights in resources when they were created' (148–57, at 149).

[7] Thus Mayhew (1993a, b); (1997) applies the term 'communism' to the property regime of the *Republic* without describing the precise nature of that regime. The same is true of the otherwise useful discussion of Dawson (1992a).

[8] For the later reception of Plato, see e.g. Burnyeat (1998); Lane (2001), with bibl.

Plato was not an entirely innocent party in all of this. His discussion of the property issue is not clear-cut and unambiguous, and, as Aristotle complained, lacks detail. Aristotle says this, however, of the ideal polity of the *Republic* (KA), not that of the *Laws* (KB). The fleeting glimpse that Plato gives us of KB is so generalized, that it is an open question whether it is a version of KA or should be credited with independent status. I will argue that the former is the case. The account provided of KA is itself not without its ambiguities, notably where tension surfaces between the principle of reciprocity (introduced at the outset at 369b and implying social differentiation) and the ideal of unity. I regard it as significant that *the same equivocations* characterize Plato's presentation of KA and KB.

It is time for us to turn to the texts, paying special attention to those relating to the property regimes of the ideal polities of the *Republic* and the *Laws*. In this and the following chapter I will have little to say about Magnesia, the second-best city of the *Laws*. This is not because it was insignificant in later times. To pick out three examples from different epochs, it is clear that Magnesia was important to Aristotle, Plotinus and James Harrington. Aristotle's own ideal polity as outlined in the later books of the *Politics* draws heavily on the Platonic model. He, like Plato, allows private ownership of property within limits imposed in terms of amount of land, location and rights accruing to owners. In the mid-third century AD the Neoplatonist philosopher Plotinus tried to interest the Roman emperor Gallienus in the foundation of a Platonopolis in Campania whose constitution would be based on Magnesia and its 5,040 citizens and heads of families. His biographer and pupil Porphyry complains that the proposal was blocked by jealous opposition at court.[9] The influence of Magnesia on James Harrington's *Oceana* (1656) is patent, especially with regard to agrarian arrangements.[10] However, it is the property regime of the *Republic* which has been most clearly associated with the name of Plato and has made the greatest impact in the History of Ideas.

THE BEST CITY OF THE *REPUBLIC*: PROPERTY ARRANGEMENTS

In Book Three Plato sets out how the Guards who will govern his ideal city are to be chosen, and outlines an educational programme for them and for the Auxiliaries from whom the Guards are drawn. That done, all

---

[9] Porphyry, *Life of Plotinus* 12.   [10] See recently Nelson (2004), ch. 3, esp. 116–17.

is in readiness for the founding of the city. A suitable location is chosen and sacrifices are made to the gods. The first matter of substance is introduced: the accommodation of the Guards. This leads immediately to a statement on property (416d–417b):

The Guards should be furnished with housing and a general standard of living which will not hinder them from becoming the best possible Guards, and which will give them no encouragement to do wrong in their dealings with the rest of the citizens ... In the first place, no one is to have any private property, beyond what is absolutely essential.[11] Secondly, no one is to have the kind of house or store room which cannot be entered by anyone who feels like it. For their subsistence, which should meet the needs of self-disciplined and courageous warrior-athletes, they should impose a levy on the rest of the citizens, and receive an annual payment for their role as Guards which leaves them with neither a surplus nor a deficiency.

Plato goes on to forbid the Guards gold and silver and to give the general rationale for this regime, which is to ensure the safety of the Guards and of the city. Only by depriving themselves of land, houses and money can the Guards truly perform their role as Guards. 'Once they start acquiring their own land, houses, and money, they will have become householders and farmers instead of Guards.' In this way too they will escape the enmities that inevitably arise between people with property, and the city will not be torn apart by civil strife, stasis, the curse of Greek civic life.

Plato returns to the property arrangements of the Guards in Book Five.[12] In the meantime he has given an exposition of the Guards' regime, including the sharing of women and children. He sets out the rationale and purpose for denying the Guards their own families, which are the same, he says, for the denial of property, now expressly linked to the family regime for the first time. The passage runs as follows (462–4, in part):

'If we want to settle this, isn't it a good starting-point to ask ourselves what is the greatest good we can think of in the organization of our city – the thing the lawgiver should be aiming at as he frames his laws – and what is the greatest evil? Then we can ask "Do the proposals we have just described match the features of this good? Do they fail to match the features of this evil?" '
'Yes, that's the best possible starting-point', he said.
'Well then, can we think of any greater evil for a city than what tears it apart and

---

[11] This must mean personal effects, basic clothing and so on, not productive property. Later, the Guards are said to possess only their bodies (464d9).
[12] There is a further, brief, summary at the beginning of Book Eight at 543a–c2.

turns it into many cities instead of one? Or any greater good than what unites it and makes it one?'

'No, we can't.'

'Is it community of pleasure and pain which unites it, when as far as possible all the citizens are equally affected by joy or grief over any particular gain or loss?'

'It certainly is.'

'And is individual variation in these feelings divisive? Things happen to the city or to its inhabitants which make some people distraught and others delighted?'

'Of course it's divisive.'

'Is this because words like "mine" and "not mine" are not applied by people in the city to the same things? The same with "somebody else's"?'

'It certainly is.'

'Does that mean the best-regulated city is the one in which the greatest number of people use this phrase "mine" or "not mine" in the same way about the same thing?'

'Much the best.'

'And the one which is most like an individual person? Take the example of someone hurting his finger. It is the whole community extending through the body and connecting with the soul ... This entire community notices the hurt and together feels the pain of the part that hurts ... '

'When anything at all – good or bad – happens to one of its citizens, a city of this kind will be most inclined to say that what is affected is a part of itself. The whole city will rejoice together or grieve together.'

. . .

'Then will our citizens, more than any others, hold one and the same thing – which they will call "mine" – in common? And because they feel the same about it, will they feel the greatest community of pain and pleasure?'

'Yes, much the greatest.'

'And the reason for this, over and above the general organization of the city, is the business of women and children being in common among our Guards?'

'Yes, that's the main reason,' he said. 'Far more important than anything else.'

'But we also agreed that this is the greatest good for a city. We said a well-regulated city was like a body in the way it relates to the pain or pleasure of one of its parts.'

'Rightly.'

'In which case the greatest good of our city has been proved to result from women and children being in common among the defenders of our people.'

'Precisely.'

'This of course ties in with what we said originally. Our view was, I think, that if they were going to be true Guards they should not have private houses, or land, or property of any kind, but that they should receive their livelihood from the other citizens as payment for their Guardship, and all make use of these resources jointly.'

'It was. And we were correct.'

'Well, then, as I say, won't these arrangements we agreed earlier, when combined

with these present ones, be even more effective in turning them into true
Guards? Won't it make them give the name "mine" to the same things, rather
than all applying it to different things and so tearing the city apart?'
. . .
'How about lawsuits and prosecutions directed at one another? Won't these
virtually disappear among them, since they have no private property apart from
their own bodies, everything else being held in common? Won't this free them
from all the disputes people run into through the possession of money, children
and families?'
'Yes, they will be absolutely certain to be rid of those.'

The property arrangements can be summarized in this way. The Guards
who govern and control the city do not collectively own, work, and enjoy
the fruit of the resources of the community. The only material resources
to which they have access are provided by others: they receive payment
(*misthos*) towards their livelihood from the rest of the citizenry, and they
are provided with housing in the form of barracks, in return for their
services to the city. This is in effect a tax regime. There is no question of
ownership, quite the contrary: there is an *absence* of ownership; at most,
there is limited common use; the Guards are said to share resources and
to eat and live together.[13] (In the same way their family life embodies the
principle of community of use; there is an *absence* of individual marital
and parental relationships and rights.) Jeremy Waldron in *The Right to
Property* has it just right. He says: 'Plato believes that in an ideal state land
will be owned privately by farmers; the farmers will provide produce to
the Guards as a class and it will be consumed by them in common.'[14]
Communism, with its implications of common or collective ownership,
is not a suitable word for these arrangements. Plato's favoured words
koinonia, *koinon*, etc., do not for him entail ownership, and should not
be translated as if they do.[15] In Aristotle's discussion of property (to be
treated below) the situation is more complex, in that he uses the same
terminology but in a wider range of senses and applications.[16] As already
indicated I prefer to employ a term such as 'communality', which is both
neutral and flexible, for property regimes that involve sharing or holding
in common in one way or another, and to reserve the term 'communist'

---

[13] 464c2: 'koinei pantas analiskein'; 458c3–4: 'oikias te kai sussitia koina echontes'.
[14] Waldron (1988), 7. However, in reporting Hegel's critical attitude to Plato, Waldron treats the
regime of the Guards as an example of a 'communist Utopia' (345–6); and see n. 6, above.
[15] In the translation of T. Griffith at 464d9 'ta d'alla koina' is rendered 'everything else is jointly
owned.'
[16] In Aristotle a polity, a polis (both institutions and site), women and children, and property can all
be *koinon* – and property which is *koinon* can be either used or owned in common.

or 'communistic' for those which actually involve common or collective ownership. This should help us avoid the confusion that sometimes occurs when the property arrangements of Plato's *Republic* are compared with others, such as the regime envisaged in Thomas More's *Utopia*. Of the two, only the latter can be called communistic. It would be inaccurate to say that More's property system in *Utopia* was similar to Plato's in the *Republic*, even if More himself thought it was (since he believed that Plato had abolished private property entirely in his polity). It would also be erroneous to say that More's *Utopia* involved an extension of Plato's arrangements for the Guards to the whole of the citizenry.

If Kallipolis A, the best city of the *Republic*, is not communistic, what about Kallipolis B, the best city of the *Laws*?

THE BEST CITY IN THE *LAWS*: PROPERTY ARRANGEMENTS

The *Laws* was composed shortly before Plato's death at the age of about seventy-five, perhaps two decades after he published the *Republic*. In between come two substantial treatises in which property is touched on, the *Timaeus* and the *Critias* (of which only a small part survives), neither precisely dated.

The *Timaeus* summarizes the arrangements for the *Republic* (17C–19A), with the difference that the polity is in two parts not three, the Guards having been absorbed back into the warrior class from which, in the *Republic*, they came. In the *Critias* Plato conjures up a primeval Athens organized and supervised by the tutelary gods, Hephaistus and Athena. The earliest Athenians, in his imagination, enjoyed a regime constructed precisely on the lines of KA:

Now at that time there dwelt in this land not only the other classes of the citizens who were occupied in the handcrafts and in the raising of food from the soil, but also the military class, who had been separated off at the commencement by divine heroes, and dwelt apart. It was supplied with all that was required for its sustenance and training, and none of its members possessed any private property, but they regarded everything they had as common to all; and from the rest of the citizens they claimed to receive nothing beyond a sufficiency of sustenance; and they practised all those pursuits that were mentioned yesterday [i.e., in the *Republic*] in the description of our Guards ... In this fashion they dwelt, acting as guardians of their own citizens and as leaders, by their own consent, of the rest of the Greeks ... [They were] famous through all Europe and Asia, both for their bodily beauty and for the perfection of their moral excellence, and were of all men living the most renowned.[17]

---

[17] *Critias* 110c–d; cf. 112d–e.

Plato, then, was still working with the property arrangements envisaged in the *Republic*. Moreover, the passage in the *Critias* gives these arrangements a Golden-Age tinge. It is clear, then, that there is nothing ephemeral about that model; Plato is thoroughly committed to it. This makes it less likely that the first-choice city in the *Laws*, or KB, is significantly different from KA. Still, KB looks different. The passage in the *Laws* runs as follows:

That city and polity come first, and those laws are best, where there is observed as carefully as possible *throughout the whole city* the old saying that 'friends have all things in common'. As to this condition – whether it anywhere exists now or ever will exist – in which there is community of wives, children, and all possessions, and all that is called private is *everywhere and by every means* rooted out of our life, and so far as possible it is contrived that even things naturally 'private' have become in a way 'shared' – eyes, for instance, and ears and hands seem to see, hear and act in common – and that *all men* are, as far as possible, unanimous in the praise and blame they bestow, rejoicing and grieving at the same things, and that they honour with all their heart those laws which render *the city* as unified as possible – no one will ever lay down another definition that is truer or better than these conditions in point of super-excellence. In such a city – *be it gods or sons of gods that dwell in it* – they dwell pleasantly, living such a life as this. So one should not look elsewhere for a model constitution, but hold fast to this one, and with all one's power seek the constitution that is as like to it as possible. (739B–D)

In contrast with KA, KB is a polity in which, apparently, *all* its members are subject to the same sharing regime, a regime which embraces property as well as women and children. Plato, the argument goes, has 'moved on', rejecting the earlier model of the *Republic*. He had come to realize and accept that KA was unrealistic and stood no chance of being put into practice. He therefore opted for a different strategy: that of presenting his first choice polity in a more extreme form (KB), admitting its unfeasibility – by characterizing it as a polity 'for gods or sons of gods' – and concentrating his attention on the detailed exposition of a new, second-best polity (Magnesia).

But not so fast: the first-choice polity of the *Laws*, KB, is quite without distinguishing features. Plato tells us nothing about it, beyond the generalization that all is shared throughout the city. There is nothing about social, economic, cultural or political arrangements. What if anything has survived from KA? Were there Guards, even, in KB? We are not informed. We cannot know for sure what Plato might have had in mind, how he would have filled out the picture, supposing he had wanted to. We are left to conjecture. There are several theoretical possibilities.

First, maybe Plato had in mind an expansion of the communality regime as outlined for the Guards in KA to encompass the whole city.[18] I foresee problems. If the whole city is involved in the scheme, there does not seem to be anybody, any group, left over to serve as producers and to do the owning of the things whose use is to be shared.

Secondly, maybe Plato was thinking of collective ownership this time around. I am not persuaded. It would be strange if this concept were suddenly to appear for the first time in Plato's thought. One might have expected him to signal so important a change from KA. As it is, he makes no attempt whatever to relate KB to KA. In addition, the abandonment of KA would carry important implications for the social and political organization of the polity – the principle of reciprocity, much heralded at the time of its introduction, would be sacrificed to unity – not to mention the implications for the structure of the soul.

I think Plato had in mind something not very different from the regime of the *Republic*. All citizens shared everything, but the workers, the artisans and the farmers, *were not citizens*, were not held to be part of the state. This seems a natural development from KA. In KA, the workers generally appear to be *in*, to be citizens. But there is the oddity that when the talk is of education, they are overlooked; and it is axiomatic for Plato that participation in a common and demanding system of education was a prerequisite for membership of any state worthy of the name. It is noticeable that in Magnesia, the second-best polity of the *Laws*, the workers have been downgraded: they are foreigners, non-citizens, and the farmers are slaves. Aristotle envisaged similar arrangements for *his* ideal state. Both philosophers excluded citizens from the workforce.

Finally, although Plato, as I said earlier, gives KB no visible institutions to make possible a detailed comparison between KB and KA, the language suggests that there is no significant distance between the two. In the first place, Plato is still using *koinon* and its cognates, and without any hint of a change of meaning. Secondly, the equivocations and qualifications of the *Laws* passage are anticipated in the *Republic*. In the *Laws*, 'the whole city' is ambiguous: it can be used metonymically, or catachrestically, for what makes the city the city it is, a matter of the citizens,

---

[18] That seems to be what Laks and Bobonich envisage. As to the nature of the regime, their views are unclear. Laks (2001), 108–9, talks of 'community of property and family ... communistic institutions in the *Republic*'; also Laks (2000), 271: 'community of goods'; cf. Bobonich (2002), 11: 'a certain kind of community of property and families'.

or alternatively for all the inhabitants.[19] The tension between the two possible senses appears to be reflected in the repeated qualification 'as far as is possible'. That polity is awarded the prize in the *Laws* in which 'as much as is possible' everything is in common (as the old saw about friends states), so that even the eyes, ears and hands act in unison 'as far as is possible', and attitudes (praise and blame) and emotions (joy and grief) are shared, again, 'to the greatest possible extent'.

These features of the discussion have parallels in the *Republic*, more especially in the second text cited above (462–4). That passage ends with a recognition that the sharing regime is confined to the Guards. But previously, in exploring the benefits of classing what is 'mine' and 'not mine' in the same way, and of having pleasure and pain in common, Socrates says that this applies to 'the citizens' 'as far as is possible', to 'those in the city', to 'the greatest number'. When anything at all happens to one of the citizens, 'the whole city' is affected by joy or grief. As in the *Laws*, a biological metaphor is employed: when someone hurts a finger, the whole community (*koinonia*) grieves. Is Plato deliberately leaving open whether the whole city is all the inhabitants, or rather, an elite within it? Or is there an unconscious slippage between the two readings? In any case, both the *Republic* and the *Laws* are affected. The tension that colours Plato's ideal polity of the *Laws* is present already in his portrayal of the ideal city of the *Republic*; the difference lies not so much in how the elite is constituted, as how it is represented: for the Guards (and Auxiliaries) of the *Republic* are the citizens of the *Laws*.

I see the gap between KA and KB as a narrow one. We don't have to say that Plato had 'moved on' significantly from the *Republic*. On the contrary, it is hard to believe that it is not a reference to the *Republic* that we now read in the *Laws*. Plato in KB has retained the basic structure of KA, while removing the ambiguity of the position of the workers by downgrading them. One might say that the *Laws* passage is the third of a trilogy of summary restatements of the regime set out in KA, the first two parts being provided by the *Timaeus* and the *Critias*.

It might also be said that by the time Plato came to write the *Laws*, he was no longer interested in giving his ideal polity any shape. Plato's KB is a dream rather than a project. His lack of commitment to it seems reflected in the neglect of the commentators. For, in the tradition of

---

[19] Aristotle's distinction between the classes that are necessary for the existence of the polis (the labouring classes) and those which are parts of the polis (the military and political leadership) is relevant. See *Pol.* 1329a35–9.

discussion of Plato's ideas of property from ancient to modern times KB arouses virtually no interest. Commentators focus almost exclusively on KA. Where they *are* drawn to the *Laws*, it's to the second-best city, Magnesia. Furthermore, in the tradition, it's KA which is classed as communistic. I will shortly be asking how this happened. But first there is a curiosity about the way Plato treats the bans on property and the family which demands attention.

THE BANS ON PROPERTY AND THE FAMILY IN THE *REPUBLIC* ARE SEPARATE AND SEPARABLE

In the bland summary of the ideal polity which is Kallipolis B, Plato presents together, as one, the sharing of wives, children and property (and feelings). In the *Republic* we find something different: the denial of property and the denial of family are introduced separately, in different ways, and far apart. Only in the second passage from the *Republic* quoted above are they brought together and revealed to be integral elements of the same system. The ban on private property comes first, well before the regulations on women and the family, and is introduced straightforwardly, without fanfare or apology. By contrast, Plato is evasive, even coy, about the arrangements for the family. He does slip in a mention of wives and children early in Book Four, but without giving any hint of what is to come: 'If the Guards are well educated and grow up into men of sound judgement, they will have no difficulty in seeing all this for themselves, plus other things we are saying nothing about – such as taking wives, marriage, and having children. They will see the necessity of making everything as nearly as possible "shared among friends", in the words of the proverb' (423e–424a). The full discussion is postponed until Book Five, and even then Socrates' interlocutors have to drag it out of him (449c).

Further, if we look ahead to the propositions that will evoke the three waves of criticism that Plato admits to be fearful of, we find that not one of them is connected with the property issue. They are: the Guards will include women; women and children will be shared; some of the Guards will be philosophers, who make the best Guards.

Plato apparently thought (and wanted his readers to think) that of the two proposals, the ban on property was less radical and would create less fuss than the ban on private families. Why? It is pertinent that the idea of an elite class doing without private property was already current in the Greek world in political and philosophical circles. Plato's Guards were selected as, and trained to be, the leaders of the ideal polity – and they included philosophers. In this connection it is worth looking at, in particular, the practice and ideology of the Pythagorean communities, going back to the regime that Pythagoras introduced into the Italian city of Croton in the late sixth century BC, and, necessarily more briefly, a proposal for an ideal city put forward by the celebrated architect and town-planner Hippodamus, in the middle of the fifth century. We will consider these in a moment.

For the present, let us note that by driving a wedge between the two bans, on property and on family, Plato gave later thinkers, whose perspectives were different, the licence to select one and reject the other.[20] So Thomas More prescribed for his *Utopia* the holding of property in common, but not wives and children. This was a typical Christian reading. Early Christian commentators such as Tertullian, Lactantius and Theodoret were scandalized by Plato's arrangements for women, but did not dismiss out of hand the absence of private property, whatever their private views on the subject, for the good reason that Christians had their own foundation text for the community of property in the Acts of the Apostles, chapters 2 and 4–5. That is why medieval glossators wondered what Gratian was up to when he brought Plato and the Acts together in two places in his *Decretum*, and in such a way as to imply a parallel between the communal property regime of the first Christians and the communal marriage bond and common offspring of the Guards in Plato's ideal state. It seems that Gratian was in fact unaware of what he was doing and of its implications.[21]

FROM TEXT TO CONTEXT

This is the moment to consider how the political and intellectual environment might have influenced Plato. In composing the *Republic* Plato could not but have had in mind, among other things,[22] an ideal constitution outlined by the architect Hippodamus, the regimes associated with Pythagoras and his followers, the Spartan polity, and Aristophanes' hilarious comedy, *Ecclesiazusae* ('Women of the Assembly').

---

[20] It was convenient and natural, but by no means essential and inevitable, for the family to serve as the central institution for the transmission of property.

[21] Kuttner (1976b).

[22] In Diog. Laert. 3.37; 53, probably from Aristoxenus of Tarentum via Favorinus, Protagoras, *Antilogica* (*Controversies*) is said (unbelievably) to be the source of 'nearly everything' in Plato's *Republic*. See Rankin (1983), 86, 176–84, 222; Dawson (1992a), 19–21.

Hippodamus, according to Aristotle,[23] imagined a city of 10,000 divided into three distinct classes of artisans, farmers and the military, with three types of land, sacred, public and private, supporting the worship of gods, the military and the farmer-proprietors, respectively. Pythagoras, about a century before Plato's birth, had installed in the South Italian town of Croton a regime of communality, which was intended to embody the principle, later attributed to Pythagoras, that friends have everything in common. The memory and to some extent the practices of the original community would have been kept alive by followers of Pythagoras in Magna Graecia and elsewhere in the Greek world in the fifth and early fourth centuries.[24] Then there was contemporary Sparta. The Guards of Kallipolis and the military class of Hippodamus recall the political/military elite of Spartiates, who experienced life in the barracks, at any rate up to the age of thirty; Spartans also practised some sharing of women and of parental care of children. Finally, Aristophanes' fantastic comedy of 393 BC or a little later has women taking over as leaders of the Athenians and legislating the abolition of private property and the sharing of women and children.

We should not be looking for one-to-one correspondences, nor do we find them. Hippodamus' is a bare-bones scheme, as presented by Aristotle, and we can do little with it beyond noting its resemblance to Plato's arrangements particularly in respect of the presence of a propertyless warrior class. In Hippodamus the revenues that support that class are drawn from common land, not the private resources of individual producers as in Plato. Aristotle puzzled over this, wondering who would farm the common land. There is a more serious discrepancy in the fact that Hippodamus' warrior class participated in government *together with the other two classes*. His paper polity was in fact a democracy.

Plato was well aware that readers would associate his scheme with Aristophanes' comic vision. Socrates is made to appear anxious lest it be laughed at. At the same time, Plato marks the differences very clearly; he was obviously confident that those who mattered to him, namely the socially and economically prominent, would take note of them. Plato's regime was a mixed economy, or better, a private property regime from which the leadership was excluded. As to families, Plato's Guards were to

---

[23] *Pol.* 1267b22–1268b4.
[24] The nature of Pythagorean communities post-Pythagoras is a contested issue. See recently Riedweg (2002), 136–49; cf. Garnsey (2005).

enjoy 'the most austere sexual regime that imagination could devise',[25] whereas in Aristophanes' plan for Athens promiscuity reigns.[26] Finally, the regime dreamt up by Aristophanes was democratic, involving not just a political/military elite, but all citizens (slaves did the work). In the *Republic* democracy is savaged by Socrates as libertarian and anarchic.[27] The idea of a regime of this kind achieving unity by any means whatsoever is treated as simply ludicrous. (Though carefully not mentioned by name, Athenian democracy is clearly the target, the regime that sentenced Socrates to death.)

Sparta is expressly linked in the *Republic*, along with Crete, with a particular order, timocracy. While Socrates is found admitting that such a regime was 'pretty generally approved', in the Platonic scheme of things it was still a form of injustice and therefore not to be taken as a model. Timocratic man is self-centred, pursuing his own interests and enrichment, with the result that disharmony reigns among the governing class, and the polity is held back from further decline only by the negotiation of a compromise according to which the free population is enslaved and land and housing privatized. This last detail is significant for us: Spartiates as individuals were property-owners, certainly in Plato's time, and probably from the beginning.[28]

Finally, Pythagoras and his disciples at Croton did not share women and children, and they held their property in common. That community deserves a second glance, in view of the ideology that guided it, the inclusion of a form of communality of property – albeit different from that proposed by Plato – and the well-established impact of Pythagorean ideas on Plato.

Pythagoras became a legend quite early on and remains a shadowy figure. The principal sources for him that survive are considerably later: they are the biographies composed in the third century AD by Diogenes Laertius and by the Neoplatonic philosophers Porphyry and Iamblichus. Some scholars believe that the Pythagorean community in Croton that we

---

[25] Burnyeat (1999), 303; and, in general, on the relationship of Aristophanes' play to the *Republic*.
[26] Token allowance is made for the unprepossessing, whether male or female.
[27] For Plato on democracy, see Schofield (2006).
[28] On timocracy, see *Rep.* 544c, 547b. The *Republic* is in dialogue form, and it is Socrates who addresses us. So Plato's own attitude is open to speculation – but only up to a point. His immense disenchantment with the politics of Athens and Greece is all-pervasive and can hardly be denied. Further than this it is hard to make progress. Plato does not make a closely argued case for the programme he has Socrates advance. This however does not permit us to hold, with the Straussians, that Plato believed the opposite of what he has Socrates expound, and that the whole creation was an elaborate joke. See Strauss (1964), ch. 2.

read about in these biographies is a construction of later epochs. Porphyry and Iamblichus drew heavily on earlier sources, often named, of which only fragments survive, but it is suggested that they added embellishments of their own, with the aim of elevating Pythagoras as a pagan holy man or son of god, in competition with Christianity.

Those earlier accounts included some that were composed by writers well placed to draw on the oral tradition preserved by people with ancestral links to the Pythagorean communities of fifth-century Italy.[29] One such was Aristoxenus, author of *Pythagorean Precepts*, and *Of the Pythagorean Life*, who sat under, among others, Plato and Aristotle (who himself wrote a work on the philosophy of Pythagoras). His city, Tarentum, in the early fourth century was the seat of the Pythagorean Archytas, the dominant politician of his day, known to the father of Aristoxenus, and a correspondent and friend of Plato: there is a story that he saved Plato from death at the hands of Dionysius. Diogenes Laertius' Life of Archytas draws, at least in part, from Aristoxenos.[30] In the generation after Aristoxenos (that is, in the early third century BC), a Sicilian historian, Timaeus, gives us the earliest information that we have of the property arrangements introduced by Pythagoras into Croton. A scholiast's note on Plato's *Phaedrus* runs as follows: 'At any rate, Timaeus says in Book Eight: "So when the younger men came to him wanting to associate with him, he did not immediately agree, but said that they must also hold their property in common with whoever else might be admitted to membership." Then after much intervening matter he says: "And it was because of them that it was first said in Italy: "What belongs to friends is common property."''[31]

This account is severely truncated, but appears to allude to a phased entry procedure, which, in Iamblichus' fuller discussion, was accompanied by a provisional surrender of property:

Since this was the education he could offer his disciples, he would not immediately accept young men who came and wanted to study with him, until he had put them through an examination and made a judgement . . . The person he had examined was then sent away and ignored for three years, to test his constancy and his genuine love of learning, and to see whether he had the right attitude to

---

[29] Burkert (1982), despite being inclined to scepticism on the sources for Pythagoras, says of Aristoxenos and Timaeus: 'Both of them had excellent information, coming from Magna Graecia themselves' (13).

[30] Diog. Laert. 8.79–83.

[31] Timaeus fr. 13a Jacoby, Schol. in Plato, *Phaedr.* 279C, transl. Kirk *et al.* (1983), 227. See also Diog. Laert. 8.10.

reputation and was able to despise status. After this, he imposed a five-year silence on his adherents, to test their self-control ... During this time each one's property was held in common, entrusted to particular students who were called 'civil servants' and who managed the finances and made the rules. If the candidates were found worthy to share in the teachings, judging by their life and general principles, then after the five-year silence they joined the inner circle: now, within the veil, they could both hear and see Pythagoras. If one failed the test, he was given double his property, and his fellow-hearers (that is what all Pythagoras' followers were called) built a grave-mound for him as if he were dead.[32]

I agree with Brian Capper that the process of provisional surrender implies a regime of community of property, and I find his comparison with the Qumran community of the Dead Sea Scrolls (and other Essene communities) fascinating and compelling. I do not however accept that the later accounts of the Pythagorean community at Croton such as that of Iamblichus drew their inspiration ultimately *from Plato* and cannot be taken back any earlier.[33] It is important here that Plato does not follow the Pythagorean example as described subsequently by Timaeus and Iamblichus (see below). Proof is unobtainable, but the Iamblichan description of the way in which the Pythagorean community was ordered seems to me to be too detailed and vital simply to be written off.[34]

Iamblichus makes strong assertions about the debt of Plato to Pythagoras; he was certain that Plato's Kallipolis was modelled on the Pythagorean community.[35] He writes: 'The origin of justice is community feeling and fairness, for all to share one soul, and for everyone to say "mine" and "someone else's" about the same thing (just as Plato also testifies, having learnt it from the Pythagoreans).'[36] Iamblichus claims elsewhere that Plato appropriated the Pythagorean idea of political structure as based on geometric proportion or equality.[37]

---

[32] *Vita P.* 71–3. The property arrangements are presented summarily in *Vita P.* 81, cf. 168. See also Hippolytus, *Ref. omn. haer.* 1.2: 'On being released, he was permitted to associate with the rest, and remained as a disciple, and took his meals along with them; if otherwise, however, he received back his property and was rejected.'

[33] Capper (1995b), 327. At 330 n. 13, he writes: 'The likelihood of an historical community of goods amongst the original disciples of Pythagoras is not great ... Neopythagoreanism was influenced in its portrayal of Pythagoras' school at Croton by the Platonic ideal state.' He leans on Philip (1966), 25, 185, among others. Others inclined to a sceptical position include Burkert (1972); (1982); Dawson (1992a), 14–18, 44 n. 10 (following Burkert); Zhmud (1997). My position is similar to that of Riedweg (2002), though for him communality of property is part and parcel of the allegedly sect-like nature of the Pythagorean organization.

[34] See Dillon and Hershbell, 1991, on Iamblichus, *Vita P.*, at 16.

[35] So O'Meara (1999), 195–6.   [36] *Vita P.* 167; cf. *Rep.* 462b–e.

[37] *Vita P.* 131; cf. *Rep.* 546b.

The attribution of the principle of communality to Pythagoras as founder and source became firmly fixed in the tradition. The Christian humanists took it as read. Erasmus refers to 'the famous saying of Pythagoras that friends have all things in common'.[38] Guillaume Budé in a letter to his English friend Thomas Lupset writes that Jesus Christ 'left among His followers a Pythagorean communion and love'.[39]

But was Iamblichus *right* to think that Plato's regime was modelled on that of Pythagoras? It is uncontested that Plato's debt to Pythagoras and the Pythagorean tradition was very considerable, involving core cosmological and psychological doctrines, quite apart from music and religious preferences – one notes in particular their shared devotion to the Muses. Iamblichus is interesting on the Muses: 'He [Pythagoras] advised them first to found a temple of the Muses, to preserve their existing concord. These goddesses, he said, all had the same name, went together in the tradition, and were best pleased by honours to all in common.'[40] The Muses, then, had a sociopolitical as well as a religious significance for Pythagoras – so it might have been also for Plato.

As to the saying 'Friends will hold things in common', much favoured by Plato, this was certainly in circulation before his time – he knew it as proverbial. That Pythagoras coined it, as the sources claim, cannot be proven; it can at least be accepted that he applied it, in his own way, and made it his own.[41]

The proverb, of course, was infinitely flexible. Aristotle could invoke it in support of common use rather than common ownership. For Diogenes Laertius citing Timaeus, it meant 'putting all their possessions into one common stock',[42] and this interpretation as we saw was followed by Iamblichus. Plato prescribed both less and more than this: less, in that his Guards had no property of their own to share; more, in that they shared wives and children.[43]

---

[38] Cited in Surtz (1957),160–1.

[39] See Adams (1992), 120. For a recent discussion of the reception of Pythagoras in later ages, see Riedweg (2002), 168–76.

[40] *Vita P.* 45. See the exhaustive treatment of the Muses by Boyancé (1937).

[41] Timaeus is twice cited as attributing it to Pythagoras. See also Diog. Laert. 10.9, of Epicurus, rejecting the maxim as implying mistrust. A famous fragment of Pythagoras' contemporary, Xenophanes, attests the value that Pythagoras set on friendship. Pythagoras tried to stop a dog being beaten with the words: 'Stop, do not beat it; for it is the soul of a friend that I recognized when I heard it giving tongue', Diog. Laert. 8.36.

[42] Arist., *Pol.* 1263a30; Diog. Laert. 8.10; the wording of 10.9 is almost identical.

[43] It is interesting, and a sign that Plato is not following Pythagoras' application of the maxim in detail, that it occurs (twice) in the *Republic* in association with the sharing of families. See *Rep.* 424a, 449c.

To conclude: the rules governing the Guards *are influenced by* rather than closely modelled on those rules laid down for the chosen few in the Pythagorean communities. Plato produced his own reading of the proverbial saying that friends will have (all) things in common, and the property arrangements he devised for his ideal polity are distinctive. In general, Plato's creativity is not to be denied, in shaping his model, and more significantly, of course, in the philosophical concerns to which the model is put in the *Republic*.

In the last section I showed that the proposal to abolish private property for the Guards of the ideal city is prior to and separated from his proposal to deny them their own wives and families, and that the former, but not the latter, is presented straightforwardly and with relative insouciance. Perhaps the abolition of the family was simply by its very nature the more radical and controversial of the two. In any case, there were precedents in the Greek world for the denial of private property to a political or philosophical elite without an accompanying sacrifice of the family, and there is reason to believe that they impressed Plato. (In contrast, the sharing of women was associated in the Greek mind predominantly with 'barbarian', that is, non-Greek, societies.)[44] Contemporary Greeks were at least familiar with the idea, even if the citizenry (and more particularly the leadership) of individual Greek cities would not readily have welcomed it. Even Sparta, whose social system had some features that interested Plato, did not deny private property to its citizens. But the proposal would not perhaps have been laughed out of court. In contrast, Plato says at one stage, of his arrangements for women: 'What we are saying now is pretty unconventional. It may well seem absurd, if our suggestions are really going to be put into practice.'[45]

All that said, Plato did recognize that both proposals were radical (even if he thought only one of them would be treated as absurd), and wanted to harness them together in a *double strike* at the conventions of the contemporary Greek polis. That is why he brought them together at the end of his discussion.

ARISTOTLE ON PLATO

As we follow the reception of Plato's ideas on property, we will discover a tendency to reduce his thinking to one unitary, integrated idea. Plato was

---

[44] See e.g. Herodotus 1.93, 199, 216; 4.172, 176; 5.3, on Lydians, Cypriots, Babylonians, Scythians, Libyans and Thracians. See Dawson (1992a), 18–21.
[45] *Rep.* 452a.

credited, from Aristotle on, with a utopian regime involving a community-wide sharing of everything. When in modern times the concept of Communism became available to describe a society where property and possessions were owned, worked and enjoyed in common, by an easy transition it became customary to apply the C-word to Plato's arrangements.

The second book of Aristotle's *Politics* contains a critical analysis of Plato's ideas of property. Aristotle begins by putting the question, what relation or balance between communal and private should, and realistically could, a well-ordered polis aim at? He proposes to take Plato's *Republic* as a test case:

> We must begin at the natural starting-point of this inquiry. All the citizens must either have everything or nothing in common, or some things in common and some not ... But should a well-ordered polis have all things, as far as may be, in common, or some only and not others? For the citizens might conceivably have wives and children and property in common, as Socrates proposes in the *Republic* of Plato. Which is better, our present condition, or one conforming to the law laid down in the *Republic*? (1261a4–9)

'The citizens', 'the city', 'having ... property in common': the terminology may be imprecise but the meaning is patent. Aristotle has already intimated that his enquiry concerns 'all the citizens'; so we can fairly assume that in the question that follows, 'the city' means 'the whole city', and, similarly, that in the summary of Socrates' proposals, 'the citizens' stands for 'the whole citizenry'. This is noteworthy, because of course the sharing regime outlined in the *Republic* embraces only the Guards and Auxiliaries, not the citizenry as a whole. But there can be no doubt about what Aristotle has in mind: in the very next sentence, he launches his attack on Socrates' proposals in this way: 'Now for *all the citizens* to have their wives in common involves a variety of difficulties.'[46] It is not till several pages later that he shows, in a casual way, that he is fully aware that Socrates' arrangements are only for the Guards: this is where he claims that, actually, a system of sharing wives and children would be better suited to the farmers than the Guards. A little later he complains that the transfer of children between ranks, as envisaged in the *Republic*, would be hard to organize.[47] Again, when he comes to consider property, he says that Socrates leaves it up in the air whether the farmers are to

---

[46] The translation in S. Everson, ed., reads: 'There are many difficulties in the community of women.'

[47] *Pol.* 1262b1; 1262b25–36.

have private property or not:[48] 'The citizens who are not Guards are the majority, and about them nothing has been determined: are the farmers too to have their property in common? Or is each individual to have his own? Or are their wives and children to be individual or common? If, *like the Guards*, they are to have things in common, in what do they differ from them, or what will they gain by submitting to their government?'[49]

This last passage shows that Aristotle's misreading of Plato extends to the nature of the property-sharing regime itself. If the farmers were to be 'like the Guards', they would neither own productive property in common, nor work the land – they would not be farmers. Aristotle has failed to recognize, or has lost sight of, the particularity of the property regime laid out for the Guards. This misunderstanding can be traced back to the beginning of the discussion of property, where Aristotle asks whether it is better to combine private ownership with common use, or common ownership with private use, or common ownership with common use.[50] This typology appears to bypass Kallipolis altogether,[51] in so far as it covers only societies in which owners, tillers and consumers are drawn from the same class; in Kallipolis the products that the class of Guards and Auxiliaries use in common are provided by a separate class of owner/producers. There follows a fleeting recognition that tillers might come from a different class, in which case the system 'would work differently and be easier', but the *Republic* is not cited here, and was not necessarily in Aristotle's mind at all. In any case, there is no follow through. Rather, Aristotle moves on to urge, evidently against a system of common *ownership*, that it will inevitably be undermined by rivalry and discord. Of course, although Aristotle has misrepresented the nature of Plato's regime, his argument about the dangers of pursuing unity above all other goals might still pose a genuine challenge to Plato, who claimed to have produced a recipe for harmony and unity in the city.

How is Aristotle's reading of Plato to be explained? We should bear in mind that our standards in source-usage were not theirs; this is not the only occasion on which Aristotle misrepresented Plato;[52] and Aristotle was not the only ancient writer to indulge in misrepresentation. Aristotle

---

[48] Or wives and children – on which matter he was not in doubt at 1262b1.
[49] *Pol.* 1264a12–19.   [50] *Pol.* 1262b38.
[51] Bornemann (1923–4), 142 long ago noted that the discussion was of doubtful relevance to the *Republic*.
[52] Lane (2006) shows convincingly that Aristotle gives an inaccurate account of the meaning of *eironeia* in Plato.

was not misremembering the *Republic*, nor had he been daydreaming during the great man's lectures. Aristotle knew what he was doing. By simplifying Plato's views he was sharpening the dialectic he was conducting with him. Aristotle always had before him his wider purpose, the defence of private property and the individual household, and he interpreted Plato from this point of view. It suited him to represent Plato's vision as that of a polis completely united. He could then argue that the single-minded and obsessive pursuit of unity in the polis involved, paradoxically, its destruction. As the polis strove to achieve the unity that can best be achieved in an individual, or, slightly less successfully in a family, it ceased to be a polis. Meanwhile, other virtues and desirable ends of a political community were being sacrificed to the all-engrossing drive for unity: reciprocity, that is to say, the mutually beneficial exchange between people who have different talents and skills; the pride and pleasure that comes from owning property and seeing it increase; and finally, the opportunities ownership of property gives to exercise liberality. Aristotle also wanted us to consider more mundane matters of practicality: a system of collectively owned property would fall apart, because no one would take responsibility for the land, leaving it to others.[53] (The limited relevance of this argument to the property regime of Kallipolis was a matter of minor significance to him.) In consequence productivity would be lower than under a private property regime, and the economy of the city would suffer. Among the joint property owners there would be dissension and discord – the opposite of what Plato had predicted.

Aristotle produced a rich seam of arguments here, which have appealed to many philosophers, political theorists and theologians in later epochs. To quote Alan Ryan: 'From Aristotle to Jefferson, and even nearer to our own time, there has been a tradition of thought which associates political virtue in the citizen and stability in the state with the ownership of land and the cultivation of the soil.'[54] Be that as it may, looking at Aristotle's confrontation with Plato from the viewpoint of a Historian of Ideas, one has to note that a serious misreading of Plato's *Republic* had been launched, with all the authority of Aristotle behind it.

LATER PLATONISTS AND PLATO ON PROPERTY

Aristotle transmitted a flawed version of Plato's ideas on property and was his pupil. How did Plato's later disciples, specifically the Neoplatonists of

---

[53] *Pol.* 1261b32–40. [54] Ryan (1987), 3–4.

late antiquity, read their master? We can attempt an answer to this question, thanks largely to an essay on the *Republic* by Proclus, the only survivor of a number of interpretations and commentaries composed in late antiquity.[55] But before we look at that text, or the relevant part of it, it is worth reminding ourselves that roughly nine centuries had elapsed between Plato and Proclus (that is, from the fourth century BC to the fifth century AD), and in this period there had been any number of summaries, florilegia, epitomes and commentaries of the works of Plato. Of this outpouring only some brief summaries survive. The limitations of such works are obvious, and hardly worth dwelling on. Yet, if relevant bits are put side by side, interesting things can emerge. A comparison of two extant specimens three centuries apart may serve as an illustration. They are *The Handbook of Platonism* (*Didaskalikos*) of the Middle Platonist Alcinous belonging to the mid-second century AD, and the *Prolegomena to Platonic Philosophy* written by an anonymous Neoplatonist in the sixth century.[56] Our two authors treat types of Platonic polities in parallel passages. Alcinous has two categories of constitutions, those 'based on the presence of certain conditions' and those that are 'emended', and finds examples in the *Laws* (he has Magnesia in mind), and in the *Letters*, respectively.[57] The Anonymus has both categories with the former renamed the 'hypothetical' state – by which he means the best possible city in some given circumstances – but he adds a third dubbed 'non-hypothetical' – the best possible city *tout court*. In this last kind of state, in which he places the *Republic*, 'nothing is regarded as given by tradition, but everything is common property, so that mine is yours and yours is mine, and the possessions of the individual are his own and at the same time not his own'.[58]

This is a sign that the property arrangements peculiar to the *Republic* have bypassed the Neoplatonists. Confirmation comes from Proclus. Proclus became head of the Platonic School of Philosophy at Athens around 435 at the age of twenty-five and held the post for half a century until his death in 485. His essays on the *Republic* (for his work is not a commentary in the sense that his *Parmenides* and *Timaeus* are) include one that survives incomplete, entitled 'Examination of objections made

---

[55] See O'Meara (2003) for a list.
[56] See Dillon, 1993, on Alcinous, *Didaskalikos*; Whittaker, 1990, on Alcinous; Westerink, ed. 1990, on Anonymus.
[57] Alcinous, *Didask.* ch. 34, in Dillon 46–7, 204–9.
[58] Transl. Dillon 1993, 203–4; cf. Dillon (2001), 244.

by Aristotle in the second book of the *Politics* against Plato's *Republic*. This is a critique of a critique, a sharply focused defence of Plato against the arguments levelled against him by Aristotle, in particular against the charge that Plato gave undue weight to the goal of unity. The detailed arrangements for the ideal state are ignored by Proclus, they clearly don't matter much to him; all the same, he says enough about them to reveal that like Aristotle, and perhaps following Aristotle, he writes as if the ideal state outlined by Socrates was one in which property is shared as well as women and children, and throughout the whole city, not just among the Guards and Auxiliaries.[59] Thus he says:

> Everyone will say the same thing and this will come about as the result of everyone calling the same thing 'mine' in the sense of 'belonging to all', for since the city is composed of all the citizens each will think of its property as his own and will call it 'mine' ... When something belongs in common to the whole city as a single entity each one will think of it and speak of it as his own property. And each calls 'mine' what the city calls 'mine', so that, as far as possible they may have one existence and one life – that of the city. We have described how this will be a practical possibility for them in the case of women and children and in the case of property.[60]

Aristotle had argued that the pursuit of the goal of unity above all else entailed the opposite of what Plato intended, the destruction of the city. Proclus retorts that Aristotle has erroneously imposed a material, physical, numerical, sense of oneness on Plato, and has missed the teleological sense, that in which oneness is the goal and final cause and unifying force of an organism, here the city.

The essential issue is whether unity is compatible with diversity. Aristotle thinks that Plato's kind of unity is not thus compatible but instead reduces to homogeneity. Proclus quite reasonably protests that this is unfair. He is on home ground here. Neoplatonist metaphysics revolved around the theme of unity and diversity, and Proclus himself made a major contribution in this area.[61] The Neoplatonist Golden Rule that 'everything is in everything but in a manner appropriate to each' is a central principle of his philosophy, and he draws on it in his rebuttal of Aristotle. Plato, he says, is quite clear that not everything can be in

---

[59] In the brief summary of the constitution of the *Republic* which is contained in his commentary on the *Timaeus*, Proclus shows that he is fully aware of division between the Guards/Auxiliaries and the other classes, but their distinctive lifestyles do not interest him. His main concern is to develop the analogy suggested in *Rep.* 592c between the constitution of Kallipolis and a paradigmatic heavenly constitution.

[60] 367.1–11 (excerpts).   [61] Siorvanes (1996).

common: this is demonstrated by his definition of the requirement of different occupations for different kinds of people. Plato laid down 'that each should follow one occupation for which he is naturally suited, and that no one should assume an occupation or task that is altogether inappropriate for him'. This acknowledgement of diversity within unity is mirrored by the organic view of the state, the idea, to which Plato subscribes, according to Proclus, 'that the city should be integrated with itself in the same way as the parts of a single body'. He writes that the city as one

is superior to the parts and joins the many individuals together in such a way as to be greater than them and to be final cause rather than a mere condition or material cause. It is the same with our bodies which are also made of many elements ... The one in its proper sense holds the body together. It is either a single physical principle or else a soul which makes the body one, in spite of its being composed of many elements.

There is more than a suspicion that Proclus' defence of Plato has carried him beyond the text of the *Republic*. It is very much a contested question how far Plato in the *Republic* committed himself to an organic view of the state, and what implications this would have held for him.[62]

The equivocations in Plato's discussion on property in the *Republic* make it a delicate exercise to decide where Plato ends and Proclus begins. In any case, Proclus has produced a misleading reading of Plato's property arrangements for his ideal city, just as Aristotle had done. Antiquity transmitted to the Middle Ages and beyond the inaccurate message that the ideal city of the *Republic* was characterized by the sharing of property as well as women and children through the entire city.

---

[62] One reason the analogy is a useful one for Proclus' purposes is that an organism is precisely the sort of unity whose evident parts (organs of sense, hands, heart, etc.) each have their own distinctive function. As to Plato, if he does not view the state as an organism, he is nonetheless committed to its 'health', and that is given a lot of work to do. Plato's ambiguity and inconsistency on the issue is nicely brought out by L. Brown (1998) in her adjudication between Popper and Vlastos.

CHAPTER 2

Plato's 'communism' from late antiquity via Islamic Spain to the Renaissance

PRELIMINARIES

'When I roll out the whole of this text of Plato's (or of Socrates') *Republic* which I have in my hands, I know very well that I won't find those words.'[1] The speaker is Pier Candido Decembrio, and the work *Dialogues against Lactantius*, written *c*.1443 by the Franciscan Antonio da Rho (Antonius Raudensis). Da Rho is putting forward Decembrio, in real life his friend and collaborator, as the defender of Plato against the early fourth-century Christian apologist Lactantius. The work as a whole belongs in the context of the contemporary debate between advocates of Plato and advocates of Aristotle. What Decembrio knew he would be unable to find, as he 'scrolled down' the *Republic*, was any statement to the effect that in Plato's ideal polity resources should be in common *among the citizens*. It just isn't there, said Decembrio. He was quite right. Platonic communality was for the Guards and Auxiliaries alone. It was Aristotle who first, for his own purposes, blandly stated that Plato's arrangements embraced the whole citizenry; and the late antique Neoplatonists told the same story, again, for their own purposes.

I'll come back in due course to Decembrio and the wider debate. For the present, let us note that it was unusual to charge Aristotle with misreading the text of Plato, with being, in effect, a bad historian of philosophy. More generally, it was unusual to apply source criticism to a text. Friends of Plato of the late fourteenth and fifteenth centuries such as Cardinal Bessarion and Marsilio Ficino organized their defence of Plato otherwise, more in the manner of the fifth-century Neoplatonic philosopher Proclus, in whose works they were well read. What mattered to

---

[1] *In Lactantium*, 555–6, Hankins (1990) vol. 2, 610.

them was not the literal detail of Plato's social and political arrangements in the *Republic*, but the deeper message: the vital importance of unity, the dangers of faction-fighting within the governing class and the destructive consequences of confrontation between rich and poor. Decembrio's discovery of Aristotle's error was of no interest to them.

The most illustrious and formidable Platonist of the fifteenth century has not yet been mentioned and can hardly be ignored.[2] This was George Gemistus Plethon, philosopher, teacher and politician at Mistra in the Peloponnesus. He became embroiled in the Plato/Aristotle controversy late in his long life (in his eighties). In fact, he started it, when he published, using for the first time the pseudonym Plethon,[3] *On the Differences between Aristotle and Plato*, a summary of public lectures delivered in Florence in 1439. My interest, for present purposes, given that *On the Differences* is devoted to physics and metaphysics rather than politics, is in two earlier compositions, memoranda written in the 'Mirror of Princes' genre, one addressed to the emperor Manuel (around 1418), the other (probably a little earlier) to the despot of Mistra Theodore. The structure and ideology of the model polity there presented, with the avowed aim of saving the Peloponnese and the empire from internal collapse and external conquest, bear the clear imprint of Plato's Kallipolis.

But first I want to show, by means of two incursions into the medieval scene, that Platonic political philosophy in the Middle Ages is by no means an empty category.[4]

PLATONIC POLITICAL PHILOSOPHY IN THE MIDDLE AGES

Proclus died in 485 after spending fifty years as head of the Platonic school at Athens. An edict of the Christian emperor Justinian of 529 prohibited philosophers from teaching in Athens.[5] Damascius and six other Platonists left for Persia; a Neoplatonist cell survived in Alexandria until *c*.610. In the West, Plato's works went out of circulation for the most part. When Gratian was compiling his digest of Canon Law in

---

[2] On the stature of the man, see the comment of Woodhouse (1986), x, referring to the Florentine lectures of 1439: 'It is probably true that he was the first competent interpreter of both Platonism and Aristotelianism to address Latin audiences in Greek for a thousand years.' See also on Plethon, Masai (1956); Nikolaou (1974), 72–97; Karamanolis (2002), 253–82.

[3] Gemistus (full) and Plethon (abundant) are synonymous; Plethon carries echoes of Plato(n).

[4] John Marenbon kindly made available to me prior to publication a paper on Peter Abelard and Platonic Politics.

[5] See *CJ* 1.5.18.4 and 1.11.10.2 (against teaching by pagans and heretics); cf. Malalas, *Chron.* 18.451 (a special decree sent to Athens against the teaching of philosophy and law). See Watts (2004); (2006).

Bologna in the late 1130s, the only available work of Plato was the *Timaeus* in Calcidius' incomplete translation of the early fourth century.[6] Otherwise Plato was known only at second hand – through Cicero, Augustine, Boethius and ps.-Dionysius. So there was little chance of any searching discussion of the property issue. The situation changed substantially only when the production of Latin translations of Plato picked up in the fifteenth century through the agency of the Christian humanists of Italy. The publication of virtually the entire works of Plato in Latin by Ficino in 1484, almost exactly a millennium after the death of Proclus, was the culmination of this development.

The flame of Platonic political philosophy did not burn bright in the Middle Ages, but nor was it extinguished. The *Timaeus*, as we saw, was available in a fourth-century translation. This was worth something. Although the *Timaeus* was primarily a work of cosmology, it began with a summary of the institutions of the ideal polity as outlined in the *Republic*.[7] There was nothing fortuitous in this: for Plato, the ideal polity was a reflection of 'a pattern or model laid up in heaven'.[8] According to the translator Calcidius, as Socrates had produced an image of the civil state, so Timaeus wanted to get to know the workings of the cosmos as if in a universal city and state.[9] The early twelfth-century Commentators and Glossators were very interested in pursuing the comparison of the city-state to the cosmos (and to the human body) that they found in Plato/Calcidius. For our present purposes, the point to emphasize is that in the *Timaeus* scholars had a workable summary of the account of the regime of the Guards. They could moreover read it direct, without the distortions of Aristotle getting in the way – for Aristotle's *Politics* was also unavailable to scholars of the twelfth century. So we find that Plato's ideal polity, in their eyes, was unequivocally hierarchical, tripartite in structure[10] and endowed with a leadership practising a communal way of life that was distinctive *and not shared with the rest of the citizenry.*

The best known and most influential of the Glosses on the *Timaeus* were composed by an anonymous author who may have been Bernard of

---

[6] Calcidius' work ends at *Timaeus* 53c. For the rough date, see Dillon (1977), 401–8. The surviving part of Cicero's translation runs from *Timaeus* 27D–47B.

[7] The summary is reasonably accurate; but see n. 10 below.   [8] *Rep.* 592b.

[9] *Timaeus a Calcidio translatus* (ed. Waszink 1962), 59–60.

[10] Plato in the *Timaeus* collapsed the Guards and Auxiliaries into a single class of Soldiers. His translator Calcidius reverted to the tripartite structure of the *Republic* (§233), and was followed in this by the mediaeval scholars. They had a special interest in applying the Platonic tripartite structure to their own society. See Dutton (1983).

Chartres[11] and by William of Conches. On the property arrangements of the ideal state, they take up opposing positions (but without detailed exposition). Anonymus is dismissive of the idea that the soldiers should be without their own possessions, which 'no one believes'. William can see the rationale behind the regulation that the soldiers should lack private property and be content with the gifts that come to them: for 'wealth makes a man dissolute and negligent'.[12] They have more to say about the regulations for women and children. Both sidestepped the literal meaning of Plato's text, in William's words, the meaning that 'certain unlearned people' gave it, which was tantamount to accusing Plato and Socrates of 'shamefulness' (*turpitudo*). What gave them an opening to reinterpret Plato was Calcidius' rendering of 'offspring' (*to genemenon* in Plato) by *affectus*, in Socrates' sentence: 'we ordained that all should have all in common, so that no one should ever recognize his own *offspring*. *Affectus* is ambiguous between the (rare) late classical meaning 'loved ones', which Calcidius must have intended, and the classical meaning 'attachments' or 'affections'. The Glossators still had to come up with an explanation of what Plato might have had in mind. Anonymus decided that women and children were common in the sense that 'everyone loved everyone else like a son or a brother or a father, and another man's wife like his own'. He further surmised that Plato's marriages were 'not for pleasure but for the *common utility*, that is, for the defence of the *Republic*'. According to William, Plato 'did not say that they should be in common, but they should be *thought to be so*, as if he were to say, let everyone love in a good way the wife and children of other people as if they were his own'. It is in this sense that 'each person does not know his loves [*affectus*]'.[13] For Peter Abelard, in his roughly contemporaneous *Christian Theology*, literal wife-sharing could not possibly have been recommended by Socrates, who (in his view) launched the study of ethics and the quest for the highest good. Socrates/Plato meant that wives would be common not 'in their use', but 'in what they produced'; in the ideal polity, love (*caritas*) would be so pervasive that no one

---

[11] The attribution by Dutton of the *Glosae super Platonem*, which exists in six twelfth-century manuscripts, to Bernard of Chartres, is widely but not universally accepted. See Marenbon (1997), 123–4, n. 37.

[12] Bernard (ed. Dutton 1991) 148 ll.75–6: 'quae dicta sunt, quia nemo aestimat milites propria possessione carere.'; William (ed. Jeaneau 1965) 77, to 18b: 'Quoniam sapientiam et animositatem sequuntur divicie que hominem dissolutum et negligentem reddunt, precepit Socrates nullam esse militum propriam possessionem sed donativis suis esse contentos.'

[13] Bernard (ed. Dutton 1991), 148 ll.75–90; William (ed. Jeauneau 1965), 78–9 to 18c–d.

would want to possess anything, including children, except for 'the common utility of everyone'. Abelard also drew an analogy between the inhabitants of Plato's ideal state and the first Christians of the Acts of the Apostles.[14]

Gratian too, in the *Decretum*, composed about a decade later, placed Plato and Acts side by side, and he credited Plato, twice, with imagining a polity in which everyone was unaware of his own *affectus*. The second of these passages which brings together Plato and Acts caused something of a panic among Canon lawyers because of its apparent endorsement of wife-sharing. It seems that Gratian was unaware of the contextual meaning of the phrase that he was quoting.[15] It can be accepted that Gratian was not closely acquainted with *Timaeus*/Calcidius and the rationalizations of his near-contemporary commentators. Gratian had aligned himself, whether deliberately or not, with a different pattern of thought – namely, the traditional Stoic or Stoicizing theme, first pagan and then Christian, of the communality of property practised by primeval humanity. By the law of nature, he pronounced, everything was common to everyone,[16] and he proceeded to illustrate and confirm the point with reference to Plato and Acts. An anonymous Decretalist writing in the 1170s, in his *Summa Antiquitate et tempore*, found these exempla inappropriate. In particular, he asserted, 'anyone who understands Plato' will be aware that 'only the soldiers of that city were to have their disbursements in common, lest they give attention to their own affairs and in consequence are less concerned with the common utility that their office of guardianship is intended to serve'. This is one of several indications that this author *was* familiar with *Timaeus*/Calcidius and the commentaries on the text.[17]

Thus for a short period in the twelfth century a succession of scholars tapped into Plato's political thinking, thanks to the presence of a translation of the *Timaeus*. They were able to do so without the mediation of Peripatetic or Neoplatonic sources, and with the aid of a guide, Calcidius, who unlike them did have direct access to the *Republic* and, furthermore, did not misrepresent it. It is paradoxical that the fifteenth-century humanists of Italy were for the most part less reliable witnesses to Plato's views on communality, although they had much more of Plato to work with.

---

[14] Abelard, ed. Buytaert (1969), 2.43–48. Abelard moreover compared the inhabitants of Plato's ideal state favourably with the monks of his own day. On Abelard, see Marenbon (1997); (forthcoming).
[15] Kuttner (1976b), 94.   [16] See Ch. 5.   [17] See Kuttner (1976b), 95–9, 110–11 (text).

Interest in the *Timaeus* flagged after the twelfth century. When classical philosophy staged a comeback in the West in the thirteenth, the main beneficiary was Aristotle. Aristotle's *Politics* surfaces in the West in the middle of the thirteenth century, and the commentaries quickly begin, among them that of Thomas Aquinas. But before we come to Aquinas, it is worth glancing at developments that occurred earlier in medieval Islam. There the study of Aristotle had continued under the patronage of the Abbasid caliphs in their newly founded city of Baghdad (from the eighth to the tenth century), and subsequently, in Spain under the Khalifate of Cordoba (929–1031) and the Almohads (*fl.* 1149/55–1212). It's a remarkable story.[18] The aspects most relevant to us are the translation of Aristotle in bulk into Arabic from Syriac (in the East), and, following on this, the large-scale commentating on Aristotle's works (in the West). These movements spawned a chain of Aristotelian scholars, running from Alfarabi (870–950) to Maimonides (1135–1204) by way of Avicenna (980–1037), Ibn Tufail (1110–85), Avempace (d.1138), and Averroes (1126–98), and there were many lesser figures. The leading light and culmination of this explosion of Aristotelian scholarship was Ibn Rushd or Averroes of Cordoba. Averroes composed no fewer than thirty-eight commentaries on Aristotle. In these and other works he sought to return to the 'pristine' Aristotle. Eastern Islamic philosophy had run Aristotle together with Plato, in this following the lead of late antique Neoplatonism in its final, Alexandrian, phase. It was a somewhat deplatonized Aristotle that was passed on to medieval scholastics, once, that is, the works of Aristotle and Averroes had been rendered into Latin (in some cases via the Hebrew) by Jewish and Christian scholars. Aristotelianism was now set to become the philosophical handmaid of Latin theology. For Thomas Aquinas, writing in the thirteenth century, Aristotle was The Philosopher, and Averroes The Commentator.

Now here's a surprise: Averroes was an avowed Aristotelian, who furthermore was concerned to separate out Aristotelian from Platonic doctrine. Yet he produced a commentary, or at least an extended essay, in which he gave enthusiastic support to Plato's regime for Kallipolis. What was going on?

The setting is the remarkable revival of intellectual life in Muslim North Africa and Spain under the Almohad dynasty in the second half of the twelfth century. Abul-Walid Muhammad Ibn Ahmad Ibn Rushd

---

[18] See, recently, Gutas (1998); Crone (2004). Also, Hourani (1975b), Fakhry (1983), Gutas (1988).

(known to the Latins as Averroes) was born in Cordoba (1126) into a family of prominent jurists and politicians, who had flourished under the Almoravids (late eleventh, first half of the twelfth century).[19] Our man changed sides and backed the dynasty that ousted them, the Almohads. His reward was a distinguished career of which the high points were his tenure of the posts of *qadi* or religious judge of Seville, chief judge of Cordoba (a post held previously by both his father and grandfather) and court physician to the caliph in Marrakesh. His career received a boost when he was introduced to the caliph through an intermediary, the scholar, physician and courtier Ibn Tufayl. The formalities of introduction over, the caliph suddenly threw him the question: 'What is their opinion about the heavens?' – referring to the philosophers – 'Are they eternal or created?' In other words, do the philosophers side with Aristotle or with Islamic religious law? Frederick II Hohenstaufen (1194–1250) a generation or so later was prone to ask even more recondite questions of his courtiers, who, incidentally, included sons of Averroes: 'In what doctrines were Aristotle and Alexander of Aphrodisias opposed?'[20]

To return to Marrakesh: Averroes at first stood by wondering what to say (since it could be unwise to display familiarity with philosophical writings in the wrong circles), while caliph and scholar debated creationism. However, he was gradually drawn into the discussion, and must have created a good impression, because before long the caliph threw down a challenge which Averroes would take up: 'If someone would tackle these books [of Aristotle], summarize them and expound their aims after understanding them thoroughly, it would be easier for people to grasp them.'[21]

The Sultan's question had been a pertinent one, pitting philosophy against the religious law. Averroes was a Muslim. Muslims already had a divinely revealed Law, a shari'a. We know that Averroes was a judge, a *qadi*, upholding the law. This was his daytime job. He was also the author of a classic work of legal interpretation. How could he serve two masters: pagan philosophy, and Islamic law and religion? I will come back to this issue later. Now I want to return to the question raised above: why was The Commentator on Aristotle writing an extended essay on Plato's

---

[19] On Averroes, see Butterworth (1975); (1985); Urvoy (1991); Leaman (1998); Endress and Aertsen (1999); Crone (2004), esp. 189–92.

[20] See Burnett (1999), 268. Alexander was a Peripatetic philosopher writing at the turn of the second century.

[21] Quoted in Leaman (1998), 3, from an account of the meeting given by A. Marrakushi, in the translation of Hourani (1961), 12–13.

Republic, especially as he was apparently anxious to distinguish between Aristotelian and Platonic doctrine? For Aristotle, as we saw, was at odds with Plato in political theory as well as in metaphysics. He had roundly rejected the regime imposed on the Guards in Plato's ideal city, and written a spirited defence of private property. So how did Averroes cope with that?

In general, it seems that Averroes saw no clash between Aristotle and Plato's ethical and political theory, so that, for him, Aristotle's *Nicomachean Ethics* and Plato's *Republic* were complementary, the former providing 'the first or theoretical part of politics', the latter 'the second or practical part'[22] – which is a nice inversion of the usual assumptions. It seems that his efforts at disentangling Aristotelian and Platonic doctrine were concentrated on the area of metaphysics and cosmology. He pointed out, for example, that Plato's theory of ideas and the Neoplatonist emanationist doctrine of creation were un-Aristotelian. He apparently did not see a parallel incompatibility in the realm of the practical sciences. A glance at his work on the *Republic* shows that Averroes has included whole chunks of Aristotle, especially from the *Nicomachean Ethics*, while ignoring large sections of the *Republic*. The verdict of modern scholars that Averroes provided an Aristotelian reading of the *Republic* would not have displeased him. He and predecessors such as the tenth-century philosopher Alfarabi were heirs of the tendency that gathered pace in late antiquity among the Neoplatonists to play down the differences between Plato and Aristotle. Averroes saw the two philosophers as basically in agreement. If one did have to choose between them, his inclination was to go for Aristotle.

But in any case, Averroes did not have to cope with the clash between Plato and Aristotle over communality, because he knew nothing of it. How so? The answer is simple: he couldn't find a copy of Aristotle's *Politics*. As he disarmingly tells us early on in his work on the *Republic*: 'It has not yet come into our hands.'[23] That's why he wrote about Plato's *Republic*. And it was the non-availability of the *Politics* that explains the Aristotelianizing of Plato in which he appears to indulge therein.

What would he have written had he possessed a copy of Aristotle's *Politics*? Would he have taken a completely different line on property, and the sharing regime in general? For he is not at all lukewarm about Plato's arrangements for his ideal city, including those for sharing women and children. One thing is clear: we wouldn't have the commentary on the

---

[22] See Butterworth (1975).   [23] Rosenthal (ed. 1956) 8, 112.

Republic at all if he had succeeded in getting his hands on Aristotle's *Politics*. It's pure accident that we have it and that he wrote it blind, without the criticisms and distortions of Aristotle getting in the way. Let us make the most of this lucky circumstance.

Two caveats are in order before we proceed. First, we are working with an English translation of the Hebrew translation of the Arabic, composed (by Samuel ben Judah) in the early fourteenth century in Provence. We are at two removes from the original Arabic text, which is lost. Second, it is uncertain what exactly Averroes had in front of him when he wrote his work. It is commonly held that he did not have the *Republic* in a proper translation of the original text, but had rather a translation of a paraphrase by Galen, the cultivated physician from Pergamum who died around AD 200, the best part of a millennium earlier. If Averroes had only a paraphrase, then it was a very full paraphrase, because he displays detailed knowledge of (some parts of) the *Republic*. However, the recent discovery of a passage from *Republic* Book Ten translated literally into Arabic, and what's more, in the original dialogue form, should force a reconsideration of this view.[24]

Averroes endorses Plato's Kallipolis openly.[25] He is forthcoming in his opinions. He makes personal appearances in his text, often speaking in his own name. His support of Plato is allied to recurring, critical comments on 'these cities of ours'.[26] He agrees with Plato's analysis of the cause of the ills, namely, the exploitative behaviour of the ruling magnates. He accepts Plato's recipe for their cure, the dissolution of private households and personal wealth. He reprimands Galen for not appreciating that the abolition of households was in the interests of the unity of the community. Averroes does not even criticize Plato's eugenics programme: he accepts that controlled mating among the Guards was necessary for the preservation of the best natures.[27] On women, he pronounces that their innate abilities and talents were not being utilized in the cities of his day:

In these cities the ability of women is not known, because they are only taken for procreation there. They are therefore placed at the service of their husbands and [relegated] to the business of procreation, rearing and breast-feeding. But this

---

[24] Though the editor, Reisman (2004), does not seem to have taken the point. Some degree of contamination in the process of transmission must of course be allowed for, whichever of the alternatives we favour.

[25] For a contrary view, that Averroes is non-committal, see Leaman (1998), 127; but cf. 130.

[26] In addition to his treatment of communality in Kallipolis, he works hard to apply Plato's discussion of the decline of constitutions to the contemporary Spanish scene.

[27] Rosenthal, 1956, 164; cf. Lerner, 1974, 57.

undoes their [other] activities. Because women in these cities are not being fitted for any of the human virtues, it often happens that they resemble plants.[28]

In his account of the property arrangements for Kallipolis he walks in step with Plato, at least at first: 'When he had set the bounds of their dwelling places he investigated whether Guards ought to possess anything by which they might be singled out from the citizens by way of their dwellings or otherwise.' He proceeds as does Plato to issue the warning that Guards must be like sheepdogs rather than wolves: they must use their superior power and strength to protect rather than exploit them to do harm. There follows a critical reference to contemporary Spain, though in fairly general terms: 'You can understand this clearly from the mighty in these States, for they turn against the subjects and devour them when the tyrant dies who subdued them.'[29]

Averroes goes on to make the case for absence of private possessions emphatically: '*It is therefore readily apparent* that it is right and proper for none of them to have possessions, whether it be dwelling, tools, or anything else. But they have [a claim] against the other citizens to such food and clothing as is sufficient for them.'[30] On the dispositions themselves he is briefer than Plato, and there are some omissions, including the provision against locked doors in the Guards' quarters, and the requirement that they eat in common messes. On the other hand he is keen to spell out the justification for the arrangements: Plato had merely said that the Guards, if allowed private possessions, would have far more to fear from internal than external enemies. Averroes elaborates the message that private ownership stirs up dissension and disunity, with a further reference to the Spanish cities of his day: 'In general, therefore, enmity, hatred and mutual deceit will break out among them in relation to the citizens and one another, as happens with the inhabitants of these states. Sometimes this is the reason they plot against the citizens and devour them.'[31] In later sections, where he is dealing with cities that have fallen away from the ideal, he makes specific, critical comments on recent and contemporary history in al-Andalus. Thus the decline from the ideal constitution to the timocratic and oligarchic (called hedonistic or

---

[28] Rosenthal 166; cf. Lerner 59. Averroes goes on to comment that the failure to use women effectively is a factor in the poverty of the cities.

[29] See Urvoy (1991), 29, for the suggestion that the background might be civil strife in Cordoba. In 1121, five years before Averroes was born, there had been a revolt in the city leading to the sacking of the governor's palace.

[30] Rosenthal 144; cf. Lerner 38.   [31] Rosenthal 146; cf. Lerner 39.

plutocratic) is illustrated from the fate of the Almoravids of which Averroes was a witness.[32]

Having set out and justified the property arrangements, Averroes considers the challenge that Plato had withheld from the Guardians 'the most exalted thing'. In the *Republic* this was *eudaimonia*, happiness. There is an interesting divergence between Plato and his commentator here. Plato allows Adeimantus to present a vision of *eudaimonia* in terms of the lifestyle of the wealthy aristocracy, without Socrates making any objection. Plato's treatment is surely ironical here. He would hardly have approved of a definition of *eudaimonia* in purely materialistic terms. Averroes seems to have missed the irony. At any rate, he twice raises the possibility that wealth is a virtue:

Even if the possession of money and wealth were a virtue, it would not be necessary for the Guards as Guards to be rich, since we do not desire the Guards to be virtuous in the absolute but rather virtuous as Guards. It is not right that we should desire for them the most excellent thing per se, but rather because of their being Guards – provided of course that wealth were a virtue.[33]

The influence of Aristotle is visible: he held that full happiness required not only the 'goods of the soul' but also corporeal goods such as health and external goods like money and reputation.[34]

A serious deviation from the text of Plato follows:

When it became evident to him that it was not right for the Guards to possess anything, he also enquired into the case of the other craftsmen and workers among the citizens of this State, whether it was right for us to allow them property so that they might accept remuneration for their work, and property accrue to them from it [in consequence]. He found the matter the same in both instances. For it was evident to him that nothing would be more harmful for this State than that poverty and wealth would enter into it. This is because if we were to allow the craftsmen property in their calling, their ultimate aim in respect of their craft would be the acquisition [of wealth] and the return they could get out of it by an improvement of their possessions; their advantage to the citizens would be incidental. As a consequence, their work will not [be done] out of duty but rather for gain. This being so, they delude themselves very much as to the ultimate and true aim, namely, usefulness to the citizens. For when they have succeeded, they loathe their craft so that they discard it or become idle craftsmen. But if they are needy, the tools and everything they need are too dear

---

[32] Rosenthal 227; cf. Lerner 125.   [33] Rosenthal 146–7; cf. Lerner 39–40.

[34] There is an interesting anticipation here of the position of Bruni, cited in Hankins (1990), 62. The status of lineage and wealth as virtues was a subject of debate a century later in the time of Thomas More, where it was clear that Aristotle's view was under debate. See Skinner (2002a).

for them so that their work will be bad. From this description it can be seen that Plato is of the opinion that in this State there should be no property for any individual specially to acquire and make use of as he wishes. This being the case, there are among them no transactions in gold and silver, nor are they at all needed in this State.[35]

That this is no slip of the pen is confirmed by a later passage in which Averroes states that the family arrangements – more specifically, the controlled procreation of children, which is designed to ensure that the Guards 'beget children like themselves' – is 'imperative not only for the Guards but also *for every [other] class of citizens*'. And he goes on to muse over whether women 'possess natures similar to the natures *of every single class of citizens*'.[36]

There was some fuzziness in Plato on the regime of the lower classes, but not such as to justify Averroes' statement. He is right about the nature of the property regime imposed on the Guards, the fact that they have no property of their own but live off a subvention from the citizens, but departs from Plato (and without Aristotle's mediation) in affirming that in the Republic the Guards' regime was extended to all citizens,[37] and in representing Plato or Socrates as having *specifically addressed* the question whether the regime of the guards was appropriate for the workers too.

To come back to the central issue, the striking position that Averroes takes on Plato's arrangements for his ideal city: we wonder how he got away with it, for he was voicing views clearly at odds with the prevailing system of values. I raised this matter earlier in connection with his secular career in the law. In fact, Averroes did not subordinate the law to philo-sophy. He seems to have believed, like the earlier scholar Alfarabi, who was a major influence on him, that law and philosophy offered different versions of the truth and were suitable for different audiences. Philosophy was an activity in which only a few gifted people could engage: unlike religion, it was not designed for a popular audience. Philosophers were a class apart, a small intellectual elite having no contact with the masses, and aware of the risks of attracting their attention and disturbing their

---

[35] Rosenthal 147–8; cf. Lerner 40–1. In the very next sentence Averroes has turned his attention to the discussion of money transactions in *Nic. Eth.* 1133a19–b28, so easily does he slide from Plato to Aristotle.

[36] Rosenthal 164; cf. Lerner 57.

[37] Nor does he ask himself how an extension of such a system to the workers would operate, if the workers both had to provide what the Guards and their families needed and received no private profit from their labours.

religious sensibilities. Averroes' careers as judge and as philosopher belonged to distinct compartments.[38]

There is nevertheless something bizarre in the spectacle of a confirmed Aristotelian backing Plato's property regime (as he read it) to the hilt. Sanity is restored when Aristotle's *Politics* finally emerges, and commentators can cite Aristotle directly. Thomas Aquinas wrote a commentary on the *Politics* and in the *Summa Theologiae* drew on some of Aristotle's arguments.

The results are disappointing. The commentary on the *Politics* is little more than a summary. Thomas sticks close to Aristotle's text. Clearly he endorses Aristotle's views, but without telling us why. Deviations from Aristotle are few and minor. One is in a Christian direction: private wealth enables one to be generous; to one's friends, guests and companions, says Aristotle, to friends, strangers *and anyone else*, says Thomas. In the *Summa Theologiae* there is a more significant drawing on Aristotle: he poses the question, *Is it legitimate for individual men to possess anything as their own?*[39] His answer is that private property is not only legitimate but also necessary for life. Part of the argument he advances is utilitarian and comes straight from Aristotle:

[Private property is necessary.] First, because each person takes more trouble to care for something that is his sole responsibility than what is held in common by many – for in such a case each individual shirks the work and leaves the responsibility to someone else, which is what happens when too many officials are involved. Second, because human affairs are more efficiently organized if each person has his own responsibility to discharge; there would be chaos if everybody cared for everything. Third, because men live together in greater peace where everyone is content with his task. We do, in fact, notice that quarrels often break out amongst men who hold things in common without distinction.[40]

This argument apart, Aquinas draws inspiration and content largely from biblical and patristic sources. But let us not underrate the significance of the contribution of Aristotle to Aquinas' thought. Aristotle had found a powerful patron in Aquinas, a prodigiously gifted theologian and philosopher whose influence has been unrivalled within the Church and profound outside it. Thomas' general endorsement of Aristotle's arguments for private property was a major factor in their transmission to later ages.

THE ITALIAN RENAISSANCE: ARISTOTELIANS VERSUS PLATONISTS

The problem facing admirers of Plato when they finally began to emerge after the period of Aristotelian dominance was how to reconcile his

---

[38] See Crone (2004), ch. 14.   [39] *ST* 2.2ae.66.2.   [40] Cf. *Pol.* 1262b38.

writings with humanistic values and Christian culture, more particularly, how to respond to the shock caused by the prescriptions in the *Republic* on the relations between the sexes and the denial of private property.[41] Here are the complaints of Leonardo Bruni of Florence, who translated several works of Plato but deliberately avoided the *Republic*:

> [Plato held] some opinions utterly abhorrent to our customs and ways of living. He believed for instance that all wives should be held in common – one can hardly imagine why – with the result that no one could tell his own children from those of a perfect stranger. Moreover, he would do away with the laws of inheritance and have all things held in common.[42]

On the other side, advocates of Plato could stress the high reputation he enjoyed in late antiquity among men of culture, both pagan and Christian. Plato's dialogues, for ancient interpreters of Plato from the third century on, were a kind of Holy Writ. Plato himself was divine, *theios*, Aristotle merely inspired, *daimonios*. What's more, the Church Fathers, as read by the humanists, provided support for the view that early Christian theology owed more to Plato than to Aristotle. Had not Augustine written in the *City of God*: 'There are none who come nearer to us than the Platonists'? As Marsilio Ficino reported in his treatise *Platonic Theology*: 'With just a few changes, he [Augustine] maintained, the Platonists would be Christians.'[43]

The protagonists in the Plato/Aristotle debate were influenced by a variety of factors, of which personal philosophical conviction sometimes seems insignificant in comparison with the competition for patronage and the struggle for influence at court, whether of Duke or Pope. Whereas Cardinal Bessarion was a 'convert' to Neoplatonism, Pier Candido Decembrio appears to have stumbled into the Platonic camp almost by accident. He needed a significant patron for his literary studies, he had to translate a great work, and because his Greek was not very good it had to be a work for which a translation already existed. The *Republic* was the obvious choice. His father Uberto had produced the first Latin translation of the work in collaboration with the Greek scholar Manuel Chrysoloras. There was also the happy circumstance that his competitor for the patronage of Duke Humphrey, Leonardo Bruni of Florence, had been offered the commission and turned it down. This personal rivalry, added

---

[41] On the contest between Aristotelianism and Platonism in the Quattrocento, Hankins (1990) provides a masterly account.
[42] Quoted in Hankins (1990), 65.
[43] Augustine, *City of God* 8.5; Ficino, *Platonic Theology*, Proem 2.

to competition between Milan and Florence and infighting at the Visconti court in Milan, contributed to Decembrio's undertaking of the translation of the *Republic*. It may also explain the line that he took, which was the direct opposite of that of Bruni (and of his own father).

Decembrio employed an unfamiliar kind of source criticism in order to expose error and inaccuracy in classical authors, more particularly those who had been unfriendly to Plato. It was no coincidence that in the faction-fighting at the Visconti court he was an ally of Lorenzo Valla, who is often regarded as the forerunner of modern historical and philological criticism. It was Valla who, amongst other things, exposed the Donations of Constantine as a forgery.[44] Decembrio insisted that textual evidence was the only basis for historical truth, and rejected the appeal to authority as irrational. When his patron Pizolpasso, archbishop of Milan, objected to his attack on Jerome's libellous criticism of Plato, he replied in forthright manner: 'I did not write this rashly, but for the sake of discovering the truth ... You adduce no argument in this letter of yours other than that the Bishop of Burgos agrees with you; on that view I might myself say that no one agrees with me except the truth, which must take precedence over all authorities.' A little later he would write in the same letter: 'There is no worse calumny than that which is set in motion by an authority.'[45]

By contrast Bessarion and especially Ficino were genuine Neoplatonists, who had immersed themselves in the works of Plotinus and Proclus, and were inclined to follow their reverential approach to Plato. Neither was interested in employing source criticism to score points off Aristotle. Let us now see how Platonic communality fared in the hands of these three men.

Pier Candido Decembrio (1392–1477)

Decembrio was the first of the Italian humanists to examine critically Aristotle's critique of Platonic communality. He complained about the errors and general injustice in Aristotle's presentation of Plato's doctrines. The specific charge that concerns us is that Aristotle claimed, wrongly, that in Plato's ideal state everything was held in common. In fact, a hard look at Plato's texts reveals that his regulations of property and family apply

---

[44] Valla was not the first to claim this, but he brought new arguments to bear.
[45] See Fubini (1966), 361.

only to the Guards. Decembrio gives (that is, he is attributed by Antonio da Rho)[46] a robust if long-winded response:

As Aristotle made objection to Socrates for proposing a rule that children, wives and resources should be in common, and as he worked up a considerable battery of reasoning and evidence against him on the point, and eventually concluded that the state of which Socrates had spoken had the problems in it which he said it did as well as others just as serious, it plainly now remains for me to say a word or so about those common resources and belongings; when I have rolled out the whole of this text of Plato's (or of Socrates') *Republic* which I have in my hands, I know very well that I won't find those words, namely, that 'resources should be in common among the citizens'.[47] The fact that there is no such sharing of resources among them can be easily established from Socrates' own words in several places. In Book Four section nine he says: 'Will you really require the Guards in the state to settle lawsuits? Surely their aim will be limited to preventing the seizing of others' property and being robbed of one's own?' If everything *were* in common, no citizen could possibly steal things of others or be robbed of his own! The wish of the great lawgiver himself for his state was that among the Guards who governed it nothing else should be in common, and as he decreed that they should have nothing of their own, so they would live more religiously. Listen, I beg you, to Socrates' words in Book Five section twelve: 'We have, then, at last made our basic statement: we have said they should not have houses of their own, or lands, or belongings. They should get their sustenance from the rest of the citizenry in recompense for their exercise of Guardship, and they should consume all of it communally together if their duty is to be true Guards.' So, for food and all the other necessities of life, they and their children are to be the object of donation.

'Decembrio' goes on, ambitiously, to make a comparison with Francis' Rule:

That sort of communality appears quite in line with the rule which St Francis laid down for his brethren. He says: 'The brethren will not take for their own a house or land or anything.' He wanted them to guide people to God, to encourage them to virtue, to draw them away from vice, and to receive alms of pence from the people while having nothing of their own at all, not even collectively.

---

[46] The case for da Rho's Decembrio accurately representing the views of the historical Decembrio is a strong one. See Hankins (1990), 150. Decembrio had himself completed one book of a diatribe of his own against Lactantius (it is lost), and there is independent textual evidence for collaboration between him and da Rho. See Zaccaria (1974–5), 207 for a letter of Decembrio in which he raises the matter, not without crudity, of the attack of Aristotle on Socrates 'de comunione mulierum et possessionum reliquarum'; cf. Hankins (1990), 144 n. 74. For an account of the debate, 148–53; for the text, see vol. 2 no. 54.

[47] It is to be noted that the assembled company had just heard the whole of Aristotle, *Pol.* 2.2, read out by the pro-Aristotelian jurist and diplomat Niccolò Arcimboli (in Bruni's Latin translation).

There follows another 'proof' that among the ordinary citizens of Kallipolis possessions are not in common. Having observed that the Guards will adjudicate such lawsuits as will arise in the city at large out of disputes over property, 'Decembrio' signals references in the *Republic* to marketplace activity.[48] And he concludes: 'If therefore, as it is charged, possessions are in common, why the attention given to traders, artisans and farmers, why the need for a market, for money and for exchange?'

The style of criticism employed in this treatise[49] is one that modern scholars can recognize and appreciate. It would not however be taken up by Decembrio's more illustrious successors.

Cardinal Bessarion (1403–72)

Bessarion wrote *Against the Slanderer of Plato* (1469) as a robust counterattack on George of Trebizond's *A Comparison of the Philosophers Plato and Aristotle* (1458), itself a vicious onslaught on Plato. By coincidence the protagonists were both Greek émigrés with roots in Trebizond on the Black Sea. Bessarion was born there, as were the parents of George: he himself was born in Crete. The quarrel was sparked off by the Neoplatonist Gemistus Plethon, philosopher and counsellor at the court of the Despot at Mistra in the Peloponnese, who in this period controlled around half of the dwindling territories of the Byzantine empire. Plethon had come to Ferrara and subsequently to Florence as part of the Eastern delegation to the Council that assembled there in 1438/9 to try to negotiate Union between Eastern and Western Churches. His lectures given in Florence in 1439 *On the Differences of Aristotle with Regard to Plato*, subsequently written up in a treatise usually known as *De Differentiis*, provoked a *Defence of Aristotle* from a fellow Eastern delegate to the Council, George Scholarius, in 1443/4, which in turn was answered in Plethon's *Reply* of 1448/9. Plethon had taken a sternly critical line on Aristotle, but when Scholarius locked swords with him a new element of personal abuse intruded. Responding to Scholarius' contemptuous dismissal of the Italian humanists, Plethon retorted:

These men should certainly enjoy your calumny on ourself, being much better qualified than you are in every branch of philosophy, and also your intellectual superiors. For you are not only vindictive but dull-witted, as your present work shows; and you are ignorant even of the doctrines of Aristotle, in which

---

[48] *Rep.* 425cd; 433e.
[49] The Aristotelian Arcimbolo was also inclined to cite chapter and verse, against his opponent.

you purport to be quite somebody. This will become clear as the argument proceeds.[50]

For his part, Scholarius and other critics of Plethon appear at least as concerned to expose their opponent as a heretic and blasphemer as to refute his criticisms of Aristotle. It was Scholarius (now renamed Gennadius) who as the first Patriarch of Constantinople under Turkish rule saw to the burning of Plethon's last work *The Laws* not long after the latter's death in 1452.

A second round of the controversy began in the 1450s. Following George of Trebizond's entry into the fray on the side of Aristotle, the criticism of Plato became as ferocious and personal as that directed at his supporters.[51] It is at this stage that the attack on Plato becomes more narrowly relevant to the matters before us at present. The exchange between Plethon and Scholarius had concerned for the most part physics and metaphysics. In the hands of George of Trebizond the charge-sheet was extended to cover the alleged enormities and the scandal of Plato's arrangements for the communal life of Kallipolis and Plato's own private life, as retailed by gossipy sources. As it happens, Plethon did have things to say which are significant for our purposes, but in earlier works, in which he tried to persuade the political authorities (the Despot in Mistra or the Emperor in Constantinople) to reform the social and economic arrangements pertaining in that part of the Peloponnese still under imperial control (see below).

The ferocious attack on Plato mounted by George of Trebizond was answered by Cardinal Bessarion. Bessarion had studied with Plethon at Mistra and come under the influence of Neoplatonism, but without succumbing to the paganism of his teacher. Soon after the Council at Ferrara/Florence, to which he came as a delegate of the Emperor, he turned to Catholicism and made Italy his permanent residence (in 1441). Thereafter his aim, or mission, was to seek a synthesis of Neoplatonism and Catholicism.

Bessarion in *Against the Slanderer of Plato* took a more conciliatory line on the contest between Plato and Aristotle than George of Trebizond had done.[52] Like the mainstream late antique Platonists to whom he looked

---

[50] Quoted in Woodhouse (1986), 166.

[51] George of Trebizond was replying to an intervention by Michael Apostolius against Theodore of Gaza.

[52] There are problems with the text of Bessarion's work. There are two texts, one in Greek by Bessarion, the other in Latin, which frequently departs from the sense of the Greek, by Bessarion's secretary, itself leaning on Bessarion's earlier, less stylish, Latin translation of his own Greek text.

back, he held the doctrines of Plato and Aristotle to be basically compatible (though Plato held the palm). Whereas George made only too evident his venomous hatred of Plato, Bessarion pronounced himself an admirer of Aristotle, and insisted that Aristotle had followed his own teacher Plato for the most part. Writing in 1470 to his friend Guillaume Fichet, rector of the University of Paris, he argued that 'a serious and steadfast philosopher should embrace both and despise neither'.[53] On unity, for Plato the prime desideratum, Bessarion's line is that everyone wanted it, Aristotle simply less intensely than Plato. He goes on to say that Aristotle the natural philosopher was more in tune with feelings, Plato with intellect, which was the nobler part of man. At one point Bessarion slyly introduces a citation from a scientific work of Aristotle to suggest that Aristotle actually approved of communality among men: 'Aristotle was very wise to call man a political and social animal. Political animals, he says, in Book One of the *Historia Animalium*, are those whose characteristic function *is one and common to all*. That is not true of all gregarious animals, but it can be said for example of *humans*, bees, wasps, ants and cranes.'[54]

Given that he is pursuing the strategy of minimizing the difference between the two philosophers, it is no surprise to find that Bessarion does not set about exposing errors in Aristotle's account, as Decembrio had done. (George's countless errors are mercilessly paraded.) Bessarion was following the lead of Proclus in concentrating on the big picture and exploring the deeper purpose and logic behind Plato's doctrines. It was not always easy to carry through this resolve, given his felt need to respond to George's often low-level polemic. Bessarion appears as a boxer in retreat, fending off the blows that rain over him, including those directed below the belt. Admittedly, he says, the sharing of women is very hard to accept. I too find it so. But then so did Plato. Look how tentatively he presented it in the *Republic*, and look how he retreated from it in the *Laws*. Plato was painfully aware of how problematic it was – this is Bessarion's constant refrain. For all that, he drives home the message of the need for unity. Bessarion advocated unity as strongly as Proclus had done. Everyone agrees with Plato, he says, that 'there is no greater good in a state than unity'.[55] It's a simple choice between unity and discord, the former condition deriving from having things in common, the latter from

[53] Bessarion, *Ep.* 71, 555 (ed. Mohler, 1942).
[54] Bessarion, *In Calumniatorem Platonis* IV. 3.11, 37, 508–10 (ed. Mohler, 1927).
[55] IV 3.2, 494 (Mohler).

the classification of things as 'mine' and 'not mine'. For Bessarion, it was the desire for exclusive possession which caused the collapse of states, even the greatest ones: Athens, Sparta, Rome. Then comes the studied *praeteritio*: 'I pass over examples from our own times, lest I cause offence.'[56] Here speaks the consummate diplomat, which Bessarion was (except when doing battle with George of Trebizond).

It is consistent with his lack of interest in the details of Aristotle's critique of Plato that Bessarion does not pick up Aristotle's gratuitous extension of the regime of the Guards to encompass the whole polity. Indeed Bessarion says nothing of the Guards, nothing of the social and political structure of Plato's Kallipolis. He talks, as Proclus had done, as if the whole citizenry were involved.[57]

There is one surprise. Bessarion knows about Kallipolis B, the ideal state of the *Laws*, and he quotes the whole passage. He does this uniquely among commentators on Plato's *Republic* to my knowledge. But then *Against the Slanderer of Plato* is not a commentary on the *Republic*. It's a total defence of Plato. And by now, in this part of the treatise, Bessarion has moved on to the *Laws*. He does this to clinch the point, which as we have seen is a leitmotiv of the whole discussion, that Plato himself had doubts about the regime of Kallipolis. So the ideal state is now agreed to be one that is divine rather than human. That is the part of the *Laws* passage that he wants to draw attention to, and that is why he quotes the passage.[58]

Marsilio Ficino (1433–99)

'To this day, Plato is unknown to Latin men.' So wrote Bessarion to Guillaume Fichet in 1470, two years before his death.[59] Unknown to him, Marsilio Ficino of Florence had one year earlier completed a translation of nearly the whole corpus of Plato from Greek into Latin, at the request

---

[56] IV 3.3, 498 (Mohler).

[57] Bessarion focuses on the sharing of women. Property is of less concern to him, until he comes to consider the *Laws*, when he can now argue (plausibly) that Plato and Aristotle see eye to eye. For Plato's second best city of the *Laws*, Magnesia, has a lot in common with Aristotle's own ideal state of the *Politics*. The explanation is presumably that George of Trebizond was calling the shots, and he, like most Christian commentators through the ages, was concerned much more with the sexual issue than the question of property.

[58] IV 3.10, 508 (Mohler).

[59] This was only partly true then. If we ignore the *Timaeus*, Chrysoloras and the two Decembrios had translated the *Republic* (in the case of Chrysoloras only Books 1–5) between 1403 and 1440, Bruni had translated five dialogues by 1423, and the *Letters* shortly after. In addition, George of Trebizond and Theodore translated the *Laws* before 1465, and George the *Parmenides* as well. On the other hand, all of these remained in manuscript and were probably not widely circulated.

of his patron Cosimo de' Medici. In so doing, Ficino brought the revival of Plato in Italy to a climax and ensured the transmission of his thought to Western Europe. By another coincidence 1469 was the final publication date of Bessarion's *Against the Slanderer of Plato*. Ficino's work was not actually printed until 1484, so Bessarion went to his grave unaware of its existence (d.1472, as did his adversary George).[60] Bessarion was thirty years older than Ficino and they moved in quite different circles. Bessarion was a high-flying papal diplomat, much of whose energies were absorbed with two missions, both unsuccessful: restoring the unity of Christendom and, after the fall of Constantinople, drumming up support for a crusade against the Turks. Ficino was a philologist, physician and philosopher, who taught Plato to the young within his own 'Academy' at Florence, and to men of culture and education in his city and beyond. Ficino was clearly indebted to Bessarion's works. They each wrote a *Platonic Theology* – with Proclus' work of the same name as the ultimate model and source. They were equally devoted to Plato and had a shared interest in constructing an 'ancient theology' out of a combination of Christianity and Neoplatonism. Their methods and approaches had much in common. In particular, following the exegetical methods of late antique Neoplatonists, they were concerned to direct the reader's attention to Plato's deep intentions and broad vision. Ficino is more successful than Bessarion in rising above the ongoing debate. Unlike Bessarion, he does not get involved in hand-to-hand combat with weapons chosen by an enemy; rather, his defence of Plato is contained in nutshell arguments and epitomes attached to individual books and works of Plato, a foretaste of the full commentaries he had wanted to write but (in most cases) never did. The opening words of his argumentum to *Republic* Book Five set the tone:

I am well aware that there are some who expect an Apologia from us, in which we defend against the malevolent or just ignorant calumny this fifth book which proposes a citizens' communality of everything. Such detractors should read Plato himself, I suggest, and should do so with care and should judge without bias: they will then want no Apologia at all, and I know what I speak of.

It was predictable that Ficino would ascribe to Plato 'a citizens' communality of everything', reproducing the same error that had occurred in friend and foe of Plato alike from Aristotle on. What makes this a little different is that it occurs in the argumentum appended to Book Five of the *Republic*, which he had just translated accurately, and which gives Plato's prescriptions as they actually were.

---

[60] A somewhat expanded version was published in 1496; see Hankins (1990), 320, for the details.

Let us return to the opening of the argumentum. It is bold. Plato, he says, needs no defence, no advocate. He may need an interpreter perhaps, because in Plato we have an inspired theologian who speaks in mysteries. Bessarion had started off on the wrong foot by making excuses for Plato and for himself for taking Plato's side, and he never fully recovered his balance. Ficino continues in the same up-beat manner:

Plato was humanity's Apolline physician: he realized that individuals and families and states are all for ever ailing, ailing seriously, all over the world, and that so far no treatment from politician doctors, vainly trying their cures for generations by now, has brought either liberation from the ailments or at least a little alleviation and a minimal convalescence. And so he devoted himself, with as much common sense as kindness, to that rule which is peculiar to physicians, by which medical authority allows that if a patient shows very little recovery when certain treatment, say a cold treatment, is applied, then in the end recourse may properly be had to hot treatments. Because of his understanding that laws dividing property into private portions brought mankind no benefit over time – indeed things were daily getting worse – he was not wrong to focus instead on rules of friendship, which said that between friends everything should be in common, so that once division and the cause of division and misery were removed we could achieve concord, oneness and happiness.

Ficino does address some of the traditional concerns of antiplatonists. He provided his own brand of special pleading for the sharing of wives and children. But the main point has already been made and it is a good one. Private property regimes hadn't worked, they had failed mankind, they had not produced concord, unity and happiness but their opposites, and things were only going downhill. Plato had seen this and like a good doctor prescribed a cure, a friendship regime involving the sharing of everything. The medical metaphor seems standard enough, but in Ficino's hands it is self-referential, for he was a physician, and the son of one, the court physician no less. As Ficino writes elsewhere:

I have had two fathers, Ficino the medicus and Cosimo de' Medici. From the one I was born, from the other, reborn. The former commended me to Galen (the doctor and Platonist); the other consecrated me to divine Plato. Both the former and the latter destined me to be a doctor, a Galen, a doctor of bodies, as well as a Plato, a doctor of souls.[61]

Ficino saw himself as performing a similar task for his city to Plato's for Athens, rescuing it from its spiritual and political ills. At the end of the argumentum on Book Five he appears to have Florence in his sights,

---

[61] *Opera* 493.

as he returns to the idea that the passion for private property is at the bottom of 'our' ills. He looks to the day when 'our own casual lack of care will get removed, as if it were a quality quite alien from us, when in all of us it is pretty well general'. He continues:

Out too will go that daily dishonesty which distracts our judgement so stupidly in our concentration upon what we think of as our own. Out will go finally that extreme of worry, concern and unhappiness which torments us because of our crazy love of property. I omit the fact that when the cause of dispute is removed, charity becomes both a shared thing and a whole thing.

There remains the question of the feasibility of the arrangements set out by Plato in the *Republic*. Bessarion had more or less capitulated on this point, constantly representing Plato as seeing no chance of their implementation. Ficino is more positive and arrives at a position which may not be far from Plato's own: 'First then: if it could not be brought into being, he shows he has not published to no purpose, since it can be an ideal to be copied in shaping citizen bodies as far as possible. Second he shows that it can only be brought into being when philosophers are the kings, and that till then there will be no respite from evil.'

A footnote: Antonio da Rho in the treatise *Against Lactantius* has Decembrio draw a comparison between Plato's communality and that of the contemporary Franciscans (of which he, Antonio da Rho, happened to be a member). Ficino goes further than this. In countering the alleged novelty of regimes of communality, he cites precedents from ancient times to the present, at the end drawing on the Christian tradition from its origins to the present day, thus: 'We have good record further that there was a similar sharing of goods among the Brahmins, the Gymnosophistae, the Essenes and the Pythagoreans, and also, to begin with, among the holy men who set up the Christian community [he's talking of Acts 2 and 4–5]. We see too in our own times that goodness and happiness are the attainment of the religious who have no private property.' In bringing together, among other things, Platonic communality and that of the first Christians at Jerusalem, Ficino is following in the tracks of Gratian's *Decretum*.

BYZANTINE NEOPLATONISM: THE 'IDEAL POLITY'
OF GEMISTUS PLETHON

Gemistus Plethon was the greatest philosopher of the age, unrivalled in his knowledge of both Plato and Aristotle. We have seen that he was an envoy of the Eastern Church at the Unity Conference with representatives of the Western Church at Ferrara, and then at Florence in 1439, and took time off to deliver lectures 'On the Differences between Aristotle and Plato', which were published soon afterwards. This work has nothing to say about political philosophy. It would be fascinating to know what Plethon thought of Kallipolis. He seems to have aired his opinions in his major work *On the Laws*. That work was held back deliberately by the author and only released after his death in 1452 – and almost immediately consigned to the flames by George Gennadius Scholarius, the first patriarch of Constantinople under Turkish rule. It is a tragedy that we have only fragments of the life's work of the man who has been regarded as the greatest philosopher since Plato and Aristotle. Scholarius was an Aristotelian and a long-term opponent of Plethon. He was convinced that Plethon was a heretic, or worse, a pagan. He was undoubtedly right. As to Plethon on Kallipolis, there is a letter of Scholarius, in which he justifies burning the book on a number of grounds, including that the author had shown himself sympathetic to such abominations as the sharing of women.[62]

Still, the cupboard of Plethon's political philosophy is not bare. He was not only a philosopher and teacher, but also a politician and courtier of consequence at Mistra in the Peloponnese, outpost of the crumbling Byzantine empire, through much of the first half of the fifteenth century. Within a decade of his arrival at Mistra (around 1409), Plethon had composed two memoranda, the first for the despot of Mistra, Theodore, the second, a few years later (and by 1418), for the emperor Manuel. In these documents Plethon put forward proposals for the salvation of the Peloponnese and the empire. His plans are presented not as a utopian dream, but as a package of severely practical measures, whose implementation is held to be essential, and feasible. Plethon challenges his addressees to find some better solution if they disapprove of his own, and he offers himself as executor of his own project, should no one else come forward. In tune with the practical nature of the project, the discussion is wide-ranging and detailed, covering such matters as currency, taxation, military recruitment and the agrarian economy.[63] Utopian or not, and

---

[62] Scholarius, *Letter to Joseph* 636B; 647C.

[63] Plethon was concerned about, e.g., tax exemptions of foreign merchants, monasteries and other large landowners, the deleterious effects of the circulation of foreign currency, the complex and exploitative tax system, the weakness of the armed forces and low agricultural production.

there is no sign that his advice was heeded, the structure and ideology of his reformed, model polity bear the clear imprint of Plato's Kallipolis.

Obviously, Plethon's model state is by no means an exact replica of or even approximation to that of Plato. The historical context and Plethon's own influential part in it, the genre of the works, and the other intellectual influences to which he was subjected, rule this out.[64] Still, the Platonic element in his construction is transparent, and striking, beginning with the tripartite structure.[65] The guiding principle of this structure is Plato's: each part is by nature suited to its own role and must not stray from it. In Plethon's polity, as in Plato's, the inference is drawn that the governing class and the military should be supported by the producing class by means of a tax so that they can protect, and save, the state.

Early in the *Address to Theodore* Plethon turns, after a historical introduction, to the sphere of the constitution and government:

In the realm of human affairs, the only way of ensuring a sure and safe recovery for any city or people is the reform of the political system. Cities succeed or fail because they are endowed with a good or bad political system. Men of good judgement rank monarchy as the best of constitutions, as being the one that is equipped with the best of advisers and also enjoys the benefit of good laws which are actually enforced. The best advisory body is a moderate number of trained and educated men ... Good laws as a general rule are laws which lay it down that each of the parts and classes of a state should discharge its own proper function; which forbid the men of each class to interfere with what is not properly theirs, whether in their actions or in the habits of their lives.

There are three such parts or classes of a state. The first, the most necessary, and the largest in almost every state is that of the husbandmen – farmers, shepherds and all others who procure any produce from the land by the labours of their own hands. A second part or class is that which ministers to the needs of the husbandmen and of the rest of the population of the state – artisans, merchants, traders and the like ... and there are also in this class some who live by hiring out the strength of their bodies in the service of others as occasional labourers. Finally, there is the ruling class – saviours and guardians of the whole city or race with the king or some leader at their head and under him others who charge themselves with the different departments of the race or polis and make

---

[64] There are various discrepancies. For example, in opting for monarchy as the best constitution, Plethon was following Plato's *Politicus* (302d–303d) rather than the *Republic*. Plato gives the lion's share of attention to the composition, recruitment, education and lifestyle of the Guards. Plethon treads lightly over these matters (while insisting that the monarch must have the best of advisers who must be well educated), but is expansive on monetary, fiscal, economic and military matters, which do not interest Plato.

[65] Plethon's three classes are the ruling class who are the military, agricultural producers, and a service sector of traders, etc.

provision for their security if anything untoward happens ... The membership of this ruling class, occupied as they are with the protection of the community, and needing the aid of others for their support, must have contributions assigned to them, drawn in the main from the several members of the husbandman class, and providing subsistence to the Guards in common and pay and reward for the work of protection. This is the origin of taxes.[66]

Plethon insists that the tripartite organization of the polity has its origins in nature, and that no part 'should exchange its way of life or mode of action for that of another; more especially, the ruling class should not engage in any of the pursuits of the ministerial class ... such as merchandise, trading and the like'. Later he will reinforce the point, with special reference to the need to keep soldiering and farmwork apart, with a *bon mot*: 'We do not use donkeys to do the work of thoroughbred horses, nor do we use thoroughbred horses to do the work of donkeys.'[67]

So far, so Platonic. When Plethon turns to detailed reform measures, he is on his own. Here are his proposals for land reform:

I would next suggest that all the land should be the common property of all its inhabitants, as perhaps it is by nature, and that no man should claim any part as his private property. Every man who wishes to do so should be allowed to plant a crop wherever he will, to erect a house, and to plough as much land as he wishes and is able to plough, on the assumption that he will have that amount at his disposal in so far as, and on condition that he does not neglect to till it while he is its occupant. Meanwhile he should pay no rent to any person, and should not be hindered by any person, other than one who has anticipated him in cultivating it, and this according to the rule regulating all common property that does not belong to any one man more than it does to another. Then, and on that basis, the occupant of the land will, if he ranks among the helots, pay to the public funds a third of the product, as I have suggested; but he will have no further obligation whatsoever to any person, and he will be counted as having paid finally and once for all the whole of his dues ... regulating all common property that does not belong to any one man more than it does to another ... All the land would be under cultivation and crops, and no part would be idle or untended, if it were equally possible for all who wished to apply their labour wherever they desired to do so; and the scheme I suggest would thus be to the greater advantage both of the community and of individuals.[68]

There are echoes here of later thinkers: Thomas More, John Locke and Jean-Jacques Rousseau – not forgetting Chairman Mao with his battle cry

---

[66] *PG* 160, 845A; 848B–849C.   [67] *PG* 160, 861C.
[68] *PG* 160, 833D–836B. This comes from the address to Manuel; in the address to Theodore there is only a hint of what is to come. See 853A.

'Land to the tillers!'[69] In the case of Thomas More, there are more than echoes.[70] More would have known of Plethon's utopian scheme from a variety of sources, including Pico della Mirandola, Erasmus and Theodore of Gaza, a younger contemporary of Plethon, who died in the year of More's birth (1478). Theodore had access to a copy of *On the Laws*, or part of it – hence some of the work has been preserved. More clearly studied Plethon carefully. The extent of his borrowings is surprising, especially in the sphere of religion. Plethon was a crypto-pagan. For our purposes, it is to be noted that More, like Plethon, ruled out private property and criticized those who had land but did not work it; he names 'nobles, gentry, yes and even some abbots'. Plethon aimed his fiercest criticism at monasteries. At one point More suggests that those living near Utopia can be forcibly deprived of their land by the Utopians if they leave it idle – an argument that was to become familiar in contexts of imperialism, but that appears in More perhaps for the first time:

By their policies the Utopians make the land yield an abundance for all, which had previously seemed too barren or paltry even to support the natives. But if the natives will not join in living under their laws, the Utopians drive them out of the land that they claim for themselves, and if they resist make war on them. The Utopians say it is perfectly justifiable to make war on people who leave their land idle and waste, yet forbid the use of it to others who, by the law of nature, ought to be supported by it.[71]

Plethon does not say how his reforms were to be implemented. It is difficult to imagine how they could have been introduced without forcible seizure and redistribution.

As to the intellectual background to Plethon, we can I think trace the influence of Stoic or Stoicizing Golden Age primitivism, according to which, by natural law, or in the state of nature, everything is common to all, and nothing is owned privately.[72] As to Plato, Plethon has taken over basic structural elements of Kallipolis, but then used them as a springboard to launch his own programme. I don't think we can say that Plato has suffered in his hands. He has not misread or misrepresented Plato. In contrast Thomas More would have us believe that Plato in the *Republic*

---

[69] Barker (1957), 204, evokes Locke's *Second Treatise on Civil Government*, ch. 5, and Rousseau's *Du Contrat Social* 1.9. Was Plethon aware that in Hippodamus' ideal polity the land was held in common? More intriguing is the apparent anticipation of the idea of Locke that labour provided justification for ownership. But Plethon appears to be thinking in terms of circulating possession rather than stable ownership.

[70] To my knowledge only Derrett (1965) has appreciated this.

[71] Adams (1992) *Utopia* 2, 41.   [72] See Chapter 5, below.

advocates, and the Utopians actually practise, the holding of everything in common *with equal shares for everyone*. The two key passages are as follows:

Though my advice may be repugnant to the king's counsellors, I don't see why they should consider it eccentric to the point of folly. What if I told them the kind of thing that Plato advocates in his *Republic*, or which the Utopians actually practise in theirs? However superior those institutions might be (and as a matter of fact they are), yet here they would be inappropriate, because private property is the rule here, and there all things are held in common.[73]

So I reflect on the wonderfully wise and sacred institutions of the Utopians who are so well governed with so few laws. Among them virtue has its own reward, yet everything is shared equally, and all men live in plenty ... When I consider all these things, I become more sympathetic to Plato and do not wonder that he declined to make laws for any people who refused to share their goods equally. Wisest of men, he easily perceived that the one and only road to the welfare of all lies through the absolute equality of goods. I doubt whether such equality can ever be achieved where property belongs to individual men.[74]

With the advancement of an idea as preposterous as that Plato was a champion of equality,[75] we seem to have entered a new phase in the manipulation of the political thought of Plato, which culminates in the modern period when Plato becomes a weapon, or a victim, in the ideological warfare between Left and Right. That is another story. Our present narrative ends with two utopian writers who in their different ways drew inspiration from Plato, but, unlike Plato, found no room for private property in their regimes.

---

[73] Ibid. *Utopia* 1, 26.   [74] Ibid. *Utopia* 1, 28.   [75] Contrast Plato, *Laws* 756e–757e.

CHAPTER 3

Renunciation and communality: thinking through the primitive Church

PRELIMINARIES

'In revolutionary France of April 1849, a banquet was held of "socialist priests", 33 of them, 3 in cassocks, and the rest dressed as lay men. 600 working men joined the festivity, and toasted Jesus of Nazareth, father of socialism.'[1]

In 1891 Pope Leo XIII issued the encyclical *Rerum Novarum*. The early chapters carry the message that socialism is unjust and deleterious to workers' interests, whereas private property is natural, blessed by God, and conducive to the common and private good. That principle once established, the Pope is now ready to pronounce on the issue of how the class struggle can be moderated, through a proper understanding of how wealth should be used. For guidance on this point, he says, the place to turn is not to philosophy but to the teachings of the Church; and the Pope now cites authorities. Thomas Aquinas receives pride of place, followed by New Testament texts urging charitable giving. We hear that in God's view, 'there is nothing disgraceful in poverty, nor cause for shame in having to work for a living': 2 Corinthians 8:9 is cited, where St Paul says of Christ: 'He who was rich became poor for our sake.' Pope Leo's particular take on Christ's poverty is that Christ was a working man, a regular member of the labour force: 'He chose to be seen and thought of as the son of a carpenter, despite his being the Son of God and very God himself; and having done so, made no objection to spending a large part of his life at the carpenter's trade.' I suspect the Christian revolutionaries of 1849 had a different Christ in mind, equally deriving from New Testament texts: Christ on the road with his chosen few, who

---

[1] Chadwick (1998), 310.

had, like him, given up everything; Christ challenging the rich man to sell all his property and distribute it to the poor.

Scriptural texts can furnish authority for contrasting points of view and very different ideological positions; they can also be edited, and used selectively. All this certainly applies to Acts 2:43–5 and 4:32–5:5 and the narratives of which they form a part, apparently composed by the Gospel writer, Luke:

> And fear came upon every soul; and many wonders and signs were done through the apostles. And all who believed were together and had all things in common; and they sold their possessions and goods and distributed them to all, as any had need.
>
> Now the company of those who believed were of one heart and soul, and no one said that any of the things which he possessed was his own, but they had everything in common. And with great power the apostles gave their testimony to the resurrection of the Lord Jesus, and great grace was upon them all. There was not a needy person among them, for as many as were possessors of lands or houses sold them, and brought the proceeds of what was sold and laid it at the apostles' feet; and distribution was made to each, as any had need. Thus Joseph who was surnamed by the apostles Barnabas ... sold a field which belonged to him, and brought the money and laid it at the apostles' feet. But a man named Ananias with his wife Sapphira sold a piece of property, and with his wife's knowledge he kept back some of the proceeds, and brought only a part and laid it at the apostles' feet. But Peter said: 'Ananias, why has Satan filled your heart to lie to the Holy Spirit and to keep each part of the proceeds of the land? While it remained unsold, did it not remain your own? And after it was sold, was it not at your disposal? How is it that you have contrived this deed in your heart? You have not lied to men but to God.' When Ananias heard these words, he fell down and died.[2]

Acts 4:32 (as we have seen)[3] is the text on the basis of which Gratian in his *Decretum* made the case, with a little help from Plato, for the holding of property in common as being in accordance with natural law. Leo XIII in his encyclical approaches the Acts texts once and with circumspection. He writes: 'So deeply did the first Christians love one another that very many among them who were well-to-do stripped themselves of wealth to bring aid to those worse off: "None of their members was ever in want." ' (Acts 4:34). That's all: there is no mention of community of property, though such a regime is undoubtedly to be read in Acts; nor does the Pope pick up the theme of friendship which percolates through the Acts passage, a

---

[2] The story of the similar fate of Sapphira three hours later follows (Acts 5:7–11).
[3] See pp. 3, 35; cf. pp. 81–2.

theme taken over from the classical philosophical tradition. 'All things in common.' 'Of one heart and soul.' 'No one calls anything his own.' We think of Plato, *Republic*; of Aristotle on friendship in the *Nicomachean Ethics*, citing what he calls the 'common tags', 'friends are of one soul' and 'friends have goods in common'; and also of Cicero in *On Duties*.[4] The Pope wants to stress the charitable behaviour of the first Christians. There is an indication too that he saw charity and friendship as in a sense in competition, for in Chapter 21 of the Encyclical he ranks the former above the latter. I shall come back to the tension between the two concepts at the end of this chapter.

The fact that Luke was tapping into an established tradition of utopic thought has been taken as a sign, one of many, that his story is unreliable as history. Several generations of biblical scholars have by now had their say and concur with this opinion. As it happens, the Pontificate of this same Pope Leo XIII (1878–1903) saw an upsurge of debate on the issue. With a few exceptions, among them a paper of Friedrich Engels,[5] the general view advanced at that time was that Luke's account could not be trusted, except in so far as it told of exceptionally generous almsgiving. This was precisely the message that the Pope extracted from Acts. The weight of scholarly opinion has not shifted since, despite the publication in 1951 of a document known as the Manual of Discipline amongst the Dead Sea Scrolls. This document contains elaborate regulations for the transference of private property into community control by stages. It is contemporaneous with the events described in Acts. Brian Capper has recently argued with ingenuity and plausibility that the nature of the first Christian community at Jerusalem was shaped by an influx of property-sharing ascetics from a local Essene group structured like the Qumran community, and that Luke's account bears the marks of its presence.[6]

It is distinctly possible, then, that there was community of property among the first Christians at Jerusalem. There is no reason to think that the Jerusalem community provided a model that was followed elsewhere; in any case, it did not itself last long. It needed fraternal assistance in order to survive (as is recorded in Acts), and it ceased to exist, probably in AD 66, at the outbreak of the war with the Romans.

---

[4] Arist., *Nich. Eth.* 9.8.2, 1168b; Cic., *On Duties* 1.16.5. See Mealand (1977).

[5] *Die Neue Zeit* 13 (1894–5), 4–13 and 36–43.

[6] Capper (1995a, b). There is a good, summary account of the community of the Essenes in Betz (1999), 444–70.

I wish I could penetrate into the mind of Luke as he put together those verses. One can see why the historical accuracy of the account is held to be suspect: it is short on detail and is generalized, an exemplary foundation story. It is nonetheless a story that contains some nuggets of fact derived from earlier sources, some hints of Essene-type property arrangements, of which Luke may well have been unaware, and for which he may well have had little sympathy. He was a Gentile Christian, not a child of the Jerusalem commune.

My business now is not biblical scholarship. I want to ask what happened to two sets of ideas which have their origin in New Testament texts: first, the renunciation of property and the community of property among Christians; and second, the poverty of Jesus and his apostles.[7] I want to ask how these ideas figured in later ages, what new justifications and explanations of private property and communality were thrown up in the various discussions, and what impact they had on the history of ideas in general.

Besides the Acts passages, there are a number of New Testament texts that address the renunciation of property, and the deliberate pursuit of poverty. They are very familiar. I offer here a selection.

Matthew 19:16–30 (excerpts): Jesus is approached by a rich man seeking salvation, but not at the cost of giving up his wealth. 'Jesus said to him: If you would be perfect, go, sell what you possess and give to the poor and you will have treasure in heaven; and come, follow me' (19:21). (The corresponding passages in the other Gospels omit 'if you would be perfect'.) The rich man goes away despondent, and Jesus comments: 'Truly I say unto you, it will be hard for a rich man to enter into the kingdom of heaven. Again I tell you: it is easier for a camel to go through the eye of a needle, than for a rich man to enter the kingdom of God' (19:23–4). The disciples are astonished, and ask who can be saved? Jesus answers: 'With men this is impossible; but with God all things are possible' (19:26). Peter, acting as spokesman for the disciples, says: 'Lo we have left everything and followed you; what then shall we have?' (19:27). He receives the welcome answer: eternal life (19:28–9).

Matt. 8:20; cf. 2 Cor. 8:9: Jesus himself renounced everything and imposed poverty on himself, before he demanded it of his disciples. He said: 'The foxes have holes, and the birds of the air have nests, but the Son

---

[7] To some extent this distinction, between what I will call *ecclesia primitiva* and *vita apostolica*, is an artificial one; but I find it useful for purposes of analysis.

of man has nowhere to lay his head.'[8] This is picked up and generalized by Paul: 'For you know the grace of our Lord Jesus Christ, that though he was rich yet for your sakes he became poor, so that by his poverty you might become rich.'

Matt. 6:25–33 (from the Sermon on the Mount): 'Therefore I tell you, do not be anxious about your life, what you shall eat or what you shall drink, nor about your body, what you shall put on. Is not life more than food, and the body more than clothing? Look at the birds of the air: they neither sow nor reap nor gather into barns, and yet your heavenly Father feeds them. Are you not of more value than they? ... Therefore do not be anxious, saying, 'What shall we eat?' or 'What shall we drink?', or 'What shall we wear?' For the Gentiles seek all these things; and your heavenly Father knows that you need them all. But seek first his kingdom and his righteousness, and all these things shall be yours as well. Therefore do not be anxious about tomorrow, for tomorrow will be anxious for itself. Let the day's own trouble be sufficient for the day.'

The texts may be said to form a single narrative. They flow into each other, together forming an image, a model, of the ideal Christian life. However, they also have individual histories which are to some extent separate and separable, and they have different roles to play in the thought and lives of Christians of later times. We will find that theologians and other interested scholars and commentators will select some texts and bypass others, and the choice is not haphazard, but appears to have a deliberate point. So, for example, the thirteenth- and fourteenth-century Franciscans sought inspiration not from Acts 2 and 4–5, but from those passages which depict the life of Christ.

In this chapter I consider texts relating to the regime of the Church of the first Christians at Jerusalem who came together after Pentecost after the departure of Jesus. The *ecclesia primitiva* (as I will call it) became a paradigm of the ideal Christian community. In the next chapter it will be the turn of those texts which project Christ in the company of the apostles, as a model of *individual* poverty and humility.

THE THIRD CENTURY: ORIGEN AND CYPRIAN

'At that time, when the perfection of the primitive church [*ecclesia primitiva*] endured inviolate among its successors ... ' So John Cassian

---

[8] This is repeated in Luke 9:58 in reply to a scribe who professed his desire to be a disciple.

begins a sentence of his *Institutes*, writing from his monastery in the south of France in the early fifth century. He is coining a phrase – for this is the first appearance of the term *ecclesia primitiva* in literature.[9] Cassian was referring to the first community of Christians, for he cites Acts 4:32 and 34–5. However, he locates it in Egypt, calls its members monks, and says that their Rule was laid down by the Gospel writer Mark as 'pontiff' of the Church at Alexandria. Cassian shows in another work, the *Collationes*, that he knew perfectly well that the author of Acts was talking about the first Christians *at Jerusalem*, but he prefers to use the 'Egyptian version' here, citing Eusebius' *Ecclesiastical History*.[10] The context explains his choice. He is addressing the matter of the monastic regimen of prayer, his aim being to promote an older, traditional model of Egyptian origin above the sundry modern variants introduced by abbots whom he dismisses as ignorant and egotistical. The Acts texts contain no hint of monastic arrangements; their connection with monasticism is a product of later interpretation.

From the third century through late antiquity and the Middle Ages to the Protestant Reformation and beyond, there were internal critics of the contemporary Church, its institutions, spiritual life and material circumstances, who found it wanting by comparison with the pristine perfection of the first community of Christians.[11] Rather than attempt to survey the whole panorama of reformist criticisms and complaints, in this chapter I will focus on the appearance of the Acts texts in discussions of monasticism, the particular form or forms of asceticism characterized by life in common. For by the early fourth century a special partnership had been forged between the Acts texts and monasticism.

Before I come to this development, I want to make brief mention of two writers from the mid-third century, Origen of Alexandria and Caesarea in Palestine (*c.*185-*c.*251), and his younger contemporary Cyprian, Bishop of Carthage (*c.*200–58). Origen and Cyprian were the earliest of the Church Fathers to make any significant use of the Acts texts. In this connection Origen's *Commentary on Matthew* and Cyprian's *On Work and Alms* are of special interest. Both homilies predate two events which are often seen as marking the opening of a new era in the history of Christian asceticism: the launching of the ascetic career of Antony in

---

[9] *Inst.* 2.5.2: 'ecclesiae illius primitivae perfectio'; cf. 2.5.1: 'primitus ecclesiam'. The bibliography on the *ecclesia primitiva* is large. The most significant contributions are the monograph of Bori (1974), and sundry articles of Olsen. See Olsen (1969, 1980, 1982a, 1982b, 1984, 1985, 1998).

[10] Cassian, *Collationes* 18.5.   [11] Ladner (1967) is a classic study.

Egypt around 270, and the foundation of the first great monastery in Egypt, by Pachomius in the early 320s. The works of Origen and Cyprian were, as it were, uncontaminated by these developments.

Some Christians in the first two centuries attempted to practise an ascetic lifestyle, influenced by the tradition handed down of the deeds and words of Jesus and the lives of the apostles and their early followers.[12] Origen in the relevant passages shows interest in the pursuit of perfection by the individual but not in group asceticism, while Cyprian is concerned with neither. Both writers conjure up the Jerusalem Church as a paradigm of unity and unanimity, but to different ends: Origen is preoccupied with the internal unity of the individual as a spiritual being, modelling himself on God; Cyprian with the unity of a structured, well-disciplined Church held together by its bishop. It is Cyprian who sets in motion themes that are associated with later usages of the Acts texts: the centrality of almsgiving, the special role of the bishop in the administration of almsgiving and the accumulation of Church property in general, and the patronal power that accrued to bishops in consequence. One passage of Origen contains hints of this, but no more.

For Origen the first Christian community is a model of unity and harmony; in demonstration of this it is enough for him to cite the phrase 'among the believers there was one heart and one soul'.[13] In so far as he gives attention to the 'communitarian' dimension, and there is little of this, it is the spiritual rather than material aspect of the *koinonia* which interests him. At times he expresses a distrust of 'multiplicity', linking it to sin, and virtue to singularity.[14] Again, in commenting on Matt. 18:19 in which Jesus envisages 'two or three' coming together, he cites 1 Cor. 1:10, in which Paul is openly critical of divisions amongst the Corinthians, and Acts 4:32a, whose message of unity and unanimity is somewhat undermined by the sceptical qualification: 'insofar as it is possible to find such a thing [i.e., having one heart and one soul] among many'.[15] Finally, in the tract against the pagan Celsus, Origen flatly rejects Celsus' claim that the Christians were few and united at the beginning and split into factions

---

[12] On Christian asceticism before the third century see, in summary, E. A. Clark (1999), 14–42.

[13] Seven of the eight texts are of this kind. The main text in question, Acts 4:32a, is usually cited en passant, and as one of a number of biblical texts. See Bori (1974), 21–61 (discussion), 214–20 (texts).

[14] *Sel. in Gen.* (Gen. 11.7), *PG* 12.112A; cf. *In Ezech. hom.* 9.1 (*GCS* 8 [33] 406): 'Where there is sin, there is a crowd, there are schisms, heresies, dissensions; where there is virtue, there is singularity, union and a single heart and soul of all believers. To put it succinctly, the beginning of all evils is the crowd, the beginning of [all] good things is limitation [*coangustatio*] and reduction [*redactio*] from a crowd to an individual.' The theme is prominent in Philo. See Bori (1974) 48ff.

[15] *In Matth.* 14.1 (*GCS* 10 [40] 275).

only when their numbers grew, with the judgement that, on the contrary, divisions were present from the beginning.[16]

In the homily *On the First Book of Kings*, 1 Cor. 1:10 and Acts 4:32a are again brought together, but this time in order to stress the need for the believer to strive for unity within himself in the face of conflicting and fluctuating opinions and desires. He must seek the perfection of an internal unity by imitating God, who is one, supremely virtuous and unchanging.

The same theme emerges on the only occasion when Origen deals with the Acts texts in any detail, in the *Commentary on Matthew* (at 15:14–15). The context is important: Origen is treating the story of the rich young man instructed to renounce everything if he wants to achieve perfection. The sheer difficulty of carrying out this exhortation 'in the name of the perfection that is in God', given the innate weakness of human beings, has led interpreters to allegorize the text, says Origen. This is branded a shameful tactic,[17] in view of the many stories told of Greek philosophers who gave up their possessions. Crates of Thebes is Origen's example, and he comments that if Greek wisdom and precepts could move men to liberate the soul in this way (as they thought), this is even more straightforward for someone *who aspires to perfection for himself*. 'Holy Scripture shows that this is quite possible, for Acts bears witness to people "who were moved by the converting power at work among the Apostles to have faith and live completely in accord with the word of Jesus".' Origen then quotes four snippets from the story: 'All that believed were together and had all things in common ... They gave thanks to God and were loved by the whole people ... Now the company of those who believed were of one heart and soul ... They brought the proceeds and laid them at the feet of the Apostles.' He goes on to recount the saga of Ananias and Sapphira, and to give it a novel twist: the couple were guilty, that is clear (and Peter can be exonerated, for it was the all-seeing God who exacted the penalty). But Origen softens the blow by allowing that theirs was a good death, for they departed life the purer for their punishment, as having believed in Christ and having surrendered a part of their wealth. Finally Origen returns to his main text, which is the story of the rich man (not that of the Jerusalem Church): 'We have said all this because we wanted to make clear that it is possible for someone to

---

[16] *C. Celsum* 3.10–12.

[17] Notwithstanding the fact that Origen was himself an artful exponent of allegory on other occasions. See Hanson (1959); Dawson (1992b).

become perfect and to respond to Jesus when he says: "Go, sell what belongs to you and give it to the poor."' He then winds up the discussion in an unexpected way:

It is, however, in my opinion the job of bishops, those who have the qualities that are appropriate to that office, to encourage people who have the capability and are persuaded by Jesus' exhortation, through guaranteeing them sustenance from the treasury, and also through urging others to adopt a similar lifestyle. In this way would be created an image of the harmony that existed among the faithful in the time of the apostles.

Origen is offering advice as to how the institutional Church might nourish and integrate the aspiring perfect. There is no call here for a return to the original Church.[18] The would-be perfect are evidently few, they are to be fed from Church funds, and the bishop will preside over the operation and provide spiritual leadership. This picture is not incompatible with that which emerges with much greater clarity from the pages of Cyprian.

Origen and Cyprian each in his own way compares the moral and spiritual values of the contemporary church unfavourably with those of the first Christians, but it is only from Cyprian that we get a sense of the Church in the grip of a full-blown crisis, which in his view reflected the travail of a world in its last throes.[19] And the Church in his time was indeed riven by discord, schism, persecution and apostasy. Cyprian's response was to construct an image of a united Church, its unity modelled on and deriving from the divine unity, and safeguarded by episcopal discipline and fraternal love, exercised above all in the support of weaker members through charitable giving. Almost invariably in Cyprian, the Acts texts are brought into service (along with many other biblical passages) for this (limited) purpose. Once only the citation of Acts is sufficiently full to include the renunciation of property by the first Christians and their sharing of everything. Furthermore, in the work in question, *On Works and Alms*, Cyprian, unlike, for example, Clement of Alexandria,[20] eschews an allegorical reading of the scriptural passages that call for the surrender of property for charitable purposes. What did he have in mind? What did he expect of his audience?

---

[18] Cf. Bori (1974), 38: 'The unanimity of Acts is presented more as an aspiration than a historically realized fact.'

[19] E.g. *Ad Demetrianum* 3: 'Scire debes senuisse iam saeculum.' See Bori (1974), 24–29 (Origen); 63–7 (Cyprian).

[20] See Ch. 4 below, p. 89.

In the homily (at Chapter Twenty-five), Acts 4:32 is the last in a parade of texts from both Old and New Testaments. The thread running through the biblical citations and giving them unity is the obligation on Christians to give alms. Almsgiving entailed the sacrifice of personal resources, that is evident. And certainly the fear of the poverty that might follow the surrender of goods for almsgiving is a repeating motif of the homily. Cyprian encourages, cajoles and finally abuses reluctant givers, who are labelled Pharisees rather than Christians. Yet there is no overt call for total renunciation. The only hint that this might be at issue comes with the citation of Matthew 19:21: 'If you would be perfect, sell up everything and give it to the poor.' This is the toughest of the scriptural texts, which vary according to the demands they appear to make. Yet even in this case there is no follow through. The story that follows concerns Zacchaeus, who earned from Jesus the promise of salvation for giving up *one half* of his goods. Cyprian, one imagines, would have been well satisfied if he had had a handful of Zacchaeuses in his congregation. Total renunciation was not on the menu. Cyprian reveals no plan to set up a monastery (here or in any other work).[21] Nor is there any sign that he was hoping or expecting to inspire individuals to head off into the desert as anchorites. Cyprian's own financial situation is something of a puzzle. It seems that he was willing to divest himself of his worldly goods, but was not successful in doing so. On his conversion he sold his properties and possessions, but received them back, apparently by the favour of God.

Cyprian did not view the primitive Church as a model that could be transplanted into mid-third-century Carthage. The truths that he gleaned from Acts were these: the obligation of almsgiving for Christians, the central role of the apostles, and the reward of salvation. It is pertinent that Cyprian was a conscientious and active bishop, keen to boost the authority of his office within the still-evolving hierarchy of the Church. We know too from his letters that he took special responsibility for running the Church's charitable programme, and that he strove to monitor and maintain it even when persecution forced him to go into hiding. If he saw himself in the position of the apostles in the Acts story, as receiver and distributor of charitable contributions, he would probably not have been the first bishop to do so: he was certainly not the last.

I now turn to the 'capture' of Acts 2 and 4 by the monastic movement.

---

[21] It may be significant that in the summary of Acts 4:32 which precedes the citation of the passage Cyprian omits the detail that all was held in common.

ACTS AND MONASTICISM: PHILO IN EUSEBIUS AND JEROME

That the Acts texts would come to be associated with monasticism was predictable. Thus Acts 4:32 is frequently turned to in the literature emanating from the monastic movement initiated by Pachomius in Egypt in the 420s, as providing a model for life of the community.[22] The desirability of imitating the primitive church was urged by Basil of Caesarea in the next generation,[23] and it became a standard theme in Greek patristic literature thereafter, and subsequently spread widely in the West, especially after the translation into Latin of Basil's Rule in *c.*400. But the connection with monasticism had been made already a century earlier. This came about by means of a bizarre piece of historical fabrication carried out by Eusebius bishop of Caesarea, who lived under Diocletian and Constantine and wrote his *Ecclesiastical History* around 300.

Eusebius in Book Two of the *Ecclesiastical History* addresses the beginnings of the Christian community.[24] He proceeds to read a passage from *On the Contemplative Life* by Philo, the Hellenized Jew from Alexandria, as if it describes a Christian cell set up in Egypt by the Gospel writer Mark. This group of Christians was obviously, according to Eusebius, an offshoot of the first community of Christians at Jerusalem. So he is able by circular reasoning to arrive at a detailed understanding of what the Jerusalem Church was like: for the lifestyle of the Egyptian group was presumably modelled on that of the Jerusalem group. But Philo was describing not Christian, but Jewish ascetics, specifically a group called the Therapeutae, known also to Josephus. Eusebius has to turn Philo into a Christian to make the story work:

They say that this Mark was the first to be sent to preach in Egypt the Gospel which he had also put into writing, and was the first to establish churches in Alexandria itself. The number of men and women who were there converted at the first attempt was so great, and their asceticism was so extraordinarily philosophic, that Philo thought it right to describe their conduct and assemblies and meals and all the rest of their manner of life. Tradition says that he came to Rome in the time of Claudius to speak to Peter ... This would, indeed, be not improbable since the treatise to which we refer, composed by him many years

---

[22] On Pachomius and his followers, and Acts, see *Life of Pachomius and his Disciples*, ed. A.Veilleux: *Pachomian Koinonia, First Sahidic Life of Pachomius*, ch.11; cf. *First Greek Life* 131; *Bohairic Life* 194; *Testament of Horsiesius* 50.

[23] Basil, *Ascetic Works*, e.g. *Longer Rules* 347E–348A, 380B–381A; *Shorter Rules* 183; *De Iudicio* 216D; etc.

[24] Eus., *Hist. Eccl.* 2.16–17 (transl. A. Bowen); Jerome, *De Viris Inlustribus* (*On Famous Men*) 8; 11. See, briefly, on Eusebius' argument, Barnes (1981), 130; Bori (1974), 145.

later, obviously contains the rules of the Church which are still observed in our time. Moreover, from his very accurate description of the life of our ascetics it will be plain that he not only knew, but welcomed, reverenced, and recognized the divine mission of the apostolic men of his day, who were, it appears, of Hebrew origin, and thus still preserved most of the ancient customs in a strictly Jewish Manner ... Philo says 'that they and the women with them were called Therapeutae and Therapeutides'[25] ...

At any rate he bears witness especially to their abandonment of property, and states that when they begin to follow philosophy they give up their possessions to their relations, and then, having bade farewell to all the cares of life, go outside the walls to make their dwellings in deserts and oases, and so on. Now also in the canonical Acts of the Apostles it is related that all the acquaintances of the Apostles sold their goods and possessions and divided them among all according as anyone had need so that none was in want among them; and as many as were possessors of lands or houses, so the story says, sold them and brought the price of what had been sold and laid it at the feet of the Apostles, so that it might be divided to each according as any had need ... To practices like those which have been related Philo bears witness and continues in the following words: 'The race is found in many places in the world, for it was right that both Greece and barbarism should share in perfect good, but it abounds in Egypt in each of the so-called nomes and especially around Alexandria[26] ... In each house there is a sacred dwelling which is called a sanctuary and a monastery, "monasterion", in which they celebrate in seclusion the mysteries of the sacred life, and bring nothing into it, either drink or food or any of the other things necessary for bodily needs, but law and inspired oracles given by the prophets and hymns and other things by which knowledge and religion are increased and perfected.'

Warming to his task, Eusebius proposes that the sacred scriptures that they read and expounded included: 'the Gospels, the writings of the apostles and some expositions of prophets after the manner of the ancients, such as are in the Epistle to the Hebrews and many other of the Epistles of Paul'. And he continues: 'We think that these words of Philo are clear and indisputably refer to our communion. But if after this anyone obstinately deny it let him be converted from his scepticism and be persuaded by clearer indications which cannot be found among any, save only in the worship of Christians according to the Gospel.' These clearer indications turn out to be the presence of 'elderly virgins who kept their chastity from no compulsion', the fact that the men and the women

---

[25] Eusebius' gloss on this is that the title of Christian was unavailable, 'since [it] had not yet become well known everywhere'. This at least could be true.

[26] The detail that Philo's communities are already dispersed throughout the world, which rules out the possibility of their being Christian, does not trouble Eusebius.

live separately in the same place, the festivals they celebrate and, to cap it all, a Church hierarchy rising to the episcopate: 'In addition to this he writes of the order of precedence of those who have been appointed to the service of the Church, both to the diaconate and to the supremacy of the episcopate at the head over all.' Eusebius concludes: 'Anyone who has a love of accurate knowledge of these things can learn from the narrative of the author quoted already, and it is plain to everyone that Philo perceived and described the first heralds of teaching according to the Gospel and the customs handed down from the beginning by the apostles.'

So there we have it: the first community of Christians described at first hand by a contemporary source. What better authentication and legitimation for the foundation story of the Church could one hope for? The irony is that if it is true that the first Church at Jerusalem received a significant contribution from Jewish asceticism, then the practices of the Therapeutae as read in Philo and Josephus might well be a useful source for the first Christian community. Meanwhile, Eusebius' fanciful reconstruction passed into the mainstream of Christian thinking on the primitive Church. His version remained highly influential, leaving its mark for example on John Cassian in the early fifth century, who as we saw traced communal asceticism back not only to Jerusalem but also to its offshoot in Egypt, and on Jerome a generation earlier, in the late fourth century. About sixty per cent of Jerome's book *On Famous Men* (392–3) is taken over from Eusebius. There are chapters on Mark and on Philo. Jerome accepts that Philo was writing of Mark's handiwork in Egypt:

Having finished writing about the Good News, he [Mark] proceeded to spread it, journeying to Egypt and preaching Christ. He established first a Church at Alexandria; a Church marked by such signal learning and continence of life that all believers in Christ were constrained to follow its example. Indeed Philo, the most eloquent of the Jews, witnessed the first church at Alexandria in its Judaizing phase, and wrote of their way of life just as if he was praising his own race. And just as Luke narrates that the faithful at Jerusalem had everything in common, so Philo perceived the same practices installed at Alexandria under the direction of Mark.

Jerome on Philo has one significant development from Eusebius, which reflects the extraordinary progress that the ascetic movement had made in the course of the fourth century. In the accounts of Philo and Eusebius *monasterion* signifies a simple room or cell; in Jerome however it means place of habitation (*habitaculum*). Furthermore, Jerome makes a direct comparison with monks of his day, who he says model themselves on the first Christians. Further, the dispersal through the Roman empire of groups of ascetics, who in Philo's day could only have been Jews, could now be accurately described as a Christian phenomenon.

The chapter on Philo begins with a confirmation of his status as an ecclesiastical historian, as a reward as it were for his glorification of the Christian congregations both in Alexandria and throughout the Roman world:

> We rank Philo the Jew, an Alexandrian by birth, and born to a family of priests, among historians of the Church. For in composing a book about the first Church founded by Mark the evangelist at Alexandria, he praised our people and not only those in Alexandria. For he also noted their presence in many provinces; and their dwelling places he named as monasteries.

Jerome proceeds:

> It is clear then that the first Church of the faithful in Christ was such as the monks of today are desirous of emulating: no one had any personal possessions; no one among them was rich, no one poor; resources were divided among the needy; they devoted themselves to praying and the singing of psalms. Just so were the believers at Jerusalem in those first times – as Luke reports.

As a footnote to this discussion, and as confirmation of the status of the Eusebian myth of the early Church as mainstream, let us note that the Venerable Bede was a keen student of the Acts of the Apostles and knew his Jerome well. He too saw the early Christians as the first monks.[27]

Let us now see how the paradigm of the first Christian community was utilized by a contemporary of Jerome, Augustine.

AUGUSTINE

Augustine before his conversion tinkered with the idea of forming a group of around ten philosophically inclined friends who would share their possessions and pursue a contemplative life. It came to nothing. Hearing and reading of St Antony precipitated his conversion to an ascetic Christianity, but it was the communal rather than eremitic style of asceticism that he aspired to follow. It seems that he founded a monastery in his home town of Thagaste in Numidia. Later he set up and presided over one in Hippo Regius, and sponsored others. What was unusual about the Hippo monastery was that it incorporated clergy as well as lay monks.[28]

---

[27] Olsen (1982b).   [28] See Lawless (1987), 1–64.

Augustine thought of himself as imposing high standards on the inmates of his monastery, though there is much less emphasis on ascetic practices than in the Rule of his contemporary John Cassian for the monastery of Lérins in the south of France, or for that matter in the sixth-century Rule of Benedict.[29] It was enough of a problem for Augustine to enforce his basic principle, that those clergy who enrolled must own nothing. His initial policy was not to ordain anyone who was unwilling to give up his property and live in the monastery, 'to be poor together with me'. And he reserved the right to deprive someone of his clerical status if he failed to carry out his obligation. However, towards the end of his life, he relaxed his line: clerics could own something, but if they did, they could not live in. Anyone who was found to have reneged on his obligations would not be defrocked, but he would be excluded from the community.

What brought about this change of mind was the behaviour of a certain Januarius. It's an interesting story in itself. I tell it here in order to show the extent to which Augustine's thought and action revolved around the Acts texts. Januarius was a priest who entered the monastery and gave up property – not all of it, however; he kept some in trust for his daughter (passing over a son). That was his excuse. On his deathbed he made a will in which he disinherited the daughter (and the son) and sought to make the Church his beneficiary. Augustine refused the offer.

In the first of two sermons dealing with the matter,[30] Augustine tells how he set up the monastery in the house of the bishop; he evokes the spirit of the first Christians with a citation of Acts 4:32, then tells of Januarius and his own reaction. In the second sermon, delivered a year later, Acts 4 comes centre-stage. Acts 5, the saga of Ananias and Sapphira, is waiting in the wings. He begins by asking a deacon to read Acts 4:31–5, 'so that you may see where the pattern is described which we desire to follow'. He then insists on reading out the passage himself, in order to drum home the point that his own community 'is the sort of community to which the reading you heard just now when we were reciting it bears witness'. Yet Januarius 'made a will as he was dying, because he had property to make a will about. There was something he called his own, while living in a community where nobody was allowed to call anything his own, but they had everything in common.' Augustine has meanwhile

---

[29] See Leyser (2000). Of the three, only Augustine's regime was inclusive of clerics as well as lay monks.

[30] *Serm.* 355 (AD 325; five years before his death), followed by *Serm.* 356 (AD 326).

been busy: to protect the reputation of the community, he has investigated the affairs of its members, and concluded that none of them had any questions to answer. Furthermore, Januarius' children, now reconciled, were in receipt of their father's legacy. So a happy ending all round – except that Augustine has something more to say to any potential transgressors, which supplements his words in the first of the two sermons. This enables us to take the link with Acts a step further.

The Januarius story as introduced in the first of the sermons seems to evoke the story of Ananias and Sapphira, who only pretended to have sold all their property, and dropped dead after being exposed by Peter. Augustine tells property-owning priests whom he is allowing to retain their status: 'Look, this is what I am saying, listen: someone who deserts the fellowship of the common life which he has taken on, *which is praised in the Acts of the Apostles*, is falling away from his vow, falling away from his holy profession. He should watch out for a judge – God, not me. I have set before his eyes what great danger he is in; let him do what he likes.' And a little later: 'If he falls away from this commitment, and remains outside as a cleric, he has fallen away from half his life. What's it got to do with me? I'm not judging him.' The same people are advised 'to consider whether they can have eternal felicity'.

'God, not me, is the judge', says Augustine. Peter accused Ananias of lying not to men, but to God; and Sapphira of conspiring, with Ananias, to tempt the Spirit of the Lord. And both of them died forthwith. It's hard not to see Januarius as an Ananias, with Augustine taking the role of Peter.

In the second sermon we learn that the priest who stays outside the monastery, described earlier as only half alive and here as crippled, is better off than the one who is inside and cheats: on the latter, Augustine appears to pass a death sentence: 'I preferred, you see, to have even crippled colleagues than to mourn over dead ones. Because anyone who is a hypocrite is dead.'

COMPETING ASCETICISMS IN LATE ANTIQUITY

What we witness in the writings and actions of Augustine and other sponsors of monasticism in the fourth and fifth centuries such as Basil, Ambrose and John Chrysostom, is the ordering of asceticism under the wing of the Church. The monasticism which is thus promoted and patronized is anchored in the foundation myth of the first Christian Church.

But the divided Christendom of late antiquity knew a number of competing brands of asceticism. We find Augustine and other Church leaders making decisions about the acceptability of particular groups and tendencies, and working in conjunction with the secular authorities to have those that were judged unacceptable labelled as heresies. These groups were usually judged heretical in terms of doctrine. One suspects however that doctrinal deviation was often an added extra, thrown in to secure condemnation at a later stage – after the group had attracted hostile attention because of their lifestyle, independence or elitism. Examples are the wandering, mendicant monks such as the Messalians who caused disruption and spread disorder, and groups which made exclusive claims about themselves like the Donatists. The Donatists were schismatics rather than heretics, until Augustine secured their reclassification as heretics on the grounds of their ecclesiology – they did not identify with the universal Church self-consciously, holding themselves alone to be the true successors of the apostolic Church. One heretical group actually called itself the Apostolici. Augustine writes:

The Apostolici have given themselves that name with great arrogance, because they refuse to admit into their membership people who make use of marriage and those who possess private property. The Catholic Church has very many monks who live this type of life. But the Apostolici are heretics because, separating themselves from the church, they think that those who make use of the things from which they themselves abstain have no hope of salvation. They resemble the Encratites and are also called Apotacticae. But they also teach some heretical doctrine or other of their own.

Augustine admits that there is nothing wrong with the style of life of these people, which they share with 'very many Catholic monks'. Their fault lies in their refusal to accept the authority of the institutional Church and their condemnation of the lifestyle of ordinary Christians.

Another strategy was open to heretical groups. Rather than take on the forces of the established Church in competition for a particular text, in this case Acts 2 and 4–5, they might avoid it or place little emphasis on it, and seek to establish their legitimacy by another route. We see this happening on one of the rare occasions in the extant literature when a heretic speaks for himself. The treatise in question is the anonymous *On Wealth* (*De Divitiis*) of around 415. I will have more to say about this text in different contexts in later chapters. It is the most sustained, vigorous and radical attack on wealth and private property that survives from antiquity.

In this treatise, which swarms with biblical citations, the Acts passages make just one cursory appearance. The anonymous author is asserting that renunciation of property is incumbent on every Christian, not just on the apostles, as has been claimed. To make his point Anonymus cites two texts. The first is Matt. 19:21, the challenge to the rich man. 'Why', asks Anonymus, 'did Christ bother to issue the challenge unless renunciation was incumbent on non-apostles as well?' The second text is Acts 4:32, which also shows surrender of property outside the apostolic circle. What Anonymus provides is a bare summary of the text, one which happens to omit, among other things, any mention of a community of property. It's as if the story concerns the actions of a number of individuals, which were exemplary to be sure, 'commended to posterity to imitate'. They renounce their property, and in some cases themselves pass the proceeds to the poor (a detail not without interest: the apostles are apparently not in total control of receipt and distribution). The text runs: 'And in the case of those who, in the Acts of the Apostles, undoubtedly sold all their possessions, some of them laying the price of what they sold at the apostles' feet, while others distributed them to the poor themselves, why were they willing to do this if they knew that only the apostles had to do it?'

Anonymus' general argument has a quite different focus: he is calling for renunciation of property on the model of Christ himself. He selects his texts accordingly, focusing on the life and the preaching of Christ. Acts is marginal to his case. There is an interesting comparison to be made here with the Franciscans. They too placed heavy emphasis on the poverty of Christ and made little use of the *ecclesia primitiva* as model.[31]

MONASTICISM AND REFORM IN THE MIDDLE AGES: FROM
BENEDICT TO JOACHIM OF FIORE

In the Middle Ages Acts 2 and 4 continue to be a leitmotif of discussions of monasticism. Benedict's Rule, composed in the mid-sixth century, and destined to serve as the definitive formulation of the monastic life for centuries to come, contains the following stern injunction with regard to private property:

Above all, this evil practice must be uprooted and removed from the monastery ... No one should presume to give, receive, or retain anything of his own, nothing at all – not a book, writing tablets, or stylus – in short, not a single item ... For their needs, they are to look to the father of the monastery, and are not allowed anything which the abbot has not given or permitted. 'All things

---

[31] Peter Olivi is a special case. See pp. 82–3. For the Franciscans, see Ch. 4.

should be the common possession of all', as it is written, so that no one presumes to call anything his own.[32]

Benedict is here echoing Augustine's Rule One.

At the turn of the sixth century, around half a century later, Augustine of Canterbury sought advice from Pope Gregory I as to how bishops should live with their clergy (among other things).[33] In reply Gregory put forward the first Church of Jerusalem as a model, before beating a partial retreat along the route prescribed by Augustine of Hippo in order to accommodate clerics with lower standards:

You, brother, are conversant with monastic rules, and ought not to live apart from your clergy in the English Church ... You ought to institute that manner of life which our fathers followed in the earliest beginnings of the Church; none of them said that anything he possessed was his own, but they had all things in common. If however there are any who are clerics but in minor orders and who cannot be continent, they should marry and receive their stipends outside the community; for we know that it is written concerning those fathers whom we have mentioned that division was to be made to each according to this need.

Reformers in the eighth and ninth centuries also summoned up earlier models, Biblical and Patristic, of an ideal Christian life, which revolved around living the common life and the absence of private property. In the process they provided explanation and justification for property-owning by the Church and its control by the bishop. An example is a chapter in the *Rule of Canons* of Chrodegang, bishop of Metz *c.*747, which begins with a summary of the regime of the *ecclesia primitiva*, and continues:

But because in our time it is not possible to be persuaded to do this, let us agree at least in this: we ought to draw our spirit in some small measure to their way of life. Because it is hardly devout to be tepid, inert and remiss; and because every community should be in harmony for the sake of the name of God, we, who ought to live by our own particular rules, should consent not merely a little to this perfection. And if we are unable to abandon all things, let us hold our possessions for their use only, so that, whether we will or no, they will descend not to our heirs of the body and our relatives but to the church, which, with God as our witness, we serve in common. We have our support from these possessions, but let us leave them to this place by inheritance. So that, if the crown of salvation is not given to us along with those perfect ones because of their perfect renunciation and contempt of the world, then at least forgiveness of sins and divine mercy may be conceded to us as to the least of humans. Thus St Prosper

---

[32] *Rule of Benedict* 33.1–6 (*SC* 182; transl. Fry *et al.* 1981). See Leyser (2000), 101–28.
[33] Bede, *Vita S. Cuthberti* 16; *Hist. Eccl.* 1.27.

and the other holy fathers have established, according to divine law, that clerics
who desire to live from ecclesiastical goods should confer their possessions by
charter to God and to the Church which they serve; and thus they will have
licence to use ecclesiastical goods without incurring grave fault.[34]

In the second half of the ninth century, the defence of Church property
ownership and its control by the bishop was given a boost by the publication of a collection of fabricated papal letters known as the *Collectio
Isidori Mercatoris*. These documents, the earliest of which purports to
have been issued by Clement of Rome in the first century, represent the
cession of property to the bishops for the support of the common life as a
natural development out of the practices of the original community of
Christians. Ps.-Isidore's Collection enjoyed wide circulation and con-
taminated a whole succession of canonical writings, including the influential *Decretum* of Burchard of Worms of the early eleventh century, not
to mention the *Decretum* of Gratian of the mid-twelfth century. The
advocacy of Church ownership and episcopal control of property formed
a significant dimension of the wider programme of reform of the eleventh
and twelfth centuries.[35]

The assertion of a natural continuity and progression in property
arrangements from the first Christian community to later periods in the
history of the Church is an example of a tendency, much favoured by
Church leaders and canonists of the eleventh and twelfth centuries, to
view the institutions of the primitive Church as immature and unformed,
requiring development beyond the prototype model.[36] Thus we find
Gregory VII in a letter of 1080 justifying the prohibition of the use of the
vernacular in the sacramental life of the Church in the following way:

It is evident to those who consider the matter carefully that it has pleased God to
make Holy Scripture obscure in certain places, lest it be vulgarized and subjected
to disrespect or be so misunderstood by people of limited intelligence as to lead
them into error. Nor can it be said in excuse that some pious persons have
yielded patiently to this demand of simple souls or let it go without reproof,
since the primitive Church passed over many things which later, when Christianity had become established and religious observances had increased, were
corrected by the holy fathers after close examination.[37]

---

[34] Chrodegang, *Reg. Canon.* 31, quoted in Ganz (1995), 22–3.
[35] Olsen (1969); (1985), with bibl.
[36] In some of the canonist literature of the period the special link connecting the *ecclesia primitiva* to
the Jerusalem Church is loosened, so that the whole pre-Constantinian period, and even at times
the whole patristic age, was classed as 'primitive'.
[37] Quoted Olsen (1969), 79.

Early Church Fathers (for example, Augustine and John Cassian) had perceived the Church as inexorably declining from the primitive perfection of the first Christians at Jerusalem, following the concession of private property to the Gentile Christians who increasingly made up the Christian congregations. The alternative, progressivist, reading of the history of the Church had already surfaced in Bede (673–735). Bede accepted the monastic status of the first Christian community (as we saw earlier), but viewed their monasticism as embryonic and immature rather than fully formed and pure. The early Church in his account went through a formative period in which it gradually shook off the Jewish practices which masked the distinctiveness of the Christian Gospel.[38]

While in the eleventh and twelfth centuries the idea of the *ecclesia primitiva* as underdeveloped and embryonic became ever more widely canvassed, the contrary supposition of the decline of the Church into decadence after the earliest days continued to be advanced by moralists such as Bernard of Clairvaux. In fact, for the most part, appeals to the *ecclesia primitiva* in general, and to the experience of the Church at Jerusalem in particular, followed time-hallowed tradition. In an age when invocations of the *ecclesia primitiva* proliferated and diversified, it remains the case that they were predominantly advanced by critics of the contemporary Church, and usually (though not invariably) in the cause of the reform of the monastic and canonical common life.[39]

Monastic reform in the mind of Joachim of Fiore (*c.*1130–1202) had a pronounced apocalyptic dimension. Bernard of Clairvaux, whom Joachim much admired, had shown the way in his vision of monastic life at Clairvaux as a prefiguration of the heavenly Jerusalem: 'She is the Jerusalem united to the one in heaven by whole-hearted devotion, by conformity of life and by a certain spiritual affinity.'[40] Joachim held out similar hopes for his Florensian community, founded on a mountain top in Calabria after his abandonment of the Cistercians, in conscious imitation of Benedict of Nursia's retreat to Monte Cassino. In Joachim's view of history, a new, virginal society would appear in a Third and Final Age (*status*) of the world, the Age of the Spirit, with a reformed

---

[38] In this Bede was developing in an original way Jerome's notion of a Judaizing primitive Church. See Olsen (1982b).

[39] Occasionally imaginative canonists defended particular features of the contemporary Church, such as papal supremacy eleventh-century style, with the argument that they originated in the primitive Church. See Olsen (1969), 75–7 on the *Quaestiones Stuttgardienses* (*c.*1154–79). The argument had already been refuted around half a century earlier by the Norman Anonymous.

[40] *Letters of St Bernard of Clairvaux* (transl. James 1953), 91.

monasticism at its centre. The Book of Revelation was obviously his main source of inspiration, but his elaborate picture of the future society of the heavenly Jerusalem as outlined in the *Liber Figurarum* carries echoes of the historical Jerusalem of the first Christians, for example, in the detail that 'at the command of the spiritual father the surplus will be taken from those who have more and given to those who have less so that there may be no one in need among them but all things held in common'.[41] The link with the primitive Church is made explicit in other works. The *ecclesia primitiva* witnessed, according to Joachim, the beginnings of monastic life; it provided the model of a common life of unity and voluntary poverty, to which contemporary Christians, lay and cleric, should conform, and was the yardstick by which their signal failure to do so could be measured.[42]

FRIENDSHIP IN THE PRIMITIVE CHURCH: JOHN OF SALISBURY AND GRATIAN

I move now to a consideration of a use of the *ecclesia primitiva* which was pre-monastic in origin, though it could be and sometimes was harnessed by spokesmen for the monastic movement.[43] One reading of Acts stressed the *friendship* of the first Christians. We saw at the outset that alongside the more specifically theological categories in Luke's account, such as that the first believers were 'inspirited' and were drawn into charity, there is another theme, which drew on the characterization of friendship in Plato, Aristotle and Cicero, as bringing together people of one heart and soul who do not call anything their own.

From Gregory of Nazianzus in the second half of the fourth century through Alcuin in the eighth century (*c.*730–804) to John of Salisbury in the twelfth, Acts was read through the eyes of a reviving humanism which stressed the bonds of friendship that sustained groups of like-minded individuals.[44]

John of Salisbury writes in 1159 to his friend, Peter, Abbot of Celle:

---

[41] McGinn (1980), 147–8; Joachin of Fiore, *Il Libro* 2.
[42] Wessley (1990), 72–3, nn. 11–16, with citations from Joachim of Fiore's works *Liber de Concordia Novi et Veteris Testamenti*; *Expositio in Apocalypsim*; *Tractatus super Quattuor Evangelia*.
[43] See e.g. John Cassian, *Collationes* 16, which influenced Anselm, on whom see Olsen (1984), 343, referring to Southern (1966), 70–6.
[44] Greg. Naz., *De vita sua* 11.227–30, 474–85; Alcuin, *Ep.* 39, 147, 237, 290. On John of Salisbury, see n. 45 below. See Olsen (1998), 455.

Virtue lays it down that all the property of friends should be shared between them, and the judgement of wisdom excludes from the shrine of friendship all those who claim even their feelings as their own rather than their friends'. Who doubts that he ought to share his goods with those who are of one single mind with him, if the truth of professed friendship is preserved by the loyalty of love? It is this which unites men's souls in the bond of charity; as Calcidius says, it causes many souls to be made one by the wondrous welling of grace; and as Plato asserts, one and the same spirit presides over the many bodies of those that love one another truly ... Since I have professed myself to be your friend, I gladly acknowledge our partnership of mind and possessions ... I do my best to secure that we should have one heart and one soul in the Lord.[45]

This is a Christian humanist synthesizing the classical virtue of friendship with the Christian virtue of charity.

Let us now glance at Gratian's *Decretum*, composed a couple of decades earlier, and well known to John, to judge from the frequency with which he cites it. It is not that all roads led to Gratian, but Gratian was certainly a milepost on the road to John of Salisbury and beyond. In *Distinctio* 8 Gratian brings together Acts and Plato in support of the principle of natural communality; in the parallel passage *Causa* 12, the question under discussion is whether clerics may have any possessions of their own. Here Gratian cites, clearly with approval, the Ps.-Isidorian Letter 5 of Pope Clement I to St James and the Brethren in Jerusalem. This latter text gave special problems to canonists, for it both baldly stated that iniquity was at the root of all private ownership and spelled out that the regime of sharing everything included 'without doubt' wives.[46] In the present context I am interested in the way communality is laid out in this text. The two texts run as follows:

The Law of Nature stands apart from Custom and Ordinance. *For by the Law of Nature everything is shared by everyone.* This is believed to have been observed not only by those of whom it is written: 'Among the multitude of believers there was one heart and one soul', etc., but it is also found in an earlier tradition handed down by philosophers. In Plato that polity is said to be most justly ordered in which each person does not know his own attachments. By contrast, by the Law of Custom and Ordinance, this is mine, while that is another's.

Many authorities pronounce that clergy should possess nothing ... *All men ought to have the use in common of all that is in this world.* It is through iniquity that one thing came to be called one man's and another thing another's. So

---

[45] *Letter* III. See *Letters* vol. I: *The Early Letters* (1955), 180–2; see also Brooke (1984).
[46] Gratian, *Decretum*, Dist. 8, col. 12; *Causa* 12, qu. I, col. 676–7.

division grew up among men. *Finally, the wisest of the Greeks said that everything should be shared among friends.* And among the everything, wives are undoubtedly included.[47]

Gratian is acknowledging his debt to the classical philosophical tradition and its doctrine of friendship. His allegiance to this tradition is not at all skin-deep. It is there in his reading of Plato, and it colours his account of the first Christians of Jerusalem. That is why he can move easily back and forth between a communality that is for everyone and a communality that is for friends.

POSTLUDE: THE FRANCISCANS AND THE *ECCLESIA PRIMITIVA*

There were Christians in all ages who were antipathetic to the wealth of the Church and the power of the hierarchy and what they saw as laxity and corruption in the common life as practised in their time, whether clerical or monastic. Notably, the Franciscans. The ideal of *ecclesia primitiva* had little appeal to St Francis and the first Franciscans. This ideal had long been the 'special possession' of monastic coenobitism operating in the shadow of the institutional Church. St Francis had moved away from, and was implicitly undermining, the established monastic tradition by his renunciation of possessions both private *and in common*. St Francis and his followers looked for another model, and found it in the poverty of Christ.

There does exist a Franciscan discussion of Acts 2 and 4–5, and within the context of a commentary of the Acts.[48] The author was Peter Olivi (1248–98), a leading light within what came to be known as the Spirituals, a rigorist group in the Franciscan Order. Olivi had apocalyptic expectations which were derived from those of Joachim of Fiore, but his vision of spiritual life in the Third Age drew its Biblical model not from the primitive Church, the *ecclesia primitiva*, but from the life of Christ and his apostles, the *vita apostolica*, which he saw as revived in St Francis and his Rule.[49] In the event Olivi produced an extremely forced and implausible reading of the community of Jerusalem as a society which

---

[47] An exegesis of Acts 4–5 follows. The italicized words run: *Distinctio* 8.12: 'nam iure naturae sunt omnia communia omnibus'; *Causa* 12: Quest. 1.1: 'communis enim usus omnium, quae sunt in hoc mundo, omnibus hominibus esse debuit . . . Denique Grecorum quidam sapientissimus communia debere ait, esse amicorum omnia.'

[48] Peter Olivi, *Acts of the Apostles*, in *Lectura Super Actus Apostolorum* (ed. Flood 2001) 88–94, 124–37.

[49] See in general Burr (2001), and for the *Commentary on the Apocalypse*, Burr (1993).

fully conformed with the Franciscan principle that property should be owned neither privately nor in common, and with his own elaboration of that principle, to the effect that the 'usus' of goods among the first Christians implied no rights over those goods, and was in any case marked by extreme poverty.

CHAPTER 4

The poverty of Christ: crises of asceticism from the Pelagians to the Franciscans

INTRODUCTION

On 7 May 1318 four men were burned at the stake in the market place of the city of Marseille. According to a contemporary writer:

They were burned because they asserted that the rule of Saint Francis was the same as Christ's Gospel, that, once solemnly promised, it enters the category of precept in the same way that the vow has the force of a precept ... It is thus beyond anyone's power of dispensation. They also asserted that the Supreme Pontiff could not concede cellars, granaries and storage facilities for oil to the Brothers Minor, who had promised to observe Christ's Gospel, and that the Pope had sinned in conceding such things, as had the brothers in accepting them.[1]

The four victims are only names to us; the writer was Angelo Clareno, a member of the Franciscan order, *Fratres Minores*, or Brothers Minor. In protest at what he saw as laxity and corruption in the Order, Clareno tried to form a breakaway group more in tune with the ideals of St Francis. He won temporary success, when Pope Celestine IV created for them a new Order called the Poor Hermits of Pope Celestine, under his own rather than Franciscan jurisdiction. However, Celestine was forced out of office after only four months (in 1294), his acts were nullified by the new Pope, Boniface VIII, and the Poor Hermits fled to Greece (in the first instance). Clareno endured several more decades of persecution of one sort of another, but survived to tell his tale in an *Apologia de vita sua*, and died an old man of around ninety (in 1337). He

---

[1] Clareno, *Liber Chronicarum* 6.433. A group of twenty-five, who were originally sixty-four, stood out against the Pope's bull *Quorundam exigit* of 7 October 1317, which required Brothers Minor to wear clothing stipulated by the Offices of their Order, and accept the principle that wheat and wine should be stored. The rebels were later asked whether they thought the Pope had the authority to issue these commands.

and the four victims of Marseille belonged to a radical wing of the Franciscan Order later termed Spirituals.[2] They held an extreme view of the already radical doctrines of the Franciscan community on the absolute poverty of Christ and the apostles and on the identity of the Gospel Message and the Rule of St Francis, and they stoutly defended their positions against their own leaders and Pope John XXII. The remainder of the original group of twenty-five recalcitrants recanted under intense pressure from the Inquisitor, Michel Le Moine, and were compelled to confess their errors in public where they had earlier preached them – with the exception of one man imprisoned for life for having displayed special pertinacity. Having pronounced the Spirituals to be heretics, John XXII moved on to examine the special claims and doctrines of the whole Franciscan Order. In 1323, five years after the Marseille incident, in the Bull *Cum Inter Nonnullos*, he pronounced it heretical to hold that Christ was absolutely poor.

The Franciscan poverty dispute was a disagreement over the *vita apostolica*. I use this as an umbrella term to take in Christ's words on renunciation and poverty and his lifestyle, together with that of the apostles. The *vita apostolica* thus defined proved at least as malleable and rather more divisive than its mate, the *ecclesia primitiva*. Christians could agree that Jesus provided a model for them to imitate. Disagreement arose once one got past the generalities and penetrated into the detail.

There was no single, accepted, reading of the *vita apostolica*. On the surface Jesus' words are unambiguous: to become a disciple, to achieve salvation, one must renounce fortune and family. But then the questions begin: was total renunciation required of *all* Christians, or only of those seeking perfection, more especially religious? Were Jesus' words to be taken literally? Was his Gospel, as reported by the Evangelists, internally consistent? Were his words compatible with his own lifestyle, and that of his apostles? On these points Christians from early days were divided. Still, there may once have been a time when civilized disagreement on these matters was possible. If so, our opening text is a stark reminder that such a time had long since passed by the fourteenth century. Further, the consequences of losing the argument were dire. The categorization of religious deviancy as heresy was a relatively early development in the history of the Church; the transformation of heresy into a criminal

---

[2] See Cusato (2002). Both 'Spirituals' and 'The Community', the name given to their more moderate confrères within the Order, emerged as recognizable entities only in the second decade of the fourteenth century.

offence followed in late antiquity.[3] But defenders of orthodoxy in late antiquity were rather less concerned than their medieval counterparts would prove to be, to hunt down those in error and to have the full penalty of the law enforced by the secular authorities. The execution by decapitation of Priscillian, bishop of Avila in Spain (about 387), was exceptional and shocking. Ecclesiastical controversies, according to Henry Chadwick, 'though from time to time producing vehement crowd reaction which led to loss of life, were not marred by actual executions of those deemed heretical'.[4]

In the thirteenth and fourteenth centuries the debate was altogether more intense, public and central to the life of the Church. In addition, it appears to have changed in character and focus. The Franciscan controversy turned on the content of poverty and what was involved in renunciation, in the past and in the present. The details mattered. Thus, for example, we find that a Pope who was friendly to the Franciscans, Nicholas III, felt it necessary to explain, in the encyclical of 1279 *Exiit Qui Seminat*, why Jesus had at his disposal a purse.[5] That would seem to give the lie to the Franciscan dogma that Jesus and the apostles had no possessions in common. Nicholas sums up in this way:

Furthermore, the said Rule states explicitly 'let the brothers not make anything their own, neither house, nor place, nor anything at all.' Our predecessor Gregory IX and several others have also declared that this point must be observed both individually and in common ... Nor let anyone think that this value is disproved by the fact that Christ is said at times to have had a purse. For Christ did everything perfectly: he so practised the path of perfection in all He did, that on occasion He stooped to the imperfections of the weak ... Christ did indeed perform and teach the works of perfection, but He also performed acts proper to our weakness, as is clear from His taking flight at times, and having a purse. Both courses, however, he carried off perfectly, so as to commend himself as the way of salvation for perfect and imperfect alike, just as he had come to save both and as he wished eventually to die for both.[6]

More than four decades later, Pope John XXII, in a brusque encyclical of November 1323, *Cum Inter Nonnullos*, gave his whole attention to the issue of whether Jesus and the apostles had renounced everything,

---

[3] Humfress (2000); (2007).
[4] Chadwick (1976), 131, of Christological controversies in particular, but his statement may be applied more generally to the treatment of heresy in late antiquity. The marked change, in his view, came with the Byzantine iconoclastic controversy.
[5] See e.g. John 12:6 cf. 13:29 concerning a common purse or money-box under Judas' control.
[6] *Exiit qui seminat*, ed. Friedberg, vol. 2, 1109–21.

individually and in common, and showed himself rather less friendly to
the Franciscan point of view:

Since it is the case that among various men of learning it is often doubted
whether the persistent assertion – that our Redeemer and Lord Jesus Christ and
his apostles did not have anything, either individually or in common – should be
deemed heretical ... we ... declare by this everlasting edict that a persistent
assertion of this kind shall henceforth be deemed erroneous and heretical, since
it expressly contradicts Sacred Scripture, which in a number of places asserts
that they did have some things, and openly supposes that the Holy Scripture
itself ... contains the seeds of falsehood ...[7]

There is an interesting development which comes to light when we
consider the way the Pope's restatement of his objection to the Franciscan
position is phrased:

Again, as to the pertinacious assertion that our Redeemer and his apostles ... had
no right to use things that Holy Scripture shows them as having, and similarly had
no right to sell, give away or exchange such things (although Holy Scripture
testifies that they did this with regard to the things in question, or it expressly
supposes that they could have done so): since this assertion clearly designates
such use and actions as unjust ... in accordance with the counsel of our brothers
we declare that this pertinacious assertion shall henceforth and rightly be judged
erroneous and heretical.

John is using a language which does not seem to have featured previously in the debates over the *vita apostolica*: the language of rights. I will
come back to this later. Let us first go back to antiquity, to witness the
firing of the first shots in the dispute over the *vita apostolica*.

THE RICH MAN'S CHANCES OF SALVATION ACCORDING TO CLEMENT OF ALEXANDRIA

Some early Church Fathers, while not being crudely defensive of wealth
tout court, asserted that people of means are not excluded from salvation.
In the process they offered explanation and justification for the holding of
private property. By contrast, we occasionally encounter in the patristic
literature the advocacy of wealth-renunciation and an extreme ascetic
lifestyle. These competing approaches had in common that they sought
Scriptural backing, and found it, not without the artful selection and
imaginative exegesis of texts.

---

[7] *Cum Inter Nonnullos*, ed. Friedberg, vol. 2, 1229–30.

I illustrate the former position from works of Clement of Alexandria in the late second century and Augustine of Hippo in the early fifth. Both offer an extended treatment of the same problem, namely, how might a rich man be saved, and in trying to solve it, they equally give attention to the story of the rich young man and his encounter with Jesus. It is of interest to compare their strategies in dealing with this awkward story.

The institutional Church, virtually from the beginning, though it promoted some counter-cultural values, by and large worked within the social system of the world in which it grew up. The Church accepted the existing social hierarchies, the patriarchal family, the subordination of women, and slavery. This was the case even before the community of Christians came to include people of social and economic prominence. As it was, for the first century and a half of its existence, Christianity was a sect, of little significance numerically or socially. The appearance in the late second century of Clement's treatise *Who is the rich man who can be saved?* (and, in the mid-third century, *On works and alms* by Cyprian of Carthage)[8] are a clear indication that Christianity was beginning to make an impact on the propertied classes.

If Clement is to be believed, the tough stance taken by Jesus in the Gospels was putting the wind up wealthy Christians and would-be Christians of his time, who were drawing the inference that they could not be saved, precisely for the reason that they were rich.[9] In response to these concerns, Clement makes a case for Christian property-owning, under certain, clearly specified conditions. Clement strongly believes in the case he is making: at one point, he presents the opposing argument in the form of the *reductio ad absurdum* that only beggars are ensured of salvation:

For it is no great or enviable thing to be simply without riches, apart from the purpose of obtaining life. Why, if this were so, those men who have nothing at all, but are destitute and beg for their daily bread, who lie along the roads in abject poverty, would, though 'ignorant' of God and 'God's righteousness', be most blessed and beloved of God and the only possessors of eternal life, by the sole fact of their being utterly without ways and means of livelihood and in want of the smallest necessities![10]

---

[8] Discussed in Ch. 3, above.

[9] Further, in ch. 3, Clement talks of some who 'behave with insolent rudeness towards the rich members of the Church', presumably taking it upon themselves to bring home to the rich the alleged precariousness of their position. Text in Clemens Alexandrinus, vol. 3 (*GCS*), translation based on Loeb ed. (G. W. Butterworth, 1919).

[10] Ch. 11.

In the following chapter he suggests that destitution makes salvation difficult if not impossible of attainment, for the sheer effort of surviving the day puts barriers between oneself and God: 'For when a man lacks the necessities of life he cannot possibly fail to be broken in spirit and to neglect the higher things, as he strives to procure these necessities by any means and from any source.' It follows for Clement that the ideal is not to strip oneself of wealth, which would throw one into precisely that state, but to use it wisely and well.

The main stumbling block is Matt. 19:16–26, the story of Jesus' encounter with the rich young man. Jesus lays down the challenge of total renunciation, and the rich man beats a retreat. There follow Jesus' gloss on the incident, that it is easier for a camel to pass through the eye of a needle than for a rich man to enter the kingdom of heaven, and his qualification, 'With God everything is possible.'

Clement has two ways of dealing with this text. One is an argument from consistency. Whatever interpretation is given to the story in question, it must be reconcilable with other crucial elements of the Gospel Message, which happen to point away from a literal interpretation of Jesus' words. It is above all the injunction to charitable giving which is in his view incompatible with total renunciation. Secondly, Clement employs allegory. 'Jesus', he says, 'taught not in a human way, but with a wisdom that was divine and mystical; it follows that his words are not to be interpreted literally, but we must search for their hidden meaning.' [11]

In Chapter Eleven he shows us what he has in mind:

'Sell what belongs to you.' What is this, then? It is not what some hastily take it to be, a command to fling away the substance that belongs to him and to part with his riches, but rather to banish from the soul its opinions about riches, its attachment to them, its excessive desire, its morbid excitement over them, its anxious cares, the thorns of our earthly existence which choke the seed of true life.

Clement was well versed in classical philosophy. He was drawing here on Stoicism, more particularly on the doctrine of the Stoic wise man, who has turned his back on worldly concerns, holding them to be 'indifferents'. Clement himself employs such technical language. True wealth and poverty are spiritual, not material. Thus physical possessions are irrelevant to salvation, while the condition of the soul is everything. This is a leitmotiv that runs through the entire treatise.[12]

---

[11] Ch. 5.
[12] See Chadwick (1966), for Clement's immersion in classical philosophy. Countryman (1980), ch. 2, discusses Clement's treatment of wealth in other works.

On this Stoic base Clement constructs a Christian position, combining Jesus' transparent distrust of wealth – which in Clement's view stops short of a blanket condemnation – with the injunction to charitable giving. Renunciation of property is simply incompatible with a lifetime of charity, which was obligatory for all Christians. So Clement answers his own question, 'Who is the rich man who can be saved?' thus: the rich man who has sufficient property and uses it well, by helping those in need, can be saved.

THE RICH MAN'S CHANCES OF SALVATION ACCORDING TO AUGUSTINE

Augustine's parallel discussion is part of a long letter to a Sicilian correspondent, one Hilary, probably a cleric. Two centuries had passed since the time of Clement. From the emperor Constantine on, the Church had steadily acquired wealth and a top echelon of well-heeled members, as it made inroads into the aristocracy of the empire. As William of Ockham was to write in the 1330s, echoing words of Bernard of Clairvaux from around a century earlier: 'In the abundance of riches, the Pope has succeeded, not blessed Peter, but Constantine.'[13] Meanwhile and on the other hand the rise and expansion of the ascetic movement from the second half of the fourth century was asking searching questions of the institutional Church and its leaders. Their response was mixed. Augustine's own life had been turned upside down by a reading of the *Life of St Antony*, and he encouraged others to seek perfection, while recognizing that only a select few would choose to do so. At the same time, he and other Church leaders subjected the various ascetic groups to close and often hostile scrutiny, setting out rules for the discrimination of good ascetics from bad. Bad monks were typically mendicants, who turned away from manual labour, kept no fixed abode, but gravitated to cities, where they brought disorder and violence; some were also judged to be doctrinally suspect.[14]

In the late fourth century a group led by a British monk Pelagius formed on the ascetic wing of the Church.[15] This group was socially as well as spiritually elitist; it forged strong connections with the aristocracy

---

[13] Ockham, *Work of Ninety Days* 93. For English translation see Ockham, *Letter to the Friars Minor* (McGrade/Kincullen 106).

[14] See Aug., *De Opere Monachorum* 32–4, for a more moderate statement on manual labour, reflecting the author's respect for social hierarchies: monks from a 'working-class' background had to work, but not those who had surrendered wealth to become monks.

[15] On Pelagianism, see de Plinval (1939); P. Brown (1972); Rees (1998).

of Rome itself, while spreading the word that perfection was available to and incumbent on *all* Christians, and that the necessary first step was the renunciation of all property. All Christians were urged to carry out Christ's instructions to the letter. The Pelagians would in due course be condemned as heretics, though not because of their stance over property, but rather because of the position they took on the Fall, sin, free will and grace. Their special interest for us is that they forced Augustine to explain and justify the possession of wealth by Christians, and that by a happy accident a Pelagian work survives which takes an opposing line.

To turn to Augustine's exchange of letters with the Sicilian Hilary (of perhaps *c.*414): Hilary was complaining about subversive doctrines that he said were circulating among 'certain Christians in Syracuse'; the doctrines are identifiably Pelagian. They included a denial of salvation to the rich:

Therefore, I ask you to be so kind as to remember me in your holy prayers, and to enlighten my ignorance on some points which certain Christians at Syracuse maintain, saying that it is possible for a man to be sinless and to keep the commandments of God with ease, if he wishes; that an unbaptized infant cut off by death cannot justly be deprived of heaven because it is born without sin; that so long as a rich man holds on to his riches he cannot enter the kingdom of God; he must first sell all that he has, and if he clings to his wealth it doesn't help him that he keeps the commandments; that we ought not to swear at all; and what is the nature of the Church of which it is written that it has neither wrinkle nor spot, whether it is the one in which we now gather or the one we hope for. Some have made it out that it is this Church into which we now gather the people and that it cannot be sinless.[16]

There was a great deal more at stake here than wealth as a bar to salvation, but our concern is to see how Augustine coped with that particular issue in his reply.[17] Like Clement, he tackles the story of the rich young man in Matthew's Gospel. However, he has recourse not to allegory, but to subtle exegesis. Jesus, he decides, is asked two distinct questions and gives two distinct answers. Augustine's reading is highly implausible – it seems ruled out by other versions of the same story, apart from other considerations – but let's see where it leads:

'What should I do to receive everlasting life?' (Question 1)
'If you wish to enter into life, keep the commandments.' (Answer 1)
'I have kept the commandments', says the rich man. He then asks:
'What else do I lack?' (Question 2)

---

[16] Aug., *Ep.* 156 (transl. W. Parsons, with corrections).   [17] Aug., *Ep.* 157.

'If you wish to be perfect, go and sell what you have and give to the poor.'
(Answer 2)

According to Augustine the questions and answers are designed for different people: ordinary Christians, and perfectionists, respectively. Whereas perfectionists *have* to renounce, ordinary Christians are not obliged to do so; they merely have to observe the commandments, that is enough to enable them to 'enter into life', to be saved.

He then moves on, as did Clement, to look for texts which appear to contradict an outright condemnation of wealth. Paul's first letter to Timothy beckons:

The apostle Paul ... wrote to Timothy, saying: 'As for the rich in this world, charge them not to be arrogant, nor to set their hopes on uncertain riches but on God who richly furnishes us with everything to enjoy.'[18] But perhaps because the Lord went on to say: 'Amen, I say to you that a rich man shall with difficulty enter into the kingdom of heaven' ... they think that even if a rich man does the things which the apostle prescribed for the rich,[19] he cannot enter into the kingdom of heaven? What is the answer?

At this point Augustine issues a challenge: on the one hand, there's this letter of Paul, on the other, in apparent contradiction, there's the camel and needle. Which to believe? It is unthinkable that Paul contradicts Jesus. Therefore the other interpretation must be wrong: 'I think it preferable for us to believe that they [the Pelagians] don't know what they are saying, than that Paul is contradicting the Lord. And why don't they listen to the words of the Lord himself when he goes on to say to the disciples who are saddened by the plight of the rich: 'What is impossible for men is easy for God?'

Augustine later produces a stirring description of the ideal rich who have heeded Paul's advice to Timothy:

Though they possess riches, they are not possessed by them, because they have renounced the world in truth and from their heart, and put no hope in such possessions. They use sound discipline in training their wives, their children, and their whole household to hold fast to the Christian religion. Their homes are swarming with guests ... they break bread for the hungry, clothe the naked, ransom the captive. They are 'laying up in store for themselves a good foundation for the time to come'.

---

[18] 1 Tim. 6:17.
[19] In verses 18–19, Paul says: 'They are to do good, to be rich in good deeds, liberal and generous, thus laying up for themselves a good foundation for the future, so that they may take hold of the life which is life indeed.'

He goes on to claim, optimistically, that such people, the good rich, will if required be ready to undergo a greater sacrifice than merely ridding themselves of their riches – martyrdom.

Augustine recognizes a distinction between those striving to be perfect, among whom he counts himself, and 'the weaker soul, less capable of the glorious perfection'. And some of the latter might turn out to be not just weaker, but bad, having to be carried along together with the good to await judgement at the end of the world. But let us not imagine that the rich as such are bad. On the other hand, two categories of Christians *do* deserve condemnation in Augustine's book. First, there are the many who look to the Christian religion 'to increase their riches and multiply earthly delights'. We are reminded of the fact that in his day the Church offered good career opportunities for the ambitious. The other class worthy to be condemned in his sight is made up of 'those wrong-headed men who preach and prate [renunciation], puffing themselves up because they have sold their riches or their insignificant little patrimony according to the Lord's command, but are really working to trouble and undermine *his* inheritance, by this unsound doctrine'. He means the Pelagians. He does not name them, any more than his correspondent Hilary had done.

Let us sum up the case for the property-owning Christian, drawing this time on the whole Augustinian corpus – for in his voluminous writings he returns frequently to the subject of wealth.[20] His views have much in common with those of Clement, and are compatible with those of other spokesmen of Christianity of the era of Augustine such as Basil, Ambrose and John Chrysostom. If I focus on Augustine, it is because his position on wealth carried a special stamp of authority, and passed down to medieval Western Christendom as orthodoxy, to be taken over and refined by Thomas Aquinas in the mid-thirteenth century.

The central points are these: The rich may retain their wealth, unless, that is, they aspire to perfection, in which case they have to renounce everything. Earthly goods are a gift from God. Lest the rich feel proud and proprietal about their possessions, they are to be reminded that they are merely tenants and managers of property, not owners. *Dominium* lies with God alone. In any case, the society of Christ, the Church, is to be seen as the treasury or fisc of Christ in the world. It is the dispenser of earthly wealth and possessions among all Christians according to their

---

[20] MacQueen (1972) collects the texts.

needs.[21] Possession of wealth carries obligations for the individual which are serious and difficult to fulfil. Wealth is mankind's to use, but to use well, to use with justice. It is not to be enjoyed for its own sake. Here Augustine's well-known contrast between to use and to enjoy (*uti/frui*) comes into play. Wealth must not be an end in itself, but a means to an end, which is to serve those in need. What is to be made available for almsgiving is superfluous wealth, that which is not required for one's own needs. Working from this base, Thomas Aquinas would argue that in a case of extreme necessity private property rights are in effect suspended: 'everything becomes common property'. Even theft is permissible as long as the proceeds are used for almsgiving, as long as those benefited are in extremis.[22] By the time of William of Ockham in the early fourteenth century, the duty of a proprietor to share his goods with the starving man has been redefined as the latter's natural right to claim what he needs in the interests of self-preservation.[23]

The issue that is not confronted in the patristic literature under consideration is how property came into the possession of *the existing proprietors*, and what if anything should be done about it if they failed to meet their obligations to the poor as laid down by God. Augustine and his colleagues were not in the business of questioning anyone's title to land – unless, that is, they were heretics.[24] In Chapters 5 and 6 I show how the prior issue of how private property came about in the first place was addressed by lawyers, theologians and philosophers with a view to establishing the legitimacy of private ownership, in the period from late antiquity to the Enlightenment.

ANONYMUS, *ON WEALTH*

The literature I have been surveying takes the line that Christ did not mean what he seemed to be saying, namely, that renunciation of property was obligatory for Christians. The early fifth-century tract *On Wealth* (*De Divitiis*) by an unknown Pelagian challenges this view.[25] The author does

---

[21] See Wilks (1962) for the emergence of this idea in Augustine and its full development and exploitation by the Papacy in the Middle Ages.

[22] Aquinas, *ST* (*Summa Theologiae*) 2a2ae32.8; and resp. 1.   [23] See Ch. 8 below.

[24] See e.g. Aug., *In Iohannis Evangelium Tractatus* 6.25, at the expense of the Donatists, a text familiar to medieval canonists (through Gratian, *Decretum, Distinctio* 8) and to later theologians and philosophers.

[25] In much of the secondary literature, it is frequently Ambrose rather than the anonymous Pelagian who is credited (or charged) with hostility to private property, and even sometimes with communist sympathies. See Ch. 5, below.

not seem to have any particular opponent such as Augustine in his sights. Similarly, Augustine was not apparently answering Anonymus specifically in his letter to Hilary of Syracuse. Rather, these are isolated shots in an ongoing exchange. What gives the debate special piquancy is that the Pelagians, our Anonymus included, presumably, would soon be condemned as heretics by Church and State. This would not come about because of their views on property and wealth, or on the value of asceticism in general, although these matters were under vigorous debate at the time. Anyway, our author gives no indication of an awareness that a storm is approaching. His treatise reeks of the rhetorical school rather than the courtroom. There is every sign that the debate is an old one, revolving around hoary old chestnuts such as the wealth of Old Testament patriarchs, and the camel and the needle. Ingenious and improbable reinterpretations of the camel go back at least as far as Origen in the early third century,[26] including the reading of 'camel' as 'rope'. In an inordinately extended passage Anonymus makes capital out of this and other feeble attempts to resolve the problem or predicament of the camel. Here is a short excerpt:

Why need we debate any further a passage whose meaning is absolutely clear – unless it is necessary to remind rich men to recognize that they will be able to possess the glory of heaven only if they find a needle large enough for a camel to pass through its eye, and a camel so small that it can go through the very narrow entrance provided by such a needle? . . . But, you will say, the reference is not to a camel, which cannot possibly go through the eye of a needle, but to a ship's rope! As if it were any more possible for such a large rope to pass through the eye of a needle than it is for that very large animal, the camel! . . . But the word 'camel', you will say, refers to the Gentiles: for in their case, though corrupted by every kind of vice and devoid of all virtue, yet because like camels, they have bowed down and surrendered themselves to Christ's faith, it is foretold that they will have an easier passage through the eye of the needle, meaning the path of the narrow way to the kingdom, than will the rich man, that is, the Jewish people.[27]

Again, at one stage Anonymus turns to 'that notorious debating-point' advanced by 'lovers of this world', to the effect that the consequence of the rich giving up everything is that there will be no good works to perform because no objects of charity remain. From another perspective, Anonymus adds, charity might grind to a halt for a different reason, that the rich have nothing left to give. Clement of Alexandria had over two

---

[26] See a fragment of Origen (*Origenes Mattäuserklarung BCS* 41, Katenenfragmente 390, 166) cited in E. A. Clark (1999) 96: *kamilos* equals ship's rope.
[27] Anon., *On Wealth* 10.5–6; 18; transl. Rees, 1998, with corrections.

centuries earlier voiced a version of this objection, with the rhetorical question: 'What sharing would be left among men, if nobody had anything?'[28]

Anonymus' argument revolves around three main points: riches and avarice cannot be separated, for one cannot acquire, possess or retain riches without avarice; Christ's demands of the rich are transparent – we should beware of those who appeal to allegory in order to escape the straightforward meaning of the texts; and Christ himself was poor and his example supersedes that of the patriarchs and kings – the New Testament trumps the Old.

A crucial matter is how to interpret Scripture, and especially how to weigh the Old Testament against the New. The Old Testament, it might be argued, shows that God approves of riches.[29] For he endowed with wealth patriarchs and kings, beginning with Abraham. Anonymus breaks the link between divine providence and wealth-creation in two stages. First, he argues there were already rich men in the world before Abraham; he was merely the first on whom God conferred riches. Further, those who preceded him assuredly secured their wealth by skulduggery, which is how wealth came into the world. Secondly, the wealth of Abraham, David and Solomon is like the irregular marriage arrangements of these and other kings and patriarchs, or the Jewish animal sacrifices. They were examples, which are now superseded by the truth. The model of the patriarchs has now given way to the model of Christ. Anonymus finds in the Old Testament the position that the ideal is to be neither rich nor poor but something in between. The wise man of Proverbs 'distributes his surplus wealth to those in need and is content with enough'.[30] We recognize the model man of means of Clement and Augustine, and he will make another appearance in Thomas Aquinas. Anonymus however does not wish to embrace a middle-of-the-road position on private property. He is pressing the ideal of poverty, not sufficiency. He resolves this issue, like the last, by pointing beyond the teaching of the Old Testament to the New. Christ, rather than the wise man of Proverbs, is the model for Christians to follow. Proverbs has to give way to the Gospel and to Paul.[31]

---

[28] Ibid. 12.1; Clem. *Rich Man* ch. 13. At 11.8, Anon. refers to a stock argument, one 'that they usually advance', to the effect that the disciples could not have dispossessed themselves, since when they left Jesus, they 'returned to their own homes'.

[29] *On Wealth* 9.   [30] Prov. 30:8.

[31] Matt. 19:16–26 (the challenge to the rich man); 8.20 (Jesus had no place to lay his head); 2 Cor. 8:9 (he who was rich became poor).

Anonymus then focuses directly on the New Testament. Christ is the example to follow: how then are we to imitate him? The answer is given: 'In poverty, if I am not mistaken, not in riches; in humility, not in pride; not in worldly glory; by despising money, not by coveting it.'[32] The author instructs us to take the texts at face value. This leads him to attack allegorical interpretations, and to try to resolve apparent inconsistencies and anomalies. On allegory he makes a good point, when he complains that his opponents have reversed the more normal and acceptable procedure of reading the Old Testament figuratively and the New Testament literally.[33] They have found in the Old Testament wealthy men whom they hold to be real, historical figures, while inventing over-imaginative interpretations of the words of Christ in order to obfuscate the plain meaning of the text.

Anonymus is less persuasive in reconciling his own thesis with New Testament passages that seem to go against it. His explanations are often ingenious but rarely convincing. Meanwhile it is noticeable that whereas he is prepared to argue over whether Jesus' instructions are consistent,[34] and whether the disciples in fact gave up everything,[35] he never analyses the poverty of Jesus himself. Thus, for example, there is no mention of the purse of Jesus entrusted to Judas, a famous crux raised in passing by Augustine more than once.[36] Anonymus never gets beyond the general statement that Jesus embraced poverty: he returns to this time and time again, it's his trump card, but he does not feel the need to explain what it means in detail, let alone admit to anomalies in the texts.

Looking ahead, we find that Jesus' material circumstances are very closely examined in the context of the Franciscan poverty dispute. Theologians such as Bonaventura, John Pecham and Peter Olivi trace in meticulous detail the life of Christ from the cradle to the grave, from the manger to the cross. The Franciscan claims to superiority over all the other orders (as Pope John XXII would put it) were, predictably, subjected to close and hostile examination, with the result that their spokesmen were forced to argue their case in full.[37]

---

[32] *On Wealth* 10.   [33] Ibid. 19.

[34] Jesus on the one hand called for total renunciation and on the other pronounced, according to Paul in Acts 20:35, that it is more blessed to give than to receive. Further, he apparently softened the requirements for rich men like Joseph of Arimathea and Zacchaeus.

[35] Thus the disciples had homes to return to after the Crucifixion, and John took Mary to his, on the instructions of Jesus.

[36] Aug., *The Lord's Sermon on the Mount* 2.17.57; *Enarratio in Psalmos* 146 no. 17.

[37] See esp. Bonaventura, *Apologia Pauperum*; Pecham, *De Paupertate*; Olivi, *Quaestio De Perfectione Evangelica* 8.

Last thoughts on Anonymus, *On Wealth*. Despite the shortcomings of this disorganized and over-rhetorical treatise, it is to be welcomed as a sophisticated statement from the opposition, a rarity in the world of late antiquity.

THE FRANCISCAN POVERTY DISPUTE

In the early thirteenth century two new Mendicant Orders were born, the Dominicans and the Franciscans, or Lesser Brothers, Minorites. Francis gave poverty special emphasis, and as source of inspiration and model he went to Jesus himself. In 1208 he began his mission, living from day to day, having given up everything. A year later, at a reception at the Papal Court in Rome, he secured from Pope Innocent III verbal sanction for his Order. Probably on this occasion he presented the Pope with his Rule; a revised Rule, the so-called Second Rule, was approved with ceremony by Pope Honorius III in 1223. The stigmata of Christ miraculously appeared on Francis' body soon afterwards, perhaps in 1224. Two years later, 1226, he was dead. Another two years on and he was a saint (1228).

The Papacy was laying up trouble for itself in taking the Franciscans so readily into the bosom of the Church, canonizing its founder and facilitating the growth of a mythology surrounding him. As we saw, Francis aspired to imitate the poverty of Jesus and the apostles. In his reading of the Gospels they had no possessions whatever, either personally *or in common*. Francis imposed on himself and his own followers the same regime. No other order had adopted such a rigorous interpretation of the *vita apostolica*. These, then, were exclusive claims, and they were soon branded as novel and suspect by critics, who in the first instance were centred on the Faculty of Theology of the University of Paris.[38]

There were now two texts to quarrel over, the Rule of Francis having taken its place alongside the Gospels as a sacred text requiring interpretation. And there were now additional questions to answer. In addition to the primary question, *did* Jesus and the apostles practise absolute poverty as defined by the Lesser Brothers? there was now a second question, doubly problematic, *was* the Rule of Francis identical to the Gospel of Christ? There was still a third issue: Were the Lesser Brothers living up to their professed ideals? The Franciscans themselves were not united on these matters: the rigorist Spirituals reacted adversely to a

---

[38] See Lambert (1961); Congar (1961–2); Burr (1989); (2001); Nold (2003).

perceived relaxation of standards in the Order. For the Franciscans were a success. The Order expanded, prospered, became institutionalized – and moved away from the strict ideals and practices of its founder.

In the prolonged battle for their special status and legitimacy, Franciscan lawyers, theologians, philosophers and administrators combined artful diplomacy with vigorous apologetic. It was crucial to their survival and success that they enjoy the favour of the Papacy. And in fact, Pope after Pope in their encyclicals fell in with the community's interpretation of the Rule and were dismissive of external criticism. Eventually Pope Nicholas III settled all contentious issues – or so it seemed at the time – in the bull *Exiit Qui Seminat* of 1279. He ruled that the Franciscan 'renunciation of property over all things, individually and in common is meritorious and holy. Christ, showing the way to perfection, both taught this doctrine by word, and strengthened it by example.'[39] This judgement comes at the end of an exhaustive, line-by-line commentary on the Rule. There could no longer be any doubt that the Rule and the Gospel were identical. The Franciscans were completely exonerated, their critics were abused and told in no uncertain terms that the argument was over.

For present purposes I am interested less in the political and diplomatic skills of the Franciscans than in the character of their arguments, more especially their use of legal terminology including the language of rights. Why did the Franciscans use the language of rights? In the first instance because it was there. The air was thick with rights talk from the twelfth century on.[40] But the language of rights and legal terminology in general had a particular appeal for the Franciscans, in so far as it enabled them to define with precision what they *did not have*. We have, they claimed, abdicated everything: ownership (*dominium*), possession, usufruct, and right of use (*ius utendi*). Others may have all these rights: we do not; we alone do not.

The Franciscan poverty dispute has been widely regarded as the crucible of Subjective Rights Theory. Michel Villey, who launched this line of thought in the 1940s, believed that William of Ockham, who was active in the Franciscan cause in the 1330s, was the prime mover.[41] Others have found inventiveness in William of Ockham, while not returning to

---

[39] *Exiit qui seminat*, ed. Friedberg vol. 2, 1112.   [40] See Tierney (1997).
[41] Villey was later persuaded by Grossi (1972) that William of Ockham's so-called innovations, e.g. his definition of *ius* as *potestas*, were already in use in earlier Franciscan discourse. I return to Villey in Ch. 7, below, where I examine his highly influential view of the Roman juristic tradition and its alleged failure to contribute to 'subjective rights theory'.

the original hypothesis of Villey.[42] The originality of the twelfth-century canonists has been strongly canvassed.[43] The debate will rumble on. I find the way legal or quasi-legal language is employed to be a sufficient source of fascination. That creativity is shown in this area, and on both sides, is clear, wherever the poverty dispute stands in the grand scheme of the development of Rights Theory. I give three examples, all arising directly out of the controversy: *usus pauper*, *simplex usus facti* and *ius abutendi*.

Usus pauper

The invention of the concept of *usus pauper* reflects a conflict within the Order itself. The background is this. After Nicholas III's bull of 1279 *Exiit*, which ruled in favour of the Franciscans, the Order entered a new period of expansion and prosperity. In direct reaction to this, a rigorist group within the Order began advancing the idea that the vow of poverty implied not just renunciation of *dominium*, ownership, but also a commitment to *usus pauper*, poor use, basic use. The main spokesman for this view was Pierre Jean Olieu, more commonly known as Peter Olivi, who came from a village near Béziers in the south of France. His treatise on the subject, *On Poor Use*, can give a false impression. On the surface at least the tone is surprisingly moderate, as Olivi appears to make concessions: obviously bishops who are Franciscans have to entertain, and in so doing are not breaking their vows. In general, immoderate consumption is tolerable and not vow-breaking, as long as it is occasional, rather than habitual. And so on. Here is a sample of Olivi's clever and rather persuasive argument:

Sixth, we must pay some attention to dissolving these people's sophistical delusions. They argue that *usus pauper* cannot fall under the vow because, in the first place, one should not make a vow concerning anything that cannot be rationally described. A great many dangers would follow from doing so, because no one would be able to determine the precise limits of obligation. A vow of *usus pauper* would be indeterminate in just that way.

In the second place, either one would then be bound to observe *usus pauper* for all time and in that case whenever one had a fancy meal one would sin mortally; or one would be bound for some sizeable period (let's say a month), and in that case whoever ate good bread or chicken or drank white wine and used anything else he could have done without would sin mortally.

Third, scholars in our Order agree that any deviation from a precept or vow is

[42] Brett (1997).   [43] Tierney (1997).

a mortal sin, and thus the least deviation from *usus pauper* would be such. If so, it would become a snare of damnation for those who vowed it ...

As for the first ... I ask them if it's always fully clear to them at what point socializing or conversing with women becomes suspect, or the degree to which it should be avoided, or how long or how thoroughly we are required to avoid carnal thoughts or desires ... I believe they'll be forced to say they cannot know this sort of thing fully. All they can offer is a probable judgment.

The same is true with precepts of the divine law. I ask if they know the precise degree of pride, envy, vainglory, sloth, gluttony or wrath required to be in mortal sin. I suspect they'll have to say they know only in a very general and confused way ...

To the second it should be said that *usus pauper* is not violated by a single good meal, for it's clear that the needy and beggarly are sometimes invited to have a first-rate dinner. On the contrary, it's perfectly fitting for an apostolic man to condescend in this way to the wishes of ill or holy hosts as long as he knows how to do it fittingly for the time and place, and it was in that way that Christ ate with publicans ... As to what is added here, that they would sin mortally whenever they used something they could do without, that would be the case only if they used it so often or so extensively that their behaviour was so inconsistent with *usus pauper* that it could be described rather as rich use, *usus dives*.[44]

Olivi's critics, which means the Franciscan leadership and the bulk of the ordinary membership, were not taken in. His crucial argument was that the vow of poverty which every Franciscan took entailed *usus pauper*. But if *usus pauper* were in the vow, then it would be a mortal sin to depart from it. And where was the line to be drawn? Where does poor use end and temperate use begin? Brothers Minor would be in a constant state of anxiety, or panic.

Usus pauper was rejected by the Franciscan leadership and community, its author sidelined and investigated for heretical views associated with the Second Coming. In death (1298) he developed cult-status, and his followers became part of the underclass of radical splinter groups who peopled the landscape of Italy and France, were hounded by the Inquisition, and enliven the pages of Umberto Eco's *Name of the Rose*.

Simplex usus facti

By refusing to accept that *usus pauper* was built into the Rule, the Franciscans were not renouncing their claim to be poorer and more

[44] Olivi, *On Poor Use* (*c*.1283), transl. D. Burr.

perfect than other mendicant Orders. On the contrary, they continued to want to have it both ways: on the one hand, they had abdicated all rights and powers over things, whether rights of ownership or of use; and on the other, the Order accumulated properties, buildings, libraries and engaged, for all intents and purposes, in a variety of economic transactions. And of course they ate the food that they needed to stay alive – all this while remaining rightless. They were able to perform this difficult balancing act through the intervention of Nicholas III and his bull of 1279. In order to head off critics of the Franciscans and to salve the consciences of members of the order, Nicholas ruled that the ownership of all the goods, mobile and immobile, that had accrued to them belonged to him and to the Roman Church. The Brothers Minor retained only *simplex usus facti*, bare use, of things, whether non-consumables or consumables. He went on to allow the sale or exchange of books to continue under the hierarchy of the Order, and to lay down that any profits were to be handled by a procurator appointed by the Pope or the Cardinal Protector of the Order. He also permitted gift-giving, whether involving members of the Order or others outside, with the approval of the officers of the Order.

The two bases of this arrangement were the fiction that the Pope and the Church of Rome owned everything that the Franciscans possessed, and that the Franciscans practised merely a *simplex usus facti*. The former goes back at least to Innocent IV, the latter appears for the first time in Nicholas' *Exiit*, having been invented by Bonaventura, one of the great theologians of scholasticism, in his *Apologia Pauperum* of the late 1260s. Bonaventura persuaded Nicholas to work it into his bull and thereby give it his blessing. *Usus facti*, as the phrase implies, is use which is factual, *de facto*, as opposed to legal, *de iure*. It is purely physical use, a mere act of using, as William of Ockham would later say. This suited the Franciscans down to the ground.

A later Franciscan apologist Bonagratia of Bergamo explains *usus facti* with reference to a horse eating chaff and a slave or a renunciate monk using bread, wine and clothing:

Just as a horse has *usus facti* of the chaff that it eats, but does not have any rights of ownership over it, so a slave and a renunciate religious has simple *usus facti* over bread, wine, clothing ... and still has no ownership over them nor any proprietal rights, nor rights of use, but simple *usus facti*, which carries no rights in the using.[45]

---

[45] Bonagratia, *Tractatus de Christi et Apostolicorum paupertate* 511.

Horse, slave, religious make a striking sequence. It was however a train of thought that was entirely rejected by Pope John XXII and his advisers, who included Hervé de Nédellec (Hervaeus Natalis). This Dominican general was one of the many divines who responded to the Pope's question as to whether it would be heretical to state that Christ and the apostles possessed nothing, singly or in common. De Nédellec argued that absolute poverty was impossible for a human being as a rational creature. It might be compatible with being a horse, perhaps, but people cannot be compared to animals. Where humans are concerned, just or licit use is inseparable from ownership. John took over this opinion, while employing the language of right (*ius*) rather than ownership (*dominium*). He told the Franciscans that they could either use something justly (and so legally), or unjustly (and so illegally). There was no third way, no category of extra-judicial use. They had to choose, and if they opted for just use, that was use with right.[46]

Ius abutendi or *ius consumendi*

The Pope made what he considered to be his final statement on the poverty issue in the bull *Cum Inter Nonnullos* of 12 November 1323. He ruled that to deny that Jesus and his apostles, as attested in the Scriptures, had the right to use, use up, sell, donate or acquire, was heretical.[47] This bull could be short and sharp because the ground had been prepared. *Quia Nonnumquam* of 26 March 1322 removed the ban on critical examination of Nicholas' *Exiit*. Then the Pope set in motion an extended period of consultation in the course of which he solicited views on whether or not to assert the absolute poverty of Christ was heretical. This exercise was interrupted by the bull *Ad Conditorem Canonum*[48] which picked apart the Franciscans' case and turned them into possessors with rights. John's mind was already made up, one may suppose, at the beginning of this process – the writing was on the wall with the issuing of *Quia Nonnumquam* – but before he issued a definitive and authoritative judgement on the heretical status of the Franciscan position, he wanted to test the waters. In particular, he wanted to be reassured that his stance

---

[46] Hervaeus Natalis, *De Paupertate* 235. William of Ockham issued a rejoinder to this and other arguments of the Pope in his *Work of Ninety Days*, of around 1332.

[47] *Extravagantes Iohannis* XXII, 255–7.

[48] This bull was first issued on 8 December 1322; a second edition, which survives, was written in response to the riposte of Bonagratia of Bergamo, and was published in 1323, but carries the earlier date.

could be represented as complementing, if not actually compatible with, that taken by Nicholas III in *Exiit*. This was a tall order, for in *Ad Conditorem Canonum* he systematically dismantled the edifice that Nicholas had built. Nevertheless, there were those who were willing to give him what he wanted. One man prepared to walk the tightrope was Cardinal Bertrand de la Tour, himself a Franciscan.[49] Much of his counsel for the Pope's benefit consists of a summary of *Ad Conditorem Canonum*, the clarity of which is in sharp contrast with the laborious convolutions of the Pope's own document. In the course of his summary Bertrand invents a new term, *ius abutendi*, the right to consume, but hardly *ex nihilo*: the term is a precipitate of the Pope's own argument.

It happens in this way. The line that the Pope takes on the bull *Exiit* in the *Ad Conditorem Canonum* is that the bull had deleterious consequences for all parties concerned, certainly for the Brothers, which Nicholas had not been able to foresee. For it permitted them to continue to 'acquire and hold on to goods', while boasting that they were more perfect than the other mendicants because they were rightless, retaining only simple use. In fact, the Pope retorts, the Roman Church's ownership has greater claim to be simple than the brother's use. 'Who could call someone a simple user of something if that user is allowed to sell it or give it away?' Yet this, he goes on to say, is indeed the practice of the Brothers in relation to mobile goods. It is obvious that their being deprived of ownerhip does not enable them to embrace a higher level of poverty than those mendicants who have things in common.

The Pope moves on to consider things that are consumed in the use. That there is just use or factual use in such things distinct from ownership over them 'is repugnant to law and to reason'. He employs ridicule and sarcasm: it is simply a nonsense to claim that the Pope owns the food that the Brothers eat from day to day:

For who in his right mind could believe that a Father so great intended the Roman Church to have ownership, while the Brothers retained the use of items that are often and at any moment given to the Brothers to consume: an egg, a chunk of cheese, a piece of bread, and other such things that are used up as they are consumed?[50]

John might have talked about the *durable* possessions that the Franciscans undoubtedly had: churches, libraries and so on. To achieve maximum

---

[49] For his role, see Nold (2003), reviewed in Flood (2004). Flood at 230–5 usefully provides a reading of 103va–106ra for which Nold drew on Tocco (1910).
[50] *Extravagantes Iohannis XXII* 236.

effect, however, he focuses on daily foodstuffs, basic consumables, and in their case he conjured up a *ius abutendi*, or *consumendi*, to be set along-side the established Roman law term *ius utendi*, now applied exclusively to things that were not consumed in the using. In doing so, the Pope was taking the advice of Bertrand de la Tour, included in his formal opinion.

John exploits his legal training in the section that follows, in which he argues that whereas use and ownership can be held over the same thing by distinct persons – and the owner can be said to derive no utility from the thing in question, whether it be immobile or mobile property – this cannot be true with respect of things that are consumed in the use, things that cease to be when they are used, or used up (*per usum vel abusum*). A little later he recapitulates: even if there is no right of using in things consumed in use, there *is* a right of using up.[51] Using up and using, *abuti* and *uti*, are opposed to each other. *Uti* is an inappropriate term to use for using up, for there can be no *ius utendi* or personal servitude (such as usufruct) in such things, but merely a 'personal right' (*ius*). John then specifies the nature of the right that is here involved: if there is not use, and there cannot be, since the thing is destroyed, then it must be own-ership, *dominium*. It remained for Bertrand de la Tour, like the good secretary that he was (he was no lawyer), to put his master's case in a nutshell, and in so doing, introduce the phrases 'act of using up' and 'right to use up' (*ius abutendi*). He writes, addressing the Pope: 'Now your constitution states that, in the matter of things which are consumed in the use, *usus simplex facti*, which is the act of use, *or rather of using up* (*actus utendi vel potius abutendi*), cannot be held by a person without ownership (*proprietas*), so that whoever has such a "use" has at the same time ownership.' He goes on: 'The constitution itself states that in the matter of things that are consumed in the use, there cannot be a right to use or [rather] to use up which is held at the same time as the act, without ownership of the consumable item in question ... '

It was of course the Pope who introduced the term *abuti* in the sense of 'use up' in the first place, in the bull *Ad Conditorem Canonum*. If he knew his Roman law, he would have known that this word and cognates occur with this sense in the *Digest* of Justinian (though more commonly with the meaning of using for a wrong or inappropriate purpose). The term *ius abutendi* would surface again in conjunction with *ius utendi*, in the definitions of property rights that appear in the French Declaration of the

---

[51] The text has *ius abuti*.

Rights of Man and Citizen and in article 544 of the *Code Civil*.[52] Curiously, John employed in later bulls not *ius abutendi* but a synonym, *ius consumendi*. The latter term occurs in some manuscripts of *Nonnullos* and is to be restored there alongside *ius utendi* with reference to the property 'rights' of Christ and the apostles. In fact in the bull of 1328 *Quia Vir Reprobus* he complains that the Michaelists (supporters of Michael of Cesena) were omitting this very term in their citations of *Nonnullos*.[53]

CONCLUSION

In concluding, I would draw a circle around the year 1323. The poverty dispute was by no means over. William of Ockham had not yet entered the fray and become the most formidable opponent that Pope John XXII would face. But the bull *Nonnullos* of 1323 was the climax of John XXII's campaign against the Franciscans. In the same year occurred the canonization of Thomas Aquinas. These events are not unconnected. Beneath the strident rhetoric and fierce polemic of the bulls of Pope John there lay a doctrine of poverty that was coherent, rational and moderate – a doctrine that recalled that advanced by Thomas Aquinas more than fifty years before. Thomas held that among the vows poverty was subservient to obedience. Rebellious Franciscans take note! He said that poverty was not an end in itself any more than wealth was; it served a higher virtue, which was charity. Further, in an argument that goes all the way back to Clement of Alexandria, he held that true renunciation and true poverty are spiritual rather than material. To quote from John's bull *Ad Conditorem Canonum*:

The perfection of the Christian life consists principally and essentially in charity, which the Apostle calls the bond of perfection, for it unites or connects human beings in some way to their final end. The path to it is prepared by the contempt of temporal goods and their renunciation, particularly in order that the anxious care caused by acquiring, maintaining and administering material goods and which thus militates against the act of charity, is thereby removed ... [54]

Thomas could not have put it much better.

---

[52] See Ch. 7 below, where the claim of French lawyers of the time that their definition of property rights was derived from Roman law is assessed.
[53] Nold (2003), 136 and n. 65.
[54] *Extravagantes Iohannis* XXII 232–3; cf. *ST* 2a2ae.188, 7. See also, on the poverty of Christ, *ST* 3a.40, 1–4.

CHAPTER 5

The state of nature and the origin of private property: Hesiod to William of Ockham

INTRODUCTION: PIERRE-JOSEPH PROUDHON AND THEODOR MOMMSEN

In 1849 a cartoon appeared in Germany depicting The Progress of Learning ('der Fortschritt der Wissenschaft') over 300 years. Three panels present scholarly figures in dress appropriate to the academic profession of their epochs, the sixteenth, eighteenth and nineteenth centuries. Each panel bears a caption, apparently drawn from Roman law.

On the left: 'Justice is the constant and unwavering determination to give to each his right.'[1] This is a citation, attributed to the classical jurist Ulpian (d. 223), from the sixth-century *Digest* of Justinian.

In the centre: 'The king is completely exempt from all law.' This is an Absolutist State's version of a statement of the same jurist, Ulpian: the emperor is exempt from the laws.[2]

On the right: 'Property is theft' (*Dominium est furtum*). No Roman jurist, we may be sure, ever made this pronouncement. The slight figure in this panel is full of nervous energy as he points emphatically at his audience. He is Theodor Mommsen, Extraordinary Professor of Roman Law at Leipzig. At the time only thirty-one years of age, he was later to become arguably the greatest historian of ancient Rome of all time. In 1840 Pierre-Joseph Proudhon of Besançon had posed the question: 'Qu'est-ce que la propriété?' and had given as his answer: 'La Propriété, c'est le vol.' Nine years later we find Mommsen being credited with a Latinized version. The message of the cartoon, then, seems to be that the Progress of Learning was actually a 'Regress' (*Rückgang*), culminating in a revolutionary slogan mouthed by a Professor of Roman Law.

---

[1] 'Iustitia est constans et perpetua voluntas ius suum cuique tribuendi.' *Dig.* 1.1.10.
[2] 'Rex omnino legibus est solutus.' Cf. *Dig.* 1.3.31: 'princeps legibus solutus est'.

Two friends of Mommsen were having a joke at his expense. It was a barbed joke. Mommsen was deeply involved in the political turmoil of the revolution of 1848–9 and sailed close to the wind.[3] But he was not a Proudhonist, any more than he would become a Marxist. So much can be inferred from his known political affiliations, and from his anonymous pamphlet of 1849 entitled *The Essential Rights of the German People* (*Die Grundrechte des deutschen Volkes*), in which among other things he defended private property, while criticizing its misuse by feudal lords and institutions, religious included.

The classical Roman jurists who provided the raw material for Mommsen's lectures – and whose works excerpted in Justinian's *Digest* he eventually produced in an edition that we still use – were as convinced as he was of the necessity of private property. Few Romans or Greeks would have thought otherwise. In the slave-societies of Greek and Roman antiquity, even *people* might be classed as property, by law.

Still, we have seen in earlier chapters that doubts were aired about private property, on political, moral and religious grounds. For Plato in the *Republic*, the unity and well-being of a polis could only be secured if the governing class were denied their own property (and families). The first community of Christians at Jerusalem held property in common to ensure that resources were distributed to all those in need. The net can be cast more widely if it is asked what were the *origins* of private property. This is a leading question: it raises the issue of the legitimacy of private ownership. Why? Because in virtually all allusions to, or accounts of, the early development of human life on earth, it is taken for granted that in the state of nature[4] the resources of the world were equally available and accessible to all, and private ownership had no place. The fruits of the earth were, in one sense or another, *communia*, shared by everyone. And this mythical age was commonly represented as ideal, a Golden Age. Primeval people got what they needed without any effort and lived peaceful, healthy and long lives.

But if nature had laid out for humanity a life so felicitous, how was the transition to a private property regime to be explained, and justified? For, according to Golden Age narratives, the human race slid into decline, becoming by stages more and more degenerate. In some (not all) of these

---

[3] For the cartoon, see Whitman (1990); on Mommsen see Wickert (1959–80); Rebenich (2002).

[4] The term 'state of nature' seems to have been used for the first time in the seventeenth century, and is commonly attributed to Thomas Hobbes. The idea of early humanity living according to nature is however as old as Hesiod. See Tuck (1999), 6.

narratives private property is given a role to play, appearing as an aspect of disintegrating society, even as an agent of decline. Golden Age mythology permeated classical poetry from Hesiod to the Augustan poets and beyond; it also appeared in philosophy from Plato through Dicaearchus (a pupil of Aristotle) before emerging in the Stoic tradition in middle and late Stoicism, and was finally adopted by Stoicizing Christian writers such as Ambrose.[5] Students of the Middle Ages and later epochs will be aware of the impact made by some of these texts on, for example, medieval millennarian movements from the eleventh to the sixteenth century, and Utopian literature from the sixteenth century on.

Golden Age mythology did not carry all before it. There was a set of narratives stressing the extreme primitiveness, chronic insecurity and relative asociability of primeval human existence. The sequence begins with the Presocratic philosophers and passes by way of the atomists Democritus and Epicurus to surface primarily (for us) in the mid-first century BC in Lucretius, *On the Nature of Things* (*De rerum natura*); a brief summary of this alternative story appears in the (roughly contemporaneous) universal history of Diodorus Siculus.[6] This is the tradition from which seventeenth- and eighteenth-century theorists from Grotius on would draw in preference to Golden Age mythology. They used it (for the most part) to fashion a story of progress, which follows (with many variations) the advance of mankind out of a miserable and lawless state of nature into an ordered civil society. Most of these thinkers regarded the transition from communality to private ownership, and specifically the status of first acquisition (*occupatio*), as issues that demanded to be addressed, and they approached them as apologists for property. Lucretius' treatment is by no means progressivist. In his account mankind undergoes a process of continuous development from its emergence from the earth to its participation in civil society, but the changes that occur are not necessarily for the better. Lucretius makes considerable use of Golden Age topoi but without idealizing the prehistory of mankind. He is paddling his own, Epicurean, canoe. The message is, that until and unless humanity embraces the enlightenment that only Epicureanism can bring, there will be no moral progress.[7] Among later writers Lucretius has much

---

[5] See the catalogue of texts assembled in the classic work of Lovejoy and Boas (1935).

[6] Diod. Sic. 1.8.

[7] Lucretius is constantly aware of the 'impoverished and darkened mentality of pre-Epicurean society'; see Furley (1989), at 209. The commentary of Lucretius *De Rerum Naturae* Book 5 by Campbell (2003) is valuable, but stops short at line 1104. Both authors argue persuasively against classifying Lucretius as a 'progressivist' or a 'primitivist'.

in common with Jean-Jacques Rousseau, who in *The Discourse on the
Origin of Inequality* (1755) similarly manipulates themes from Golden Age
mythology for his own purposes (which do not of course include pressing
the virtues of Epicureanism), and distinguishes between technological and
cultural advances, and moral progress; Rousseau finds the latter to be
lacking not only in the state of nature but also in contemporary societies.[8]

These various accounts of early humanity have in common that they
are, in one way or another, commentaries on existing society, as distinct
from being serious attempts to reconstruct prehistory. Beyond this,
interpretation is by no means straightforward. How are we to approach
those narratives in which private property is excluded from the state of
nature but is a structural feature of a society in moral decline? Is the
message that a private property regime is inherently antisocial and
morally suspect, and that a return to primeval communality is desirable?
A glance at, for example, Virgil's use of the Golden Age theme should
warn us against making such a simplistic assumption. Virgil conjures up
an idyllic primeval world in which communality was practised, but he
does this within a poem, the *Georgics*, whose theme is the virtue of the
small landowner and the dignity of agriculture. Further, in a poem
composed earlier, the fourth *Eclogue*, Virgil appears to be playing politics,
as he looks forward to a new Golden Age marked by the birth of a boy,
probably to be identified with the son of the aristocrat Asinius Pollio, or, as
Christian writers would later say, Jesus Christ. Virgil started something
here. It became routine to praise incoming Roman emperors, and in later
ages other rulers, for restoring the Golden Age.[9] Anyway, it is quite clear
that the return of a regime of communality was far from Virgil's mind.
All those writers who present narratives of mankind at the dawn of
history have in common that they are manipulating traditional stories for
their own purposes.

Whatever their specific agendas might have been, such writers, in so far
as they address the issue of property, expose a contradiction between the
status of private ownership in myth and in their own worlds. In their
stories private property is tainted by its association with corruption and
decline, whereas in life it is the cornerstone of an ordered society. To
reveal a contradiction is not the same as deliberately to draw attention to
it, let alone to try to resolve it. While some writers appear to avert their
gaze, there are others, in the medieval period and later ages rather than in

---

[8] See pp. 159–65, below.   [9] DuQuesnay (1976); Virgil, *Ecl.*, ed. Clausen (1994), 119; Piccaluga (1996).

antiquity, who are both fully aware that there is a problem and anxious to puzzle it out. This is just as true of the early Enlightenment thinkers Grotius, Pufendorf and Locke as it is of medieval canon lawyers.

Christianity is at least in part responsible for the closer attention that is given to this problem. From late antiquity, a Christian interpretation was grafted onto the traditional narratives of the state of nature, according to which God, the Christian God, was responsible for the original state of affairs: it was He who in the act of Creation had given all things to men in common. Humanity might therefore appear to be interfering with the purpose of God in introducing a regime of private ownership.[10] Gratian in the *Decretum* (c. 1140) set the cat among the pigeons by appearing to reject the institution of private property as contrary to natural law.

I begin the discussion with a consideration of some testimonia from antiquity, giving special attention to Stoic or Stoicizing treatments of the Golden Age myth. When I come to discuss the Middle Ages and, in the next chapter, the Early Modern Period, I will confine my treatment to the way lawyers, philosophers and theologians argued for the legitimacy of a private property regime against perceived challenges raised by the traditional narratives. What holds my discussion together is the fact that it focuses on the moment, or the process, of the birth of private property. The question of how the transition from communality to private ownership was effected serves as a litmus test of attitudes to private property. Among ancient authors a wide spectrum of viewpoints emerge, ranging all the way from those who saw no problem at all about the status of private property (for example, Cicero, and, it would seem, Roman jurists), to the anonymous Pelagian writer of the fifth-century treatise *On Wealth*, who is as close to a Proudhonist as the ancient world has to offer. I begin with authors who found the transition from communality to private ownership unproblematic: first, Cicero, then the Roman jurists.

CICERO AND THE JURISTS

Cicero

Cicero was a contemporary of Lucretius and Posidonius, a Stoic philosopher, who as we shall see produced a version of the Golden Age myth,

[10] The Book of Genesis provided Christians with their own (Judaeo/Christian) Golden Age narrative, and the interpretation of this narrative becomes a contested area during the Franciscan poverty dispute in the thirteenth and fourteenth centuries. Before that time Christian thinking about property draws for the most part on traditional classical discussions about communality.

one which Seneca, his fellow-Stoic who lived around a century later, was unhappy with.[11] Yet Cicero rarely refers to the constructions of primeval society that I have been talking about. A passage from the oration *For Sestius* shows awareness of both traditions, Epicurean and Stoic. One might say that the picture of early man that he paints has an Epicurean base with a Posidonian topping – the wise men who rise above the chaos and teach humans the ways of justice and humanity look like the philosophers of Posidonius' Golden Age.[12] The passage runs as follows:

How then is it that, in this matter of getting together a bodyguard, you make it a crime in Sestius, while at the same time you make it a merit in Milo? ... For which of us, gentlemen, does not know the natural course of human history – how there was once a time, before either natural or civil law had been formulated, when men roamed, scattered and dispersed over the country, and had no other possessions than just so much as they had been able either to seize by strength and violence or keep at the cost of slaughter and wounds? So then those who at first showed themselves to be most eminent for merit and wisdom, having perceived the essential teachableness of human nature, gathered together into one place those who had been scattered abroad and brought them from that state of savagery to one of justice and humanity. Then things serving for common use, which we call public, associations of men, which were afterwards called states, then continuous series of dwelling-places which we call cities, they enclosed with walls, after divine and human law had been introduced. No, between life thus refined and humanized, and that life of savagery, nothing marks the difference so clearly as law and violence. Whichever of the two we are unwilling to use, we must use the other ... [13]

Cicero's treatment is of course highly rhetorical and tendentious. Maybe Sestius *was* no worse than Milo (of whom the prosecutor of Sestius approved), but both look to us like men of violence rather than stout law-abiding citizens.[14]

Cicero's thoughts about property are introduced in the main in *On Duties (De Officiis)*, to which we may add an isolated passage in *On Ends (De Finibus)*. Both are works in which Stoic influence is strong, and

---

[11] Seneca, *Ep.* 90.

[12] Unless the source is Hermarchus, who succeeded Epicurus as head of the school in 271 BC; according to Porphyry, *On Abstinence* 1.7.1–2, 10.2, he credited men of exceptional talent with the introduction of prudent moral behaviour and legal rules. On primeval man in Cicero see also *De Inventione* 1.2.

[13] Cicero, *For Sestius* 90–92 (excerpts).

[14] Cicero shows little interest in property in this fragment. In his version of the state of nature (in anticipation of Hobbes) each man takes what he can and defends it by force. There may also be implications for property in the reference to the 'enclosure' of, among other things, 'things serving for common use, which we call public'.

herein lies a problem. According to recent authoritative discussions, Cicero in these works is little more than a mouthpiece for, respectively, Panaetius and Chrysippus.[15] In which case there is no specifically Ciceronian view of property. Julia Annas writes: 'When Cicero (that is, presumably Panaetius at this point) talks of the origin of property rights at *De Officiis* 1.21, we find that, although he is very sure that people have just entitlements to what is theirs, he has no criterion for deciding whether an entitlement is just.'[16] As for *On Ends* 3.67, Annas, again: 'Cicero quotes Chrysippus as claiming that, just as in a theatre the space is public, but I can rightly be said to own the seat which I have paid for, so in the world at large the fact that everything is common is compatible with people's owning things.'[17] Tony Long refers to this 'fascinating comment of Chrysippus', and in a footnote rebukes Jeremy Waldron for attributing this same passage 'only to Cicero … without reference to Chrysippus or Stoics'. He goes on: 'This is a typical example of the way Stoicism continues to be marginalised in our intellectual tradition.' Long says this in an article which makes very bold claims about the alleged Stoic anticipation of Hegel and Locke.

Incidentally, this passage is practically universally assigned to Cicero by later writers, and it is an exceedingly popular text, receiving attention from, among others, Seneca, Epictetus, Thomas Aquinas, Grotius, Pufendorf, Thomas Reid and Proudhon. Proudhon (writing in 1840) astonishingly pronounced: 'This is all that ancient philosophy has to say about the origin of property.'[18]

On the matter of how far Cicero's opinions emerge from his writings, there is no certain answer. I am going to adopt the following position, at least as regards *On Duties*:[19] Cicero was subject to two main influences, Greek philosophy and Roman aristocratic values, and it is the latter which is prominent, and certainly when he is talking about property. It is a theme of *On Duties* that the prime duty of the state was to defend private property, and it is primarily the Roman state that is being talked about. The key passage, *On Duties* 1.21–2, has a strong Roman flavour, with its

---

[15] It has also been claimed that Cicero was dependent on Posidonius, whose treatise *On Duties* he had called for and read, but found brief and disappointing: *On Duties* 3.18, 34.

[16] Annas (1989), 170; cf. Long (1997), concerning *On Duties* 1.22: 'probably drawing on Panaetius'.

[17] Annas (1989), 167; Long (1997), 24, n. 30.

[18] Proudhon 2.2 (Kelley and Smith 44–6). Cf. Kelly (1992), 76: 'Cicero, in the only explicit ideology of property that Roman literature seems to contain, compares the world's goods to the seating in a theatre.'

[19] Here I am influenced by Margaret Atkins, in her treatment of *On Duties* in particular. See, most recently, Atkins (2000); briefly, Cic., *On Duties* (Griffin and Atkins, xx–xxi).

references to imperialism and legal processes, not to mention the evocation of Cicero's home town of Arpinum, together with Tusculum.[20] It is hardly surprising that Cicero took the line that it was vital to defend private ownership. In Rome, property gave access to social status and prestige, in a word *dignitas*. Cicero was a senator who had recently been deprived of both property and *dignitas* by his political enemies. The passionate defence of private property in this treatise is his own.

The *On Ends* passage is trickier, and I don't place so much store on its being directly Ciceronian. The passage comes in the midst of an exposition of Stoic moral philosophy which is put in the mouth of Cato. Reference has just been made to views of Chrysippus, so it is easy to credit him with what follows also. The syntax however suggests that the citation of Chrysippus stops before the exemplum of the theatre.[21] That exemplum and the assertion of the legitimacy of *occupatio* could well be Cicero's own.

To turn to the texts: first, *On Duties* 1.21–2:

The first office of justice is that each person should do no harm to another unless provoked by injustice; the second is that one should treat common goods as common and private ones as one's own. *Now, no property is private by nature, but rather by long occupation (as when men moved into some empty property in the past),* or by victory (when they acquired it in war), or by law, by settlement, by agreement or by lot. The result is that the land of Arpinum is said to belong to the Arpinates, and that of Tusculum to the Tusculani. The labelling of private property is of a similar kind. *Consequently, because proprietorship develops over what used to be by nature common*, every proprietor may keep what has fallen to his lot. If anyone is acquisitive in his own name, he will be violating the law of human association.[22]

Cicero recognizes that private property was carved out of land that had been common, open to all. Property was not private by nature. We might expect him to follow up this statement with some argument for the legitimacy of *occupatio*, first acquisition. He could, for example, have taken the vision of the history of early man in *For Sestius* a stage further, with an argument to the effect that the stabilizing of private ownership was the consequence of, and the reward for, abandoning a regime of violence for

---

[20] On the agrarian laws, which he bitterly opposed, see *On Duties* 2.72–4, 78–84.

[21] At the words: 'iniustum fore'.

[22] I use the translation of Griffin and Atkins (1991), though reading, on the advice of Anthony Bowen, *descriptio* = labelling, rather than *discriptio* = distribution. The italicized words read: 'Sunt autem privata nulla natura, sed aut vetere occupatione, ut qui quondam in vacua venerunt ... Ex quo, quia suum cuiusque fit eorum, quae natura fuerant communia.'

one based on law and justice. There is nothing of this. Instead Cicero merely describes *the process* of privatization – it happens through 'long occupation, as when men moved into some empty property in the past', to which is added war, and various contractual transfers according to Roman civil law. Cicero rushes on to insist that people have a right to hold on to any property they have acquired, and to declare that any encroachment on another's property was an attack on the very foundations of society. The way *occupatio* occurs is apparently of no significance to him.

Cicero does say that it is *long-term occupatio* that establishes property rights.[23] But this is not to be seen as a sign that he had qualms about the legitimacy of *occupatio*. The issue is a practical rather than a moral one – whether the occupier can defend his possession against rival claimants. In the state of nature there was no civil law with which to defend ownership claims. First and foremost, the occupier had to be seen to be the occupier, and over an extended period of time. Otherwise the land became available to another first taker.

It is relevant that in the Roman civil law, which Cicero knew well, the problem of protecting ownership was resolved by the device of *usucapio*, which gave a possessor the status of owner if he remained in possession for a certain period of time, two years for land. There was of course no civil law rule in place at the time of first possession, in the state of nature. However in Rome in Cicero's day, Roman civil law did underpin property rights, and Cicero's main business in this passage, and elsewhere in the work, is to remind his readers of the fact.

There is a question we can ask of Cicero which might be revealing as to his attitude to first acquisition. What did he understand by things that were 'common by nature'? It might be helpful to bring into play the notions of negative and positive community (or in my terminology, communality) aired by the early Enlightenment philosopher and jurist Samuel Pufendorf, in his *On the Law of Nature and of Nations* of 1672 (*De Iure Naturae et Gentium*).[24]

Original communality might be conceived negatively. The resources of the world were nobody's: they were *res nullius*, in Roman legal terminology. *Occupatio* when it took place in this setting cannot be said to have

---

[23] In *On Duties* 2.81–3, Cicero cites with approval the recognition by Aratus tyrant of Sicyon that those who had held land for fifty years by courtesy of a previous tyrant, and also those dispossessed by that tyrant, had a genuine claim to the same land – he also applauds Aratus' solution of the problem.

[24] Pufendorf, esp. 4.4.1–5. See Hont (2005b), chs. 1, 6.

wronged anybody, and the matter of its legitimacy is not raised sharply or even at all.

Alternatively, one might hold that in the state of nature things were possessed collectively, so that people had access to resources in common and no one could be excluded from using anything. As models of such an arrangement of what might be called positive community, Pufendorf, following Grotius, designates the Essenes, the first Christians at Jerusalem, and ascetic groups of his day. Such an arrangement or claim *would* put a question mark over the *occupatio* which disrupts it: it would be easy to characterize first acquisition under such a regime as unilateral appropriation or usurpation.[25]

Looking at the two regimes side by side, it would appear that first acquisition would have less to answer for were it to be imposed on a regime of negative as opposed to positive communality. The privileges of others might be reduced, but rights would not be undermined, for there are none. Cicero, I would propose, had something like negative community in mind in *On Duties*. For him, the land in the state of nature is vacant, empty, *res nullius*. First acquisition in this environment would injure or wrong nobody, for there are no claims on the land, communal or private. So there is no need to harbour doubts about *occupatio*. Nor does Cicero raise any such doubts.

We can now glance at *On Ends* 3.67 about a spectator at the theatre:

People think that the ties between man and man are part of a proper system, but they don't also think that there are any such ties between man and beast. Chrysippus put it very well, in saying that all the rest of creation was there for the sake of men and gods, whereas men (and gods) were created for what they could share in their own togetherness, and so a man could put beasts to his own use without doing them a wrong; and since man's nature was such that a citizen's system, as it were, guided his relationship with mankind as a whole, anyone who observed the system would be a just man and anyone who diverged from it would be unjust. *Nevertheless, though a theatre (for instance) is a shared amenity, it can still be right to say that a seat in it belongs to the man who takes it; by the same token, the system is not against a man having things of his own within the community of a state, or of the world at large.*[26]

---

[25] Pufendorf 4.4.9. Note that the negative/positive community distinction is not made by Grotius in *On the Law of War and Peace* (*De Iure Belli ac Pacis*) (originally published 1625).

[26] The italicized passage reads: 'Sed quemadmodum, theatrum cum commune sit, recte tamen dici potest eius esse eum locum quem quisque occuparit, sic in urbe mundove communi non adversatur ius quo minus suum quidque cuiusque sit.'

The theatre is public territory, any seat can be taken. But when someone does occupy a seat (*occuparit*), he may treat it as his own. The communality envisaged here appears to be something akin to Pufendorfian negative community. In a community of this kind there were no rights to be challenged or undermined. There was, rather, a rights- or claims-vacuum.

Negative community, in the analysis of Pufendorf, is inherently unstable, constantly straining to evolve into something else, whether positive community or private ownership.[27] The first to take up the theatre exemplum after Cicero was Seneca, in *On Benefits* from 7.2. Here the occupied seat in the theatre is located in a restricted zone available only to members of the equestrian order, the second aristocracy of Rome. The innovations are two: the equestrian seats are acknowledged to be collectively owned, a feature of a Pufendorfian positive community; and a principle of exclusion has been established. These moves have not been made in Cicero, *On Ends*.[28]

Both *On Ends* and *On Duties* appear to have in mind negative community. A note of caution should be sounded here. Problems would arise if we tried to bring the two texts into close alignment with each other. The theatre as a public amenity does not seem to provide an appropriate model for the acquisition of land, as opposed to, say, the hunting/gathering of the fruits of the earth. The seat is presumably the spectator's own only as long as the entertainment lasts. He could not claim it as his own in permanency, for all future theatrical shows. Seneca in his use of the theatre exemplum did not have in mind private ownership according to the civil law. His argument is that the possession of everything, by the wise man, or for that matter, by God or the emperor, is quite compatible with civil law ownership: it was simply a different kind of ownership. Grotius does however seem to have read the passage as envisaging first acquisition of land.[29]

---

[27] Cf. Pufendorf 4.4.13. There was an element of proprietorship in negative community, as soon as individuals made use of things that were supposedly accessible to all.

[28] Pufendorf is interested in the Senecan passage and not expressly in that of Cicero. He does not say outright that it exemplifies positive community, but the discussion implies as much. See 4.4.2; cf. 4.4.9, where he uses Epictetus' version from 2.4.8 for another purpose, to establish the existence of a 'tacit agreement' that each man could help himself to things. The Epictetus passage makes a clear distinction between that which is 'by nature common' and that which has been assigned to individuals by the legal authorities. Pufendorf's own version of the exemplum (4.4.10) confirms that he saw the situation as a step up from negative community.

[29] See *On the Law of War and Peace* 2.2.1; cf. Tully (1980), 71.

To sum up: If Cicero did have in mind *occupatio* intruding on a Pufendorfian negative community, then this might help to explain the lack of justification of first acquisition, in what is of course a highly abbreviated account of the transition from communality to private ownership. My suggestion remains hypothetical, and perhaps it is an optional extra anyway. The fact is, Cicero was so set on pressing home the argument that the security of private property was essential to the stability of the state, that any doubts he may have had about its origins are simply buried; he could introduce the matter of the origins of private property without even considering the issue of legitimacy.[30]

The same cannot be said of St Ambrose, bishop of Milan in the late fourth century (374–97), who wrote a treatise *On Duties* in conscious imitation of and rivalry with Cicero's work of the same title. Ambrose has a version of Cicero's key sentence which carries a different message altogether. For Cicero's neutral *occupatio* as acquisition, Ambrose substitutes the pejorative *usurpatio* as illicit appropriation.

Looking ahead to the Early Enlightenment we find that Grotius, Pufendorf and Locke were much exercised over the legitimacy of private ownership. Grotius and Pufendorf produced the notion of consent: the community as a whole had to agree to admit private ownership. Locke resolved the issue to his satisfaction with the argument that the labour of the occupier, his working of the land, established rights of ownership over it. Neither idea is present in Cicero, nor to my knowledge in any other writer from antiquity.[31]

If Cicero betrays no particular concern over the transition from communality to a private property regime, he shared this insouciance with the Roman jurisprudential tradition – in so far as this tradition can be reconstructed from the highly fragmentary evidence of the legal sources.

---

[30] Two further texts of Cicero are relevant to the issue of inequality: *Rep.* 1.54–5 and *On Duties* 3.21. In the first, Cicero, through Scipio, imagines a primitive state in which there is already inequality, but any ill effects are checked by the paternalistic king. A careful separation of the discussion of political power from property enables him to skirt the issue of the establishment of inequality. In the second passage, Cicero says: 'It is permitted to us – nature does not oppose it – that each man should prefer to secure for himself rather than for another anything connected with the necessities of life.' What nature is against is increasing 'our means, our resources and our wealth by despoiling others'.

[31] The closest parallel I can find to Grotian and Pufendorfian consent in ancient texts is Lucretius, *De Rerum Natura*, from 5.1019, on a stage in the development of humanity in the state of nature. However, property is not mentioned in connection with the friendship pacts. For the centrality of friendship in Epicurean doctrine, see Long and Sedley (1987), vol. 1, 137–8, with texts.

The Roman jurists

Roman jurists, on the face of it, had very little to say of a philosophical or historical nature. Their concerns, it is generally agreed, were thoroughly pragmatic. As regards property, they were interested above all in expounding and interpreting the highly elaborate and complex Roman law of property. Whether private property was legitimate was simply a non-question for them. They saw it as a structural feature of their society, an economic and political necessity, and that was that.

It is worth bearing in mind that the compilation of the *Digest* under the direction of the emperor Justinian involved, by his own admission, the deliberate elimination of a vast body of juristic literature, for the most part from early periods.[32] This extraordinarily destructive operation must have cut into whatever the legal treatises had contained of theoretical speculation and historical reconstruction. There are however some surviving traces. Thus, for example, right at the beginning of the *Digest*, a passage excerpted from the *Institutes* of Ulpian sets out some basic concepts of *ius*.[33] On the basis of this and other fragments, one can begin to reconstruct a plausible picture of how the jurists might have set out to justify and explain the origins of private ownership, supposing they had wished to do so.

There are signs of a recognition of natural law (*ius naturale*) as a distinct category from, on the one hand, the law of nations (*ius gentium*), that is, 'the law that the inhabitants of the nations observe', and the civil law (*ius civile*), which according to Ulpian drew from the law of nations. The mid-second-century jurist Gaius in his *Institutes* operated with a *dichotomy* between *ius gentium* and *ius civile*.[34] But he was not above characterizing particular rules of the *ius gentium* as 'natural'.[35] It may be that the action of the emperor Caracalla in 212 of bestowing citizenship on virtually all free inhabitants of the Roman empire liberated the jurists of the Severan period, Ulpian among them, to 'indulge in more purely philosophical remarks about the various types of law'.[36] In any case *ius naturale* did emerge in Ulpian's writings as a separate category of law. Furthermore, Ulpian in another work stated that 'with respect to the civil law, slaves are held to have no standing. But as regards natural law, that is not the case: according to natural law all men are equal.'[37] We cannot tell

---

[32] See Chapter 7, below.   [33] *Dig.* 1.1.1.3–4; cf. 1.1.6 pr.   [34] Gaius, *Inst.* 1.1.
[35] For relevant texts see Johnston (2000), 620 n. 16.
[36] For this conjecture, see Johnston (2000), 621.   [37] *Dig.* 50.17.32 (*Sabinus* 43).

whether this scrap that escaped the 'shredder' of the compilers was in origin a throwaway remark or part of a substantive discussion. It happens that Ulpian was anticipated in his remarks on slavery by Florentinus, a jurist of the late Antonine period, writing therefore at least a generation before the edict of Caracalla. 'Slavery', said Florentinus, 'is an institution of the law of nations, whereby someone, against nature, is made subject to the ownership of another.'[38] Florentinus was a jurist of no great significance, known only by his textbook of Roman law (*Institutes*). Yet his comment was saved for posterity, whether deliberately or by chance.

It is pertinent to ask how much weight the jurists placed on considerations of natural law. The jurists refer to natural law and natural reason not infrequently. But such references 'rarely seem to be essential to the argument: where natural law conflicts with positive law, it does not prevail.'[39] In the view of the jurists, the Roman civil law which regarded slaves as non-persons was to be preferred to natural law by which all men are equal. Looking ahead to the twelfth century, we find Gratian deciding otherwise in his *Decretum*. Natural law is said to 'prevail in antiquity and dignity over all laws', so that 'whatever has been recognized by custom or set down in writing must be held null and void if it conflicts with natural law'.[40] This declaration understandably created a dilemma for succeeding canonists, as we shall later see.

Certain jurists, then, discussed the origins of slavery and, no doubt under the influence of philosophy, conjured up a primeval age when man was free and natural law reigned. Was there a parallel juristic discussion of the origins of the private ownership of things as distinct from humans?

Two substantial chapters in the *Digest* (41.1–2) are headed 'On acquisition of ownership of things' (*De adquirendo rerum dominio*) and 'On acquisition and loss of possession' (*De adquirenda vel amittenda possessione*). At the beginning of the second of these, Paul, a contemporary of Ulpian, in his commentary on the praetor's *Edict*, cites a jurist from the first century, the younger Nerva, for the view that private property originated in 'natural possession'. Nerva went on to say that a relic of this idea survives in the current legal regulations concerning 'things that are taken on land, sea or in the air, for such things forthwith become the property of those who first take possession of them.'[41] The reference is to *occupatio*, the taking of things that have no owner. It turns out that the juristic discussion revolves around the appropriation of 'wild things',

---

[38] *Dig.* 1.5.4 (*Institutes* 9)   [39] See Johnston (2000), 621, citing Levy (1949), 15.
[40] *Decretum* (*Corpus Iuris Canonici* vol. 1) 5.1; 8.2.   [41] *Dig.* 41.2.1.1.

whether birds, bees, fish or wild terrestrial animals, which might in principle move from one 'first taker' to another. Bees and doves receive special attention as animals with a homing instinct.[42] (The jurists also show a keen interest in these same chapters in the issue of who was entitled to 'acquire', which was a matter of legal status.) This may seem to us bizarre, but in Italy and the more settled provinces of the empire in the period of the Principate, landed property for 'first taking' must have been virtually an empty category.

In any case, thanks to Nerva (via the later jurist Paul who cited him), we can see that there *was* some juristic treatment of the origins of property. Nerva's comment (to use his own or Paul's example) is 'a gem on the beach', and we are entitled to take it for our own.[43]

How are we to evaluate this putative juristic discussion of the origins of property? In the case of slavery, we saw that there were jurists who held that slavery was incompatible with natural law. This did not however amount to a 'liberal' concession, let alone a revolutionary statement.[44] For the same jurists would have ranked natural law below the civil law that it was their duty to administer and explain. Similarly, if they had held that private property issued out of a natural order in which all things were enjoyed in common, any pronouncement to that effect would not have constituted an adverse judgement about the legitimacy of private ownership. I suggest that Nerva the Younger, whom we know to have paused to think about these matters, envisaged a time when all the earth's resources were open to all and were *res nullius*, and furthermore that he felt no need to justify the advent of *occupatio*. If so, his position was similar to that of Cicero.

Let us now look at a pattern of thought on the origins of private property that was current in Cicero's time and subsequently, was markedly different from his, and from which he held himself aloof: I refer to the Golden Age narratives.

PRIMITIVISM FROM HESIOD TO SENECA

Golden Age narratives are typically pessimistic.[45] Primitive men might have lived happily and in harmony with nature, but they had fallen from

---

[42] See Daube (1991a).
[43] The natural law philosophers of the seventeenth century, in particular Pufendorf, were well acquainted with these passages from the jurists and built them into their accounts.
[44] See also Garnsey (1996), 48, 64–5.
[45] For a comprehensive account of Golden Age literature, see Gatz (1967).

this privileged state, and there was no going back. When Golden Age mythology makes its first appearance in Greek literature, in Hesiod's *Works and Days*, it was the gods who did the damage, fashioning a succession of short-lived races of men, each more decadent than its predecessor.[46] The poets of the classical period of Latin literature thought the seeds of decay were internal and traceable to moral decline. Moreover in their narratives the introduction of agriculture in conjunction with private property frequently surfaces as a feature of a post-Golden Age, disintegrating society. According to Virgil in *Georgics* Book One, in the primeval world 'it was not even right to mark the land or portion it with boundaries; all need was met in common, and Earth yielded everything, of herself, more freely, when none begged for her gifts'. It was Saturn's successor Jupiter who introduced agriculture and private ownership, and together with them, toil and want. A generation later Ovid wrote in *Metamorphoses* Book One that in the age of Saturn 'men used to cultivate good faith and virtue spontaneously, without laws ... Earth herself, untroubled and untouched by the hoe, unwounded by any ploughshare, used to give all things of her own accord ... ' But with the succession of Jupiter, 'shame and truth and good faith fled away: and in their place came deceit and guilt and plots and violence and the wicked lust for possession ... And the wary surveyor marked out with long boundary lines the earth which hitherto had been a common possession like the sunshine and the breezes ... ' In both poets the introduction of private property belongs to an inferior age, in which skills and technology were on the advance but morality and happiness in retreat. In their accounts private property was tainted, because it was linked to an economic system that was labour-intensive yet inadequately productive, and to social disorder and war.[47]

Turning from poetry to philosophy, we find the theme of corruption and decline already surfacing in Plato in connection with a Golden Age myth. Plato, who had his own distinctive utopia to canvass, was not persuaded that Golden Age man was happy, for he lacked philosophy to guide him on the path to virtue and was therefore prey to the passions and to vice.[48] In a world where, according to Platonic speculation, human

---

[46] Hesiod has fused together two myths, that of the reign of Cronos, and that of the races of man. Latin poets of the classical period commonly refer to the Golden Age rather than Race. See Hesiod, *Works and Days* 109–120, ed. West; Baldry (1952).

[47] Virgil, *Georgics* 1. 125–8; 3.458–540; cf. *Ecl.* 4; *Aen.* 6.791–3; Ovid, *Met.* 1. 89–150; cf. Germanicus, *Aratus* 115–19 (ed. Gain).

[48] See Dillon (1997); Boys-Stones (2001), 3–14.

culture was periodically wiped out by natural cataclysms, new beginnings, and therefore new primitive ages, regularly appeared – and as regularly disintegrated – in a cyclical sequence.

Dicaearchus (*fl. c.*300 BC) at first sight appears progressivist as was his master Aristotle, though Aristotle had no truck with Golden Age mythology. In his cultural history of Greece from earliest times down to his day (of which only a few fragments survive), Dicaearchus describes how humanity developed in three stages from a gathering society to a pastoral and then agricultural society.[49] Hugo Grotius writing in 1625 had read Dicaearchus and probably derived from him his own, progressivist three-stage theory.[50] However, Dicaearchus' story had a dark side. As men developed a competitive possessiveness first over animals, then over land, there was an inevitable descent into internal discord and warfare between men and states. Agricultural society was a bellicose society.

The Father of Stoicism, Zeno, was a contemporary of Dicaearchus. Early Stoic thinking about the first days of man and property in general is shadowy. Only fragments of their works survive in later writers. An important document is *Letter* 90 of the late Stoic Seneca (d. 66). The letter is set up as an attack on the claim of the middle Stoic Posidonius (d. 51 BC) that philosophers were responsible for inventing the technological arts. Seneca outlines two alternative versions of the early history of mankind. According to the first, which is attributed to Posidonius, primeval society was presided over by philosophers who ruled wisely and generously over willing subjects without any need of formal laws. In Seneca's rival account, early men lived in a state of prephilosophical innocence. They were not wise. Rather, 'they did what wise men should do', instinctively following nature, being ignorant of virtue. They also lacked technological skills (in Seneca's account, though not in Posidonius'). Seneca rounds on Posidonius for crediting the philosophers who ruled in the Golden Age with teaching their subjects technical and artistic skills, and so turning them away from the ways of nature. The two accounts converge at the second stage of the evolution of society: the arts were invented, humanity fell captive to avarice and vice, and society gradually fell apart. It has been plausibly argued that in the second account Seneca is returning to early, classical Stoicism, while adding

[49] The main fragments are from Porphyry, *On Abstinence* 4.2.1–9 and Varro, *On Farming* 2.1.3–9. See Fortenbaugh and Schütrumpf (2002), 56a, 54. In the same volume Saunders and Schütrumpf provide contrasting readings of the fragments. See also Boys-Stones (2001), 14–17.

[50] See below, pp. 139–40.

glosses and embellishments and updates of his own.[51] In any case, it is Seneca's version that pinpoints the transition from communality to private ownership, as follows:

There was once a fortune-favoured period when the bounties of nature lay open to all, for men's indiscriminate use, before avarice and luxury had broken the bonds that held mortals together, and they, abandoning their communal existence, had separated and turned to plunder ... There is no other condition of the human race that anyone would regard more highly; and if God should commission a man to fashion earthly creatures and to bestow institutions upon peoples, this man would approve of no other system than that which obtained among the men of that age, when: 'No ploughman tilled the soil, nor was it right / To portion off or bound one's property, / Men shared their gains, and earth more freely gave / Her riches to her sons who sought them not.'[52] What race of men was ever more blest than that race? They enjoyed all nature in communality. Nature sufficed for them, now the guardian, as before she was the parent, of all; and this her gift consisted of the assured possession by each man of the common resources. Why should I not even call that race the richest among mortals, since you could not find a poor person among them? But avarice broke in upon a condition so happily ordained, and, by its eagerness to lay something away and to turn it to its own private use, made all things the property of others, and reduced itself from boundless wealth to straitened need.

Seneca goes on to give a rhetorical account of the desperate state of contemporary society as avarice and luxury run riot.

What is to be made of this? On a literal reading, private ownership comes in on the skirt tails of avarice, as a central feature of a society that is falling apart. But let us not lose our heads. Seneca was one of the richest Romans of his time. It was reported, by hostile sources to be sure, that he single-handedly caused the revolt of Britain under Boudicca by calling in his loans. His written works provide ample evidence, if we need it, that he took the existence and necessity of private property for granted. Neither our passage, nor others like it, calls for the abolition or redistribution of private property.

Seneca was no social radical. He was however a moralist. His sharpest weapons, here as elsewhere, were aimed at the extravagantly rich, especially *nouveaux riches*, who included freedmen, that is, emancipated slaves, the Trimalchios of Petronius' *Satyricon* of his day. This was not pure rhetoric. Seneca liked to think of himself as a man of restraint. As a letter-writer, he wanted his correspondents to know that he was inclined

---

[51] Boys-Stones (2001).   [52] Virgil, *Georgics* 1.125–8.

to asceticism, experimented with vegetarianism, habitually bathed in cold water and preferred hard beds.[53] Seneca was offended by the way wealth was used, not by its existence. The well-known *Letter* 47 on slavery provides something of a parallel, in its vigorous attack on the brutality of certain slaveowners, which at the same time manages to avoid criticism of the institution of slavery itself.

In our *Letter* 90, then, Seneca is a moralist. He is also and above all a Stoic philosopher, and the two roles or *personae* are closely connected. His specific purpose in this letter is to present a critique of Posidonius, who was wrong about the golden age, because he located philosophers within it, and ascribed to them the invention of technology, with the unhappy consequence that man abandoned the ways of nature, including communality. In knocking spots off an illustrious predecessor, Seneca was setting out his own credentials as a spokesman and practitioner of Stoic orthodoxy. The Golden Age myth served this purpose very well – and that is why it is present in *Letter* 90.

AMBROSE

Moving across the religious divide to Christian literature, we come first to St Ambrose. The transition is smoother than might have been anticipated. Ambrose, *On Duties* is a kind of commentary on Cicero, *On Duties*. Where Ambrose touches on the origins of private property, he has Cicero before him – and is consciously deviating from him. On the other hand, he is very close to Seneca. Let us put Cicero and Ambrose (in that order) side by side:

The first office of justice is that each person should do no harm to another unless provoked by injustice; the second is that one should treat common goods as common and private ones as one's own. Now, no property is private by nature, but rather by long occupation (as when men moved into some empty property in the past), or by victory (when they acquired it in war), or by law, by settlement, by agreement or by lot. The result is that the land of Arpinum is said to belong to the Arpinates, and that of Tusculum to the Tusculani. The labelling of private property is of a similar kind. Consequently, because proprietorship develops over what used to be by nature common, every proprietor may keep what has fallen to his lot. If anyone is acquisitive in his own name, he will be violating the law of human association.

---

[53] Hines (1995), 96.

The next expression of justice, they have thought, is that a person who holds common, that is to say public, property, should regard it as public, and a person who holds private property should regard it as private. This is not even in line with nature, for nature generously supplies everything for everyone in common. God ordained everything to be produced to provide food for everyone in common; his plan was that the earth would be, as it were, the common possession of us all. Nature produced common rights, then; it is illicit appropriation that has established private rights. In this connection, we are told, the Stoics believed that everything the earth produces is intended for men's benefit, and that men were created for the sake of other men, in order to serve one another.[54]

For Cicero private property has its origin in *occupatio*, for Ambrose it springs from *usurpatio*. I read *usurpatio* as 'illicit appropriation'. Was Ambrose condemning private property outright? Was he a 'communist'? Such questions are frequently asked in all seriousness, and many have leapt in to save the saint's reputation. But Ambrose was no more a Red Bishop than Seneca was a Proudhonist.[55]

An escape route much favoured by Ambrose's self-appointed defenders involves taking *usurpatio* in the neutral sense of 'usage' or 'custom'. So the key sentence would read: 'Nature produced common rights, then; common usage established private rights.' This clearly would narrow the distance between Ambrose and Cicero, whose term *occupatio* is also neutral. *Usurpatio can* mean 'usage', but not I think here. The context shows that Ambrose is self-consciously distancing himself from Cicero, as he does elsewhere where he judges it appropriate. Here he finds fault with Cicero's analysis of the two 'offices' of justice. There are a number of parallel passages in other works, and he often employs *usurpatio* and other forms of the word in a negative sense.[56]

The way forward is to recognize that in *On Duties* Ambrose was operating within the parameters of traditional Stoic thought. This was a Church Father who found a classical, pagan myth congenial to work

---

[54] Cicero, *On Duties* 1.21–2; Ambrose, *On Duties* 1.132: 'Deinde formam iustitiae putaverunt ut quis communia, id est publica, pro publicis habeat privata pro suis. Ne hoc quidem secundum naturam: natura enim omnia omnibus in commune profudit. Sic enim Deus generari iussit omnia ut pastus omnibus communis esset et terra ergo foret omnium quaedam communis possessio. Natura igitur ius commune generavit, usurpatio ius fecit privatum. Quo in loco aiunt placuisse Stoicis quae in terris gignantur, omnia ad usus hominum creari; homines autem hominum causa esse generatos ut ipsi inter se aliis alii prodesse possint.'

[55] There is ample evidence from his other writings that Ambrose accepted the institution of private property. For example, in *Naboth* he champions the cause of the small farmer Naboth against the rich proprietor Achab. See Davidson's commentary, on 1.132.

[56] For references, see Davidson, comm.; Wacht (1982); Vasey (1982). However Vasey opts for *usurpatio* as 'usage'.

with. More particularly, as I have already suggested, there is a close affinity between the discussions of Ambrose and Seneca. Cicero had been writing against the background of Stoic thought, but had managed to remain uncontaminated by it. Ambrose however aligned himself with the position outlined in Seneca, which I have suggested represents Stoic orthodoxy. In the narratives of both Ambrose and Seneca, prehistoric humanity moved straight from felicitous communality to the avaricious division of property between individuals. No room is left for an intermediate stage of the licit *occupatio* of resources that had once been open to all.

True, Ambrose does not leave the Stoic primitivist narrative exactly as he found it: he Christianizes it. For nature, read God, for the law of nature, the law of God – the God of the Christians. Then, while Ambrose notes with approval the Stoic belief that the earth's resources were intended for all men, and that men were created for each other, he insists that the Stoics were borrowing here from the Scriptures. Moses got there first. *On Duties* is full of such assertions. Ambrose is a firm believer in the idea that pagan thought was dependent on and derived from the Hebrew scriptures, which Christians had now annexed to their religion.[57] Further, in his view the Stoic doctrine of mutual support remained just that, a doctrine: there was no follow through. By contrast, charity was both a central plank of Christian doctrine and a living institution.

We can now see why Ambrose found the Stoic version of the Golden Age myth 'good to think with'. The exploitation of the bountiful resources of the earth brings with it a duty to ensure that they are distributed to those in need. As he put it in an earlier passage in *On Duties*:

Nothing commends the Christian soul so much as mercy. First and foremost, it must be shown towards the poor: *you should treat nature's produce as a common possession; it is all the fruit of the ground, brought forth for the benefit of all alike.* You should give what you can to a person who is poor, and offer assistance to one who is by nature your brother and your fellow.[58]

To sum up: the Senecan account of early human history or mythology furnished Ambrose with an example and a rhetoric which he could use to press his own point, a theological point with practical, that is, pastoral significance. Ambrose was not of course looking for a change in existing

---

[57] For the dependency thesis, see Boys-Stones (2001), 176–202.

[58] *On Duties* 1.38: ' ... ut communes iudices partus naturae quae omnibus ad usum generat fructus terrarum ... '

property arrangements; he *was* urging a change in the behaviour of men of property. They must keep their hands off the property of others, for it is *that* which is against nature, not property-owning in itself;[59] and they must respond to their obligation as Christians to show mercy to the poor. God's intentions may have been thwarted because of human selfishness and possessiveness, but the divine plan could be salvaged, if the bounty of the earth which was intended by God for all was shared with the poor.

It was hard for a Christian theologian to formulate this message without talking of sin and the story of the Fall, in other words, without invoking the Judaeo-Christian primitivist myth of the Garden of Eden. One might say that the Fall is an invisible presence in the *On Duties* passage. In fact, Ambrose was capable of bringing the Fall into play, as he does in a passage from the *Hexaemeron*:

And God said: Let the waters bring forth creeping things that have life, and birds that fly above the earth in the firmament of heaven ... Alas, even before the arrival of man, there had appeared worldly allurements, the source of our extravagant living. Pleasures came first, man afterwards. Man's temptations were in place before man made his appearance ... *However Nature was not at fault: it furnished nourishment for man but did not not lay down that he should be vicious. Nature provided things for you to share, not to claim as your own.*[60]

LACTANTIUS AND ANONYMUS, *ON WEALTH*

Private property as the product of the Fall, private property as conventional rather than natural: some thinkers in late antiquity were not entirely comfortable with these ideas. As we shall see in the next section, the discomfiture of medieval thinkers – lawyers, philosophers and theologians – appears more acute and they rally to the cause of protecting or raising the status of private property. But not all of them. One thinks in particular of certain radicals among the Franciscans. William of Ockham, as part of an argument with Pope John XXII against the existence of *dominium* in the sense of ownership in the age of innocence, stated quite baldly that: 'The lordship called "ownership" therefore did

---

[59] Cf. Ibid. 1.122; 3.28. There is an echo of Cicero, *On Duties*, 3.21.
[60] *Hex.* 5.1.2: 'Dixit atque deus: "Producant aquae reptilia animarum viventium secundum genus et volatilia volantia secundum firmamentum caeli." ... Vae mihi! Ante hominem coepit inlecebra, nostrae mater luxuriae, ante hominem deliciae. Prior ergo hominum temptatio, quam creatura. Sed nihil natura deliquit; alimenta dedit, non vitia praescripsit. Haec communia dedit, ne tibi aliqua velut propria vindicares.' Cf. *Comm. Ps.* 61 (= *CSEL* 64. 396. 22–32) at 32: man lost the *ius commune* because of sin.

not exist in any way in the state of innocence and never would have existed if our first parents had not sinned, because nothing would have been appropriated in such a way to any single person or any particular group.'[61]

There were several ways of defending private property. Some of them are adumbrated, if not fully expounded, in late antiquity. One possible tactic was to emphasize the role of private property as a key institution of civil society in securing ends such as peace, stability and good order, that could be agreed to be valuable, indeed essential, in a post-Fall society. Book 19 of Augustine's *City of God* might be thought to encompass this line of argument, even if private ownership is not one of the political and social institutions that he specifically pinpoints.

Moreover, Augustine again, and also Ambrose, liked to think of the law of God (identified with the law of nature) as extending beyond the Fall into later stages of human development. Notoriously, Augustine, in *City of God* 19, ch. 15, represents slavery, though a product of the Fall, as part of God's plan for mankind, an aspect of the judgement of God. If this was the case with slavery, then it was even more true, one might imagine, of other institutions of politics and society, including private ownership.

Ambrose, as we saw, viewed charitable giving as a way of recovering something of nature's order before it was undermined by the sinfulness of man. In one treatise he talks of natural and written law as 'twins', and of written law as a necessary consequence of the failure to preserve natural law.[62] In addition he sometimes implies that the not giving of excess to the poor is a failure of justice, which suggests some modification of the status of property. This idea becomes explicit in Thomas Aquinas.

A more radical solution of the problem of legitimacy was to take private property *back into the Golden Age*. The advantage of this was that private property could then be said to have received God's special blessing, indeed to have replaced communality as His preferred order. This was the solution of Lactantius in the *Divine Institutes*, composed in the first decade of the fourth century in the midst of the Great Persecution of Diocletian.[63] Lactantius found fault with the poets' vision of the Golden Age. He singled out Virgil for special criticism, for his assertion

---

[61] Ockham, *Work of Ninety Days* ch. 26, quoted from Ockham, *A Letter to the Friars Minor* 36 (McGrade and Kilcullen).

[62] *Fuga* 3.156: 'lex autem gemina est, naturalis et scripta'; *Ep.* 73.2.

[63] Lact., *Div. Inst.* 5.5–7 (Bowen and Garnsey, 36–40).

in *Georgics* Book One that there was no private property in the Golden Age, the age of Saturn. This is quite simply wrong, says Lactantius. Private property *did* exist in the Golden Age. There were 'haves', and they shared their surplus generously with the 'have-nots'. The private property regime as we witness it is a product of the reign of Jupiter, not Saturn. Jupiter ended the Golden Age abruptly when he supplanted Saturn with violence and expelled justice from the earth. Jupiter introduced avarice, the greedy expansion of private property by the few at the expense of the many, and Jupiter provided laws to protect the new-style, exploitative land-ownership. Lactantius went on to say that the Golden Age was golden because there was no worship of gods, Saturn and the rest being mere men,[64] but only of the one true God. In this respect the Golden Age of the past was a preview of the higher carat Golden Age that is to come, when Christ returns to earth. This too escaped Virgil and the poets, according to Lactantius.[65]

This crude rewriting of the Golden Age myth appears to have fallen on stony ground, or at least nobody in late antiquity seems to have taken it up. Lactantian-style millennarianism on the other hand belonged to a strong tradition in early Christian thought and consciousness. In linking the Golden Ages of past and future, Lactantius was walking in step with the author of Revelation.[66]

Next, we come to a truly radical solution to the dilemma of the apparent illegitimacy of private property. Property is tantamount to theft. We should admit it, and give everything up. We should do what Christ told us to do. So says the anonymous author of *On Wealth* (writing *c.*415), whom I earlier flagged as a proto-Proudhonist. According to Anonymus, sin, the sin of avarice, lies behind the *acquisition* of wealth as well as its maintenance and expansion. This is as true of the past, as it is true of the present:

Rich Man: What of those born to riches?

Anonymus: I think their riches can hardly have been acquired without some injustice.

Rich Man: How can you know the source, when you don't know when they began?

Anonymus: I divine the past from the present, and I also understand what I have not seen from what I do see. If you were to ask me how men or herds or flocks or all the manifold variety of living things were

---

[64] Cf. *Div. Inst.* 7.24.10.　　[65] *Div. Inst.* 7.2.1; 24.　　[66] See e.g. Rev. 22.

born a thousand years ago, I would reply that in every case it was by coition. And if you were to say to me 'How can you know that?', I would answer that I infer the past from the present and am confident that every effect that I see to have a certain cause now had the same cause then too, when I could not witness it.[67]

Riches are to avarice as babies are to sex.

Later on Anonymus concedes with heavy irony that the rich man might just happen to be the only man who had ever lived, or very nearly the only man, who had inherited wealth 'left by godly parents, amassed by grandparents, great-grandparents, great-great-great grandparents and great-great-great-great grandparents and acquired with no sin incurred by themselves and no hurt or pain inflicted on others'.

Anonymus owes nothing to pagan primitivism; he is operating within an entirely Christian discourse, grounded in the Scriptures. That's what makes his argument radical and threatening in a way that Ambrose's could not be. Anonymus, not Ambrose, denies that divine providence had anything to do with wealth-creation, and he backs up his identification of wealth with avarice by pointing to the words and lifestyle of Christ.

GRATIAN AND HIS LEGACY

Thomas Aquinas' discussion of private property is included, provocatively, under Question 66 of his *Summa Theologiae, On Theft and Robbery with Violence* (*De furto et rapina*). In the second section he poses the question: 'Is it legitimate for individual men to possess anything as their own?' His initial response, with which he would subsequently take issue, is: 'It would seem not. For everything that is against natural law is wrong. But according to natural law everything is common to all, and this is contradicted by the individual holding of possessions. Therefore it is wrong for any individual to appropriate any material thing.'[68]

In this Thomas was presenting a faithful summary of the discussion of Gratian in his *Decretum*. According to Gratian, 'by the law of nature everything was in common'. Gratian went on to say without ambiguity that private property was introduced not by the law of nature but by human law, by convention and enactment. He rubbed it in by going on

---

[67] *On Wealth* 7.4.
[68] *ST* 2a2ae66.2 (p. 68). In Aquinas generally legitimate acquisition is *(prae)occupatio*, illegitimate *usurpatio*.

to declare that human law was to be rejected where it clashed with natural law. All that is in *Distinctio* 8. As we saw in Chapter 3, in *Causa* 12 of the *Decretum* Gratian allows Ps.-Isidore to declare that private property came about 'through iniquity'. Private property, it seems, was damned. Gratian was working within the Stoic or Stoicizing tradition from which Ambrose also had drawn. According to that tradition, nature was normative. Moreover, nature's special status and authority could only be accentuated when natural law was identified, as it was by Christians, with Divine law, the law of the Christian God. This was the dilemma that Gratian bequeathed to generations of lawyers and theologians.

How did the canon lawyers, who used and interpreted the *Decretum*, react? A preliminary observation was that nature and law, and therefore natural law, can mean a number of different things, and they compiled long lists of those meanings.[69] This ambiguity, they claimed, must have escaped Gratian, and accounts for the problems and inconsistencies of his *Decretum*. Most canonists went on to make a distinction between two fundamental senses of nature, as, on the one hand, primordial and primitive, and, on the other, as the intrinsic character of humans as rational beings. The regime that prevailed in the age of innocence, which included communality, it was urged, was not normative. Communality was not prescriptive – merely permissible.[70] The advent of private property could thus be seen as a mark of progress. Rufinus painted a graphic picture of humans dragging themselves out of a post-Fall chaos and developing the skills and institutions, including ownership of property, that would enable them to fulfil their potential as rational beings.

Thomas Aquinas in making his case for private property combined utilitarian arguments drawn from Aristotle with an Augustinian emphasis on humans as suitable managers of resources that belonged to God in the interests of all. Alluding (without reference to any particular ancient source) to the Ciceronian image of the man who secures a seat for himself at the theatre without barring others from access, he reasons that: 'a rich man who takes prior possession of something that was common before is not doing anything wrong provided he is ready to share it; he sins only if he unreasonably prevents others from using it'. He concludes: 'The individual holding of possessions is not, therefore, contrary to the natural

---

[69] Tierney (1997), from 58.
[70] This was the view of Rufinus (*c.* 1160) and Huguccio (*c.* 1190). See Tierney (1997), from 62.

law; it is that which rational beings conclude as an addition to the natural law.'

On the other side there were those who clung to the view that the law of nature in the age of innocence *was* normative, and claimed that private property was already present in that age. Lactantius (writing in the first years of the fourth century) had done just this, when he annexed the Golden Age of Saturn for the God of the Christians and for private property. He does not appear to have ruffled any feathers (or gained any supporters) in late antiquity. It was otherwise when the idea surfaced again in the early fourteenth century in the midst of a furious controversy. That controversy threw up two new developments that relate to the present discussion. First, the story of the Garden of Eden in Genesis provided the setting for an argument about the origins of private property, for the first time. Secondly, one of the protagonists, Pope John XXII, made a strategic strike. In his bull of 1328, *Quia Vir Reprobus*, he declared that Adam received *dominium* from God in two senses, not just rule or control over the rest of creation but also property rights. The Pope went on to pronounce that in the Garden of Eden private property preceded common property, Adam being proprietor when he was on his own before he became joint owner with Eve. After the Fall, a private property regime was reinstituted (and on more than one occasion). All this happened by God's direct command.

The Pope was conducting a running battle with renegade Franciscans who were still reeling under the blows delivered to their order in his earlier bulls. They threw charges of heresy back at him. One of their leaders, William of Ockham, claimed to have found in John's three anti-Franciscan constitutions, 'or rather heretical destitutions', 'a great many things that were heretical, erroneous, silly, ridiculous, fantastic, insane and defamatory'.[71] He was soon (in 1328) to retreat to the court of the emperor at Munich, together with two other prominent Franciscans, Bonagratia of Bergamo and Michael of Cesena. It was in fact Bonagratia who brought the Book of Genesis into play for the first time in the poverty dispute in his treatise *On the Poverty of Christ and the Apostles* (1322). Bonagratia set out to prove that there was no private property in the age of innocence. He argued, not without circularity, that Christ's life had been a reenactment of that blessed state, just as St Francis' life had been a revival of Christ's. A crucial element of this reenactment had been

---

[71] *A letter to the Friars Minor* (McGrade and Kilcullen, 3).

the total renunciation of property. On conditions in Eden, he had this
to say:

But before the Sin no one had held lordship over those things which are consumed by use, nor of any other thing. Because there had not been 'mine' and
'yours', but rather a common use of all things by men, such as a common use of
air by all men, and of the riches of the land, and the sea, and the sea shores, and
similar things. And just as no individual was able to say, or indeed did say, to
anyone 'this air is mine', or 'this splendour of the land is mine', so no one had
said 'this bread is mine' or 'this garment is mine', because, as it was said, there
was no 'mine' or 'yours'.[72]

In due course there followed two further statements of this position, one
from Michael of Cesena drawing on a treatise of Duns Scotus (d. 1308),
and another from William of Ockham.[73] The latter was contained in the
Work of Ninety Days (c. 1332–34), a massively detailed riposte to the Pope's
bull of 1328, *Quia Vir Reprobus*. In a very intricate legal analysis of the
historical state of evidence Ockham reintroduced legal or quasi-legal
categories thrown out by the Pope in earlier encyclicals, such as *usus facti*,
that is to say, *de facto* use. Ockham insisted that Adam had exercised
'factual use' over the resources of the earth, not proprietorship or any
other kind of usage that implied rights:

The appellant [Michael of Cesena] says: 'The first man, and his posterity, if they
had not fallen, would have had the use of things consumable in use without
ownership and lordship of them.' In these words he indicates clearly that he
speaks of the lordship which in law is called 'ownership', and our first parents
had no such lordship in the state of innocence. Thus, although it must be
conceded that in the state of innocence our first parents had lordship in some
sense over temporal things, yet it should not be conceded that they then had
ownership of temporal things.[74]

This for Ockham as for Bonagratia was an important subsidiary argument
in defence of their position that 'the Friars Minor are simple users, that is,
they use things without having any right by which they could litigate in
court.'[75]

Over 300 years later Robert Filmer's *Patriarcha or The Natural Powers
of Things* was published posthumously (in 1680). Filmer's argument for

---

[72] *Tractatus De paupertate Christi et Apostolorum, Arch. Franc. Hist.* 22 (1929), 506–7. See Geltner
(2001), 74.
[73] Cited Geltner (2001), 75–7.
[74] Ockham, *Work of Ninety Days*, ch. 26, quoted from Ockham, *A Letter* 37.
[75] Ockham, *Work of Ninety Days*, ch. 2, quoted from Ockham, *A Letter* 34.

royal absolutism took off from the very position that Pope John XXII had staked out in 1328, namely that God gave proprietal rights over the world to Adam and his line – to which Filmer added that God granted absolute sovereignty over mankind to Adam, and so to kings. Filmer's main achievement was to provoke John Locke's *Two Treatises of Government* (of 1690). Locke confronted the traditional problem of the legitimacy of private property, and answered it with the claim that labour is its origin and justification.

CHAPTER 6

The state of nature and the origin of private property: Grotius to Hegel

THE EARLY ENLIGHTENMENT

Hugo Grotius (1583–1645), Samuel Pufendorf (1632–94) and John Locke (1632–1704) all sought to give private property the status of natural law by locating its emergence in the state of nature. The problem they faced was that they were working within a tradition, stretching right back into antiquity, according to which the primeval condition was a form of communality in which all humanity had equal access to the resources of the earth. Moreover, late antiquity and the Middle Ages had produced a Christian reading of this tradition, by which the Christian God had ordered things in this way. Their response to the challenge was twofold. First, in order to counter the possible charge that mankind had thwarted God's purpose, they argued that the establishment of private property, while not a direct consequence of a dictate of God, was man's rational response to the divine command to use the resources of the world for his self-preservation and increase. Secondly, in order to justify the apparent breach of the principle of equal access to material resources, Grotius and Pufendorf proposed that agreement, tacit or express, must have preceded first *occupatio*; while for Locke the crucial step in the establishment of rights over unoccupied land was creative labour.[1]

The contributions to property theory of these philosophers of the early Enlightenment should be seen as part of a wider concern with the great political issues of the time, domestic and international. On the one hand, they were interested in the origins, character and authority of civil

---

[1] The position of Thomas Hobbes (1588–1679) is that there were no property rights prior to civil society. In this he had more in common with philosophers of the eighteenth century than those of his own century. Mankind in the state of nature had the right to necessities but no more. See *On the Citizen*, 3.9 (Tuck and Silverthorne 48); *Leviathan*, ch. 15 (Tuck 106); in general, Lopata (1973).

government and not just in property and law; and on the other, they wrote with more than one eye to the controversy over the legitimacy of the colonial enterprise. Thus, for example, John Locke's *Second Treatise of Government* (1690) which contains his main statement on property, and the separately composed *First Treatise*, were an attack on absolute rule in general, and the claims of the royal government of Stuart England in particular. In addition, Locke used a single logic to argue for the justice of both the acquisition of property in the state of nature and the seizure of land from the native peoples in America. In the latter instance, Locke was following the lead of Grotius, who had argued in *On the Law of Booty* (*De Iure Praedae*) – or, as Grotius himself called it, *On the Indians* (*De Indis*) – of 1607, that the natural rights of people and of states were identical. As natural law entitled each man to preserve and protect his own existence, and to acquire for himself and retain those things that were needed and useful for life, so it laid down the same rights for each and every state. The treatise, we should note, was composed primarily to defend the aggressive commercial policies of the Dutch in the East Indies.[2]

Grotius gives first acquisition brief mention at various points of *On The Law of Booty*, and some connected thoughts in the context of a discussion of 'the question of the sea', that is to say, whether the sea can be brought under the jurisdiction of any particular nation.[3] His principal and more accessible discussion[4] of the evolution of private property is contained in his larger work *On the Law of War and Peace* (1625). This work shares the main premises and subject matter of the earlier treatise, but this time Grotius devotes a section near the beginning of the second chapter of Book Two to 'the origin and development of private property'. Men began as gatherers of the fruits of the earth. Life was easy and involved no toil. God had conferred on mankind superiority over other created things in the world, and each man could take what he needed. Nor could he, without injustice, be deprived of what he had taken. As an illustration of what Grotius calls a 'universal right which took the place of ownership', he summons up the exemplum of the spectator at the theatre from Cicero's *On Ends* Book Three. (He had cited this exemplum already in *On the Law of Booty*, but in the version of Seneca.)[5] He goes on to say that primeval communality might have lasted, had men remained

---

[2] Tuck (1999), ch. 3.   [3] Grotius, *On the Law of Booty*, from 226 (Williams and Zeydel).
[4] The earlier work remained in manuscript except for ch. 12, printed as *Mare Liberum* in 1609 at the request of the East Indies Company, until it was discovered in 1864. See Tuck (1999), 81.
[5] Grotius, *On the Law of Booty* 229.

satisfied with living in caves and wearing animal skins or the bark of trees, or had the bonds of charity held firm. In setting out this second condition, Grotius was giving voice to his conviction that early man had a natural 'desire for society, that is community', which acted as a check on his instinct to seek his own interests.[6] Thomas Hobbes in *On the Citizen* (*De Cive*, 1641) and *Leviathan* (1651) advanced the opposing thesis that the state of nature would inevitably be a state of war and chaos rather than peace and community.[7] Pufendorf would later distance himself from Hobbes and expand Grotius' idea into a more generous theory of sociability.[8] Be that as it may, according to Grotius, primeval man became dissatisfied with a life that was 'simple and innocent', men and animals grew in number and it proved inconvenient to bring things into a common store. So individuals began to appropriate things for themselves and private ownership followed.

Grotius imagines that private ownership when it came was not the result of a unilateral decision, an 'act of will', but was achieved by means of 'a kind of agreement (*pactum*), either expressed, as by a division, or tacit, as by occupation'.[9] He cites a passage from Cicero, *On Duties*, Book Three, which however does not give him what he needs (nor, incidentally, does the passage in Book One discussed in my Chapter 5). By introducing the idea of a pact Grotius was departing from Cicero (and other ancient authors[10]) and betraying a degree of sensitivity at the disruption of primeval communality by private ownership. A 'tacit agreement' justifying *occupatio* might not seem to us to amount to very much,[11] but it is not in *On the Law of Booty*, and its introduction in the later work suggests that it did have some significance for Grotius. He seems to have found somewhat disturbing the idea that primeval men had rights that were

---

[6] See prolegomenon to 2nd ed. of 1631: 'appetitus societatis id est communitatis'. Grotius goes on to invoke the Stoic doctrine of *oikeiosis*, on which see Pembroke (1971); Long and Sedley (1987), vol. 1, 346–54. The word is virtually untranslatable; 'appropriation', 'familiarization', 'fellow-feeling' have all been canvassed. The influence of Stoic thought on the natural law theorists is amply documented in their works. Two sixteenth-century writers helped spread Stoic teaching widely, namely, Guillaume de Vair (1556–1621) and Justus Lipsius (1547–1606).

[7] For Hobbes on the state of nature, see Skinner (2002b), 134–5, 216–20.

[8] On sociability see Hont (2005a); Hochstrasser (2000), 40–71.

[9] Grotius, *On the Law of War and Peace* 2.2.2.

[10] The idea was however canvassed by some medieval thinkers, e.g. Ockham, arguing against John XXII in *Work of Ninety Days* 434–5: where a system of common ownership prevailed the consent of the community was required for any appropriation. See also 661, with Tierney (1997), 163–6.

[11] Tuck (1979), 77, while acknowledging that it is a new development in Grotius' thought, is inclined to downplay it. It is worth noting however that Filmer's attack on consent was directed specifically at Grotius. See Buckle (1991), 161–7.

being challenged or set aside by *occupatio/divisio*. Grotius could have reduced the level of his embarrassment (such as it was) by placing the beginning of the movement towards private ownership in a regime of negative rather than positive community, to use a distinction introduced later by Pufendorf. The significance of this is that only in positive community were there rights to be challenged and undermined. In a Pufendorfian negative community there was a rights- or claims-vacuum. That the style of regime envisaged by Grotius fits Pufendorf's picture of positive community follows from the fact that Grotius attributes to it a common store, and finds comparison appropriate with the Essenes, the first Christians at Jerusalem and the monastic movement of his time.

The traditional, pessimistic reconstruction of the early history of the human race as a downward spiral from a Golden Age of ease and plenty did not appeal to Grotius and succeeding natural rights theorists. In particular, they saw private ownership, which in the Golden Age narratives often played a compromising role, as, if not a God-given natural right, at least a product of the natural reason which God had given to man. Thus, the context that they created for the transition from primeval communality to private ownership was one of progress rather than decline. Humanity was moving forward towards ever higher levels of achievement. In the economic sphere this process of advancement is viewed in terms of the passage from hunter-gatherer to pastoral and then agricultural society, with humanity at each level gaining an additional layer of knowledge and new technological skills. This three-stage process is already to be found in Dicaearchus, Aristotle's pupil. Aristotle's *Politics* had provided the raw material for such a theory – and for that matter for its extension into a four-stage process with the addition of a commercial society – in the account of the various ways of life open to and practised by humans.[12] However Aristotle did not come up with a stadial theory of society. In fact, it was only around the middle of the eighteenth century that a sophisticated and comprehensive four-stage theory of human development was elaborated, by Adam Smith and his contemporaries.[13]

---

[12] Arist., *Pol.* 1258a20–b8.

[13] On the four-stages theory, see Stein (1988), ch. 22; Kerr (1993); Hont (2005b). Note however that not all stadial theories of society were along these lines. Thus Adam Ferguson (1723–1816) in his *Essay on the History of Civil Society* (1767) produced a theory, drawing from Montesquieu, which is much less strongly connected to variations in forms of property than Smith's. His main categories are 'savage' (only personal possessions such as tools and weapons), 'barbarian' (first rudiments of private property), and 'civilized' ('the state'). See *Essay*, esp. II.ii–iii, III.ii. I owe this information to

Grotius was aware of Dicaearchus' evolutionary account and cites him for the first stage, the age of the hunter/gatherer. At another point he places the private acquisition of moveables before immoveables, which may imply a progression from a primarily pastoral economy to one with an agricultural base. Elsewhere however there is stage-conflation, as where he attributes to 'the first brothers' (and note the order) 'the most ancient arts of agriculture and grazing not without exchange of commodities'.[14] One might say that in Grotius (and Pufendorf), the stadial evolution of society is underdeveloped and limited in scale, being tied, and that rather loosely, to an explanation of the origin and growth of private ownership.

Grotius does give the Golden Age myth an airing. However, he chooses to cite it from Dicaearchus, who had himself rationalized and scaled down the Hesiodic vision, with the consequence that he represented the life of primeval man as one of extreme simplicity and frugality verging on want. For Grotius the sheer primitiveness of that life guaranteed its impermanence. His picture was not bleak enough for Samuel Pufendorf. Writing in *On the Laws of Nature and of Nations* (1672), Pufendorf says that men in the state of nature were like 'miserable animals', living a 'life most wretched'. That is, if 'state of nature' is not an empty category, Pufendorf more or less defines it out of existence by denying it everything 'added to it by human institution'.[15] The influence of Thomas Hobbes, with whose *On the Citizen* and *Leviathan* Pufendorf was in constant dialogue, is palpable. Among authors from antiquity Pufendorf prefers Horace, Lucretius and Diodorus Siculus, for their stress on the extreme primitiveness of the first men, to the Augustan poets and Lactantius, who in his view exaggerated their degree of advancement.[16]

As I have already indicated, Pufendorf clarifies and corrects the account of Grotius by introducing a distinction between negative and positive community.[17] The defining feature of negative community is that 'all things lay open to all men and belong no more to one than to another'; positive community, on the other hand, presupposes the introduction of use-rights and institutions such as a common store, which are enjoyed

---

Iain McDaniel. In addition, Ferguson was much less optimistic than Smith (or Hume) about the historical fate of commercial society. See Hont (2005b), 296–8.

[14] Grotius, *On the Law of War and Peace* 2.2.2.

[15] Pufendorf, *On the Law of Nature and of Nations* 2.1.8; 2.2.4. On Pufendorf, see Tuck (1999), 140–65; Hochstrasser (2000); Hont (2005), 38–47, 159–84.

[16] Pufendorf 2.2.2, citing Hor., *Sat.* 1.3.99; Lucr. 5.925; Diod. Sic. 1.8; etc. See also 4.4.8, on Lactantius, *Div. Inst.* 5.5.

[17] Pufendorf 4.4.9.

by a specific group or community to the exclusion of everyone else. Pufendorf did applaud Grotius for understanding the necessity of agreement before communality could give way to private property.

Pufendorf himself spins out that transitional process: 'Now men left this original negative community of things and by a pact established separate dominions over things, not indeed all at once and for all time but successively, and as the state of things, or the nature and number of men, seemed to require.'[18] But why should primeval society undergo development at all? What was the motor for change? Of the state of nature he writes that 'nature could never have intended man to spend his days in that state'.[19] Negative community too was destined to give way to other regimes. This might take time, if resources were plentiful and could easily go around a small population. But negative community contained the seeds of its own destruction. It would fall apart as soon as people began to acquire things for themselves; and 'things are of no use to men unless at least their fruits may be appropriated'. But such appropriation becomes problematic (he says 'impossible') 'if others as well can take what we have already by our own act selected for our uses'.[20] Pufendorf is going some way to meet Hobbes in conceding that conflict was inevitable in a situation where no one owned or had exclusive rights to anything. However, against Hobbes, he sees the concession of use-rights to individuals or groups, and ultimately, private ownership, as an effective safety valve. Against the 'old saying', 'Mine and thine are the causes of all wars', he retorts: 'Rather it is that mine and thine were introduced to avoid wars.'[21] Also against Hobbes' view that conflict would be endemic in the state of nature, he holds that men were capable through their innate sociability of steering away from hostile confrontation. Further, they could do this without having recourse to the protective and coercive apparatus of civil society, let alone the dictates of an absolute monarch.

How did these transitions from one regime to another take place? They were not engineered by God. God did allow men the use of the products of the earth, but 'He did not determine at that same time what things should be held individually, and what in common.' He did not impose dominion, and certainly did not designate Adam as sole proprietor.[22]

---

[18] Ibid. 4.4.6.   [19] Ibid. 2.2.4.   [20] Ibid. 4.4.5.
[21] Ibid. 4.4.7. This follows a jibe at the Utopians More and Campanella for advocating community of property (*communio bonorum*), 'I suppose because perfect men are more easily imagined than found.'
[22] Ibid. 4.4.9–12, against Filmer, who is not named.

Rather 'he left to the judgement of men, that they should dispose of the matter according as it seemed to work for peace'. Men by the use of sound reason (*sana ratio*) would decide how to head off the apparently inevitable collisions between individuals as they competed for God-given resources. The solution lay in the pact. 'Dominion presupposes absolutely an act of man and an agreement, whether tacit or express.'[23] Pufendorf insists that at every stage of societal development a prior agreement or pact had to be arrived at, a convention or pact negotiated within the community. Why? A convention was needed if people were going to be excluded. As he puts it: 'Assuming an original equal faculty of men over things, it is impossible to conceive how the mere corporal act of one person can prejudice the faculty of others, unless their consent is given.'[24]

In conceding the necessity of pacts, in allowing that 'occupancy of itself, before the existence of pacts, does not confer any rights',[25] Pufendorf is giving a hostage to fortune. The pact is made to bear too much weight. If it was scarcity that forced change, as he thinks,[26] then it needs to be explained how placing exclusive rights over resources in the hands of some at the expense of others could be expected to improve the situation; how 'the rest', those whose access to resources has been reduced, could benefit from the changes, and why they should ever agree to such a reduction.[27] Aristotle is brought into service to show that ownership was beneficial to mankind 'when it had grown numerous'.[28] But Aristotle bypassed the issue of competition for, or scarcity of, resources, and in general spoke as one of the 'haves' and reflects their interests.

Locke contended that private property rights were natural rights tenable independently of government and law. He allowed no role to pacts or agreements in the process of the creation of private property:

He that is nourished by the acorns he picked up under an oak, or the apples he gathered from the trees in the wood, has certainly appropriated them to himself. Nobody can deny but the nourishment is his ... And will any one say, he had no right to those acorns or apples he thus appropriated, because he had not the consent of all mankind to make them his? Was it a robbery thus to assume to himself what belonged to all in common? If such a consent as that was necessary, man had starved, notwithstanding the plenty God had given him.[29]

In this Locke saw eye to eye with his opponent and sparring partner, Sir Robert Filmer (1588–1653), and was in fact using one of Filmer's

[23] Ibid. 4.4.4.   [24] Ibid. 4.4.5.   [25] Ibid. 4.4.5.   [26] Ibid. 4.4.6.
[27] For criticisms of consent, see Waldron (1988), 149–53, 232–41.
[28] Pufendorf 4.4.7.   [29] Locke, *Second Treatise of Government* 28.

arguments against consent. This argument depended on the assumption that the first men were joint owners of the resources of the world, and that the agreement of 'all the men in the world at one instant of time' was required before anyone could have access to any of them. Filmer, and Locke in this passage, were working with a model of positive community, but it was not one that they shared with Grotius and Pufendorf. The latter were thinking rather, at least in the first instance, of agreements made on a local level in the setting of individual communities.

In any case, Locke's example of the gathering of the fruits of the earth (rather than the acquisition of land) fits more naturally into the context of a Pufendorfian negative community. In a lecture on Grotius delivered in Cambridge in 1754, Thomas Rutherforth, Regius Professor of Divinity, offered a solution to Locke's dilemma which distinguished between access to moveables (which man had as of right), and immoveables (for which the consent of mankind was needed):

When he gathered them [the apples and the acorns] and was eating them, he exercised his common right of using and enjoying, out of the joynt stock, what his occasions called for. Though therefore we contend, that he could not acquire an exclusive right of property in them, or in anything else, without the consent of mankind, either express or tacit, yet there is no fear of his being starved, while he is waiting for this consent; because in the mean time the exercise of his common right will sufficiently provide for this subsistence.[30]

Locke and Filmer had different reasons for rejecting a conventional basis for property. Locke wanted to protect property rights from political interference, while Filmer held that property rights and absolute dominion over all mankind were a gift of God to Adam and his line, through which the authority of the Stuart monarchs had descended.[31] Locke's own theory of appropriation, according to which first occupants established their rights to land simply by cultivating it, is itself rooted in his view of God's plan for man, which was that he survive and increase. Mankind had not merely a right to appropriate the means by which these

---

[30] Goldie (1999), vol. 6, 243.
[31] On Filmer's criticisms of an original agreement, see Buckle (1991), 161–71. It is worth noting that Locke was prepared to bring consent in by the back door when it suited his argument. Thus he argues that men agreed to the introduction of money and the resultant 'disproportionate and unequal possession of the earth' (*Second Treatise* 36; 47; 50). This suggestion is at odds with the 'sufficiency proviso' which Locke attached to first acquisition: 'at least where there is enough, and as good left in common for others' (27). As to its plausibility, Waldron (2002), 176, calls it 'one of the worst arguments in the *Second Treatise*'. Note however that David Hume was quite prepared to countenance the introduction by human convention of gold and silver as means of exchange. See *Treatise of Human Nature* Book III part II, 490 (Selby-Bigg/Nidditch).

ends could be achieved, but also a duty to God to carry out His purposes.[32] In a post-Lockean world dominated by secular values, this argument can be rephrased in terms of a concern that natural resources be exploited in such a way that a proper balance is maintained between the liberty of individuals to use or appropriate them, and the preservation of the environment.[33] Such a formulation however rips the heart out of Locke's theory, for without the transcendental dimension it does not work.[34] The specific arguments that he advances of course have to be evaluated on their own terms. Locke writes:

Though the earth, and all inferior creatures, be common to all men, yet every man has a property in his own person; this no body has any right to but himself. The labour of his body, and the work of his hands, we may say, are properly his. Whatsoever then he removes out of the state that nature hath provided, and left it in, he hath mixed his labour with, and joined to it something that is his own and thereby makes it his property. It being by him removed from the common state nature hath placed it in, it hath by this labour something annexed to it, that excludes the common right of other men: for this labour being the unquestionable property of the labourer, no man but he can have a right to what that is once joined to, at least where there is enough and as good left in common for others.[35]

Critics have been quick to notice, with reference to the so-called 'sufficiency proviso' of the last clause, that Locke's theory would apply only where unoccupied land is in plentiful supply, which it was not in the England of his day. John Stuart Mill wrote in his essay on 'Property in Land': 'It is some hardship to be born into the world and to find all nature's gifts previously engrossed, and no place left for the newcomer.'[36] Locke it is clear had his eye on the opportunities for settlement in America. In the *Second Treatise* he insists that labour, the labour that justifies first acquisition, entails *cultivation*. By this yardstick the native inhabitants of America had no title to the land they inhabited.[37] Locke's argument suffers from other basic weaknesses.[38]

---

[32] Waldron (2002), 160.   [33] See Clarke and Kohler (2005), 90.

[34] Cf. Waldron (2002), 184.

[35] Locke, *Second Treatise* 27. This passage gives the basic content of his theory. See also 31 (the spoliation proviso: 'as much as anyone can make use of to any advantage of life before it spoils, so much he may by his labour fix a property in'; cf. 46); add 40–1 (the value-added argument).

[36] Mill, *Principles of Political Economy*, Book II, ch. 2, 6.   [37] See *Second Treatise* 32; 41–3.

[38] Locke's argument has been picked over by so many expert commentators from the eighteenth century to the present day that one might say there are no unallocated acorns or apples to be garnered, no spare wasteland to be cultivated. A selection of the more recent, major, studies might include Dunn (1969); Tuck (1979) and (1999); Tully (1980); Waldron (1988) and (2002); Sreenivasan (1995); Kramer (1997). I have learned much also from the discussions of Buckle (1991); Harris (1996); Clarke and Kohler (2005).

The concept of self-ownership may have made some kind of sense in an era where slaves were being made every day, albeit far from the shores of England, as Locke was aware. Kant, who wrote in such an era, was one who rejected the idea, though without offering a full critique – this in *The Metaphysics of Morals* of 1797:

An external object which in terms of its substance belongs to someone is his property (*dominium*), in which all rights in this thing inhere (as accidents of substance) and which the owner (*dominus*) can, accordingly, dispose of as he pleases (*ius disponendi de re sua*). But from this it follows that an object of this sort can be only a corporeal thing (to which one has no obligation). So someone can be his own master (*sui iuris*) but cannot be the owner *of himself* (cannot dispose of himself as he pleases) – still less can he dispose of others as he pleases – since he is accountable to the humanity in his own person. This is not, however, the proper place to discuss this point ... [39]

In our world, inasmuch as slavery cannot be accepted as a feature of a just society, talking of humans as property, even of themselves, seems to be a category error.[40] Modern lawyers, when faced for example with the problem of how to define a patient's interest in a cell removed from his body and used for medical research (with windfall profits for doctors and pharmaceutical companies a possible outcome), are inclined to talk in terms of personal rather than property rights.[41]

The idea that labour can give entitlement to the product seems fair and reasonable. It appeared so to Aristotle (it is implicit in his critique of common ownership in the *Politics*) and equally to Pufendorf.[42] Locke was often at odds with Pufendorf's account of property, but the latter had produced an argument linking the necessity of labour for making the resources of the earth usable to the claims of the labourer to the fruits of his work: 'Moreover, most things require labour and cultivation by men to produce them and make them fit for use. But in such cases it was improper that a man who had contributed no labour should have the right to things equal to his by whose industry a thing had been raised or rendered fit for service.'[43]

---

[39] Kant, *Metaphysics of Morals*, 56 (Gregor).   [40] Cf. J. Harris (1996), 184–9.

[41] Clarke and Köhler (2005), 3–16. Coleman (2006a) correctly emphasizes the novelty of Locke's argument. Lockean ownership of self and Marxist sovereignty over oneself are easily conflated. For Marxist views, see Cohen (1995). For self-ownership in Hegel, see next section.

[42] And to certain medieval scholars such as John of Paris. See *On Royal and Papal Power*, ch. 7 (Watt, 103): 'Lay property is not granted to the community as a whole ... but is acquired by individual people through their own skill, labour and diligence ... ' Quoted in Coleman (2006a), 143, n. 16.

[43] Aristotle, *Pol.* 1263a12–15; Pufendorf 4.4.6.

That labour should give rights to the land itself and not merely to its product, which is Locke's central thesis, seems an extravagant claim. It happens that Pufendorf in the lines that follow the above quotation goes on to anticipate the sequential introduction of *dominium* of things 'such as require labour and cultivation by men'. He appears to be preparing the ground for Locke here. The difference is that for Locke the acquisition that is legitimated by labour has both logic and morality on its side, whereas in the case of Pufendorf acquisition is the empirical outcome of the need for peace and the reality of population growth. It must also be preceded by a pact or agreement.

Later in the *Second Treatise* Locke raises the stakes with his 'value-added' argument. 'Labour,' he says, 'puts the difference of value on everything'.[44] No less than ninety per cent (or ninety-nine per cent) of the value of land, or other things that are useful to us, can be attributed to the work we have done. The same difficulty rears its head: why should the producer be entitled to permanent ownership of the asset in question, rather than merely the product of his labour, or at best, temporary possession?

Finally, it was open to sceptics to say that, if Locke had been hoping by means of the labour argument to justify first acquisition retrospectively, he had not succeeded. First acquisition still had to be justified, on its own terms. This was the point of Rousseau's outburst in *Discourse on the Origin of Inequality* (1754–5): 'No matter if they said: It is I who built this wall; I earned this plot by my labour. Who set its boundaries for you, they could be answered; and by virtue of what do you lay claim to being paid at our expense for labour we did not impose on you?'[45]

Kant in *The Metaphysics of Morals* insisted that first acquisition of land and its exploitation required separate analyses.[46] As Proudhon was to say in *What is Property?* (1840), citing his older contemporary Victor Cousin: 'In order to labour it is necessary to occupy.'[47] The labour theory could not be used as a cover-up for or escape-route from the (equally unsustainable) principle of first occupancy.

THE RECEPTION OF LOCKE: HUME TO HEGEL

Locke's labour theory of acquisition had a chequered career. It was twisted in an anti-establishment direction by thinkers whom Locke would

[44] Locke, *Second Treatise* 40.   [45] Rousseau, *Second Discourse*, 2.30 (Gourevitch, 172)
[46] Kant, *Metaphysics of Morals* 2.15 (Gregor, 52).
[47] Proudhon, *What is Property?* 67 (Kelley and Smith; cf. 84, citing Comte).

have regarded as his ideological opponents, and was given short shrift by most leading theorists of property. Among the latter, Hegel was exceptional in making positive use of it, though for him it was only the starting point for a much more elaborate and ambitious argument for private property.[48]

Locke's theory was received positively by *opponents* of the status quo. Thomas Rutherforth (in 1754) predicted that the theory might be used to argue the cause of the labourer against the landlord, but thought (or hoped) it would not be taken up:

Now the labour of the occupyer puts the chief value upon the land, and without this labour it would be worth little; for it is to this, that we owe all its useful production ... But no one will be led to conclude from hence, that because, according to this reckoning, in the value of an acre of land ninety nine parts in a hundred are owing to the labour of the occupyer, the property, which he has in his own labour, will swallow up the property which the landlord has in the soil; and that the land, because he has cultivated it, will for the future become his own.[49]

This was overoptimistic. In the late eighteenth and the early nineteenth centuries a number of English radicals, including Spence, Ogilvie, Thelwall and Hodgskin, deployed Locke on behalf of the labouring poor and communal access to land. The arguments of course surface again, with elaboration and development, in the works of the classic 'subversives', Proudhon and Marx.[50]

The most eminent property theorists of the eighteenth century distanced themselves from Locke. Rousseau could see that occupants were likely to claim rights to land they had appropriated on the basis of labour – first to the produce of the land, then to the land itself: 'For it is not clear what, more than his labour, man can put into things he has not made, in order to appropriate them.' But, 'regardless of how they painted their usurpations', they remained just that, usurpations. No one had invited them to build walls, mark out plots and expend labour on them.[51] In his *Treatise of Human Nature* (1739–40) Hume made a brief but telling statement on the issue of the nature of the relationship between person

---

[48] However, Locke's views on property were influential in France in the Age of Revolution. See Ch. 8, pp. 229–31.

[49] Rutherforth, in Goldie (1999), vol. 6, 248.

[50] Marx cites with approval in *Capital* Book I the last of them, Thomas Hodgskin (1787–1869), author of *The Natural and Artificial Right of Property Contrasted* (1832).

[51] Rousseau, *Second Discourse* Part II, 24; 30 (Gourevitch 169, 172).

and property.[52] At one point he states, in passing: 'A man's property is some object related to him. This relation is not natural, but moral, and founded on justice.' He follows this up a little later, in a footnote. He does not attribute the argument from labour expressly to Locke, and in fact does not mention him at all:

Some philosophers account for the right of occupation, by saying, that every one has a property in his own labour; and when he joins that labour to any thing, it gives him the property of the whole; But, 1. There are several kinds of occupation, where we cannot be said to join our labour to the object we acquire: As when we possess a meadow by grazing our cattle on it.[53] 2. This accounts for the matter by means of *accession* which is taking a needless circuit. 3. We cannot be said to join our labour to anything but in a figurative sense. Properly speaking, we only make an alteration on it by our labour. This forms a relation betwixt us and the object, and thence arises property, according to the preceding principles.

Hume had just set out his view that there is no property, or property right, until civil society has been established. Finally, Kant in *The Metaphysics of Morals* is forthright and damning:

Moreover, in order to acquire land is it necessary to develop it (build on it, cultivate it, drain it, and so on)? No. For since these forms (of specification) are only accidents, they make no object of direct possession and can belong to what the subject possesses only insofar as the substance is already recognized as his. When first acquisition is in question, developing land is nothing more than an external sign of taking possession, for which many other signs that cost less effort can be substituted.[54]

Kant goes on to denounce as fraudulent the sequestration of the land of native peoples which ignores their first possession. His examples are 'the American Indians, the Hottentots, and the inhabitants of New Holland':

Should we not be authorized to do this, especially since nature itself (which abhors a vacuum) seems to demand it, and great expanses of land in other parts of the world, which are now splendidly populated, would have otherwise remained uninhabited by civilized people or, indeed, would have to remain forever uninhabited, so that the end of creation would have been frustrated? But it is easy to see through this veil of injustice (Jesuitism), which would sanction any means to good ends. Such a way of acquiring land is therefore to be repudiated.[55]

---

[52] Hume, *Treatise* 491; 506–8 n. 1 (Selby-Bigge/Nidditch).
[53] Locke had interpreted labour narrowly in terms of cultivation.
[54] Kant, *Metaphysics* 52; cf. 55 (Gregor).   [55] Ibid. 53 (Gregor).

Georg Wilhelm Friedrich Hegel (1770–1831)

Hegel produced a distinctive account of property, for which he is to some extent indebted to Locke.[56] In contrast with the eighteenth-century philosophers considered above, he builds labour into his theory of property. In addition, and of central importance – therefore to be discussed first here – the germ (at least) of Hegel's idea that the person of the owner is embodied in his property is to be found in Locke.

Locke's argument went along the following lines: If I am not a slave, nobody owns my body. Therefore I own myself. Therefore I own all my actions, including those which create or improve resources. Therefore I own the resources, or the improvements, that I produce.[57]

What happens between the agent and the object is a 'mixing' and a 'joining': 'Whatsoever, then, he removes out of the state that nature hath provided and left it in, he hath mixed his labour with, and joined to it something that is his own, and therefore makes it his property.' Locke talks also of labour as achieving the 'fixing' of 'my property' in resources removed from what was 'commons'.[58]

Hegel works the concept of self-ownership into his discussion of the first 'phase' in the relationship of person (or 'will') to the 'thing', which is the act of taking possession:

The human being, in his immediate existence in himself, is a natural entity, external to his concept; it is only through the development of his own body and spirit, essentially by means of his self-consciousness comprehending itself as free, that he takes possession of himself and becomes his own property as distinct from that of others. Or to put it the other way round, this taking possession of oneself consists also in translating into actuality what one is in terms of one's concept (as possibility, capacity or predisposition). By this means, what one is in concept is posited for the first time as one's own, and also as an object distinct from simple self-consciousness, and it thereby becomes capable of taking on the form of the thing.[59]

The self-ownership idea is crucial in allowing a slippage between 'mine' in the sense of my person, body and actions, and 'mine' in the sense of the external things that I own. Both philosophers make use of the same

---

[56] For Hegel on property, see e.g. Knowles (1983); Waldron (1988), ch. 10; Patten (1995); J. W. Harris (1996), chs. 13–14; Thomas (2003). A comprehensive treatment of Hegel's views would naturally have to consider his thought in relation to that of Kant. See, briefly, Ilting (1978).

[57] Cf. Harris (1996), 189.   [58] *Second Treatise* 27–8.

[59] Hegel, *Philosophy of Right* 57 (Wood/Nisbet 86). A discussion of slavery follows, not inconsequentially. It is noteworthy that there is a similar juxtaposition in Locke, though in his discussion slavery precedes property.

metaphysical idea that an agent is embodied in an external object. It is just that Locke's metaphysic is simple and undeveloped, Hegel's ambitious and all-encompassing.

Locke leaves it unclarified what it is of the agent that goes out from him into the thing owned. In Hegel, it is the will which is embodied in the thing. The human being is a free will, or spirit, a rational being. Or at least he is potentially so. Freedom in its completeness is displayed in the embodiment of the will in external objects – which are things that lack everything that a free spirit has: freedom, personhood, rights.[60]

The difference goes deeper than this. For Locke, there is an active agent which does something to a thing; Hegel, on the other hand, does not begin with an individual who can be isolated at the start, and who then takes action. Rather, an 'I' exists only as a process of moving 'back' from the will embodied in the thing. Meanwhile, the will itself exists retrospectively: I have a will only when there is a social context which recognizes my will as embodied in something (see below).

At this level of abstract right, then, a person has a *right* to property: 'A person has the right to place his will in any thing. The thing thereby becomes mine and acquires my will as its substantial end (since it has no such end within itself), its determination, and its soul – the absolute right of appropriation which human beings have over all things.' Hegel goes on to say that Plato's *Republic* contains 'a wrong against the person, inasmuch as the person is forbidden to own private property'; and to approve of the dissolution of monasteries where it has occurred 'because a community does not ultimately have the same right to property as a person does'.[61]

And Hegel also believed that *only property* can provide an appropriate stage on which a person's freedom can be acted out. His discussion of property begins with the following sentence: 'The person must give himself an external sphere of freedom in order to have being as Idea.'[62] At the same time he allowed that at other levels, those of the family, society and the State, there were institutions in addition to property through which persons could fulfil themselves. These other levels of analysis were in fact of crucial importance to Hegel's theory. Property enables a person to show himself distinct from other persons, to mark out boundaries

---

[60] Cf. ibid. 45: 'The circumstance that I, as a free will, am an object to myself in what I possess and only become an actual will by this means constitutes the genuine and rightful element in possession, the determination of property.'

[61] Citations: ibid. 44; 46.   [62] Ibid. 41.

between himself (his will) and others, and *to be recognized* as rational. The social context of property is absolutely essential. Society has to recognize the person as agent, and the person holds his property in accordance with the regulations of civil society. It is the social, rule-grounded recognition that transforms the possession of property into ownership, not the physical relationship to the object. Similarly, abstract right might have to give ground to the higher sphere of right embodied in the State in line with political, legal or moral considerations. Above all, abstract right is subservient to the absolute right represented by the World Spirit. As Hegel wrote:

Right is something utterly sacred,[63] for the simple reason that it is the existence of the absolute concept, of self-conscious freedom. But the formalism of right, and also of duty, arises out of the different stages in the development of the concept of freedom. In opposition to the more formal, that is, more abstract and hence more limited kind of right, that sphere and stage of the spirit in which the spirit has determined and actualized within itself the further moments contained in its Idea possesses a higher right, for it is the more concrete sphere, richer within itself and more truly universal.[64]

Hegel's thought is deeply theological, and at the centre of his philosophical theology is the Trinity. Within the Trinity it is the Third Person whom he favours. God is immanent. This is the animating spirit that inspired the first Christian communities and has guided the course of human history thereafter. Hegel's *Lectures on the Philosophy of History* conclude with the following paragraph:

That world history, with its changing spectacle of [individual] histories, is this course of development and the actual coming into being of the spirit – this is the true theodicy,[65] the justification of God in history. Only this insight can reconcile the spirit with world history and with actuality – the insight that God is not only present in what has happened and what happens every day, but that all this is essentially his own work.[66]

Hegel has left Locke far behind. Locke takes agent and object and looks at the relationship between the two. Hegel sees property as a social category: the crucial component is not the physical act of working the land,

---

[63] While *that there be right* is sacred, it does not follow that any particular entitlement to a specific object or piece of land is 'sacred'.
[64] Ibid. 30.
[65] It is true theodicy in two senses: it is a true account of what happened; and philosophy can present this account in such a way as to demonstrate that it is a theodicy.
[66] Hegel, *Lectures* 224 (Dickey/Nisbet).

or the seizure of the land that precedes it, but the recognition of the person as agent by the society, and the rules which society applies. Locke's agent does not need societal recognition – at most he wants civil society to protect his rights to the land which is his by natural law. Locke's agent is assured of *divine* recognition – in the sense that he is assured that ownership is consistent with God's command to exploit the resources of the world. The God in question however is the First Person of the Trinity, the God of the Old Testament, who is separate from his creation, not the God of the Third Age, the Spirit that is working among men and guiding human society. That Locke provided Hegel with a launching pad for his property theory is however beyond question.

We turn now to the subsidiary matter of the role allocated to labour in Hegel's theory of property. Hegel allows for three 'phases' of property: possession, use and surrender. His account allots a significant role to both of the two first, and central, phases: acquisition and labour (in his terminology, 'possession' and 'use'). Indeed Hegel's presentation of the first 'moment' entails the interweaving of the two. There are three aspects to possession: physical seizure of the thing, giving it form and designating it as owned. Physical seizure may be 'the most complete mode of taking possession, because I am immediately present in this possession and my will is thus discernible in it', but it is 'in general merely subjective, temporary, and extremely limited in scope ... ' The second mode, the giving of 'form', is clearly viewed as complementary and essential: 'To give form to something is the mode of taking possession most in keeping with the Idea, inasmuch as it combines the subjective and the objective ... The effects that I have on it [the objects] do not remain merely external, but are assimilated by it.'[67] This brings to mind Locke's metaphors of 'mixing' and 'fixing'. Moreover, Hegel's prime examples concern the working of the land: 'the tilling of the soil, the cultivation of plants'. He goes on (as Locke conspicuously failed to do) to include the pastoral economy, 'the domestication, feeding and conservation of animals', as well as the exploitation of whatever raw materials are available, and the introduction of technology, for example, a windmill (which uses the air without forming it, so without establishing a claim to it).

The consideration of the second 'phase', that is, the use of the thing, suggests that in Hegel's thinking, Locke's 'mix-and-fix' (always supposing that Hegel is in dialogue with Locke) can only be a first stage in a process

---

[67] Hegel, *Philosophy of Right* 54; 56 (Wood/Nisbet).

which leads to the complete absorption of the thing: 'Use is the realization of my need through the alteration, destruction, or consumption of the thing, whose selfless nature is thereby revealed and which thus fulfils its destiny.'[68] This idea is filled out in the Addition to the same section:

While I take complete possession of a thing in a universal way by designating it as mine, its use embodies an even more universal relation, because the thing is not then recognized in its particularity, but is negated by me. The thing is reduced to a means of satisfying my need. When I and the thing come together, one of the two must lose its [distinct] quality in order that we may become identical. But I am alive, a willing and truly affirmative agent; the thing, on the other hand, is a natural entity. It must accordingly perish, and I survive, which is in general the prerogative and rationale of the organic.

Hegel has interposed between these passages what amounts to a reminder that use is secondary to seizure. This takes the form of an attack on the view that land that was unutilized was properly regarded as wasteland and fair game to appropriation by another. This was Locke's idea. Locke had written:

Whatsoever he tilled and reaped, laid up and made use of, before it spoiled, that was his peculiar right; whatsoever he enclosed, and could feed, and make use of, the cattle and product was also his. But if either the grass of his inclosure rotted on the ground, or the fruit of his planting perished without gathering, and laying-up, this part of the earth, notwithstanding his inclosure, was still to be looked on as waste, and might be the possession of any other.[69]

Hegel 'replies':

That use is the real aspect and actuality of property is what representational thought has in mind when it regards disused property as dead and ownerless, and justifies its unlawful appropriation of it on the grounds that the owner did not use it – But the will of the owner, in accordance with which a thing is his, is the primary substantial basis of property, and the further determination of use is merely the [outward] appearance and particular mode of this universal basis to which it is subordinate.[70]

Apart from putting labour in its place as subsidiary to acquisition (for the will could hardly have been brought to bear on the object in the absence of physical seizure), this passage shows that in Hegel's thinking, the process of 'assimilation' or embodiment is initiated in the act of physical seizure (or *occupatio*), and does not wait on the use of the object taken, as it does in Locke's account. The embodiment of the owner in the

[68] Ibid. 59.   [69] Locke, *Second Treatise* 38.   [70] *Philosophy of Right* 59.

thing has begun at the first stage of occupation. In Locke it is apparently an accompaniment of labour, exclusively.

However physical seizure and use, acquisition and labour, are to be ranked against each other, and there are passages that suggest uncertainty over this,[71] the central point is that Hegel, alone of Locke's successors, has provided an integrated treatment of these two central modes of possession.

Hegel produced an argument for the necessity and legitimacy of private property as such, rather than for first occupation in particular. He treats first occupation in one sentence, which is followed by a brief Addition.[72] It was a trivial truth that no one can lay claim to property which is already occupied: 'That a thing belongs to the person who happens to be the first to take possession of it is an immediately self-evident and superfluous determination, because a second party cannot take possession of what is already the property of someone else.' That the first occupant is the owner doesn't follow from the fact that he is the first, but from the fact that he is a free will.

For Hegel (as for Locke) first acquisition was virtually a non-question. His theory of property had eliminated the need to discuss it. Grotius and Pufendorf had apparently expended their energies on the issue for nought. We may wish to reply that unilateral *occupatio* is not an issue that can be side-stepped in this way, that Hegel has shown insufficient concern with the inequality that arose inevitably out of it, and that he has failed to see that his argument that 'free person entails owner of property' has implications for all free people, not just a few.[73]

Hume, Rousseau and Kant, despite holding that property rights were a matter of convention rather than natural law, were willing, as Hegel was not, to engage with the natural jurists of the seventeenth century to a greater or lesser extent, which means that they were prepared to confront first acquisition and explore its 'historical' background. It is to their narratives that we now turn.

---

[71] Ibid. 61 Addition: 'The field is only a field in so far as it produces a crop'; cf. 64 Addition: 'Prescription is based on the assumption that I have ceased to regard the thing as mine. For if something is to remain mine, continuity of my will is required, and this is displayed in the use or conservation of the thing in question.'

[72] Ibid. 50.

[73] For critiques of Hegel on such points, see Waldron (1988), 383–6; Harris (1996), chs. 13–14. On the issue of economic inequality, Hegel's view is that it was relevant only to the extent to which it leads to other bad consequences such as starvation. See *Philosophy of Right* 49; cf. 241.

FROM THE STATE OF NATURE TO CIVIL SOCIETY:
HUME, ROUSSEAU AND KANT

David Hume (1711–76)

Natural rights theorists located the right to property in the state of nature, with the understanding that the human race gave tacit or express consent to the intrusion that it represented. Hume's account apparently does not allow for consent anterior to the conventions introduced by civil society (but we would do well to look at this again). Those conventions or laws are the laws of justice, no less: 'Our property is nothing but those goods, whose constant possession is establish'd by the laws of society; that is, by the laws of justice.'[74] Hume's treatment of property is embedded in an extended discussion of virtues (and vices), which is in large part devoted to justice. Justice and property are very closely related, if they are not Siamese twins. To discuss the origin of one is to discuss the origin of the other.[75] His reasoning is that 'the stability of possession' is the bedrock of civil society, and that once the rules of property were laid down, there was 'little or nothing' left to do in order to achieve a just society, one marked by 'perfect harmony and concord'.

Justice according to Hume is not a natural virtue, and property is not a natural institution, for both have their origins in human convention. The consequences of this finding are worked out, and the origins of both justice and property are identified, in the course of a discussion of man's experience in a pre-social setting. Hume held that before the advent of civil society possessions were chronically insecure, and that this was closely related to the absence of justice at that time.

Hume regarded the state of nature as a figment of the imagination of philosophers, and the Golden Age as an invention of poets. He holds back this judgement, however, until he has made good use of the state of nature as a heuristic tool, and has more or less completed his analysis of natural humanity: 'This no doubt is to be regarded as an idle fiction; but yet deserves our attention, because nothing can more evidently shew the origin of those virtues, which are the subjects of our present enquiry.'[76]

Hume sets out to graft his own psychological theory based on 'common experience and observation' (an application, as he saw it, of the method of Newton to the realm of human behaviour) onto the received

---

[74] *Treatise* Book III, part II, 491 (Selby-Bigge/Nidditch). See Moore (1976).
[75] Cf. *Treatise* 491.   [76] Ibid. 494.

narrative of the evolution of humanity in the state of nature. The result is a distinctive and highly individual analysis; it is nevertheless one carried out on the same terrain as that traversed by the natural jurists. This means that he is in constant dialogue with the latter. In fact, in his *Enquiries concerning the Principles of Morals*, which appeared more than a decade after the *Treatise* (1751), and contained in an Appendix a summary of his views on justice and property, Hume claims that his thesis is 'in the main the same with that hinted at and adopted by Grotius'. Tongue in cheek? He does not explain himself, instead quoting *in extenso* from Grotius' discussion. And there was some explaining to be done. His account diverges from those of Grotius and Pufendorf in a number of significant respects. In the cited passage alone we note that in the final sentence Grotius states that humanity managed the transition to a regime of ownership through the device of 'a pact, either express, as in division, or tacit, as in occupation'.[77]

Hume's natural man is easily recognizable from the accounts of the natural jurists, in particular that of Pufendorf. Man in the state of nature was 'rude and savage', his condition 'savage and solitary', his state 'wild and uncultivated', his character marred by 'rough corners and untoward affections'. It is through society and society alone that 'all his infirmities are compensated' and he becomes 'in every respect more satisfied and happy'. Hume the behavioural scientist now gets to work. Natural man is torn apart by countervailing forces, on the one hand selfishness, on the other limited generosity.[78] Here he was taking on Grotius (in the first instance), though he does not name him.[79] According to Grotius natural man had an *appetitus societatis*, a sense of community with the human race, 'which the Stoics call *oikeiosis*'. Hume provides a rival interpretation of *oikeiosis* (without using the term): 'Now it appears that in the original frame of our mind, our strongest attention is confin'd to ourselves; our next is extended to our relations and acquaintance; and 'tis only the weakest which reaches to strangers and indifferent persons.'[80]

Hume's interpretation is correct, as a glance at a substantial fragment of a work of the late Stoic philosopher Hierocles (*fl. c.*100 AD) shows.[81]

---

[77] *Enquiries* 307, n. 1 (Selby-Bigge/Nidditch), citing Grotius, *On the Law of War and Peace* 2.2.4–5.
[78] *Treatise* 486–94.
[79] Cf. Haakkonssen, in his edition of Hume, *Political Essays* (1994), xxvi: 'Hume thus combined Hugo Grotius' ideas of sociability and Thomas Hobbes's idea of unsociability as the fundamental characteristics of the active side of human nature.' With respect to Grotius at any rate, I arrive at a different conclusion.
[80] *Treatise* 488.   [81] Long and Sedley (1987), vol. 2 59G, 349–50, with comment.

The message of Hierocles, which Hume reproduces accurately, is that humans instinctively regard themselves as the prime object of concern, then have regard for family and other relatives, and treat others as increasingly alien. This being the case, 'while the opposite passions of men impel them in contrary directions', without any convention or agreement to restrain them, possessions will be inherently vulnerable. Chronic instability together with scarce resources will produce without fail social dislocation and destruction. But in those very same factors Hume has also found what he was looking for, the source of justice: 'Here then is a proposition which, I think, may be regarded as certain, *that 'tis only from the selfishness and confin'd generosity of men, along with the scanty provision nature has made for his wants, that justice derives its origin.*'[82]

Hume is adamant that it is 'the nature of our passions' rather than reason which provides the impetus for humanity to embrace justice.[83] Pufendorf's *sana ratio* is sidelined. As to the Divinity, Grotius had written, famously: 'What we have been saying would have a degree of validity even if we should concede (*etiamsi daremus*) that which cannot be conceded without the utmost wickedness, that there is no God, or that the affairs of men are of no concern to Him.'[84] Hume's response was to bypass God altogether.

Hume, then, seems to be deliberately distancing himself from his natural jurist predecessors. Yet he makes a significant concession which reduces the gap between them, though he does not draw attention to it. Pufendorf had strung out the developmental process by which humanity moved towards civil society, marking off the various stages with a series of acts of consent – consent was not a one-off for Pufendorf as it had been for Grotius. Hume, I suggest, allows for something similar. He acknowledges that there is a movement towards justice, which takes time and proceeds by trial and error: 'Nor is the rule concerning the stability of possession the less deriv'd from human conventions, that it arises grad- ually, and acquires force by slow progression, and by our repeated experience of the inconveniences of transgressing it.'[85]

One wonders how a 'rule' of civil society establishing property rights can 'arise gradually', if not by means of ad hoc and provisional agree- ments between individuals and larger groups. Hume also writes (a few sentences earlier): 'I observe, that it will be for my interest to leave another in the possession of his goods, provided he will act in the same

---

[82] *Treatise* 495, original emphasis.   [83] Ibid. 496.
[84] Grotius, *On the Law of War and Peace*, prologue 11.   [85] *Treatise* 490.

manner with regard to me. He is sensible of a like interest in the regulation of his conduct. When this common sense of interest is mutually
express'd, and is known to both, it produces a suitable resolution and
behaviour.' Hume even adds: 'and this may properly enough be call'd a
convention or agreement betwixt us, tho' without the imposition of a
promise'. He follows this up with an example of two oarsmen, whose
(essential) cooperation is traced to 'an agreement or convention', again
short of a promise. Hume seems so anxious to insist on the absence of a
promise (which itself would 'arise from human agreements'), that he has
admitted the concepts of convention and agreement, so dear to the
natural jurists, by the back door.[86]

Hume makes a second, closely related, concession to the natural jurists,
which is to recognize that society makes its appearance, at least in a
vestigial form, in the state of nature, together with elementary property
conventions. The *fons et origo* is the mutual attraction of the sexes, giving
rise to a conjugal and then family unit.[87] In a later section dealing with
the source of allegiance (to government, whose origin he has just discussed), Hume interposes an intermediate stage of social development,
namely, tribal society, looking sideways at the 'American tribes, where
men live in concord and amity among themselves without any establish'd
government'. He goes on to conclude: 'The state of society without
government is one of the most natural states of men, and may subsist with
the conjunction of many families, and long after the first generation.'[88]
Pufendorf would have been entirely comfortable with this statement
(Hobbes not at all).

Hume has already anticipated this conclusion in the earlier discussion
of the origin of justice and property, where he follows the logic of his own
argument to the conclusion that natural man was always, and from the
beginning, social: 'If all this appear evident, as it certainly must, we may
conclude, that 'tis utterly impossible for men to remain any considerable
time in that savage condition, which precedes society; but that his very
first state and situation may justly be esteem'd social.'[89] If Hume thought
he was striking off on a path not traversed by his natural jurist predecessors, he was mistaken. Pufendorf had already elided the putative state
of nature, for similar reasons.

---

[86] For Hume on convention, see Wiggins (2006), 71–82; also, Forbes (1975), 26–7.
[87] Cf. *Treatise* 486: 'the first and original principle of society'.
[88] Ibid. 541.   [89] Ibid. 493.

Society without government was fated eventually to collapse; it was the competition for resources that brought it down, driving humanity to seek stability in civil society. Given that men entered civil society with possessions in tow, what should become of those possessions? Hume views the 'difficulty' as in fact quite unproblematic:

This difficulty will not detain them long; but it must immediately occur, as the most natural expedient, that every one continue to enjoy what he is at present master of, and that property or constant possession be conjoin'd to the immediate possession. Such is the effect of custom, that it not only reconciles us to any thing we have long enjoy'd, but even gives us an affection for it, and makes us prefer it to other objects, which may be more valuable but are less known to us.[90]

In footnotes Hume adds to the rule already stated, that property follows the present possession, two other principles, 'that it arises from first or from long possession'.[91] In addition, he muses rather casually over the origin of these rules as to whether motives of public interest are in question, or whether they are not the fruit of the 'workings of the imagination'. The mind', he explains, 'has a natural propensity to join relations, especially resembling ones, and finds a kind of fitness and uniformity in such a union.'

Hume, then, does not agonize over the legitimacy of first occupancy, any more than he concerns himself over the issue of inequality.[92] This was a member of the class of 'lairds', well content with existing property relations, and optimistic about the prosperity that an expanding commercial economy would bring to all sections of the population.[93]

Jean-Jacques Rousseau (1712–84)

Rousseau, on the other hand, was a son of a watchmaker, an autodidact and a provocateur. The *Second Discourse*, that is, *The Discourse on the Origins of Inequality* (1755), contains a conjectural reconstruction of the state of pre-political mankind.[94] His outline of an ideal state, *The Social Contract* (1762), is also of major relevance to our theme.[95]

---

[90] Ibid. 503.   [91] Ibid. 509, n. 2.
[92] Cf. *Enquiries* 305, over the necessity for the laws governing property to be 'inflexible'.
[93] See Hont (2005a); briefly, Forbes (1975), from 87.
[94] *Oeuvres Complètes* III 111. See e.g. Wokler (1978); (2001); Moran (1993). See Gourevitch's editions of Rousseau's works for extensive bibliography. A full study of Rousseau's ideas on early mankind would have to take in *Essay on the Origin of Languages*, within which is tucked away (in ch. 9) an interesting treatment of the stadial theory (three-stage in this case) of the development of society. See *Oeuvres Complètes* V, from 375.
[95] *Oeuvres Complètes* III 347.

Rousseau in his Preface to the *Second Discourse* openly admits that his first and main matter of interest is in 'civilized' social and political institutions and relations of his own day: 'It is no light undertaking to disentangle what is original from what is artificial in man's present nature, and to know accurately a state which no longer exists, and perhaps never did exist, which probably never will exist, and about which it is nevertheless necessary to have exact notions in order accurately to judge of our present state.'[96]

In order to bring present actualities into sharp focus, he conjures up an 'other' which is set in the past, the life of early humanity in the state of nature. Thus far (but no further) he was following in the tracks of his predecessors. What he doesn't quite say here, but will soon become evident, is that he is framing natural society as the *opposite* of modern civilized society as he sees it,[97] and furthermore, that the latter will come off *worse* in the comparison – for Rousseau is a fierce critic of contemporary society.[98] Already in the Preface there are rumblings, presaging a sequence of outbursts that punctuate the text.[99]

His story is not one of linear progress from primitive beginnings to civilized society, as sketched out by the early Enlightenment thinkers in their various ways. Mankind may have made substantial progress in learning, science and the arts, but has regressed in the realm of moral, social and political behaviour. Equality, which 'by common consent' was the natural condition of men, has been supplanted by gross inequality. Certainly the state of nature in its last stages was falling apart in a Hobbesian state of war. But the civil society which replaced it was not what it was made out to be. Instead of being 'the moment when, Right replacing Violence, Nature was subject to Law', it was a coup by the rich to safeguard their power, influence and inordinate share of the earth's resources.[100]

Rousseau has a second line of attack on the culture of civilized, European society. Present-day society comes up short by comparison not only with what was, but also with what might have been, and might still be, namely, the state that Rousseau sketched out in the *Social Contract* a

---

[96] *Second Discourse*, Pref. 4 (Gourevitch 125).

[97] Nature/civilization is a 'binary opposition' and Rousseau is here using a methodology shared by other contemporary writers, albeit to different effect.

[98] Rousseau had already shown his hand in the *Discourse on the Sciences and Arts*, or *First Discourse*, of 1751. Both were submissions in competitions organized by the Academy of Dijon, but only the former won the prize.

[99] Pref. 3; 12; *Second Discourse* 1.9, 137–8; etc.   [100] Pref. 3; Exordium 4.

decade and a half later. The latter is a 'perfect moral commonwealth', an ideal form of government wherein man's true nature is realized, a regime that has never come into existence, because human history in its very first episodes took a wrong turning. It is worth investigating the role or roles that Rousseau assigns to private ownership in the two imaginary societies and in the one that is caught in the middle.

In the process of building up his picture of primeval man in the state of nature, Rousseau sets about stripping him of all the artificial or conventional qualities which, in his view, he could only have acquired after leaving the state of nature; they are, in particular, those qualities associated with the 'moral' as opposed to the 'physical' aspect of life.[101] 'The philosophers', he says, 'have regularly transposed into the state of nature concepts and institutions that properly belong in civil society. 'They spoke of Savage Man and depicted Civil Man.'[102] The two principles that survive the purge are 'amour de soi-même', that is, self-love, or interest in self-preservation; and pity, repugnance at seeing others suffer.[103] Rousseau makes a point of excluding sociability, which is associated in particular (though not expressly here) with the narrative of Pufendorf.[104] Nature has simply not prepared man for this quality, and in any case it is unnecessary: 'Indeed it is impossible to imagine why, in that primitive state, a man would need another man any more than a monkey or a wolf would need his kind ... '[105] Rousseau goes on to criticize the idea, also Pufendorfian, that primitive man without sociability would have been miserable:

I know that we are repeatedly told that nothing would have been as miserable as man in this state ... Now I should very much like to have it explained to me what kind of misery there can be for a free being, whose heart is at peace, and body in health. I ask, which of the two, civil life or natural life, is more liable to become intolerable to those who enjoy it?

---

[101] For this distinction, see Exordium 2.

[102] Exordium 5; cf. *Second Discourse* 1.25; 1.35 (a critique of Hobbes for improperly importing 'a multitude of passions' into the state of nature).

[103] On the difference between 'amour de soi-même' and 'amour propre', see Rousseau's note to *Second Discourse* XV, 218; more refs. at 377n. On pity, see *Second Discourse* 1.35. Pity of the weak was a quality attributed to primeval man in a proto-Epicurean phase of the state of nature in Lucretius 5.1023.

[104] *Second Discourse*, Pref. 9; 1.33. In the latter passage he is interested in making the wider point that it was not nature's purpose to bring men together through mutual needs. This is a theme of *Essay on the Origin of Languages*, where Rousseau is concerned to stress the role of man's natural passions in the formation of primeval society. See e.g. 2.3 (*Discourses*, ed. Gourevitch, 253). On Rousseau and Pufendorf, see Wokler (1994).

[105] *Second Discourse* 1.33.

A sideswipe at contemporary society follows. This is one of several occasions where the reader is suddenly put on the spot and invited, or forced, to compare himself unfavourably with a savage. Rousseau's primitive man was just that, a savage: naked, without habitat, leading a solitary and idle way of life, closer to the other animals than to civilized man. Rousseau does not rule out the possibility that 'more accurate investigations' will reveal that orang-utans are men.[106] Man is superior to other animals only in so far as he is a free agent, capable of 'willing, or rather of choosing', and in being aware that he has this capacity. That however is the sum total of the qualities that can be subscribed to him on the 'metaphysical and moral' as distinct from the 'physical' side.[107]

Rousseau was not a 'primitivist', in the traditional sense. He did not idealize a Golden Age in the past at the dawn of human history.[108] He was well aware of the existence of this alternative narrative, now sidelined by philosophers, and was not above flirting with it, and teasing and provoking his audience in the process.[109] There is a 'golden' *episode* in his state of nature (see below), and moral decline is a leitmotiv of his narrative, as it was in the classic Golden Age mythology.

By the same token, he did not reject the idea of progress altogether. His case was that progress in the realm of *mores* ought to march in step with the expansion of knowledge and the cultivation of reason, whereas *in practice* it had fallen far behind. He concludes a passage comparing the tranquillity of natural man with the mental torture that modern man inflicts on himself, with the recognition that natural man had the potential to develop, and that such development could be 'providential', as long as man's capacities continued to be tailored to his needs:

It was by a very wise Providence that the faculties he had in potentiality were to develop only with the opportunities to exercise them, so that they might not be superfluous and a burden to him before their time, nor belated and useless in time of need. In instinct alone he had all he needed to live in the state of nature, in cultivated reason he had no more than what he needs to live in society.[110]

This developmental potential in natural man is encapsulated in the quality of 'perfectibility', 'the faculty of perfecting oneself', which a little

---

[106] See Rousseau's note to *Second Discourse* VI 6, 208.   [107] *Second Discourse* 1.14–16.
[108] Lovejoy (1948) is too literal an attack on this notion.
[109] Cf. *Essay in the Origin of Languages* 9.6: 'These times of barbarism were the golden age, not because men were united, but because they were separated.'
[110] *Second Discourse* 1.33.

earlier in the *Discourse* he had introduced as distinctively human.[111] That this word entered the vocabulary of the history of political thought during the Enlightenment is less surprising than that it was introduced by Rousseau, scourge of the Enlightenment.[112] It was 'the last of the philosophes', Condorcet (1743–94), who gave perfectibility full rein in his *Sketch for a Historical Picture of the Progress of the Human Mind* (1795). It is ironical that Condorcet put the finishing touches to this hymn to progress shortly before his death in a prison cell, a victim of the Revolution. Rousseau was ambivalent about perfectibility. In his account the positive attributes are matched, or outweighed, by the negative. 'Wise Providence' needed to give a guiding hand, though in fact luck is allotted a more significant role.[113] On the positive side Rousseau allows for a developmental stage within the state of nature, which he hails as 'the happiest and most lasting epoch', and 'the genuine youth of the world'. He thinks that most native peoples of his time had arrived at this state.[114] But humanity continued to evolve. A dark age of conflict and warfare came next, followed in its turn by a flawed civil society in which human reason was perfected, but at the cost of 'the deterioration of the species'. Rousseau did however retain the belief that progress and enlightenment were possible on his terms, that individual perfectibility and the perfection of civil society could be achieved by the Social Contract. Furthermore, Rousseau's perfectibility was not ahistorical, as was, for example, Plato's.[115] Plato's ideal of moral perfectibility was realizable only through the individual's grasping of the timeless and eternal world of intelligible forms, through the use of his own practical imagination and highly developed rational capacities.

Part I of the *Second Discourse* has little to say about private property; it deals in the main with the pure state of nature, in which not even 'the slightest notion of thine and mine' had intruded.[116] Part II begins with an explosion:

---

[111] Ibid. 1.17; 30.

[112] There is the germ of this idea perhaps in the doctrine advanced by some canon lawyers in the twelfth century, that human nature was inherently rational and morally responsible. See Tierney (1997), ch. 2. More relevant for Rousseau is likely to be the influence of Genevan Calvinism. See Rosenblatt (1997), esp. 82, 172–4.

[113] *Second Discourse* 1.51; cf. 2.18.

[114] Ibid. 1.44 on the Caribs and Rousseau's note XVI, 218, an appraisal of the way of life and attitudes of the savages.

[115] He holds out hopes for Corsica: see *Social Contract* 2.10.6 and the treatise *The Constitutional Project for Corsica*: *Oeuvres Complètes* III.

[116] *Second Discourse* 1.39.

The first man who, having enclosed a piece of ground, to whom it occurred to say *this is mine*, and found people sufficiently simple to believe him, was the true founder of civil society. How many crimes, wars, murders, how many miseries and horrors mankind would have been spared by him who, pulling up the stakes or filling in the ditch, had cried out to his kind: Beware of listening to this impostor; You are lost if you forget that the fruits are everyone's and the Earth no one's.

In chapter 27 he lists other evils, moral, social and economic, which were all the 'first effect' of property, and its running mate 'nascent' inequality – nascent implying that there was much more and worse to come.

Property came onto the scene at the last stage of the state of nature after significant antecedent 'progress', 'industry' and 'enlightenment', a process that culminated in the introduction of an agricultural economy. Agriculture brought in its train division, the recognition of property, and 'the first rules of justice', which are: to each his own, and to the cultivator the fruits of his labour. These feeble structures could not arrest the growth of inequality. The 'right' of the first occupant could not withstand the 'right' of the stronger. 'Nascent society gave way to the most horrible state of war.' With the world 'at the brink of ruin', the rich closed ranks and established a political and judicial system that stabilized society on the basis of existing inequalities of power and wealth, and with a further 'progress of inequality' all but guaranteed:[117]

Such was, or must have been, the origin of society and of laws, which gave the weak new fetters and the rich new forces, irreversibly destroyed natural freedom, forever fixed the law of property and inequality, transformed a skillful usurpation into an irrevocable right, and for the profit of a few ambitious men henceforth subjugated the whole of mankind to labour, servitude and misery.[118]

If we now fast-forward to Rousseau's ideal state as outlined in the *Social Contract*, we find a system of private property in place, and the right of the first occupant enshrined.[119] Has Rousseau changed his position on property? He has not. Rather, society has undergone a revolution. Mankind has been brought together into an association 'which will defend and protect the person and goods of each associate with the full common force, and by means of which each, uniting with all, nevertheless obeys only himself and remains as free as before.'[120] And again, a little later, summing up the social contract, Rousseau says: 'Each of us puts his

---

[117] Rousseau allows for three stages in the development of civil society, as there were three in the state of nature, each one more corrupt, and culminating in despotism.
[118] *Second Discourse* 2.33.　　[119] *Social Contract* 1.9.　　[120] Ibid. 1.6.4.

person and his full power in common under the supreme direction of the General Will; and in a body we receive each member as an indivisible part of the whole.'[121] The terms are quite different from those dictated by the cunning few to the hoodwinked many at the inauguration of *real* civil societies. As to property, the right of the first occupant is the basis of the property arrangements, but that right is recognized only on certain conditions: that the land is not yet taken; that only so much land be held as is necessary for subsistence; and that the land be worked. It is a first occupancy carried out by men whose reason has been 'moralized' that receives the blessing of Rousseau, not the first occupancy of the state of nature. With his gaze fixed firmly on 'civilized' Europe, Rousseau concludes that its state of corruption can only have sprung from a first occupancy that amounted to unilateral usurpation, that took place before mankind was ready for it, and that did not respect the principle of equality, specifically, the equal access of all to the resources of the world. There is an implication that the property arrangements of *real* societies, which had in the first instance been carried over from the state of nature, and had subsequently undergone further development, would have to be transformed at the introduction of the ideal state of the Social Contract.[122] It is difficult to imagine such a transformation taking place without an element of coercion. Rousseau famously allowed for the forcible submission of the individual will to the general will: 'Whoever refuses to obey the general will shall be constrained to do so by the entire body: which means nothing other than that he shall be forced to be free; for this is the condition which, by giving each Citizen to the Fatherland, guarantees him against all personal dependence.'[123]

Immanuel Kant (1724–1804)

Kant lectured in philosophy at the University of Königsberg (now Kaliningrad). Among his students in the 1760s was Johann Gottfried

---

[121] Ibid. 1.6.9.

[122] See Bertram (2004), 89–96, who cites other statements on property in Rousseau's works, of which the most interesting are *Discourse on Political Economy* 46 (Gourevitch 23), a ringing endorsement of private property but in purely general terms; and *The Constitutional Project for Corsica: Oeuvres Complètes* III: 930–1: 'Far from wanting the state to be poor, I should like, on the contrary, for it to own everything, and for the individual to share in the common property only in proportion to his services ... In short, I want the property of the state to be as large and strong, that of the citizens as small and weak, as possible.'

[123] *Social Contract* 1.7.8. See Tuck (1999), 197–207, for similarities (and differences) between Rousseau and Hobbes; and below, p. 170 for compulsion in Kant.

Herder, a friend of Goethe and an icon of the German literary revival of the 1770s. Herder's correspondence includes an engaging pen-picture of his teacher: 'In the prime of his life, he had the joyful cheerfulness of a young man which, I believe, remains with him in his most advanced years. His broad brow, built for thought, was the seat of an indestructible serenity and joy. Words, full of ideas, flowed from his lips, jocularity, wit and humour were at his disposal, and his didactic discourse was like the most entertaining conversation ... I recall his image with pleasure.'[124]

In the mischievous cartoon of 1849 with which I introduced this topic of the origins of property (in Chapter 5), a teacher of Roman law at the University of Leipzig, Theodore Mommsen, is shown at the podium, vigorously propounding the thesis that 'Property is Theft.' The message that the young Herder is likely to have heard from Kant is: 'Property is Freedom.' Kant held that it was the right and duty of a man, as a rational, autonomous individual, to own property.

Kant's discussion of property is concentrated in *The Metaphysics of Morals* (1797). It would be best to begin our discussion with *The Grounding of the Metaphysics of Morals* (1785), wherein Kant sets out the underlying premises of his moral philosophy, above all his concept of a moral law grounded in Reason, and his vision of a moral society composed of individuals who are moral authorities in their own right and respect the moral agency of their fellows. Private property was a central institution of the Kantian moral society.

Kant as moral philosopher set himself the task of enunciating principles or laws to serve as the basis of morality. His leading ideas were freedom and equality.[125] The individual is a free, independent and rational person or will, who is capable of making his own decisions about what he ought to do, and is duty-bound to do so. His freedom is a right, deriving from his intrinsic worth.[126] All other rights follow from this right. Further, they are held by us as persons equally, commoners included. Kant had learned from Rousseau that ordinary people were worthy of respect. He was himself the son of a harness-maker, who by sheer talent had climbed up the academic ladder in his local university, and gradually attracted attention and finally fame in the world outside, into which he did not

---

[124] Herder, *Briefe zu Beförderung der Humanität*, no. 79, quoted Reiss/Nisbet 193 in their edition of Kant's *Political Writings*.

[125] For Kant as 'the philosopher of the French Revolution', see *Political Writings* (Reiss 3). The third ideal of the Revolutionaries, fraternity, is perhaps picked up in Kant's notion of the 'kingdom of ends'. Kant of course followed with dismay the degeneration of the Revolution into the Terror.

[126] *Grounding of the Metaphysics of Morals*, 434–5 (Ellington 40).

venture. One can express the same idea of human worth or dignity by characterizing an individual as an end in himself, and furthermore as a member of a 'kingdom of ends'. By this is meant 'a world of rational beings', 'a systematic union of different rational beings governed by common laws',[127] in short, a moral community of free and equal members each of whom behaved as autonomous individuals while living in harmony with one another.

In so far as we are rational and free we are morally autonomous: we dictate the moral law to ourselves.[128] This is a universal law. 'Just this very fitness of his maxims for the legislation of *universal law* distinguishes him as an end in himself.'[129] Kant calls his law 'the categorical imperative',[130] and expresses it as follows (there are a number of variants): 'Act only according to the maxim by which you can at the same time will that it should become a universal law.' Or, in a different formulation (which may not be equivalent): 'Act so that you treat humanity, whether in your own Person or in that of another, always as an end and never as a means only.' The categorical imperative, while directed at ourselves, carries rights and duties for other people as well. It lays down rules and formulates claims which must be consistent with the innate right to freedom of all those who might be affected by them.

It is Reason that gives us the laws of morality. No other basis for moral law is acceptable. 'There is no genuine supreme principle of morality which does not rest on pure reason alone.'[131] Any external source of authority has to stand before the Tribunal of Reason. The founder of Christianity is himself subservient to the moral rule springing from the legislating intelligence which is the rational agent. 'Even the Holy One of the Gospel must first be compared with our ideal of moral perfection before he is recognized as such.'[132] As an instance of the defectiveness of Jesus' law, Kant cites the 'trivial' Golden Rule, 'Do not do to others what you do not want done to yourself.'[133]

---

[127] Ibid. 438; 433.

[128] 'Kant invented the conception of morality as autonomy.' So Schneewind (1998), 1, in his first sentence.

[129] *Grounding* 438.

[130] See Ibid. 414 for the categorical/hypothetical imperative distinction. On the categorical imperative, Paton (1947) is still useful. For a brief critique of the concept, see McIntyre (1998), 186–91.

[131] *Grounding* 409.   [132] Ibid. 408.

[133] Ibid. 430 n. 23: 'It is merely derived from our principle, although with several limitations. It cannot be a universal law, for it contains the ground neither of duties to oneself nor of duties of love toward others ... Nor finally does it contain the ground of strict duties toward others, for the

It would be equally mistaken to ground our ethical system as the classical Greek philosophers had done on happiness or the good. That would be to substitute inclination for Reason, and therefore to build our house on shifting sands. Happiness is an indeterminate concept: 'Unfortunately, the concept of happiness is such an indeterminate one that even though everyone wishes to attain happiness, he can never say definitely and consistently what it is that he really wishes and wills.'[134] But also, whether or not our desires will be fulfilled depends on something that is not in our control, namely the constitution of the world, and so moral evaluation would have a contingent element, which was anathema to Kant.

As for a 'mixed' moral philosophy, 'compounded both of incentives drawn from feelings and inclinations and at the same time of rational concepts', that was no solution, because it would be seriously dysfunctional. It 'must make the mind waver between motives that cannot be brought under any principle and that can only by accident lead to the good but often can also lead to the bad'.[135]

Kant strips us down to pure intelligence, discarding all our empirical properties. We can be certain that we are rational beings. We can be equally certain that there is one thing and one thing only that is morally good without qualification, a good will. (Kant begins *The Grounding* with this dictum.) The will does not waver, 'it can never conflict with itself'.[136] Equipped with a reason-directed will, one can arrive at maxims for behaviour that are not contradictory, and one can begin to put together a picture of what a society would look like which is peopled by individuals who legislate moral laws for themselves, even if they cannot always abide by them (as Kant readily concedes).

So much for Kant's conceptual apparatus, in brief summary. He does raise the issue of proof at several points of the *Grounding*, but only to palm it off.[137] His construction, he tells us, depends not on any proof, logical or empirical, but on the conviction that the mass of ordinary people accept the necessity of moral behaviour and recognize in themselves a capacity, as autonomous agents, freely to choose between the morally good and bad. A sceptical age such as ours does not share his confidence.

---

criminal would on this ground be able to dispute with the judges who punish him; and so on.' One wonders whether Kant knew that Gratian's *Decretum* began with a pronouncement that *ius naturale* was identical with the Golden Rule.
[134] *Grounding* 418.   [135] Ibid. 411.   [136] Ibid. 437.   [137] Ibid. 444–5.

A feature of the Kantian moral society, as already intimated, is that rights of property are guaranteed and protected. These rights rest on a postulate of moral reason, according to which there is an integral relationship between the possession of private property and the exercise of freedom. This has the status of an a priori proposition. It is a mixed proposition because it embraces the empirical notion of property. *It is a synthetic, a priori proposition of right that every free person has a right to private property.* Because a universal law is in question, everyone else is placed under an obligation to refrain from using the particular external objects, and the individual imposes on himself a reciprocal obligation to respect the rights of others to external objects of their choice.

Property rights are 'conclusive' only within the framework of civil society. 'It is only a will putting everyone under obligation, hence only a collective general (common) and powerful will, that can provide everyone with this assurance [i.e., that one's freedom as a property owner will not be infringed].'[138] This casts a shadow over first acquisition, which is a unilateral act. Unless first acquisition is in some way authorized by the moral law, continuity of possession between the pre-civil and the civil condition is in jeopardy. Kant does not follow the natural rights theorists of the seventeenth century in fixing property rights in the state of nature.[139] His way round the difficulty is to admit a category of 'provisionally rightful' (as distinct from 'conclusive') possession, which is 'possible' prior to civil society, as long as it proceeds 'with a view to', and is 'leading to', the civil condition. Such 'compatibility' with the introduction of a civil society means that the individual is 'the better placed' in any conflict over his act of acquisition.

How is it exactly that the individual gets an edge over any challenger? How does his act achieve the status of compatibility with the law of a moral society? Kant answers that 'provisionally rightful' acquisition does not consist merely in empirical possession, but engages the will, the rational, free will of the individual.[140] It is a will that has set its sights on entering civil society.

---

[138] *Metaphysics of Morals* 6:256. At the tail-end of the whole discussion, Kant introduces for the first time the word *dominium* instead of *possessio*, to underline the point that right to property is consummated only in a civil society. See 6:270.

[139] Equally, Kant rejects their view that prudential motives provide a sufficient and satisfactory explanation for the institution of civil society.

[140] A closely related idea is that the will establishes 'intelligible' (*noumenon*) rather than 'physical' (*phaenomenon*) possession, inasmuch as, e.g., an apple from my tree is mine even if it is not in my grasp. See 6:247.

As the argument proceeds it is disclosed that the involvement of the will makes external acquisition a duty as well as a right. It is a duty which binds others: they have an obligation to give their consent. Their consent to external acquisition, however, carries with it consent to the establishment of a civil society, in which alone possession is based on (public) law. Finally, and remarkably, any who are opposed to entering civil society may be forced into it, 'since leaving the state of nature is based upon duty'.[141]All in all, provisional acquisition in the state of nature is *true* acquisition.[142] The state of nature can be seen as a civil society-in-the-making.

The admission of the 'principles of right' into the state of nature, if only in a provisional way, produces another, striking consequence, that the concept of *res nullius* is condemned as incoherent. To classify a thing as belonging to no one, to put something which is usable beyond the possibility of being used, is to deny us our freedom to acquire. Thus first acquisition necessarily presupposes possession in common: 'Unless such a possession in common is assumed, it is inconceivable how I who am not in possession of the thing could still be wronged by others who are in possession of and are using it.'[143] Similarly, I can only bind another to refrain from using a thing if he is a possessor-in-common, and joins with others who possess it in common to accept an obligation not to use the thing.

What Kant calls 'original possession-in-common' is not an empirical concept and has nothing to do with any historical or pseudo-historical community. It is 'a practical rational concept which contains, a priori, *the principle* in accordance with which alone people can use a place on the earth in accordance with the principles of right'.[144] Kant had stated in the introduction of *The Metaphysics of Morals* that his search for moral laws was not to be confused with 'moral anthropology', which deals only with 'subjective conditions in human nature'. He goes on to give the assurance that he will not be founding his moral law on the laws of nature, but rather on the laws of freedom.[145] Kant was distancing himself from David Hume, who mistakenly looked for the origins of justice in man's pre-social psychological and cultural development.

---

[141] *Metaphysics of Morals* 6:267; cf. 265; 312.   [142] Ibid. 6:265.   [143] Ibid. 6:261.
[144] Ibid. 6:262. For that reason, Kant's dictum on the impossibility of *res nullius* is not a *direct* challenge to the Pufendorfian negative community, out of which mankind is supposed to have progressed, via positive community, into a regime of ownership.
[145] Ibid. 6:217–218.

So it is worth paying attention when Kant manages to escape from the straitjacket of his conceptual scheme, as he does briefly in two essays, *Idea for a Universal History with Cosmopolitan Knowledge* (1784), and *Conjectures on the Beginning of Human History* (1786), published in a learned periodical out of Berlin, a year before and a year after *The Grounding*.[146] In the earlier essay he states that his subject matter will not be metaphysics but history, not the concept of the free will, but the operation of the will 'in the world of phenomena, that is, human actions'. But he has in mind 'universal history' rather than 'history proper'; he is not offering a narrative of events, but will be attempting to lay down general historical laws. He is not optimistic about the possibility of achieving in the realm of human action what Kepler or Newton did in the field of science (a comment at Hume's expense?), but still manages to come up with nine propositions. The later of the two essays is introduced as a *jeu d'esprit*, an 'exercise in the imagination', 'a healthy mental recreation', a 'pleasure trip'. We are grateful for the essays, however slight they might appear in the eyes of their author. They bring Kant into closer contact with his predecessors from Grotius to Rousseau than his quasi-theological dogmatic is able to do.

The later-composed of the two essays tells the story of human development in the state of nature, and I take it first. Kant takes the Bible as a guide. This in the Age of the Enlightenment is something of a surprise, but Kant is dogging the footsteps of Herder, the first instalments of whose *Ideas on the Philosophy of the History of Mankind* (1784–91) he had recently reviewed in critical vein (causing a breach in their relationship which was never repaired).[147] Kant also (more significantly for us) is in dialogue with Rousseau. The story begins with a man and a woman in a garden, happy in 'the womb of nature'. Kant imagines them 'not in their wholly primitive state, but only after they have made significant advances in the skilful use of their powers', over, he presumes, 'a significant interval of time'.[148] Kant is following Rousseau's lead in placing his Golden Age after a primitive stage of savagery. In this way he neatly weaves together into one story the two distinct traditional narratives of the Golden Age and the state of nature.

[146] *Berlinische Monatschrift* IV and VII. The essays are translated with notes in Reiss/Nisbet 41–53, 221–34. See also their editorial introduction to Kant's Review of Herder's *Ideas*, and to *Conjectures*, 192–200.

[147] *Conjectures* 192 (Reiss/Nisbet).   [148] Ibid. 222.

Reason disturbs the peace of the couple, showing them how to be inventive in diet, to choose between alternative ways of life, to think constructively about the future, and above all, to appreciate that mankind is an end in itself. This first 'taste of freedom' carries the 'penalty' that they must depart from the garden and follow the path towards perfection under the guidance of reason. Rousseau's doctrine of perfectibility comes to mind, and its author soon surfaces in the discussion and is given sympathetic treatment. The tension between man's 'aspiration towards his moral destiny' and his nature as a physical species engenders conflict and misery, which are exacerbated as the economy evolves through the traditional stages. The arrival of agriculture is accompanied by permanent, defensible settlements and the private ownership of land. In such communities sociability acts as a unifying, and inequality as a divisive, force.[149] Rousseau, we are told, did not appreciate that inequality may have produced evil in abundance, but is also the 'source ... of everything good'.[150] Kant provocatively draws a parallel with international affairs: war between nations is 'an indispensable means' of securing cultural advancement.

The correct response to man's predicament is not to sink into a malaise as do some 'thinking men' (as Rousseau did?). So to the upbeat conclusion: 'We should be content with providence and with the course of human affairs as a whole, which does not begin with good and then proceed to evil, but develops gradually from the worse to the better. Each individual for his part is called upon by nature itself to contribute towards this progress to the best of his ability.'[151]

The *Idea for a Universal History* goes some way toward bridging the gap between the empirical and the metaphysical Kant, because it 'to some extent follows an a priori rule'.[152] In *Conjectures*, Kant had seen early humans depart from paradise and set off on the path of progress. In *Idea for a Universal History*, he looks ahead to their entry into civil society. The Fourth Proposition holds the key:

The means which nature employs to bring about the development of innate capacities is that of antagonism within society, in so far as this antagonism becomes in the long run the cause of a law-governed order. By antagonism, I mean in this context the unsocial sociability *of man, that is, their tendency to come together in society, coupled, however, with a continual resistance which constantly threatens to break this society up.*[153]

---

[149] Kant mentions property only here, at 229; in Rousseau's *Second Discourse* it plays a leading role.
[150] *Conjectures* 230.   [151] Ibid. 234.   [152] *Idea* 53 (Reiss/Nisbet).   [153] Ibid. 44, original emphasis.

In Rousseau rivalry and emulation are seen as utterly destructive. Kant disagrees: 'Without these asocial qualities (far from admirable in themselves) which cause the resistance inevitably encountered by each individual as he furthers his self-seeking pretensions, man would live an Arcadian, pastoral existence of perfect concord, self-sufficiency and mutual love.' He would be as 'good-natured' – and empty of value – as the sheep he tended, his rational nature 'an unfilled void'. Nature deserves our gratitude for promoting 'social incompatibility, enviously competitive vanity, and insatiable desires for possession or even power'. These qualities, and the conflict and misery they produced, forced humanity out of 'the state of savagery' (alias the 'state of nature') into a civil constitution in which their capacities would no longer lie dormant.

There is a catch. Civil society would remain defective and the human species less than perfect so long as antagonism *between states* is maintained. Kant offers a final bouquet to Rousseau.[154] If we bear in mind the present state of international affairs, 'Rousseau's preference for the state of savagery [over existing civil society] does not appear so very mistaken … '[155]

CONCLUSION

Two basic narratives of the life of early man were laid down in classical antiquity: one told of decline from a primeval Golden Age (and there was a Judaeo-Christian version of this theme derived from Scripture); the other traced man's development from savagery through barbarity to civilization. Neither story was without ambiguity: thus, for example, Golden Age storytellers exposed and exploited a tension between technological and cultural progress and moral regress. Some writers, Lucretius, Grotius and Rousseau, for example, drew from both traditions, and their accounts were the more equivocal and complex as a result. The history of these traditional narratives as they passed through the hands of philosophers, theologians and lawyers over many centuries is itself a fascinating subject; my main preoccupation has been to explore attitudes to property in so far as they emerge in the pertinent works. It goes without saying that there is a great deal of variety in the way property is treated, reflecting the differing aims, ideologies, backgrounds and historical contexts of the writers in question.

[154] See *Idea*, Proposition VII; and the essay of 1795 (rev. 1796), *Perpetual Peace, a Philosophical Sketch*, in Reiss/Nisbet 93–130.
[155] *Idea* 49.

In a number of these imaginative reconstructions of primeval society a role is given to first acquisition (*occupatio*). First acquisition is symbolic of the arrival of private ownership in the world. It is the first act in the dissolution of primeval communality, the order which, in one form or another, was universally agreed to have prevailed at the dawn of history. Some writers, certainly, did not give first acquisition their serious attention. Cicero in *On Duties* afforded it only a cursory glance, moving on with speed to press upon the governing class of Rome, at a time when the political order was visibly crumbling, the urgent necessity of respecting and safeguarding private property. Hobbes and Hume (among others) held that property institutions were purely conventional and existent only in the context of civil society. Accordingly they had only limited interest in tracing their origins. For Locke and Hegel property rights did not hang on first occupation as such, but on the fact that the agent actively worked the land (Locke), and that he was a free will (Hegel).

Through much of the period under survey, Christian doctrine played a crucial part in shaping the discussion. The consequences of its influence were not uniform. In one set of narratives, ownership was labelled a creation of fallen man, an institution of a corrupt society, and allowed no part in the state of nature. The authoritative first digest of canon law assembled by Gratian in the mid-twelfth century stated quite baldly that private property was wrong, being in contradiction of the original communality established by divine law (equals natural law). Caught up in Gratian's slipstream, medieval canon lawyers moved to salvage the reputation of private property by characterizing communality as non-normative, and placing the institution of private property within a narrative that followed the advance of man out of a state of extreme primitiveness, guided by God-given reason. Natural jurists of the early Enlightenment such as Grotius, Pufendorf and Locke, especially Locke, were still under the spell of Christianity. They too followed a progressivist trail, structuring their narratives around a three-stage development of early man as successively hunter/gatherer, pastoralist and agriculturalist. And, in a break from the medieval tradition, they located property in the state of nature, thus giving it the status of natural law, even if of a lower order.[156] Grotius and Pufendorf (not Locke) introduced the significant innovation that the establishment of private ownership was conditional

---

[156] See Ch. 8.

on the whole community's giving its consent. They evidently felt that first occupation without agreement, tacit or express, was not morally defensible. Locke eluded the problem of first acquisition with or without consent (or so he may have thought) with the argument that there was both a right and a duty to own property, in accordance with God's plan for man that he survive and increase – the main condition being that the land in question must be actively worked.

In the eighteenth century two accounts of first acquisition stand out, each idiosyncratic. Rousseau's treatment of first acquisition and the emergence of property in general was hostile through and through. He denied the legitimacy not only of *occupatio* in the state of nature but also of the property arrangements (based on first acquisition) of an unreformed civil society. That Kant should have given attention to first acquisition at all is unexpected, given his conviction that the property institutions and rights were 'conclusive' only in the framework of civil society (cf. Hobbes), and that the free, rational and autonomous will was the source of property rights (cf. Hegel). It seems that he was so concerned that the transition from natural to civil society be an orderly one that, in a tortuous argument, he conferred on first acquisition the status of 'true' acquisition, despite its 'provisionality'.

Our survey of state of nature narratives through the ages has not led us to a solution of the problem of first acquisition. There is no Holy Grail. 'It can fairly be said that no adequate theory of initial acquisition exists.' 'It is very hard to find a satisfactory principle of justice in acquisition. Perhaps it is impossible.'[157] For Proudhon it followed that property is theft. Other theorists have 'moved on', to confront another challenge, that of arriving at a satisfactory formula for the distribution of the resources of existing society. Organizing principles such as liberty, the happiness of the greatest number, and justice are among those that have been canvassed. Responses have ranged all the way from Karl Marx's demand that private property be abolished altogether as a constraint on liberty, to John Rawls' endorsement of the arrangements and principles that governed American constitutional, political and economic arrangements in his day.[158] Few of the thinkers whom we have been considering

---

[157] Gray (1986), 63; Wolff (1996), 158.
[158] See Geuss (2005), 29–39, at 32. Rawls' theory issues out of a discussion conducted by all members of the society 'in the original position'. This calls to mind the Pufendorfian notion of agreements arrived at by early men in the state of nature. Marxist communism is obviously an echo (but no more) of primitive communality.

seriously addressed the problem of existing inequalities of wealth. It was standard practice, especially among those writers (pagan as well as Christian) who worked with the Golden Age myth, to expose in their narratives the *abuse* of wealth in contemporary society. Rousseau was unusual in advocating the equal distribution of property (so long as the General Will was in favour).

I have left a number of loose ends, among them the important matter of property *rights*: when and how the language of rights came into use, and how the sense and application of the term varied and was transformed. For surely the concept of 'rights' did not carry the same meaning for Cicero, Ockham and Hegel. To these matters I now turn.

CHAPTER 7

Property as a legal right

HISTORIOGRAPHICAL BACKGROUND

In 1840 Pierre-Joseph Proudhon of Besançon, a printer and an autodidact, published *What is Property?* and answered his own question: 'Property is Theft.' Karl Marx was twenty-one years of age at the time, and writing his dissertation for the University of Jena on the difference between the natural philosophy of Democritus and of Epicurus. After a brief opening chapter on methodology, Proudhon moves on to definitions. He begins in this way:

'Roman law defines property as the right to use and abuse a thing within the limits of the law' – and he provides the Latin: 'Jus utendi et abutendi re sua, quatenus iuris ratio patitur.' Abuse of property, he says sardonically, is really indistinguishable from *use* of property. One way or another, the proprietor can do what he likes with his land. He can 'let the crops rot underfoot, sow his field with salt, milk his cows on the sand, turn his vineyard into a desert, and use his vegetable garden as a park'.[1]

Further definitions follow. According to the Declaration of Rights, published as a preface to the French Constitution of 1793, property is 'the right to enjoy and dispose at will of one's goods, one's income, and the fruit of one's labour and industry'. And in article 544 of the *Code Civil des Français* of 1804, renamed the *Code Napoléon*, it is written: 'Property is the right to enjoy and dispose of things in the most absolute manner, provided we do not act against the laws and regulations.'[2] 'These two definitions,' Proudhon declares, 'do not differ from that of the Roman law.'

---

[1] Proudhon ch. 2, 85 (James) cf. 35 (Kelley and Smith). It seems that for Proudhon the *ius abutendi*, and the *ius disponendi* amount to the same thing. In this he was in harmony with the juristic tradition (though not himself a jurist), going back at least to the German humanist Zasius. See p. 198, below.

[2] *Code Civil*, art. 544: 'La propriété est le droit de déjouir et de disposer des biens de la manière la plus absolue, pourvu qu'on n'en fasse pas un usage prohibé par les lois et par les règlements.' This formulation appears in Robert Pothier's *Traité du droit de domaine de propriété* (1772), 1.1.4, and indeed whole sections of that work were taken over into the *Code*. It was however by this time

There is a puzzle here. Professional Roman lawyers are familiar with the fact that their major text, the *Corpus Iuris Civilis*, compiled by order of the emperor Justinian in the sixth century, does not include a definition of property.

Proudhon was not making this up: he was leaning on law books composed by jurists, including some of those who had worked on Napoleon's codification. Napoleon had linked his project with the great compilation of Justinian. He saw himself as a second Justinian, with his committee of redaction as the equivalent of the team of jurists who put together the *Corpus Iuris Civilis*. It does not follow that the French code was authentic Roman law.

Commentators from the German Romanist Frederick Karl von Savigny (1779–1861) to the modern historian Donald R. Kelley have been unimpressed by the calibre of Napoleon's team of jurists. So Kelley, writing of the authoritative early commentary on the Napoleonic code by Charles Toullier, writes: 'For the most part, his presentation was, like the code itself in many respects, a rehash of modern Roman law as it had been taught for generations and was still being taught in France through the textbooks of Heineccius.'[3]

It's a plausible case. Roman law had not remained static in the period that elapsed between the rediscovery of the Justinianic *Corpus* in the late eleventh century in a library in Pisa and Napoleon's codification at the beginning of the nineteenth century. Seven centuries of scholarly glosses and commentaries had done their work in developing and transforming the law while retaining its Roman base. One can therefore understand the judgement that the law of property in the *Code Napoléon* is more properly described as *modern* Roman law (Kelley's phrase) than Roman law.

And there is an additional consideration. A law of Constantine included in Justinian's *Code*, which was held by the French jurists (and by Proudhon) to underpin the definition of property in the Napoleonic code, appears not to do so. The law actually concerns the Roman contract of mandate, and runs as follows:

In mandate there is a possible danger not just of a pecuniary sort, though that is what a suit under mandate is certainly about, but also a danger to reputation: because when it is a matter of one's own affairs, everybody is his own moderator and decider, and we carry out our own affairs – most if not all – according to our

---

regarded as a standard definition of property, occurring e.g. in the massive work of Pierre-Jean-Jacques-Guillaume Guyot, *Répertoire universel et raisonné de jurisprudence* (1775–83), vol. 16, 14.
[3] Kelley (1984), 49. Heineccius was a German Romanist of the early eighteenth century.

own judgment, whereas other people's affairs are carried out with precise attention to duty and nothing that is neglected and left undone in *their* administration is free from blame.[4]

The leading modern commentator on the Napoleonic code, André-Jean Arnaud, picked up the 'failure' of article 544 of the code to replicate the Constantinian law, and added that there is no other Roman legal text that does the job. I shall return to this matter of the apparent lack of connection between the law of Constantine and article 544, for there is more in this than meets the eye.[5] I will show that, while the text as a whole cannot be dressed up as the equivalent of article 544, *a key phrase within it* was used, and very appropriately, by the famous late medieval jurist Bartolus, in order to explain his own definition of property, which happens to be very close to that of article 544. For the present, however, I want to follow Arnaud's discussion a stage further, because his argument now takes an interesting turn. He says, not just that there is no text which gives a definition of property in the Roman law books, but also that there would be *no point* in looking for such a text, because the Romans did not have a concept of property rights at all, let alone the concept of subjective rights, which he says implies an association of right and power.[6] All this, he says, has been demonstrated by M. Villey. This is Michel Villey, Professor of the Philosophy of Law at the Sorbonne from the 1950s to the 1980s. Arnaud's book receives a preface from Villey and is dedicated to 'mon maître, M. Villey'.

Villey's doctrines have carried a lot of weight in recent years among historians of political thought and philosophers of law. They accept his view that Roman law made no contribution to the development of subjective rights theory.[7] This is relevant to us, because from the Middle Ages (at least) to the present day, scholarly disputes over rights have

---

[4] *CJ* 4.35.21: 'Imp. Constantinus A. Volusiano pp. In re mandata non pecuniae solum, cuius est certissimum mandati iudicium, verum etiam existimationis periculum est. nam suae quidem quisque rei moderator atque arbiter non omnia negotia, sed pleraque ex proprio animo facit: aliena vero negotia exacto officio geruntur nec quicquam in eorum administratione neglectum ac declinatum culpa vacuum est.' The date is uncertain because it depends on the identity of the addressee, Volusianus, which is uncertain. Seeck attributed it to 315, but 355 is also possible, in which case it is a law of Constantius II. See the Volterra database on the law: www.ucl.ac.uk/history/volterra.

[5] See pp. 197–9 below.

[6] Arnaud (1973), 181: 'La Rome classique n'a jamais connu ni la "propriété à la romaine", ni le concept de "droit subjectif", qui suppose l'association de pouvoir et de droit.'

[7] E.g. Tuck (1979), 7ff.; Tierney (1997), esp. 13–42. At p. 8, Tierney writes: 'Among modern scholars, probably the most widely accepted account of the origin of natural rights theories is the one presented by Michel Villey.' See Villey (1946–7); (1949); (1950); (1956); (1962); (1969); (1975); etc.

commonly revolved around *dominium*, ownership, an individual's right to own and control property.

A subjective right has been defined as a justifiable claim, resting with someone who has it, to act in a certain way.[8] An individual takes this or that action because he 'has a right' to do so. I do not find this definition satisfactory, but will let it stand for the moment, for it is part of the conceptual apparatus of a modern rights theorist, Richard Dagger, who endorses the position of Villey.

Roman jurists, we are told, did not have the concept of a right to property, or of subjective rights in general, because they were preoccupied not with rights, but with actions. Their interest was focused on a system of remedies, principally judicial actions, that were available to Roman citizens. Central to the argument is the assertion that there is no Latin word for right, in the sense of subjective right. The most obvious candidate, *ius*, we are told, does not fulfil this function. Particular legal texts are interpreted as showing that even ownership, *dominium*, was not conceived of as a *ius*, in the sense of right; that *ius*, rather, was held to be a thing, *res*, an artificial legal construct; and that this excludes the meaning of right in these contexts. I will come back to the texts in question later.

What the same scholars agree *can* be attributed to the Roman jurists was a concept of objective right, taken over from Greek philosophy, from Aristotle and the Stoics. That is to say, Roman jurists held that there was an objective standard of justice, of what is right, against which one can measure human laws and actions. It was according to this standard that each man was assigned what was appropriate to him. So, when, for example, Ulpian (in the early third century) defines justice as 'a steady and enduring will to render to each man his *ius*',[9] *ius*, it is claimed, is to be read in an objective sense. Dagger has this to say on the Roman lack of the vocabulary and concept of subjective right: 'Even the words with the greatest claim – *dikaios* ... *ius* – betray the absence of the concept because in the classical period both words mean right primarily in the objective sense. Where we say: "I have a right to this book " ... They usually said "It is right that I have this book." '[10]

As I have already indicated, this elaborate argument against the existence of a Roman concept of property rights, and more generally, subjective rights, can be traced back to Villey, who launched it in the mid-1940s. And historians of political thought and philosophers of law

---

[8] Dagger (1988), 294. [9] 'ius suum cuique tribuendi.' See *Dig.* 1.1.10 pr. (Ulpian, *Inst.* 1).
[10] Dagger (1988), 297–8; cf. Brett (1997), 3.

accept his doctrine. Brian Tierney in his comprehensive study of Rights Theory from the twelfth to the sixteenth century wavers a little. He feels that Villey may have been 'too narrowly selective in the texts he chose to illustrate the meaning of *ius* itself'. At one point he concedes that 'in some forms of discourse from classical times onwards, the word *ius* could mean a right'.[11] There is however no follow through. Above all, he does not cast doubt on Villey's interpretation of key Roman law texts, those on the basis of which Villey separates *ius* and *dominium*.

By contrast, Villey's own reconstruction of the origins of Subjective Rights Theory has not found favour. Villey put forward William of Ockham, the Franciscan theologian of the early fourteenth century, as the pioneer. Meanwhile, his systematic elimination of Roman law from the story still stands.

In this chapter I want, first, to show that the Romans had the concept of the right to property, as one of a number of individual rights. This is not the same as attributing to them the modern concept of subjective rights. As I understand it, a central component of a subjective right as the term is employed in modern rights discourse is that the right is lodged specifically in a human subject. It is not derived from some position or status in society, but relates to man as subject. It is connected with the essential, intrinsic aspect of being human, which may be summed up as the ability to think, reason and make decisions. The problem with the definition of subjective right that I considered earlier, according to which a subjective right is a power or capacity to act in a certain way, typically, to assert or defend one's legitimate interests, is that it is not sufficiently clear by virtue of what the right is exercised, from what source the right derives. A subjective right without a clear definition of the subject does not make any sense. For this reason, and because of the ambiguity of the term,[12] I would prefer to sideline the idea of subjective rights altogether, at any rate in talking about the ancient Romans. A subjective right as

---

[11] Tierney (1997), 17–19.

[12] The term subjective right (and for that matter its correlate objective right) is given a different meaning in the legal positivist tradition. Thus for example Rudolf von Jhering in *Der Kampf um's Recht* (*The Struggle for Law*) of 1872 writes (at 6): 'The term *Recht*, it is well known, is used in our language in a twofold sense – in an objective sense and in a subjective sense. This *Recht*, in the objective sense of the word, embraces all the principles of law enforced by the state; it is the legal ordering of life. But *Recht*, in the subjective sense of the word is, so to speak, the precipitate of the abstract rule into the concrete legal right of the person.' See Angle (2000) for an interesting comparison of von Jhering with a leading Chinese thinker, Liang Qichao (1873–1929). This sense of 'subjective right' has persisted in the German legal tradition. See for example Coing (1959), who talks in terms of 'material subjective rights'. See below.

I have defined it is hardly different from the idea of a natural right, later to be called a human right, a right accruing to an individual as a human being. To anticipate the argument of Chapter 8, I accept that such a concept does seem to be post-Roman and un-Roman. The Romans can however be ascribed a doctrine of positive legal rights, rights that people can exercise in a given society as full members of that society. The distinction between legal and natural (or human) rights is regularly employed in the modern rights literature and is unproblematic.[13] In the case of the Romans, they possessed legal rights under the civil law (*ius civile*) in so far as they were Roman citizens: these were rights held *ex iure Quiritium*, Quirites being a name traditionally applied by the Romans to themselves as citizens. This brings me to the second aim of this chapter. If the Romans turn out to have had the concept of property rights, as one of a bundle of positive legal rights accruing to an individual citizen, then it will be necessary to rewrite the history of the development of the legal right to property. In the first instance, adjustments will have to be made to the view, associated for example with Helmut Coing, according to which the first traces of what he calls 'material subjective rights' (which I take to be roughly equivalent to my individual legal rights), including the right to property, are to be located in the Middle Ages, in the glosses and commentaries on the lawbooks of Justinian.[14]

THE JURISTIC SOURCES REVISITED

There is a preliminary question: whom do scholars have in mind when they make claims about what Roman jurists were interested in, or that they possessed or lacked a certain concept? Let us draw closer to the juristic sources. This means, in the main, the *Digest* of Justinian.[15] The *Digest* is a massive work of compilation put together very fast in the early sixth century. Over three years, a team of jurists under the orders of the emperor Justinian attacked with scissors and paste the huge volume of juristic texts still extant at that time from the classical period of Roman law, roughly from the first century BC to the mid-third century AD. The compilers however drew especially from the jurisprudence of the

---

[13] As a glance at the essays included in Waldron (1984) will show.

[14] Coing (1959) is widely regarded as authoritative. Brett (2003) is a valuable study of the development of citizen rights.

[15] Though Gaius, *Institutes*, a textbook from the mid-second century, also comes into the reckoning, as do various minor late Roman juristic sources.

mid-second to the mid-third century AD, the period of the Antonine and Severan dynasties. The extracts that survived their labours, grouped under fifty titles, constitute approximately one-twentieth of the material with which the compilers began, as Justinian in effect tells us in the preface. These are (some of) his words: 'Nearly 2,000 books and more than 3,000,000 lines had been produced by the ancient authors, all of which it was necessary to read and scrutinize in order to select whatever might be best ... We have given these books the name *Digest* ... and taking together everything which was brought from all sources, they complete their task in about 150,000 lines.'[16]

Let us stand back for a moment and contemplate the work of Justinian and his team. The *Digest* was a superb achievement. Where would we be, what would we know of Roman law, without it? On the other side, it is worth taking a second glance at Justinian's sums. By his own calculation, an amount equivalent to *ninety-five per cent* of the existing juristic writings were eliminated. What happened, one may well ask, to the rejected 2,850,000 lines? Was this like the tidying up of one's papers which everyone does? Or was it rather an act of vandalism? One way or another, an enormous quantity of Roman jurisprudence was removed from the scene, denied any authority, permanently shelved, taken out of circulation, consigned to the dustbins of history.

I return to my initial question: which jurists are we, should we be, talking about? Several layers or stages of juristic activity come into the reckoning. First, there are the jurists of the Justinianic age, who selected the material. We know little of their principles of selection, but it should be noted that they were under orders to eliminate inconsistencies between texts. In consequence there are real doubts as to how far we have the words of the classical jurists in their original form.[17] Next, there are the classical jurists whose treatises provided the raw material for the *Digest*. Which classical jurists? The discussion usually centres on the jurists of the second and third centuries, more or less coinciding with the Antonine and Severan periods. This is inevitable, because their works dominate the *Digest*. The Roman juristic profession flourished as never before at this time: its leading practitioners were high-placed imperial civil servants with significant power and influence, and they wrote prolifically.

Roman jurisprudence however had a long history, going back four centuries or so, into the Republican period. And only scraps of these

[16] *C. Tanta* 1, *Corpus Iuris Civilis: Digest*, ed. Mommsen and Krueger, 13.
[17] See Johnston (1989) on the problem of interpolations.

earlier works survive, embedded in the writings of the jurists of the Antonine and Severan eras. Those later jurists had in effect carried out a sifting process on early juristic material that was comparable in scale to that which Justinian's jurists in the sixth century were to inflict on *them*. The loss of those earlier works may well be crucial. I'll come back to this matter shortly. For the moment, I will stay with the jurists whose works make up the bulk of the *Digest*, and try to make something of them.

Meanwhile there is a point to be made arising out of the preceding discussion. In view of the nature of the sources, and the wreckage which is Roman jurisprudence of the middle and late Republic, and to some extent that of the early empire, we should think twice before making confident statements about what interested the jurists, and especially what did *not* interest them.[18]

ARE THERE PROPERTY RIGHTS IN JUSTINIAN'S *DIGEST*?

We have seen how historians of political theory and philosophers have answered this question, under the influence of the legal philosopher Villey. But what of professional Roman lawyers? It is their primary texts, after all, that the argument is about. There was initially some hostility to Villey's thesis, but most Romanists have simply got on with the business of exploring and unravelling the knotty problems of Roman property law and substantive Roman law in general. I have found no extended treatment of the whole issue by a Romanist since Pugliese in the 1950s, though Villey restated his position many times over a forty-year period.[19]

At the same time enough has been written in brief statements and footnotes to enable us to put together a position-statement which I believe most leading Romanists would subscribe to. A distinguished German Romanist (who might not wish to be named!) sent me the following

---

[18] Villey accepted that in the post-classical period (fourth to sixth centuries) there are signs of a concept of property emerging. See Villey (1950), 188–9, 196; cf. Tuck (1979), 11 and Tierney (1997), 17, both referring to Levy (1951). Indeed Villey (at 196) is prepared to locate the beginning of the 'transformation' in an earlier period, which can only be the classical period of Roman law, without apparently realizing that this undermines his case. He thinks the introduction of the legal procedure of *cognitio* alongside the formulary system was instrumental in bringing about the change. This development was certainly already occurring in the first two centuries AD. The older system was an action in two stages, the first before the praetor, the second before a judge, who received from the praetor a formula containing the factual and legal grounds on which the case was to be decided. Under the newer system, the magistrate or delegated judge heard the whole case and enforced his decision.

[19] Pugliese (1951).

remarks after reading an earlier draft of this chapter: 'In my opinion his [Villey's] thesis is so absurd that it hardly seems worth taking issue with it. But as you are engaging with authors who are attentive neither to the position held by Romanistic scholars nor to interdisciplinary research, then (I suppose) you have to take up the old argument again.' The writer goes on to observe that 'the Romans were aware of the phenomenon of subjective rights. Their use of the word *ius* covers a linguistic field which *includes* the subjective aspect. They had no *theory* [of subjective rights].'[20] This seems to me consistent with the verdict of other Romanists. David Johnston in his chapter on Roman jurists in the *Cambridge History of Greek and Roman Political Thought* addresses the question of whether they had anything to contribute in the area of political thought, and concludes: very little. They were uninterested in theory, philosophy or historical jurisprudence. They were essentially experts in the workings of the law.[21]

It seems to follow that we should not expect to find a theory of property in their texts. Johnston again, at the beginning of the chapter on property in his valuable book *Roman Law in Context*, writes: 'Ownership (*dominium*) in Roman law is difficult to define, and the Romans themselves did not trouble to do this. The best approach seems to be to deal with the main ingredients of ownership and from that allow the meaning of the term to emerge.'[22]

David Daube has some apposite remarks in his paper, 'The Self-Understood in Legal History'. He defines his subject thus: 'By self-understood I mean something so much taken for granted that you do not bother to reflect on it or even refer to it.' He argues that 'the phenomenon is met not only in codes and surveys not aiming at exhaustiveness, but also, though in a less degree, where this objective is indeed pursued; be it that the thoroughly accustomed is overlooked, be it that it is felt to be just too platitudinous for mention.' He goes on to give examples, which happen to relate to the Roman law of property. But first off, he mischievously introduces an illustration from another era:

The sort of thing I have in mind is illustrated in fairly recent times at All Souls College ... The very first paragraph of its statutes runs: 'The College shall consist of the Warden and such number of Fellows as is in these Statutes provided. No woman shall become a member of the College.' The clause about women, paradoxically, is among the latest additions to the statutes; it is not

---

[20] Note that 'subjective rights' is being used here with the sense attributed to it by Jhering. See above, n. 12.
[21] Johnston (2000).   [22] Johnston (1999), 53.

found in the pre-twentieth-century versions. But not because women were then eligible. On the contrary: their rejection was so much a matter of course no one thought of formalizing it. That was done when, at the beginning of this century, the danger of female dons first appeared on the horizon. One day, with further advance of molecular biology and brain transplants, yet another clause will be appended to keep out monkeys. At the moment, as their participation in academic life does not enter consciousness even to a minimal extent, they are contemplated by no rules express or tacit.[23]

Daube, a former Fellow of All Souls, wrote this in the early 1970s from the safe haven of Berkeley.

In sum, professional Roman lawyers hold that the Romans did have a concept of property and of property rights: but that they did not spell them out, because they did not see the point of doing so.

This seems to me to be a perfectly reasonable 'default position'. Still, I would prefer to see it as a basis from which to move forward. For there is more that can be done. There has been little genuine debate, and there is a case for a reconsideration of the whole issue. The juristic sources need to be reassessed, both key texts, and the whole nature of the juristic enterprise, the assumptions and methods of the jurists. The non-juristic sources need to be brought into play to provide additional data as well as background and context. Finally, the argument of Villey that there are legal texts which *rule out* a concept of property and property rights remains unchallenged. I can only launch such a project here. What I offer now is a sketch of how the argument might proceed.

A good place to start, since we are interested in property, is with servitudes. A servitude is a burden on property obliging the owner to allow someone else to use it for some purpose – or preventing the owner from using it in a way that inconveniences another person. The property thus burdened is the servient property. The Roman jurists are very interested in servitudes in both a rural and an urban context. They give servitudes careful definition. And they characterize them, each one of them, as a *ius*.

So, usufruct. 'Usufruct', writes the jurist Paul, 'is the right to use and enjoy the things of another without impairing their substance.'[24] Other servitudes commonly discussed by the jurisconsults are set out in a passage from Ulpian:

---

[23] Daube (1991b), 1277–8, first published in 1973; the citation is from the *Private Manual for All Souls College*, 1958, 2.

[24] *Dig.* 7.1.1 (Paul, *Vit.*): 'ususfructus est ius alienis rebus utendi fruendi salva rerum substantia.'

The rustic praedial servitudes are these: *iter, actus, via,* and *aquae ductus. Iter* is the right permitting a man to go on foot and to walk, but not to drive a beast of burden as well. *Actus* is the right to drive either a beast of burden, or a vehicle ... *Via* is the right to go on foot, to drive, and to walk; in fact, *via* embraces both *iter* and *actus. Aquae ductus* is the right to channel water across another's land.[25]

There is one servitude that provided Villey with special ammunition for his argument that *ius* does not mean right: *ius non tollendi altius,* 'the right against building higher'. Tierney, summarizing Villey (with approval), writes:

> In discussing urban servitudes, Gaius wrote of a *ius altius tollendi.* At first glance it seems clear enough that Gaius was writing about a right in the modern sense, a 'right of building higher'. But Gaius went on to mention a 'ius ... *non* extollendi.' We cannot possibly translate this as 'a right of not building higher'. So Gaius' concept of a *ius* is just not congruent with our concept of a right.[26]

This reasoning rests on a misconception. Gaius' text runs: 'Urban praedial servitudes are as follows: the right to build higher and obstruct a neighbour's light or the right to prevent such building; the right to discharge eavesdrip on to a neighbour's roof or vacant ground or the right to prevent such discharge ...'[27] Each *ius* lies with the owner of the dominant property and impacts on the servient property. The '*ius* to build higher' allows the owner of the dominant property to add height to his dwelling, though in doing so he cuts off the light of the *servient* property. The '*ius* not to build higher' prevents the owner of the servient property from raising the height of his house so as to cut off light from the dominant house. Gaius writes in the same work, and with a different turn of phrase: 'Suppose, for example, your house is burdened with a servitude in favour of my house, preventing it from being raised in height, lest it obstruct my light ...'[28]

There are other relevant passages that might be adduced. For example, the jurist Pomponius states that a servient owner cannot be 'required to

---

[25] *Dig.* 8.3.1 pr. (Ulpian, *Inst.* 2): 'Servitutes rusticorum praediorum sunt hae: iter actus via aquae ductus. Iter est ius eundi ambulandi homini, non etiam iumentum agendi. Actus est ius agendi vel iumentum vel vehiculum ... Via est ius eundi et agendi et ambulandi; nam et iter et actum in se via continet. Aquae ductus est ius aquam ducendi per fundum alienum ...'

[26] Villey (1946–7), 217; Tierney (1997), 16.

[27] *Dig.* 8.2.2 (Gaius, *Prov. Ed.* 7): 'Urbanorum praediorum iura talia sunt: altius tollendi et officiendi luminibus vicini aut non extollendi: item stillicidium avertendi in tectum vel aream vicini aut non avertendi ...'

[28] *Dig.* 8.2.6 (Gaius, *Prov. Ed.* 7): 'veluti si aedes tuae aedibus meis serviant, ne altius tollantur, ne luminibus mearum aedium officiatur ...'

do something', like improve the view. 'He can only be required to allow something to be done or to refrain from doing something.'[29] In passages excerpted from two separate works, Ulpian envisages the possibility of a servitude to prevent the servient owner from doing anything to diminish the access of light to the dominant owner's property.[30]

What of ownership, *dominium*, itself? Is it identified as a *ius*? In fact, *ius dominii* does occur in the texts.[31] But, and this is the thing to notice, the phrase occurs normally in a context in which ownership confronts a(nother) *ius*, such as usufruct. The point is that a servitude cuts into *dominium*: it takes something away from the owner's absolute control of his property. In other circumstances it was pointless to add *ius* to *dominium* (or synonymous words and expressions such as *proprietas*, or *meum esse*). That *dominium* was a *ius* was normally taken as read by the jurists.

Using individual texts, one can build up, stage by stage, the content of *dominium*. Take the right to alienate. In no legal text is it stated that an owner has this power. However, when Gaius cites an exceptional case where an owner *cannot* alienate, we are entitled to infer that owners as a rule *do* have the *ius alienandi*.[32] Again, where Ulpian specifies that someone holding a usufruct cannot misuse or spoil the property or thing in question, there is the implication that the owner can do just that to what is his own, if he so wishes. Ulpian's word for misuse, spoil, or use up, is *abuti*, which recalls the *ius abutendi* in Proudhon's version of a Roman law definition of property.[33]

However, according to Villey and those who agree with him, there are passages which demonstrate that *dominium* was *not* a *ius*. There are two principal texts. In the first of them, Gaius writes:

The rights of those who are absent in good faith are not prejudiced in a stipulation against anticipated injury; rather, on their return, they have the power of giving a *cautio ex bono et aequo* whether they be owners themselves or have any *ius* in the matter, for example, as creditor, usufructuary, or superficiary.[34]

---

[29] *Dig.* 8.1.15.1 (Pomponius, *Sab.* 33).   [30] *Dig.* 8.2.9 (Ulpian, *Ed.* 53); 8.2.15 (Ulpian, *Sab.* 29).

[31] See e.g. *Dig.* 7.1.7.1; cf. 49.14.2.2; 27.2.68; 27.9.5.3; 36.1.61 pr.; 48.6.5.1; 50.16.18.1; *vat. fr.* 86; plus several texts from the Code of Justinian dating from the first half of the third century, i.e. the end of the classical period.

[32] Gaius, *Inst.* 2.62.

[33] For the use of the term in the context of the Franciscan poverty controversy, see pp. 103–6, above. For *abuti* in the *Digest*, see 7.1.15.1; 7.1.27.1; etc.; Buzzacchi (2002), 12, n. 34.

[34] *Dig.* 39.2.19 (Gaius, *Ed. Urb. Pref.: de damno infecto*): 'Eorum, qui bona fide absunt, in stipulatione damni infecti ius non corrumpitur, sed reversis cavendi ex bono et aequo potestas datur, sive domini sint sive aliquid in ea re ius habeant, qualis est creditor et fructuarius et superficiarius ...'

This text sets out an alternative between ownership of property and various *iura*, including usufruct. Villey takes the *whether/or* as an exclusive disjunction: he claims that Gaius is deliberately withholding the designation of *ius* from *dominium* on the grounds that it was not a *ius*. But this is to press too far what is admittedly a loose use of language.

Comparison with another text helps resolve the difficulty. Again there is an *either/or*: Javolenus in his treatise *From the Posthumous Works of Labeo* writes: 'Whenever a right of way [*via*] or any right which attaches to land is being purchased, Labeo thinks that an undertaking should be given to the effect that you [the seller] will do nothing to the detriment of the exercise of that right, seeing that there can be no clear delivery of such a right.'[35] This is an *inclusive* disjunction, demonstrably so. For *via*, right of way, was undoubtedly a *ius*; it appears in texts alongside other praedial servitudes which are *iura*. Hence no contrast is intended, no incompatibility of the two alternatives is implied. Nor is it necessary or reasonable to extract anything such from Gaius' text. The second text which is crucial for Villey is from Ulpian:

The only person who can claim at law that he has the right to use and enjoy property is the man who has a usufruct of it. The owner of the estate cannot do so, as a man who has the ownership does not have a separate right of use and enjoyment; [The fact is that a man's estate cannot be subject to a usufruct in his own favour]. For a man who brings an action must do so with reference to a right of his own and not that of another.[36]

Villey reads this as a denial that a proprietor *qua* proprietor has the right to use and take the produce from his estate. But that is unnecessary and implausible. The owner will lack the right to use and take if a servitude of usufruct lies against the estate, *but not otherwise*. Ulpian says that the owner does not and cannot use and take through an additional, 'separate', servitude. As the bracketed (supposedly interpolated) sentence explains: a man's estate cannot be subject to a servitude in his own favour. A *dominus* cannot plead from a right of usufruct, any more than a *usufructuarius* can plead from a right of ownership.

---

[35] *Dig.* 8.1.20 (Javolenus, *post. Lab.* 5): 'Quotiens via aut aliquid ius fundi emeretur, cavendum putat esse Labeo per te non fieri quo minus eo iure uti possit, quia nulla eiusmodi iuris vacua traditio esset.' 'aliud' has been conjectured for 'aliquid' (Hoffmann) in the Javolenus text, though not in the parallel text of Gaius.

[36] *Dig.* 7.6.5 pr. (Ulpian, *Ed.* 17): 'Uti frui ius sibi esse solus potest intendere, qui habet usum fructum, dominus autem fundi non potest, quia qui habet proprietatem utendi fruendi ius separatum non habet; [nec enim potest ei suus fundus servire]. De suo enim, non de alieno iure quemque agere oportet.'

The references here to defending one's *ius* at law are a reminder of the fact that ownership and servitudes both conferred on an individual holder a right to proceed at law. This is implied by Ulpian's statement: 'It is clear that conveyance and protection of servitudes will attract the protection of the praetor.'[37] In addition, the jurist Celsus states without ambiguity that action at law itself was a right: 'An action is nothing else but the right to recover by judicial process that which is owing to a person.'[38]

We have examined the Roman jurists' alleged failure to identify *dominium* as a *ius*, which has been thought to entail that they had not grasped the concept of property rights. Let us consider now the association of right and power, *ius* as *potestas*; this is at the centre of the idea of subjective rights as conceived by Villey. A subjective right, as he understands it, is a power or capacity to act in a certain way, typically, to assert or defend one's legitimate interests. Villey holds that *ius* as *potestas* was an innovation of the Middle Ages. There is an argument over who was the first to produce this definition: was it William of Ockham in the early fourteenth century (Villey), Jean Gerson in the early fifteenth (Tuck), or the canonists of the twelfth (Tierney)?

IUS AND *POTESTAS*

In the Roman law of persons, the male head of the household (the *paterfamilias*) had *ius* and *potestas* over his dependents, whether children or slaves. The former were held to be under another's *ius* (*alieni iuris*), the latter under his *dominium*. Anyone who was not subject to another's *ius* (and was thus *sui iuris*), if he had not yet reached puberty, had to have a guardian (*tutor*), as did all females, at least during the Republic and early Empire. A jurist of the late Republic Servius Sulpicius Rufus (*fl.* mid-first century BC) described guardianship (*tutela*) as 'right and power [*ius ac potestas*] granted and permitted by the law of the state over the person of a free man with the object of safeguarding him while he is too young to look after himself'.[39] This was evidently a famous definition, for Justinian's lawyers (in the sixth century) included it in both the *Institutes* and the *Digest*, having found it in a treatise of the jurist Paul (first half of the third century).

---

[37] *Dig.* 8.3.1.2 (Ulpian, *Inst.* 2): 'traditio plane et patientia servitutum inducet officium praetoris.'
[38] *Dig.* 44.7.5.1 (Celsus, *Dig.* 3): 'Nihil aliud est actio quam ius quod sibi debeatur iudicio persequendi.'
[39] *Inst. Just.* 1.13.1; cf. *Dig.* 26.1.1 pr. (Paul, *Ed.* 38). On Servius, see n. 43, below. The virtual equivalence of *ius* and *potestas* is shown by the fact that within the Roman family those who were not *sui iuris* (in their own *ius*) were *in potestate* (of the *paterfamilias*).

The same Paul is the source for a statute of 40 BC, the Lex Falcidia, which limited the amount of an estate that could be given in legacy to three-quarters. In his treatise on this law, excerpts of which are preserved in the *Digest*, Paul twice quotes the phrase 'ius potestasque'. So in one instance he writes: 'Any Roman citizen who, after the promulgation of this statute, makes his will, shall have the right and power, under the general law, to give and bequeath money to any Roman citizen.'[40]

A statute issued a little before the Falcidian law, the Lex Ursonensis, has partially survived inscribed on bronze at the site of one of Julius Caesar's Spanish colonies, Urso. This was the foundation law of the colony and includes a clause granting the right and power (*ius potestasque esto*) of judicial process (*actio petitio persecutio*, that is, action, suit and claim) 'to whoever of them shall wish' against anyone who breaches the rules governing seating at festivals, or sundry regulations governing religious ceremonies. This calls to mind the text of Celsus cited above identifying action at law as itself a right. The same charter confers certain powers on the magistrates and city council of the new colony. They had by virtue of their office the right and power (*ius potestasque*) to have certain staff, wear particular clothing, and authorize the passage of public water over certain lands. Later in the same law it is laid down that private individuals could use overflow water with the authority of the council. 'There is to be *right and power* for him to use that water in that way, insofar as there be no damage to private individuals.' There is a partial parallel in an administrative manual composed at the end of the first century AD by Sextus Julius Frontinus, a leading senator, who was curator of the water supply of Rome in AD 97. He wrote in a treatise on the duties of his office that the 'right to an allocation of water' from the imperial aqueducts 'does not run to an heir, a purchaser, or any new owner of the land'.[41] This text gains a special piquancy from the fact that its author was himself a former praetor (in AD 70), who had very likely presided over disputes involving landowners over access to water supplies and servitudes. Around a century later the jurist Ulpian wrote: 'It is clear that conveyance and protection of servitudes will attract the protection of the praetor.'[42] The *ius* in question here was not a servitude – for one thing,

---

[40] *Dig.* 35.2.1 pr. (Paul, *leg. Falc.* 1). On the Falcidian law, see Watson (1971), 170–4. Gaius, *Inst.* 2.224, for whom the Falcidian law is 'the law observed today' (i.e. in the mid-second century AD), cites laws on legacies going back to the *Twelve Tables* (mid-fifth century BC). The clause quoted from the *Twelve Tables* has *ius*, but not *potestas*: 'uti legassit suae rei, ita ius esto.' For *ius potestasque*, see also *Dig.* 47.10.24; 50.17.59.
[41] Frontinus, *De Aquaeductibus* 2.107.   [42] *Dig.* 8.3.1.2 (Ulpian, *Inst.* 2).

it was not transferable, as Frontinus notes. It was, even more obviously than a servitude, a right conferred upon and possessed by an individual.

TEXT AND CONTEXT: CITIZEN RIGHTS IN THE ROMAN REPUBLIC

The *ius* and *potestas* texts take us back at least to the middle of the first century BC, the last decades of the Republic. The *Digest*, as we have already seen, allows us to salvage very little from the Republican period. It is dominated by an enormous mass of jurisprudence from the Antonine and Severan periods, 200 or more years after the collapse of the Republic. Yet the volume of juristic material composed in the Republican period is likely to have been very substantial. Here is an indication of what has gone missing: I cited above a definition of guardianship as a *ius* and *potestas* from Servius Sulpicius Rufus, an eminent jurist who was a contemporary and friend of Cicero and died in 43 BC. This Servius is reputed to have composed 180 books of law.[43] Ulpian, jurist under the Severan dynasty, wrote over 200 books and contributed around forty per cent of the *Digest*. All that survives of Servius' corpus is a few scraps. And he comes at the tail end of the Republican period. Wise heads among professional Roman lawyers of today believe that the Republic was a creative period of Roman jurisprudence, perhaps the most creative period of all.

That is likely enough to be true. The Republican period saw the expansion of Rome into a mighty empire, the growth to maturity of Rome's political, social and legal institutions, and the concomitant development and definition of citizen rights. The rights to trade and to marry according to Roman law (*ius commercii, ius conubii*), the right of appeal against the arbitrary actions of a magistrate (*ius provocationis*): all this and more was achieved, and defined, in the middle Republic. What of a *ius dominii*, a right to property?

The idea that the Romans lacked a concept of property rights in the Republican period would come as a surprise to any reader of Cicero. Though a barrister rather than a jurist, Cicero was knowledgeable about the law. We saw in an earlier chapter that in his treatise *On Duties* Cicero took time out to insist that the defence of private property was a prime duty of Rome's statesmen: 'In particular, any who holds office in the state

---

[43] *Dig.* 1.2.2.43 (Pomponius, *Ench.*). On Servius see Stein (1978). Servius, according to Stein (p. 184; cf. 182) 'delighted in precise verbal explanations, sharp distinctions . . .'

should make it his responsibility that everyone retains what is his, and that private individuals suffer no reduction in their properties by an act of the state.'[44] In a disintegrating Republic his plea had special relevance. Besides, Cicero had himself suffered the seizure and destruction of his own house in Rome through the intervention of political enemies. There was however nothing novel about the case he was arguing. Behind him lay several centuries of historical development in the course of which there evolved the idea and the practice of ownership of private property held according to Roman law by Roman citizens (*dominium ex iure Quiritium*).[45]

The key to this development was the fundamental role played by ordinary citizens, the peasant farmers of Rome, as soldiers in the imperialistic enterprise. Put simply, the right to own property and to protect this right in law, was a quid pro quo for fighting for Rome.[46] Renaissance Republican writers culminating in Machiavelli, holding the example of the Roman Republic before them, were convinced that part-time soldiers, who had somewhere to go when they finished their term of service, were infinitely preferable to a mercenary army, both militarily and politically. Further, they stressed that soldiers must already be citizens, for only the citizen could be a good soldier. As it happens, the equation of good soldier and *good farmer* (which finds its classic exposition in the preface to the elder Cato's treatise on agriculture) does not receive their express endorsement.[47]

The rewarding of Rome's soldiers with land that they could call their own was not pure altruism on the part of the wealthy few who made up Rome's governing class. They knew that Rome was dependent on a citizen militia, but in addition, they made sure that the land which was allocated to returning soldiers was taken from public land (*ager publicus*), land seized from the conquered people of Italy. Also, this land was located

---

[44] Cicero, *On Duties* 2.73: 'In primis autem videndum erit ei qui rem publicam administrabit ut suum quisque teneat neque de bonis privatorum publice deminutio fiat.' See also 2.85.

[45] It is a regular formula in the legal documents that something 'is mine' (*meum esse*) 'by right of citizenship' (*iure Quiritium*), be it a slave (e.g. Gaius, *Inst.* 1.119) or land (e.g. *Inst.* 4.34).

[46] For property under the Republic, including the development of *ager privatus* in the context of Rome's conquest of Italy, the work of Capogrossi Colognesi is fundamental and comprehensive, e.g. (1969); (1999); (2000); (2002). See also Rathbone (2003).

[47] See Pocock (1975), from 87. (Petrarch, Bruni); from 114, 138–9 (Guicciardini); 199–203 (Machiavelli); also Bock, Skinner and Viroli (1990), 58–9 (Silvano); 173–80 (Mallett). Machiavelli wanted soldiers to have a home and an occupation to return to after terms of service rather than to be career soldiers, but there is no suggestion of land as a reward for service, as in Republican Rome. See Nelson (2004), 74–86, for some astute comments on Machiavelli's 'idiosyncratic' views on wealth, with special reference to agrarian laws.

in areas where a continued Roman presence was considered to be strategically desirable, typically in newly conquered regions. Further, the Roman aristocracy became meaner as time went on: public land had increasingly to be wrested from their control through the intervention of renegade aristocrats, like the Gracchi brothers of the late second century BC.

An agrarian law of III BC survives carved on stone, albeit in a fragmentary state. The law grants ownership of some land with full rights (*optuma lege*), land that was public until the passage of the agrarian law of Tiberius Gracchus of 133 BC. Our law states that no one is to prevent a person from 'using, exploiting, having and possessing' the land (or 'piece of land, building or possession') that is his.[48] This cannot be a full definition of ownership: in particular, nothing is said about entitlement to dispose of the land by means of one of the regular procedures of Roman law. An almost contemporary inscription dated to 115 BC helps plug the gap. Two Roman senators named Minucius, acting on behalf of the senate of Rome, adjudicate a dispute between the city of Genoa and one of its dependent communities, that of the Langenses Viturii. The two senators mark off 'private land' (*ager privatus*) of the Langenses Viturii, which they can sell and pass down to heirs, from 'public land' (*ager publicus*), which they can (only) have and exploit, and on which they must pay a rent to the people of Genoa at a rate that is stated.[49]

These inscriptions between them provide a working definition of ownership. The language is official and traditional: the magistrates in charge of drafting them were not coining phrases. There would have been definitions or glosses of ownership in earlier texts. Roman governments had been assigning private land to individuals for centuries. What was entailed in this was surely spelled out in senatorial debates and resolutions and in many a statute now lost. Legal recognition of ownership rights goes right back to the *Twelve Tables* of the mid-fifth century BC, while the Lex Aquilia of around 286 BC gave an owner the means of recovering damages from anyone who wrongfully injured or damaged his property.[50]

I conclude that the Romans did possess the concept of property rights and individual rights in general, while conceding that they did not

---

[48] 'Neive quis facito quo, quoius eum agrum locum aedificium possesionem ex lege plebeive scito esse oportet oportebitve, eum agrum locum aedificium possesionem is minus oetatur [= utatur] fruatur habeat possideatque neive quis de ea re ad senatum referto . . .' Crawford (1996), vol. 1, 2, line 9; cf. 11; 27.

[49] For the inscription, see *Fontes Iuris Romani Antejustiniani*, vol. 3, no. 163.

[50] Johnston (1999), 55.

elaborate its content. This position is a clear and preferable alternative to the view that they lacked altogether the concept of rights, in property or anything else.

GLOSSATORS AND POST-GLOSSATORS

The rediscovery of the Justinianic *Corpus Iuris Civile* in Italy in *c*.1070 led to a period of intense intellectual activity, as jurists centred on Bologna set about exploring the text and releasing its secrets. The 'Glossators' proceeded by making brief comments ('glosses') on individual words or phrases between the lines of the text or in the margin. The most creative phase in their study of the *Corpus* ran from Irnerius (d. *c*.1150) in the first half of the twelfth century to Accursius (d. 1260) in the first half of the thirteenth.[51] Irnerius was the first to study the *Corpus* systematically; Accursius assembled (*c*.1240) a collection of glosses on all five volumes of the *Corpus*, on the basis of selections made from his predecessors' work, supplemented by his own extensive glosses. The whole amounted to around 96,000 glosses. The result of Accursius' handiwork, the *Glossa Ordinaria*, was passed down to succeeding generations as an essential, authoritative supplement to the *Corpus* itself (which did not mean that it escaped revision and interpretation). From the second half of the twelfth century, schools in Roman law were established at other centres in the north of Italy, in the Rhône valley, and in the Anglo-Norman kingdom (founded by Vacarius). After the time of Accursius, Orléans became for a period the main centre for the study of Roman law, but in the fourteenth century the pendulum swung back again to Italy, which produced the leading post-Glossators or Commentators (so-called for the extended commentary they provided on Justinian's texts) in the persons of Bartolus of Sassoferrato (1314–57) and his pupil Baldus de Ubaldis (d. 1400). Bartolus began and ended his career at Perugia. His stature within the legal profession was such that there was agreement among jurists that no one who was not a follower of his could aspire to a career in the law (*nemo jurista nisi Bartolista*).[52]

---

[51] See in general Kuttner (1982); Stein (1997); Lange (1997). The earliest known teacher of Roman law at Bologna was Pepo, who cited a *Digest* text in a case in 1076. He remains a shadowy figure.

[52] Stein (1999), 73. Needless to say, Bartolus' reputation was earned by his total contribution to jurisprudence and political thought, not by his thinking about property as such. See e.g. Ryan (2000). On the political thought of Baldus, see Canning (1987).

To the Glossators and post-Glossators the Justinianic *Corpus* was a sacred text. Their aim was to understand and explain rather than correct it. Their attitude to the *Corpus* was not unlike that of the classical jurists to the *Edictum Perpetuum*. That was the final, consolidated edition of the *Edict* of the praetor (the senior judicial magistrate of Rome in the distant Republican and early Imperial eras), put together by the jurist Julian under orders from the emperor Hadrian (117–38). Thereafter (and we are talking about the century or so that followed the death of Hadrian), anyone with any pretensions of being a jurist wrote a commentary on the *Edict*. Such commentaries were invariably works of practical law following closely the subject matter of the *Edict*, namely the civil law more or less in its entirety. The authors of such commentaries, who are known to have included some of the great jurists of the Golden Age of classical jurisprudence, were not interested in probing the theoretical underpinnings of the law, or for that matter filling in any lacunae they might have spotted in the *Edict*. So the Glossators, when they came face to face with the *Corpus* of Justinian (eight centuries or more after the classical period of jurisprudence, and four centuries or more after the Justinianic age), did not set about identifying and remedying its deficiencies.

In any case, what might seem to modern political theorists and legal philosophers to be deficiencies in the Justinianic *Corpus* were not necessarily held to be such by the Glossators. We should not assume, for example, that medieval jurists counted against the classical jurists (those whose works were excerpted in the *Digest*) a shortage of definitions of key legal concepts. Nor do we find in the *Glossa Ordinaria* a raft of such definitions. The formulation of legal rules was, on the other hand, a particular interest of medieval jurists, and in particular the post-Glossators, taking their cue from the last chapter of Justinian's *Digest*.[53] Such rules were not innovative, at least in the area of property or rights. For instance, an exemplary rule that happens to be about property, to the effect that things belonging to no one became the property of the occupant, was simply found by the Glossators in the text of the *Digest*, and confirmed in its status as a *regula iuris*. In general, it would not have occurred to the medieval jurists that their illustrious predecessors had not conceptualized *dominium*, nor given to the term *ius*, along with various other meanings, the sense of the *right* of an individual to own, dispose, exchange, inherit and use property.

---

[53] Stein (1966), 134–52. Book 50.17 of the *Digest* bears the title 'On diverse rules of ancient law'.

We have to wait till the post-Glossators before we encounter a definition of *dominium*.[54] Bartolus in fact provided two. They are brief, incomplete and presented without any trumpeting. Bartolus was reacting to the distinction between ownership and possession that he found in the *Digest*. This was a standard distinction in classical Roman law. Its very familiarity may help to explain the approaches taken to one of the texts by two of the classical jurists, Paul and Ulpian (both early third century), whose texts attracted his attention. Paul begins his discussion with a piece of etymologizing and continues with some imaginative historical reconstruction, drawing for these purposes on, respectively, Labeo and younger Nerva (early-to-mid-first century). He writes: 'Possession is so styled, as Labeo says, from "seat" (*sedibus*), as it were "position" (*positio*), because there is a natural holding by the person who "stands on" (*insistit*) a thing. The younger Nerva says that the ownership of things originated in natural possession . . .'[55] At the other extreme the snippet from Ulpian contains an idea of real sophistication that might have been appreciated by Immanuel Kant: 'There is this difference between ownership and possession: that a man remains owner even when he does not wish to be, but possession departs once one decides not to possess. Hence, if someone should transfer possession with the intention that it should later be restored to him, he ceases to possess.'[56] Bartolus, writing for an audience rather less cognizant of Roman law than the readers of Paul and Ulpian, is more down to earth. It is one thing, he says, to set one's foot upon (*insistere*), another to have *dominium* over, *dominium* being 'the right of disposing and of claiming' (*ius disponendi vel vendicandi*). It is worthy of note that, while Bartolus dropped the *ius vindicandi* for his second formulation (see below), it remained on hand for use in later juristic discussions of *dominium*; it is there, for example, in a definition that Grotius gives the term.[57]

---

[54] For Bartolus on *dominium*, see Coing (1953); Feenstra (1978); Seelmann (1979), 39–43. For the views of the Glossators, see Landsberg (1883).

[55] *Dig.* 41.2.1 pr.-1 (Paul, *Ed.* 54).

[56] *Dig.* 41.2.17 (Ulpian *Ed.* 76). See Kant on 'intelligible' as opposed to 'physical' possession, in *Metaphysics of Morals* 6, 249, with p. 169, above. Of course both Paul and Ulpian produced close-grained analysis of Roman property law elsewhere in their works.

[57] See Grotius, *Jurisprudence of Holland* (1620), 2.3.1: 'dominium est ius in re quo quis rem, etsi non detineat, a possessore vindicare potest'. *Vindicatio* is (as in Grotius) a claim of ownership made against a possessor. See also, written a generation earlier, Donellus, *On The Civil Law* 9.14.27: the *ius dominii* lies, amongst other things, 'in jure revocandae et sibi vindicandae rei'. For *vindicatio* in classical jurisprudence, see Gaius, *Inst.* 2.24; 4.16; *Dig.* 44.7.24.; in general, *Dig.* 6.1. For *vindicatio* as *ius*, see *Dig.* 42.1.63 (Macer, *On Appeals* 2). Bartolus does little to explain his first definition, in contrast with the second. He merely goes on to distinguish 'insistere' from 'usufructus', without defining the latter.

Bartolus' second definition of *dominium* reads: 'Ownership is the right of full disposal over a corporeal thing except insofar as this is prohibited in law.'[58] Many jurists in later times were drawn into tinkering with this definition and exploring its implications.[59] One of the more interesting comments is provided by the German humanist Ulrich Zasius (1461– 1535). His own formulation differs from that of Bartolus only in the substitution of *libere*, 'freely', for *perfecte*, 'absolutely'. But then he adds that the 'right of free disposal' means that an owner can *uti et abuti*, 'use and abuse', the thing that is his, just as he pleases.[60] The term *abuti* is not absent from the works of the classical jurists (*uti* is of course very common). It appears with two distinct meanings, to use up or consume, and to use for an inappropriate purpose. Ulpian gives an instance of the latter use in writing of the misuse of a slave by a *usufructarius*:

> For example, if he sends a scribe into the country and makes him carry a basket of lime, or if he makes an actor do the work of a bath attendant or a singer perform the duties of a household servant, or if he takes a man from the wrestling arena and sets him to clean out the latrines, he will be held to be making a wrong use of the property of the owner (*abuti proprietate*).[61]

There is a strong implication that if the owner himself chose to treat his slave in any of these ways, it was, quite simply, his business. The terms *uti/usus* with *abuti/abusus* occur in conjunction, with the latter as a synonym of *consumere* ('to use up'), in the context of the Franciscan poverty debate.[62] *Dominium* as *usus et abusus*, where *abusus* betokens the exercising of total control over things, appears to receive a first airing from Zasius. It evidently carries this latter sense in Proudhon and in the French jurists that he was following. The *droit de disposer* of the definition of property in the French *Code Civil* means just this, as does Bartolus' *ius disponendi*. In fact, it is essentially Bartolus' definition that was incorporated into article 544 of the *Code*. The absence from his definition of *ius fruendi*, the right to exploit (or enjoy), which does occur in article 544, is easily

---

[58] 'dominium est ius de re corporali perfecte disponendi nisi lege prohibeatur.' Bartolus on *Dig.* 41.2.17.1.

[59] Feenstra (1978) names (among others) Vitoria, Soto, Molina, Lessius and Grotius.

[60] See Zasius' *Commentary on the Pandect in Opera*, vol. 3, *ad l. si quis vi, Diferentia*, n. 11. See Grossi (1985), 508.

[61] *Dig.* 7.1.15.1 (Ulp. *Sab.* 18). Compare Proudhon's 'list' of fanciful things that an owner could do with his property, cited at the beginning of this chapter. *Digest* texts include *Dig.* 5.3.25.11; 7.1.27.1; 7.8.12.1; 12.2.11.2; 24.3.22.8; 26.7.54; 27.9.5.13; 48.20.6. See Buzzacchi (2002), 12 (whose interpretations differ in some cases from my own).

[62] See above, pp. 103–6.

explained. Bartolus was intent on setting out the *differences* between various rights over land, not signalling areas of overlap. More particularly, he was concerned to distinguish between different kinds of *dominium*, as we shall see in a moment.

Meanwhile it is worth pointing to an aspect of Bartolus' legacy which has been misunderstood. French jurists of the turn of the eighteenth century (as was observed at the beginning of this chapter) were of the allegedly erroneous opinion that a law of Constantine on mandate (*Code of Justinian* 4.35.21) provided a basis for article 544. Grotius writing about two centuries earlier had not been aware of any problem: he brought precisely the same text into play in *On the Law of Booty* (1604) in the course of linking *libertas* and *dominium*. Zasius had done the same around half a century earlier.[63] It was in fact Bartolus who cited the Constantinian law in the course of explaining his own definition. The law includes the following sentence: 'When it is a matter of one's own affairs, everybody is his own moderator and decider, and we carry out our own affairs – most if not all – according to our own judgement.' Bartolus introduces these words, *extracting them from the law as whole* which was of no direct relevance to him,[64] as in effect a 'gloss' on *disponendi*. This seems an eminently reasonable thing to do, especially given that the term was not much in favour with the classical or post-classical jurists, and a word or two of explanation might therefore have seemed appropriate. This example serves as confirmation, if it were needed, that the Glossators and post-Glossators were intent on grounding their opinions and interpretations in the Holy Scripture that was Justinian's *Corpus*.

Bartolus' definition is best approached in the light of his thoughts on *dominium* viewed in the round. The French jurists at the turn of the eighteenth century used his words, but without taking over the baggage with which it had originally been encumbered. For the *dominium* of the definition encompassed only a part of what Bartolus understood by the term. His *dominium* was a divided *dominium*. He, and the Glossators before him, assigned *dominium* a broader and a narrower sense.[65] In the broader sense, *dominium* in classical Roman law stood for a *ius* over things both corporeal and non-corporeal. Corporeal things were tangible: they included land, a person (*homo*, which must refer to a slave), clothing, precious metals and so on; incorporeal or intangible things were legal

---

[63] Grotius, *On the Law of Booty* 18: 'quoad libertas in actionibus idem est dominium in rebus. Unde illud: suae quisque rei moderator et arbiter'; Zasius, l. *In re mandata C. mandati*, see Grossi (1985), 508.

[64] See p. 179 above.   [65] See esp. Coing (1953).

constructs such as usufruct, inheritances and contracted obligations.[66] In a phrase much used by the Glossators, anyone with a right over a thing, *ius in re*, had *dominium* over that *ius*, and a *ius in re* covered *res incorporales* as well as *corporales*.[67] In consequence, for instance, usufruct and other servitudes came under the (broad) umbrella of *dominium*. The medieval jurists arrived at this conclusion through a careful selection of *Digest* texts which appeared to treat usufruct as 'a part of *dominium*', while overlooking texts that stated the opposite.[68] *Dominium* in the narrow sense applied only to ownership rights over tangible things, property in the conventional sense. This is the *dominium* of the *Digest* title, 'On the acquisition of ownership of things', for example.[69] In brief, Bartolus was defining only *dominium* in the narrower sense.

Another way of expressing the idea of a split *dominium* was to distinguish between *dominium directum* and *utile*.[70] This distinction was already known to Glossators of the third generation such as Pillius and Johannes Bassianus (*fl.* late twelfth century), but might well have been introduced earlier. Where did the term come from, and why was it introduced?[71] The jurists in their commentaries on the feudal law that governed relations in their own societies employed the term *dominium utile* for the relation of a vassal to the land of which he was in long-term occupation. In so doing they were making creative use of the Roman sources. These sources provided them with both technical terms and parallel cases. The terms *directum/utile* (and their opposition) were lifted from the law of actions, which knew of an action that was *directa* and another that was *utilis*.[72] As for precedents, they were drawn from emphyteutic, superficiary and other long-term or perpetual leases known already from the Justinianic *Corpus*. A key text is *Code* 11.62.11 of 434, which describes the holders of such leases as *domini* of their farms.

---

[66] See Gaius, *Inst.* 2.13–14.   [67] Bartolus 3 on *Dig.* 45.1.58 and 4 on *Dig.* 41.2.17.

[68] *Dig.* 17.7.1.4 (Paul, *Ed.* 2: 'pars dominii'); cf. 50.16.25 (Paul, *Ed.* 21). The author and the work are the same, the statements contradictory.

[69] Landsberg (1883), 88. The Glossators used *Dig.* 7.6.3 here, in order to posit *dominium* of a usufruct.

[70] Bartolus envisaged a third kind of *dominium*, namely, *quasi dominium*, to cover the category of possession through *usucapio*, entitling its holder to the *actio Publiciana*. See Bartolus 3 on *Dig.* 21.2.39.1; Coing (1953), 365–6.

[71] Feenstra (1978) is an exhaustive study.

[72] For the meaning of *utilis*, see Buckland (1963), 588: 'the praetor gave an *actio utilis*, or one *in factum*, to persons with lesser *iura in rem*, e.g. usufruct'. See *Dig.* 9.2.11.10; cf. 687: 'every *actio utilis* was an extension, on grounds of utility, of an existing action'.

The pertinent clause does not occur in the version of the law that appears in the Theodosian Code (of 438), and was presumably added by Justinian's lawyers when they put together their own code around a century later. The medieval jurists saw the *Corpus Iuris Civilis* as a unity. Texts emanating from the *Digest* and therefore originating with the classical jurists were vested with no greater authority than those of the post-classical *Institutes* and the largely post-classical *Code*.

To sum up: we should not look to the medieval jurists for major conceptual advances in the area of property theory. The main task that they set themselves was to elucidate the meaning of the complex legal documents they had inherited, on a word-by-word, phrase-by-phrase basis. As in the famous definition(s) of Bartolus, they were capable at times of bringing out and giving form to ideas that were immanent in the *Digest*. To this extent jurists of the revolutionary period (and Proudhon who accepted their conclusions) were not wrong in claiming that article 544 had a basis in Roman law. But we have also seen that the Glossators and post-Glossators were not above manipulating texts in order to accommodate the legal thought and economic practice of their own times. The Justinianic *Corpus* invited such treatment. On the one hand, it was, relatively speaking, lacking in systematic, theoretical discussion; and on the other, there was a fuzziness and an inconsistency at the margins – which has something (but not everything) to do with the history of the original texts and the way the *Corpus* was assembled. All this gave the medieval jurists opportunity and excuse to *develop* the civil law at the same time as they were elucidating it. Humanist lawyers, looking back on the work of the medieval jurists, undertook to remove some of the excrescences[73] that had been introduced, and to return to principles that they found to be operative, even if understated, in classical law. One of these principles was a division between, on the one hand, *dominium*, which belonged exclusively to the owner, and on the other, *ius in re aliena*, which might be held over things belonging to another. This distinction, minted by the humanist Hugues Doneau or Hugo Donellus (1527–91), was destined to become the central plank of the modern civil law of property; in the intervening period it was by no means universally

---

[73] The humanist Hermann Vultejus, in *Inst.* 2.1 nr. 24 (1598), uses more forthright language to express his critical opinion of the *dominium directum/utile* distinction. He says it 'is not consonant with the purity of jurisprudence; rather, it has seeped out of the faeces of the latter centuries'. Quoted in Feenstra (1978), 233.

accepted.[74] As it happens, both the terminology and the notion itself could have been teased out of the *Digest*.[75]

In the area of rights, too, it was Donellus, rather than, say, Accursius, or Bartolus, who made a significant breakthrough.[76] Whereas the traditional civil law was constructed around procedure (that is, actions), Donellus gave centrality to rights, that is, what was due to each individual. He regarded the legal procedures through which an individual sought to obtain his due as secondary. And he rearranged the civil law accordingly. In addition, at the level of individual texts, Donellus filled a gap in the list of meanings of *ius* given by the classical jurist Paul in Book One of the *Digest*, by adding *ius* as an individual's right. The absence from this text of *ius* in that sense has been taken by many scholars as proof that the Romans lacked the concept of subjective rights altogether.[77]

In his addendum to Paul on *ius*, Donellus uses two different expressions for an individual right. He says first that rights are 'things belonging as an individual possession to each person, assigned to him by law'; and second, that right is 'a capacity and power assigned by law'.[78] The second formulation uses language that rarely occurs in the medieval glosses and commentaries. Donellus was here tapping into a rich vein of ideas stemming from theology rather than jurisprudence and passed down by canon lawyers rather than by civil lawyers. The two systems, having run more or less in parallel from the eleventh century, gradually came together to form a *ius commune*. The closing of the gap is symbolized in the fact that Bartolus' most prominent pupil, Baldus, wrote a commentary on both civil and canon law. Baldus also commented on the feudal law, but in this he was following a tradition begun by the early Glossators.[79] Looking ahead to the early seventeenth century, we find that

---

[74] The basic article is Feenstra (1978). See also Stein (1993); (1999), 82. The apposite texts occur in Book 9 of Donellus' *Comm. on the Civil Law*, at chs. 10, 13, 17, 21.

[75] One can start with the definition of usufruct taken from Paul, *Vitellius* Book 3, which begins *Digest* 7.1: 'Usus fructus est ius alienis rebus utendi fruendi salva rerum substantia.' 'Usufruct is the right to use and enjoy the things of another without impairing their substance.' Of constant concern to the classical jurists was the clash between the interests and rights of owners, on the one hand, and of those who held subsidiary rights to other people's property, especially servitudes, on the other.

[76] Coing (1959), 13–14, can only cite the Gloss *quam ius* on *Inst.* 4.6. pr.: 'Nota quod actio est ius, quo persequimur, sed obligatio est ius, propter quod persequimur.' This is nicely put, but the antithesis is already present in Justinian's text: 'actio autem nihil aliud est, quam ius persequendi iudicio quod sibi debetur', not to mention the excerpt from the second century jurist Celsus in *Dig.* 44.7.5 (see p. 190, above).

[77] Donellus, *Comm. on the Civil Law* 1.3 on *Dig.* 1.1.11 (Paul, *Sab.* 14). See Coing (1959), 10–11, 15.

[78] 'ea quae sunt cuiusque privatim iure tamen illi tributa'; 'facultas et potestas iure tributa'.

[79] The thirteenth-century *ordo iudicarius* was however a far more substantial and important work on feudal law.

strands of thought deriving from theology, philosophy and jurisprudence came together in Grotius' discussion of *dominium*. Grotius even makes use of the term *usus facti* coined by the Franciscans, attributing it to 'Scholastics'.[80] In the medieval period Glossators and Commentators were already betraying in their work a degree of exposure to canon law, but their treatment of property and rights was little affected.[81] Yet it was from the canonistic tradition that the idea of natural rights emerged, giving a very significant extra dimension to discussions of *dominium*. And in the French Revolution property was claimed as a natural right of man as well as a legal right of a citizen.

[80] See Feenstra (1978), 226–7, citing Grotius, *On the Law of Booty* 214–5.
[81] See Ch. Lefebvre (1968); Le Bras (1968); Weigand (1967), pt. 1. For the early penetration of canon law by Roman law, see Legendre (1968).

CHAPTER 8

Property as a human right

INTRODUCTION

When Aristotle was launching his enquiry into the end of political science, he resolved to consider first the opinions of ordinary people rather
than philosophers, or at least 'those [opinions] which are most prevalent
or have something to be said for them'.[1] Taking a leaf out of his book, I
begin with a quotation from the *Guardian* of 10 January 2007:

> Isn't it funny how quickly new human rights get established? Once upon a time
> we used to make do with the right to life and property. Then came the right to
> drive (at any speed), and, more recently still, the right to fly (any distance). A
> generation ago, most people would have been content to plod along to Weston-
> super-Mare and hope for some August sun. Now a long-haul flight to Thailand
> or Barbados is such a God-given birthright that the prime minister himself
> thinks it is 'a bit impractical' to ask families to consider holidaying closer to
> home for the sake of something so unimportant as global climate.

My interest is less in the proliferation and trivialization of human rights
in the modern world (to which this citation bears eloquent witness),[2] than
in the representation of property as an established natural right, worthy
company for the right to life itself. In this chapter I put this judgement or
assumption to the test with the aid of philosophers, theologians, jurists
and politicians from the middle of the twelfth century to the end of the
eighteenth.

Natural or human rights, as they are understood today, are those basic
entitlements that each and every person has, or is judged worthy of having,

---

[1] *Nic. Eth.* 1.4, 1095a29–30.
[2] See e.g. Bobbio (1996), ch. 4. The bibliography of modern rights theory is large. The essays
collected in Waldron (1984) are a useful introduction. For a recent critique of natural rights see
Geuss (2001), ch. 3.

by virtue of their status as a human being, irrespective of gender, age, race, religion, background or social and economic status.[3] Rights of such a kind are to be distinguished from the legal rights considered in the preceding chapter, which accrue to individuals as full members of a civil society.

Ideas of what constitute natural/human and legal rights overlap to a degree. As regards the right to property, all democratic societies hold that there are certain basic legal rights that attach to the ownership of property (while equally acknowledging that these rights are qualified to an extent by considerations of public utility). Such rights and the means by which they may be exercised and defended are spelled out in national law codes. But in addition, the right to property is widely regarded as a human attribute, which a person should or must have if he or she is to live with freedom and dignity. In general, agreement is not to be expected as to what constitutes a human right, because rights reflect values that people hold to be important, and those values differ widely. Property turns out to be a case in point. It is a central argument of this chapter that the status of private property as anything more than a legal right within civil society was regarded as suspect, and at best uncertain, from the Middle Ages through to the Age of Revolution. In the French Declaration of the Rights of Man and Citizen of 26 August 1789, property appears in article 2 as one of the 'natural and imprescriptible rights of man', after liberty, and before safety and resistance to oppression. In article 17 property is termed 'inviolable and sacred'. On the other hand, the preamble to the American Declaration of Independence, which along with the rest of the document was accepted by Congress on 4 July 1776, contains no reference to property among the 'inalienable rights' of man: 'We hold these truths to be self-evident, that all men are created equal, that they are endowed, by their Creator, with certain unalienable rights, that among these are Life, Liberty, and the pursuit of Happiness.' The list is avowedly incomplete ('*among these* [unalienable rights] *are* . . . '). Still, property is not present, and this was no slip of the pen, no oversight, on the part of Thomas Jefferson, who drafted the document.

The elevation of the right of property to the status of a natural right is often regarded as an achievement of the leading early Enlightenment philosophers of the seventeenth century, Hugo Grotius, Samuel Pufendorf and John Locke (not, however, Thomas Hobbes). But, Grotius and

---

[3] Hoffmann and Rowe (2006), intro.

Pufendorf did not accord it the status of a primary natural right, one bestowed directly by God on man. Rather, they conceded that it was derivative, adventitious, fashioned by man himself, albeit in line with the wisdom of God as ascertained by reason.[4] Further, in order to make the case for property as a natural right, Grotius and Pufendorf – also Locke – felt impelled to bring to bear additional considerations, which happen to be far from telling. These were arguments from consent, formal or tacit, in the case of Grotius and Pufendorf. Locke considered that labour conferred on property the status of a natural right, without qualification.

Prior to the seventeenth century, the notion of property as a natural right received only tentative and sporadic support. The humanist jurist Donellus, an older contemporary of Grotius, held that nature had given each person four attributes: life, security, liberty and reputation, while property and obligation were creations of the civil law.[5] Property had been similarly classified by Gratian in his *Decretum* more than 500 years previously. Further, Gratian had pronounced that private property was the product of sin and contrary to natural or divine law. A succession of canon lawyers tried to soften or circumvent his message, but the best that they could come up with was a classification of private property as natural, but of a lower order than primary natural rights, which alone were inalienable. This was the line of thought taken up by Grotius and Pufendorf (amongst others) centuries later.

Further, the idea of natural rights itself is relatively new. Ancient classical societies did not have it. It began to evolve in the Middle Ages. My interest is not so much in writing a biography of Natural Rights Theory, as in looking at the way the *content* of natural rights evolved, with special reference to the ambiguous status of property rights. It will emerge that the concept of natural rights was a slow developer, retaining an elemental, fledgling status well into the early modern period.

RIGHTS: FROM ANTIQUITY TO THE MIDDLE AGES

The origins of Natural Rights Theory are disputed. If we follow the account of Brian Tierney in his magisterial study *The Idea of Natural Rights: Studies on Natural Rights, Natural Law and Church Law 1150–1625*

---

[4] Grotius, *On the Rights of War and Peace* 1.1.10; cf. Pufendorf, *On the Law of Nature and Nations* 1.1.7; for the earlier history of this idea, see below.
[5] Donellus, *De Iure Civili* 2.8.

(1997), and it is a very persuasive account, the theory in its earliest phase was a precipitate of a renascent jurisprudential culture that arose in consequence of the rediscovery of Roman law (*c.*1070) and the 'codification' of canon law in Gratian's *Decretum* (*c.*1140).[6] The prime movers were the Decretalists, the canon lawyers who pored over Gratian's work in the generations that followed its publication. They were provoked, amongst other things, by the denunciatory pronouncements he made therein about the status and origins of private property and its incompatibility with the law of nature. The Decretalists, striving to reconcile Gratian's stance with their own values and those of the institutional Church, noticed that he used *ius naturale* in several different ways, and saw the solution to the problem in separating out the many possible meanings of the term. This they proceeded to do with great industry and ingenuity. There is no need for us to survey their handiwork, but one distinction they came up with is of relevance to us. It was agreed that natural law laid down certain commands and prescriptions which it was the duty of humans to obey. However, the term *ius naturale* did not only refer to such mandates, which in any case did not govern the entire realm of human behaviour, but could also be applied to human conduct and relations which were permissible rather than mandatory. It was in this sphere of permissive natural law that canonists discovered a power or capacity to act, or not to act, with freedom and autonomy, with the aid of reason and within the limits set by the law of the land and divine law. One of the results of their rationalizations was the classification of property as both *a right* and *natural*: as a natural right, then, albeit one of a lower order. For Alanus Angelicus writing around 1200, it was a relative (*respectivum*) rather than absolute right, while Ockham about a century later called it 'supposititious', and derived it from a third class of natural law: 'In a third way, natural law is said to be what can be gathered by evident reason from the law of nations or some other law or from some act, divine or human, unless the contrary is established by those concerned, and this can be called natural law by supposition.' The idea surfaces again in the Spanish Jesuit Suarez in the sixteenth century, in Grotius and Pufendorf in the seventeenth and in Hutcheson and Burlamaqui in the

---

[6] The growth of a new juristic culture is seen as part of a more general 'renaissance and renewal', marked by 'a new emphasis on personalism or humanism'. See Tierney (1997), esp. ch. 2, and the classic paper by Benson (1982). Tierney criticizes the thesis of Villey that natural rights theory had its origins in the fourteenth-century nominalism of William of Ockham. He also rules out a seventeenth-century origin for the theory, linked to the stirring of an entrepreneurial economy.

eighteenth, by which time the favoured word for the status of the right to property was 'adventitious' (apparently coined by Pufendorf).[7]

It is perfectly reasonable to begin the story of Natural Rights Theory in the Middle Ages. But before we accept this, the conventional, view, it is worth considering the possibility that ancient societies made a contribution to the development of the theory. It is one thing to say that the concept of natural rights was absent in ancient societies, another that those societies made no contribution to its later development.

The claim or assumption that the concept was lacking in antiquity has been contested. Some have detected natural rights in Aristotle, or have seen the Stoics as proto-Hegelian in their thinking on persons and property, or have represented the Roman jurist Ulpian as a precocious humanitarian.[8] I see ancient societies as locked into a morality of duties and obligations rather than rights: duty to the polis, duty to walk in step with the forces of the universe, whether spoken of as providence, nature, gods or God; and I find that, when Stoic philosophers or early Christian theologians thought about what it meant to act from moral principles, they put the emphasis on the duties of the agent rather than his rights or the rights of others. As for the Roman jurists who observed that by nature all men are equal, one has to ask what they meant by the word 'equal'. Equality, like liberty, is a slippery concept, whose meaning has not remained fixed over time. Ulpian and Florentinus were referring in all probability (the texts in question are mere scraps wrenched out of context) to a mythical age inhabited by *statusless* humans who shared with each other (only) a basic humanity. And one should ask what these jurists thought they were about when they made their observation that slavery was a product of international and civil law not natural law. In my view they were not discussing whether or not slavery was unjust, much less whether the institution should be abolished. They are rather more likely to have been engaged in making distinctions between the different kinds of systems of law, and arranging those systems in a hierarchy. There is no question but that they ranked civil law, the *ius civile*, above natural law. Gratian eight centuries later took the opposite stance, with significant

---

[7] Alanus, quoted in Tierney (1997), n. 32; Ockham, see ibid., 175, using the text in Offler (1977); Grotius, *Rights of War and Peace* 1.1.10; Pufendorf, *Law of Nature and Nations* 1.1.7, 8; F. Hutcheson, *A Short Introduction to Moral Philosophy* 4.147, with Wills (1978), 229–39; J.-J. Burlamaqui, *Principles of Natural Law* 1.4.1.

[8] Miller (1995); cf. Schofield (1999), 149–52 with notes; Long (1997); cf. Frede (forthcoming); Honoré (2002). I broadly agree with Burnyeat (1994).

consequences for the status attributed to property rights in the canonistic discussions.[9]

It is worth pursuing the matter of slavery a little further. If one is inclined to take up a negative stance on the contribution of antiquity to Natural Rights Theory, one might be tempted to back this up with an argument that ancient societies by their introduction of chattel slavery *blocked* or at least *held back* the development of natural rights.

Slavery

Slave societies treated a significant proportion of the human race (perhaps thirty per cent of the inhabitants of classical Roman Italy, for example) as things rather than people. The existence of slavery might be enough in itself to explain the failure of Greeks and Romans to develop the concept of natural or human rights.

Chattel slavery was invented in classical antiquity and passed on as a *damnosa hereditas* to later societies. The ancients bequeathed not just the institution of slavery, but a potent, supporting ideology: Aristotle's theory of natural slavery.[10] This was the idea that slavery was necessary and beneficial for some people because of their innate intellectual and moral weaknesses. Aristotle's dogma, paradoxically, received far more attention and active backing in later ages than had ever been the case in antiquity. Thus, for example, Thomas Aquinas endorsed it (thus adding substantially to its popularity), while William of Ockham at the very least missed the opportunity to distance himself from it.[11] The Aristotelian doctrine was influential among Christian humanists and scholastics of the sixteenth century and natural rights thinkers of the seventeenth. Christian Europe, itself by now virtually free of slavery, condoned the enslavement of the native peoples of the New World, bringing Aristotle into service for the purpose. It is a strange testimony to the persisting influence of Aristotle that Franciscus de Vitoria (d. 1546) in his treatise *On the Indians* introduced Aristotle as an advocate *for the defence* of the indigenous peoples (arguing specifically for their right to own their property), with the use of remarkably twisted logic.

---

[9] Johnston (2000), 621–2, drawing on Levy (1949).   [10] See e.g. Garnsey (1996), with bibl.
[11] On Aquinas, see Finnis (1998), 170, 184–5. For Ockham, see e.g. *Dialogus* 3, Tract 1 in *A Letter to the Friars Minor* (McGrade and Kilcullen 133–4).

The slow movement toward abolition began to stir in the sixteenth and seventeenth centuries.[12] There was now an argument over slavery. Neo-Aristotelians had to justify their stance, and there were dissenting voices. Las Casas confronted Sepulveda in a famous debate of the mid-1550s, while around a century later, Pufendorf carved out for himself a relatively liberal position on slavery at the expense of Hobbes.

This was new. There had been no debate over the justice of slavery in antiquity. Aristotle produced his theory as part of a dialectical exchange of some sort. We only know what he tells us about it, which is very little. In any case, no one answered back. For that matter, as far as is known, no one in antiquity, not even those who were patently influenced by his theory, expressly cited it in support of their own arguments. The question of whether slavery was just or not aroused little interest among Greeks and Romans.[13]

A crucial factor in determining the attitude of Greeks and Romans was that slavery was deeply embedded in their economy, society, culture and mentality. They could not do without slaves. This being the case, it is not surprising to find that in their societies whether one was a slave or not was thought to be a matter of chance: justice had nothing to do with it. Being a slave was *tough*, everybody agreed about that. It was tough *luck* as well. And one's luck could change. Warfare, kidnapping, piracy or poverty could turn a free man into a slave from one day to the next. This was because slaves were in high demand. For Greeks and Romans, therefore, the necessity of slavery and the ever-present risk of enslavement blotted out any thought of a universal right to liberty.

This conclusion does not take us as far as might have been hoped, for it does not rule out the possibility of *any* kind of concept of human rights having existed in antiquity: it simply makes problematic the formulation of a natural right of *liberty*, and, moreover, of a natural right to property too. For slaves were property, 'corporeal' property, along with land, clothing, precious metals and so on.[14] Nor does it explain how it was that the idea of human rights was able to arise and make progress from the medieval period on. The fact is that the *physical liberty* of the individual was not under consideration as a natural right in the period from the

---

[12] It was only from around the middle of the eighteenth century that the tide turned against the traditional philosophical and theological arguments for slavery. See Davis (1966), 480. For the sixteenth and seventeenth centuries see Pagden (1982); Tuck (1999), 65–76. The citation from Vitoria is from *On the Indians* 1.335–6.
[13] See Williams (1993), 106–17.   [14] Gaius, *Inst.* 2.13.

Middle Ages to the Age of Revolution, although the liberty of *the subject* in the face of the arbitrary will of a sovereign or other political authority was actively canvassed and debated, notably in seventeenth-century England – with its advocates drawing support from the Roman historians Sallust, Livy and Tacitus.[15] Notoriously, slavery was not expressly prohibited in any declaration of rights before 10 December 1948, when the General Assembly of the United Nations proclaimed, in article 4 of the Universal Declaration of Human Rights: 'No one shall be held in slavery or servitude: slavery and the slave trade shall be prohibited in all their forms.'[16]

Slavery, in other words, until well after our period, proved to be not incompatible with the development of Human Rights Theory, though it is likely that it slowed down that process. It was an *underdeveloped* idea of natural rights which evolved in the period from the twelfth to the end of the eighteenth century, one that could and did coexist with an acceptance of slavery.

The way forward, in arriving at an assessment of the contribution (if any) of ancient societies to Natural Rights Theory, is to look for ideas already present in antiquity which might have served as building blocks for the construction of the concept, as yet undeveloped, of a natural right. Promising candidates for such a role might include Roman law and natural law, as systematized by the Stoics and transmitted by the Christians.

Roman law

In articulating the rights of the individual citizen of the Roman state, Roman law provided a platform and a paradigm for the construction of the rights of individuals as such. The rights and duties laid down by law of nature or divine law could be measured against and contrasted with the rights and duties prescribed by the civil law. Franciscans such as William of Ockham were particularly anxious to specify the respective spheres and requirements of what he called the *ius fori* ('law of the forum') and the *ius poli* ('law of heaven').[17] The classical jurists, moreover, had provided a terminology which the medieval scholars could use. The language of *ius*, and more particularly, the expression *ius et potestas* ('right and power'), is important here. The conjunction (and virtual equivalence) of these terms

---

[15] Skinner (1998).
[16] The Catholic Church did not pronounce that slavery was morally illegitimate until 1965. See Maxwell (1975).
[17] Ockham, *Work of Ninety Days* 65 in *A Letter to the Friars Minor* (McGrade and Kilcullen 55–7). The distinction appears centuries earlier in Augustine, *Serm.* 355.

in the writings of the medieval canonists is regularly regarded as a turning point in the development of the concept of subjective rights. Yet when Johannes Monachus, an early fourteenth-century canonist, was defining a third meaning (among many) of *ius* as equivalent to *potestas* or *facultas*, he had beside him Justinian's *Digest* and Accursius's *Ordinary Gloss* on the *Digest*, both open at the title on guardianship. As it happens, the legal texts have a variant reading at this point, as between guardianship as *ius* and as *vis* ('violence' or 'force'). Accursius, evidently trying to work with *vis*, called guardianship 'violent power'. Johannes disagreed, preferring to construe *vis* as *vis intus* ('inner force'), from which he derived *virtus*; *vis* is construed as 'virtuous power'. A certain kinship has been found between Johannes' 'virtuous power' and Ockham's 'licit power' – and indeed the modern philosopher Gewirth's 'rightful power'. The association of ideas is somewhat loose; still, it would be something to savour, if it turned out that this long trail leads back to a variant reading in an excerpt from a Roman juristic treatise of the early third century.[18] *Dominium* would have been an ideal model for the canonists, because ownership in Roman property law was absolute.[19] Johannes presumably went to guardianship rather than *dominium* because, as we have seen in Chapter 7, there is no simple definition of the latter in the classical and post-classical texts. The entitlements of a Roman proprietor have to be pieced together from fragments scattered through the surviving sources. The job can be done – the late medieval jurist Bartolus did it – and the French *Code Civil* reflects his handiwork.[20]

Natural Law

What is implied in the concept of natural law is a system of law which has its basis in the natural order and whose legitimacy is therefore established on the firmest possible foundations, because it is something eternal and outside time. Furthermore, natural law is universal in its outreach, transcending all accidents of social, ethnic and political identities; it is valid for the whole human race. We have seen that Natural Rights Theory emerged out of debate among canon lawyers from the twelfth century

---

[18] *Dig.* 26.1.1; cf. *IJ* 1.13. For the passage from Johannes Monachus, see Tierney (1997), 41, n. 95, where the link is made with Ockham and Gewirth (1978).

[19] Birks (1985).

[20] The point that the Roman jurists provided later thinkers with a linguistic and conceptual base for their discussions could be elaborated, with reference to key terms such as *occupatio* ([first] acquisition) and *res nullius* (no one's property).

over the meaning of *ius naturale*, natural law. Natural Law Theory, however, had ancient origins. The doctrine in its systematic form is a Stoic creation of the early third century BC. It is conveniently accessible, as is so much of Stoic moral philosophy, in the works of Cicero composed around two centuries later. In *Laws* Book One Cicero argues for the existence of such a natural system of law (*ius naturale*) which is the origin of the virtue of justice, itself to be identified with reason. The interlocking triad of reason, law and justice, further, is shared by gods and men, who participate in the same community. 'Hence we must now conceive of this whole universe as one commonwealth of which both gods and men are members.' This points to the cosmic city of classic Stoic doctrine, though Cicero's vision of that community is more sanguine than that of the founding fathers of Stoicism. The 'cosmopolis' of Zeno and Chrysippus did not include all mankind along with the gods, but only those who had achieved the goal of virtue, that is, wise men, and they were few; the rest of mankind were only potentially 'cosmopolitan', and no great optimism was felt about their prospects. The cosmic city was universal primarily in the sense that the wise men might be located anywhere.[21] However, the natural law certainly made moral demands on the whole human race, even if only a few wise men were able to satisfy them. Cicero writes in his *Republic*, in words ascribed to the Stoic Laelius:

True law is right reason, in agreement with nature, diffused over everyone, consistent, everlasting, whose nature is to advocate duty by prescription and to deter wrongdoing by prohibition ... There will be one master and ruler for us all in common, god who is the founder of this law, its promulgator and its judge. Whoever does not obey it is fleeing from himself and treating his human nature with contempt; by this very fact he will pay the heaviest penalties, even if he escapes all conventional punishments.[22]

There is no talk of rights in this passage, or anywhere else in Stoic or Stoicizing literature – only of duty, obligation and obedience.

Early Church Fathers such as Ambrose and Augustine absorbed the Stoic doctrine of natural law and at times were capable, in the manner of Cicero, of identifying natural law with reason as laying down universal principles of morality.[23] But in addition they Christianized the Stoic doctrine. For Ambrose (though not for Augustine), the Christian Church

---

[21] Schofield in Rowe and Schofield (2000), at 452; cf. Schofield (1991). See Cic., *Laws* 1.1–35; the citation is from 1.22.
[22] Cic., *Rep.* 3.33.
[23] See Colish (1990), with bibl. For later periods, see Finnis (1980); Hochstrasser (2000).

takes the place of the ideal republic of Cicero as a model of the cosmic city. In the thought of Thomas Aquinas, in whom Christian natural law doctrine reached its consummation, the Stoic cosmopolis becomes the great 'republic under God' in which the whole human race participates.[24] In Ambrose, the Stoic instruction to work in step with nature is characterized as Pauline, and is used to back up the apostle's order to the Christian women of Corinth to wear veils as they pray to God: for 'the veil is a natural thing'.[25] Again, Ambrose accepts that the Stoics 'believed that everything the earth produces is intended for man's benefit, and that men were created for the sake of other men', but claims that they cribbed it from Moses and David.[26] This is the passage (treated earlier in Chapter 5) in which Ambrose set about subverting Cicero's account of the origin of private property. Greedy men, he says, were responsible for introducing private property. Ambrose's target is Cicero, for his views on the origin of private property, rather than the Stoics, who are credited here with believing in natural communality. But this passage does hint at an inconsistency in the Christian treatment of the Stoic doctrine of natural law which is never resolved. For the Christians, natural law can be presented as an orderly nexus of causes associated with a rational and benevolent deity, or as a new covenant of grace for a fallen world, emanating from a loving God and embodied in Christ.

A full discussion of the contribution to the development under survey of these two creeds, both born in antiquity, is not called for here. The impact of Stoicism on the early Enlightenment (to single out one highly creative period in the development of Natural Rights Theory) can be read in the major texts of the period. One could cite, for example, Grotius' evocation of the Stoic idea of *oikeiosis* (fellow-feeling) in introducing his own doctrine of sociability in *On the Right of War and Peace*, or the heavy use made by Pufendorf in *On the Law of Nature and of Nations* of late Stoic philosophers of the Roman period, not to mention Cicero, not himself a Stoic, but singularly important as a transmitter of Stoic doctrine.[27] As for Christianity, there are those for whom 'the Christian belief in the autonomous status and irreplaceable value of the human personality' is the source of the whole notion of natural or human rights.[28]

---

[24] Ambrose, *On Duties* 1.142: 'The Church is as it were the outward form of justice'; for Aquinas, see Finnis (1998), 136; 226.

[25] Ambrose, *On Duties* 1.223.   [26] Ibid. 1.132.

[27] Pufendorf's *On the Law of Nature and of Nations* has 155 references to Cicero, 109 to Seneca, 12 to Marcus Aurelius and 34 to Epictetus. See Hochstrasser (2000), 62.

[28] Kolakowski (1990), 214.

An alternative view might be that Natural Rights Theory could only mature and take on its modern form, as centred on rights rather than duties, once the hold of Christianity on the Western mind was broken, that is, from the period of the Enlightenment. Certainly Christianity made an indelible imprint on Natural Rights Theory *in its developmental stage*, in respect of the two key elements of the theory identified above: a reading of natural law out of which a correlative concept of natural rights could be extracted, and a reading of *ius* as the subjective rights of an individual.[29] Both elements are present, for example, in the formula arrived at by Jean Gerson, Chancellor of the University of Paris in the early years of the fifteenth century, when he defined *ius* as a 'dispositional capacity or power, appropriate to an individual and in accord with the dictates of right reason'.[30] Significantly, but predictably, Gerson goes on to ground his theory in the 'sacred Scriptures' and to explore specifically Christian concerns such as whether we have the capacity or power to inherit eternal life, or a right to harm ourselves.

In the section that follows I present a short case-study of a particular natural right, the right to life, showing how it grew out of a particular Christian doctrine, the obligation to give alms. This example takes us to the heart of both Natural Rights Theory and Christianity. The right to life is conventionally and properly regarded as the primary natural or human right, while the duty of Christians to give alms to the poor is, and has always been, a central plank of Christian doctrine. It will emerge that the recognition of the right to life, or self-preservation, has significant, negative, implications for the status of the right to property.

RIGHT TO LIFE – AND PROPERTY

In the late fourth century, perhaps in 369, Basil, Bishop of Caesarea, Cappadocia, in east-central Asia Minor, delivered a homily on Luke 12:16–21, 'I will knock down my barns.' This was one of several sermons in which he pressed on the rich the duty of almsgiving.[31] Basil uses two

---

[29] The central role of natural law theory in nurturing the early development of Natural Rights Theory within a predominantly Christian intellectual culture is emphasized by Haakonssen (2002), Mäkinen (2006), Coleman (2006b) and Korkman (2006). Tierney (2006) is concerned lest the existence of 'Subjective Rights Theory' in the formative period be overlooked or underemphasized.

[30] Quoted in Tuck (1979), 25–6. See Gerson, *Oeuvres Complètes*, vol. 3, 141.

[31] Rousseau (1994) on Basil; Finn (2006) is an exemplary study of almsgiving in late antiquity, its theory and practice; Basil is discussed at 223–38. The citations are *I will knock down my barns* 264–5, 276–7, transl. R. Finn. See *PG* 31; Courtonne (1935).

principal arguments to undermine their complacency and whip them into action. They are: that the rich person is not so much an owner as a manager and distributor acting on God's behalf; and that what is withheld by the rich is *stolen* from the poor. First, man is the custodian and dispenser of property that is actually God's:

Realize, man, who it is who has done the giving. Remember yourself, who you are, what you manage, from whom you received it, why you were chosen over many others. You have been made the servant of God in His goodness, the manager of your fellow-slaves. Do not imagine that everything has been prepared for your stomach. Look on what is yours to handle as if it were other people's property. These things give you pleasure for a short time. Then, having slipped through your fingers, they will have vanished, and you will be required to produce detailed accounts for them.

The ground prepared, Basil moves up a key, and aggressively targets the principle of first occupancy. In doing so he twists Cicero's image of the theatre (see Chapter 5) in such a way that the first occupant is calling 'mine' not just a single seat, but the whole theatre:

'To whom am I doing an injustice', he asks, 'by keeping what is mine?' Tell me, what kind of things belong to you? Where did you get them from, when you brought them into this life? It is as if someone catching a show in the theatre were to stop other people from coming in, in the belief that what was put on in public for everyone's enjoyment was his property. That's the rich for you. They get first hands on common property and make it theirs because they got it first.

Basil's tone becomes ever more pugnacious, as the rich man, already found guilty of avarice, is invited to choose for himself the label of 'atheist' or 'robber':

If each person would only take for themselves what would meet their own needs and then relinquish what was left over to someone in need, no one would be rich, no one poor, no one in need. Were you not naked when you left the womb? Will you not be naked when the earth covers you again? Where do your present belongings come from? Say it is an accident of fate and you are an atheist, ignorant of the Creator, with no gratitude to show your benefactor. Admit, on the other hand, they come from God, tell us the reason why you got them. God is not unjust, is he, when he divides up unequally what keeps us alive? Why are you rich, but this man poor? Surely, above all, so that you may receive the reward for your goodness and trustworthy provision, while he is honoured with great prizes for enduring in patience. But do you think you are wronging nobody in depriving them of everything you sweep up into the bottomless pockets of your avarice? Who is a greedy person? The one who does not settle for self-sufficiency. Who is a robber? The one who makes off with everyone else's property. Aren't you greedy? Aren't you a robber? Making your own private property what you took to administer? Isn't the man who strips someone bare called a thief? And does the man who refuses to clothe the naked, when he is capable of doing so, deserve any other name? The bread you hold onto belongs to the hungry person. The cloak you guard in the store-cupboard belongs to the person who goes naked. The shoes rotting in your house belong to the person who walks barefoot. The silver you dug up and hoard belongs to the needy person. So you wrong as many as you could provide for.

When the issue of extreme poverty surfaces in the Middle Ages we encounter what is for the most part a familiar charge expressed in familiar rhetoric. In Gratian's *Decretum* the obligations of private owners to the poor are expressed in dramatic (but Basilian) language: 'A man who keeps more for himself than he needs is guilty of theft ... The bread that you hold back belongs to the needy, the clothes that you store away belong to the naked.' One pronouncement stands out as different: 'When a person is dying of hunger, necessity excuses theft.' The novelty is threefold: the situation is considered for the first time from the point of view of the poor man; the accusation of theft hangs over the poor man, not the rich man; and the poor man is transparently starving.[32]

The Decretalists took up the baton.[33] Huguccio (Hugh of Pisa, d. 1210) thought the starving man would not be guilty of theft. He had no explanation to offer, apart from the starving man's reasonable expectation that the rich man would respond positively: 'because he believes or should believe that the owner will grant him permission'.[34] Alanus (writing in the 1190s) took original communality as the starting-point, as Gratian had done, but understood this to imply that goods were shared in times of dire necessity: 'Since by natural *ius* all things are common, that is, they are to be shared in time of need, he is not properly said to steal.'[35] Thomas Aquinas did not advance beyond this position. Writing in his massive *Summa Theologiae* (therefore sometime in the late 1260s or early 1270s), he declares that theft on behalf of the man in extreme want is permissible. For in extremis, property rights are in effect suspended, and everything reverts to common property, as in God's original dispensation.[36]

---

[32] Gratian, *Decretum Dist.* c. 21; 47 c. 8;

[33] Some medieval scholars investigated the right of self-preservation and its limits by way of another theme, whether the criminal who has been justly condemned to death has the right or duty to try to escape. The first main discussion is by Henry of Ghent (d. 1293). The issue was still of interest to major philosophers of the seventeenth century. See Tierney (1997), 78.

[34] Tierney (1997), 71 n. 92. Tierney, leaning on Couvreur (1961), gives a useful summary of the main canonistic discussions. See also the detailed account of Swanson (1997).

[35] Tierney (1997), 73 n. 98.   [36] *ST* 2.2ae.66.7.

Thomas does not talk in terms of a moral right of the starving man, but his contemporary the canonist Hostiensis (Henry of Segusio, d. 1271) did, if rather tentatively: 'He who suffers from dire necessity seems rather to be making use of his right than to be planning a theft.'[37] In another significant move Godfrey of Fontaines and John of Paris, colleagues at the University of Paris and writing in the 1280s, ascribe to the starving man *property rights* in the food that he takes in order to stay alive. The first quotation is from Godfrey, the second from John:[38]

For the reason that each and every man is bound by the law of nature to sustain his life, which cannot be done without external goods, so also by the law of nature each and every man has dominion and a certain *ius* in the common external goods of this world, which right also cannot be licitly renounced.

Human life is ruled by natural and positive law. Natural law never alters but positive law loses its force in certain cases where it does not remain in accord with the natural law upon which it is founded. Natural law does not determine that a thing be mine or yours, for natural law recognizes the common possession of all things ... That everyone is bound to preserve his own life is natural; therefore, according to natural law, an individual who would not otherwise survive except by taking the property of others may do so. Positive law has no force in this case, and the property which he takes no longer belongs to others but becomes his own. This is true whenever he might not otherwise be able to provide for himself ... And this resolves the problem because whoever makes use of *his own goods and not another's* does not commit theft.

Godfrey and John had between them defined the category of a *natural property right*, an entitlement to the goods required to sustain life, in addition to and above the conventional *civil property right*, an entitlement to exclude others from the resources that are owned. This move was contested. The era of the Franciscan poverty dispute had arrived, or the first stage in that dispute, and this is reflected in Godfrey's language. The position of the Franciscans had come under critical scrutiny from secular theologians such as Godfrey. The Franciscans had renounced all *dominium* and other civil law rights over the food that they needed to stay alive. They had not renounced the right to life, and claimed licit access to necessary provisions (and other fungibles). Their argument was that the

---

[37] Tierney (1997), 38; cf. 75. Thomas Aquinas' use of *ius* is much discussed. See Tierney (1997), 22, who argues against Villey that Aquinas sometimes used *ius* in a 'subjective sense'; elsewhere (e.g. 69, 258) he refuses to attribute to Aquinas 'the definition of *ius* as a subjective right'. Finnis (1998), 136, writes: 'Though he never use a term translatable as "human rights", Aquinas clearly has the concept.'

[38] Godfrey: *Quodlibet* 8 q 11; John: quoted in Mäkinen (2006), 48–9, my emphasis.

right to nourish, protect and preserve the body is a (natural) right of self-preservation, not a right to property. Their critics claimed in their turn that the Franciscan position was incoherent, because in order to exercise the undoubted and unrenounceable right to stay alive, they had to establish *dominium* over the very goods that would enable them to exercise this right. In the next round of the contest (in the 1320s and 30s) what had been a relatively civilized scholarly disagreement broke out into open warfare between Pope John XXII and the Franciscan Order. The point to be stressed here is that the leading opponent of the Pope, William of Ockham, while resisting any attempt to fuse the natural right to life with a natural right to property, was forced into a detailed analysis of the nature of *dominium* and its status as a right, and came up with a characterization of the right to property as natural in a subsidiary, conditional sense – his word (as we saw) is 'supposititious'. In this he was tapping into a line of thought that can be followed from the twelfth century to the eighteenth. Its advocates included leading thinkers of the sixteenth and seventeenth centuries, whose views on the right to life and its relation to the right to property I now briefly sketch.

On the matter in question, theorists of the sixteenth century such as the Jesuit Suarez and the Dominican Vitoria on the whole walked in step with their predecessors, invoking above all the authority of Thomas Aquinas, to whom they appear to ascribe a doctrine of individual rights. A further sign of Vitoria's allegiance to the founder of his Order is his turning of Thomas' labelling of the unresponsive rich man as a murderer into the advice that the starving poor man could not just steal from a rich man who did not release food to him, but *kill* him.[39]

The primacy of the right of self-preservation received renewed emphasis in the seventeenth century. Grotius pronounced it the only universal moral principle on which the whole of humanity could agree.[40] For Hobbes, it was *the* right of nature:

The Right of Nature, which Writers commonly call Jus Naturale, is the Liberty each man hath, to use his own power, as he will himselfe, for the preservation of his own Nature; that is to say, of his own Life; and consequently, of doing any thing, which in his own Judgement, and Reason, hee shall conceive to be the aptest means thereunto.[41]

---

[39] Suarez, *On the Laws* 3.2.17.2, 100; Vitoria, *Commentarios* 3: 64; 340; 5: 264–5 (cited Tierney (1997), 301).

[40] Tuck (1999), 9–10. For the relation between self-preservation and sociability in Grotius and Pufendorf, see Hont (2005b), 173–8.

[41] *Leviathan* 1.14.64 (Tuck 91).

Grotius' main innovation was his extension of the claims of necessity from the safety of individuals to the safety of states. Otherwise he stuck to traditional doctrine fairly closely. For example, he went along with the thesis that in extremis the original regime of communality made a temporary return at the expense of ownership rights. At such moments the poor acquired a property right in the superfluous resources of the rich in consequence of the failure of the latter to live up to their obligations, and this was done in full accordance with natural law.

Some natural law theorists found in this proposition a recipe for anarchy. Pufendorf manoeuvred his way by tenuous logic into a compromise position which took the pressure off the rich, whose duties to the poor were now characterized as 'imperfect' and less than obligatory, and allowed those in extremis access to necessary goods but no actual right to them.[42] Locke's attitude to the poor was similarly less than magnanimous. There was an obligation on the rich, but this was merely a side-constraint on existing property arrangements. It came into operation only in extreme necessity, and only as a last resort after the poor man had made an attempt to *work* his way out of trouble; further, only the bare necessities were to be furnished. Locke's long-term solution was the same as that of Adam Smith: economic growth. Through the achievement of higher productivity in the context of an expanding economy dire necessity could be brought to an end. The problem of the rights of the poor to the property of the rich would simply evaporate.

Having resolved to his own satisfaction the age-old problem of the right to life of the starving poor, Locke brought back that same right in a positive new role, that of establishing the status of property as a natural right. His argument is a simple one, resting on God, the creation and the teleology of natural resources:

God having made Man and planted in him as in all other Animals, a strong desire of self-preservation, and furnished the world with things fit for Food and Rayment and other Necessaries of Life, subservient to his design, that Man should live and abide for sometime upon the Face of the Earth, and not that so curious and wonderful a piece of Workmanship by its own Negligence, or want of Necessaries, should perish again, presently after a few moments continuance: God, I say, having made Man and the World thus, spoke to him (that is) directed

---

[42] *On the Law of Nature and Nations* 2.6.6. On both Pufendorf and Locke, see Hont (2005b), 424–35. Burlamaqui, *Principles of Natural Law and Political Law*, transl. Nugent (1763), 1.1.7 (and see below) writing in the 1740s took a hard line on the issue: 'Thus, notwithstanding reason authorizes those who are destitute of means of living, to apply for succour to other men; yet they cannot, in case of refusal, insist upon it by force, or procure it by open violence.'

him by his Senses and Reason ... to the use of those things which were ser-
viceable for his Subsistence, and given him as means of his Preservation ... And
thus Man's property in the Creatures was founded upon the right he had to make
use of those things that were necessary or useful to his Being.[43]

The Earth, and all that is therein, is given to Men for the Support and Comfort
of their being. And tho' all the Fruits it naturally produces, and Beasts it feeds,
belong to Mankind in common, as they are produced by the spontaneous hand
of Nature ... yet being given for the use of Men, there must of necessity be a
means to appropriate them in some way or other, before they can be of any use,
or at all beneficial to any particular Man.[44]

These paragraphs could have been written by one of a number of medieval to
early modern jurists steeped in natural law. But whereas others might have
hesitated over questions that surfaced in these texts, Locke does not allow
himself to be sidetracked. Original communality is mentioned, as is the
private ownership that undermined it, but without comment. The slippery
phrase 'God ... spoke to him (that is) directed him by his Senses and
Reason' (to use and possess resources) glides over a major debate concerning
the proper classification of the right to property. Later in the *Treatise* Locke
unfolds his theory of labour as a trump card to dispel all doubts and suspi-
cions about ownership. His broad strategy meanwhile is to expand those
rights whose status as natural is beyond dispute to include the right to
property. In this connection let us note the following passage on liberty:

To understand political power right, and derive it from its original, we must
consider, what state all men are naturally in, and that is, *a state of perfect freedom*
to order their actions, and dispose of their possessions and persons, as they think
fit, within the bounds of the law of nature, without asking leave, or depending
upon the will of any other man.[45]

Two chapters later Locke adds *security* for 'life, health, liberty or
possessions'. The French Declaration of the Rights of Man and Citizen is
just around the corner.

THE AGE OF REVOLUTION

Property is not among the inalienable natural rights listed in the preamble
to the American Declaration of Independence of 4 July 1776; it *does* have a
place in the French Declaration of the Rights of Man and Citizen of 26
August 1789. Why did the Americans leave it out and the French put it in?

---

[43] *Treatise* 1.86. [44] Ibid. 2.26. [45] Ibid. 2.4.

America

It might have been anticipated that Thomas Jefferson, who drafted the American document, would include property. The Bill of Rights of Jefferson's home state of Virginia, passed on 12 June only a few weeks earlier, did find space for property, in a statement (drafted by George Mason) whose content is otherwise similar to Jefferson's: 'That all men are by nature equally free and independent, and have certain inherent rights, of which, when they enter into society, they cannot, by any compact, deprive or divest their posterity; namely, the enjoyment of life and liberty, with the means of acquiring and possessing property, and pursuing happiness and safety.' Other states modelled their own bills of rights on that of Virginia in this respect.

Jefferson's omission of property was deliberate and highly significant.[46] His reasons, whatever they were (for no source informs us), were enduring, for as ambassador in Paris in the late 1780s he advised Lafayette, with whom he was in close contact, to drop property from *his* draft Declaration of Rights of June 1789. Jefferson put brackets around two phrases, thus: 'Every man is born with inalienable rights; such are [the right to property,] the care of [his honour and] his life, the entire disposal of his person and industry, as well as his faculties, the pursuit of his own good, and resistance against oppression.'[47]

Lafayette stuck to his guns and retained *propriété* and *honneur* in his third and final 'projet de déclaration' of July 1789.

Jefferson was not alone in believing that property could or should be dispensed with in any catalogue of human rights. Among the advisory pamphlets submitted in the run-up to the Declaration of Independence was one composed by James Wilson of Pennsylvania, entitled *Considerations on the Nature and Extent of the Legislative Authority of the British Parliament*. The work was written in 1768 and published in 1774. It contains a statement of rights, and its content overlaps significantly with that of Jefferson. Again there is silence over property:

All men are, by nature, equal and free: no one has a right to any authority over another without his consent: all lawful government is founded on the consent of those who are subject to it: such consent was given with a view to ensure and to

---

[46] Huyler (1995), 247, thinks otherwise: 'Not very much need be made of Jefferson's decision to substitute "the pursuit of happiness" for Locke's own formulation of "life, liberty and property".' For a view on the omission of property which is quite different from mine see Bassani (2004).

[47] Jefferson, *Papers* (ed. Boyd), 15, 230, quoted in Wills (1978), 230. For Lafayette's three 'projets', see Rials (1988), 528, 567, 590.

increase the happiness of the governed, above what they could enjoy in an independent and unconnected state of nature. The consequence is, that the happiness of the society is the *first* law of every government.[48]

Jefferson's decision to leave out property might have had something to do with slavery. To accord property the status of a human right at a time when humans constituted a significant form of property in America might seem to be legitimizing the institution. Jefferson, along with other Founding Fathers, was schizophrenic about slavery. He was a major slaveowner who was opposed to slavery. His draft document for the Declaration of Independence included a direct attack on slavery and the slave trade, characterized later by John Adams as a 'vehement philippic'.[49] Jefferson's comment on the excision of the paragraph in question by Congress is suggestive of the sensitiveness of the issue among the politicians of the time, Northerners as well as Southerners:

The clause too, reprobating the enslaving of the inhabitants of Africa, was struck out in complaisance to South Carolina and Georgia, who had never attempted to restrain the importation of slaves, and who on the contrary still wished to continue it. Our Northern brethren also I believe felt a little tender under these censures; for tho' their people have few slaves themselves, yet they had been pretty considerable carriers of them to others.[50]

Slavery might be sufficient explanation for the absence of property in Jefferson's document. But there were also the 'Indians' (Native Americans).[51] American leaders could not stop settlers from taking over Indian land, nor did they want to. Jefferson writing in 1801 as President to the Governor of Virginia spoke of his dream that white farmers would 'cover the whole northern if not the southern continent, with a people speaking the same language, governed in similar forms, and by similar laws; nor can we contemplate with satisfaction either blot or mixture on that surface.'[52] Jefferson himself together with associates had been acquiring Indian land from the 1760s. As for Indians who did not cede their lands peacefully, they could be forced to do so in a 'just war'. Warfare was in progress on

---

[48] Wilson, *Works* (ed. McCloskey 1967), 2, 723.
[49] Becker (1922), 212–34; Adams, *Works* (1851–6), 2, 512.
[50] Quoted in, Becker (1922), 171–2. The Virginians confined rights to those deemed to be members of society ('when they enter society'), thereby excluding slaves. In this way they showed a willingness to make the distinction between slave and free, but not to make the distinction explicit. The Americans in their unwillingness to make the distinction were employing a deeper level of evasion. The explanation of the difference lies in the different constituencies, situations and attitudes of the decision-makers.
[51] See e.g. Wallace (1999); Sheehan (1973).   [52] Wallace (1999), 17.

the frontiers of Virginia just when Jefferson was preparing his draft for the Declaration of Independence – fomented, he charged, by the British. At the same time Jefferson and many other leading politicians did not claim that the Indians, though primitive peoples, had no natural rights, including the 'right of soil'. However, if there was a natural right to property, virtually all property held by descendants of European settlers would have been put under suspicion. Jefferson was as inconsistent over the Indians as he was over slavery.

Slaves and Indians might provide sufficient explanation for Jefferson's reluctance to include property. Alternatively, or in addition, Jefferson was swayed by the writings of a natural law theorist. This was not John Locke, whose influence on the American Revolution has been strongly asserted and as strongly denied,[53] but Jean-Jacques Burlamaqui (1694–1748). Burlamaqui was Professor of Natural and Civil Law at Geneva from 1723 until his death, and wrote up his lectures as *Principes du droit naturel* (*Principles of Natural Law*, 1747) and *Principes du droit politique* (*Principles of Political Law*, published posthumously, 1751). He was a disciple of Jean Barbeyrac of Lausanne (1674–1745), the eminent translator and commentator of Grotius and Pufendorf.[54] Burlamaqui's work was translated into English and circulated widely among American politicians in the decades leading up to the Revolution. James Wilson owned a copy in the original French. In his influential position-paper of 1774, *Considerations*, there is a quotation from Burlamaqui in the paragraph that follows the statement on natural rights cited above. In his law lectures, and *On the Law of Nature* in particular, he quotes Burlamaqui in the text, and refers to him repeatedly in the footnotes. Jefferson knew and drew on Wilson's *Considerations*. He too had a copy of Burlamaqui (in French) in his library.

Jefferson and Wilson would have found in Burlamaqui a very clear message about property and rights. Following in the tracks of earlier natural law theorists, Burlamaqui distinguishes between the primitive and original state of man 'in which man finds himself placed by the very hand of God, independent of any human action', and adventitious states 'wherein he finds himself placed by his own act'. The 'property of goods'

---

[53] For the debate see Huyler (1995), with bibliography.
[54] For Burlamaqui in his Genevan setting, see Rosenblatt (1997), and in general, Gagnebin (1944). The 'American connection' was first observed by Chinard (1926) and studied in detail by Harvey (1937). White (1978), 213–28 gives a penetrating analysis. Huyler (1995), 247–8 is a recent endorsement. See also, with special reference to 'the pursuit of happiness', Korkman (2006).

is one such adventitious state. The natural state of man comprises both primitive and adventitious states. He goes on:

Let us not forget to observe ... that there is this difference between the primitive and adventitious states, that the former, being annexed as it were to the nature and constitution of man, such as he has received them from God, are, for this very reason, common to all mankind. The same cannot be said of the adventitious states, which, supposing a human act or agreement, cannot of themselves be indifferently suitable to all men, but to those only that contrived and procured them.

On rights, Burlamaqui lays down with equal clarity a parallel distinction between natural and acquired rights: 'The former are such as appertain originally and essentially to man, *such as are inherent in his nature, and that he enjoys as man,* independent of any particular act on his side. Acquired rights on the other hand are *those which he does not naturally enjoy,* but are owing to his own procurement.' He gives illustrations. They are, of a 'natural' right, the right of self-preservation, and of an 'acquired' right, 'sovereignty, the right of commanding a society of men'. He might equally have cited the right to property as an exemplary 'acquired' right.[55]

Jefferson left out property (with the connivance of colleagues) because he held that to designate it as an unalienable human right was philosophically unjustified and politically unwise.[56]

France

It was not a foregone conclusion that the National Assembly of France would issue a 'Déclaration des droits de l'homme et du citoyen' in 1789. The demand for a Declaration of Rights came out of the Lists of Grievances ('cahiers de doléances') brought to the King by the Deputies of the Three Estates, and these typically addressed themselves to the rights of *citizens.* The 'cahier général du Tiers de Nîmes' is representative:

---

[55] Burlamaqui, *Principles of Natural Law and Political Law,* vol. 1, pt. 1, chs. 4 and 7, 43–4 and 73 (in reprint of 1972 at 31 and 51). Wills (1978) argues forcefully, but not to my mind persuasively, that the main influence on Jefferson came from the Scottish Enlightenment, and in particular from Francis Hutcheson. Burlamaqui was doubtless influenced by Hutcheson as well as by Grotius and Pufendorf, but what is at issue is their respective popularity among the Founding Fathers. I find it significant that James Wilson, though a Scot and educated in Scottish Universities, cites with regularity Grotius, Pufendorf and Burlamaqui, but of the Scottish thinkers only Thomas Reid. See Hamowy (1979) for a devastating attack on Wills' thesis.

[56] It is of interest that Abraham Lincoln wrote in a letter of 6 April 1859 to H. L. Pierce and others, of 'the Jefferson party formed upon the supposed superior devotion to the personal rights of men, holding the rights of property to be secondary only and greatly inferior'. See Lincoln, *Collected Works* (ed. Basler), 2, 374–6.

The purpose of the laws being to safeguard *for all citizens*, under the protection and through the vigilance of the monarchy, the blessings that they bestow on society in common, the deputies shall never lose sight of the fact that the laws must be conducive to the preservation among men of the liberty to act, to speak, and to think; of the property in their persons and goods; of their honour and of their life; of their tranquillity, and finally, their safety. Nor shall they forget that the highest point of perfection in the laws is to procure for those who are placed under them the greatest summation of happiness that is possible.[57]

Some 'cahiers' talk in terms of 'des droits de l'homme et du citoyen'. In addition, men of influence such as the Marquis de Lafayette, the Abbé Sieyès and Jean-Joseph Mounier in their Draft Declarations ('Projets de Déclarations'), issued in the run-up to the period of concentrated debate in the National Assembly (late July through August), had addressed the rights of man and citizen.[58] Nevertheless, a number of the thirty or so declarations that were submitted to the Assembly for discussion limited themselves to the 'rights of mankind *in society*', in effect, to the rights of citizens. The committee of five under the Comte de Mirabeau that was entrusted by the Assembly on 12 August with the task of finding a route through the maze of proposals, reported back on 17 August with a 'Projet de Droits *de l'homme en société*'. Article 11 of their proposal guaranteed '*to every citizen* the right to acquire, possess, manufacture, trade, employ his abilities and his industry and dispose of his properties as he wishes'.

Mirabeau's report fell flat, satisfying neither supporters of a Rights Declaration nor its critics, of whom there were a significant number among the 1,200 deputies.[59] In introducing his document Mirabeau adopted a defensive tone. His committee's task, he says, had been to lay out some general principles which were applicable to all forms of government. What was needed was a formula of conspicuous simplicity on which all could agree and over which one could harbour no doubts. In fact, the ancient and decrepit state of the existing political order and the need to take account of local circumstances dictated that only a 'relative perfection' could be hoped for. To arrive at a Declaration of Rights in such circumstances was 'a labour fraught with difficulty'. Specifically, his committee had found it difficult to distinguish 'that which belongs to the nature of

---

[57] *AP* (*Archives Parliamentaires*) 240; Rials (1988), 115, my emphasis.
[58] See Rials (1988), Dossier nos. 17, 27, 33 (Lafayette); 34, 38 (Sieyès); 35 (Mounier), and ch. 1 for the sequence of events of spring and early summer 1789. For biographies of the 'Constituents' see Lemay (1991). The events of July and August 1789 are well covered by Rials (1988), ch. 2; Baker (1990); Tackett (1996).
[59] See Jennings (1992) on the critics.

man from those modifications introduced on his behalf in one society or another'. Mirabeau evidently thought that to impose such a distinction was not worth the effort, and he illustrated his point with reference to liberty. 'Liberty has never been the fruit of a doctrine arrived at by means of philosophical deduction, but rather out of everyday experience.' A side-glance at the American revolutionaries follows: 'they deliberately steered clear of "science", preferring to present the political truths that they wanted to enact in a form that could easily be taken up by a people. For liberty matters only to a people, and only by a people can liberty be maintained.'[60] Mirabeau had betrayed a certain lack of interest in human rights as early as April 1788, when he circulated his own 'projet de déclaration'. After a terse opening – 'all men are free and equal' – Mirabeau got down to the business that interested him, which was to set out the rights of the citizen in civil society.[61] When the Deputies showed their displeasure at his report, Mirabeau retaliated by proposing that the drafting of the Declaration be postponed until other parts of the constitution had been settled. We can sympathize with his attitude. As the Old Order entered its terminal phase, the moderate reformers in the Assembly moved to counter the threat of revolution from below and counter-revolution from above. The priority, in the eyes of many of them, was to spell out in concrete terms the rights of citizens within the protective framework of a new constitution. And they had within their ranks or readily at hand a battery of lawyers armed with the expertise that was needed for this specific task.[62]

In the event, after the disappointment of the Mirabeau report, the movement for a comprehensive Declaration of Rights picked up again, and the Assembly after only a week's debate reached a successful conclusion. What drove the 'Rights Movement' then, as before, was the desperate state of France. In the summer of 1789 the situation had worsened through a sudden combination of political tensions and acute food shortages. Poor harvests, a dramatic rise in the price of bread (peaking on 14 July), and the 'Great Fear' of a conspiracy to stop the revolutionaries in their tracks by denying them food, resulted in a dramatic rise in the level of violence in the countryside and on the streets of Paris. The National Assembly responded to the emergency by abolishing seigneurial privileges and

---

[60] *AP* 8, 438. Also on America, see esp. *AP* 8, 452 and 518. See, briefly, G. Lefebvre (2001), 140. The classic comparative work is Palmer (1959–64). The Virginian and French Declarations are placed side by side in his Appendix 4.

[61] Rials (1988), 519–22.

[62] Kaiser (1994) makes a powerful case for the contribution of Old Regime jurisprudence to the redefinition of property relations in the revolutionary era.

ending the tithe – and the fate of Church properties lay in the balance.
This was the deputies' main business in early August; it is remarkable that
they were able to give any attention at all to Rights and a Constitution.
But now (in mid-August) the nation was in greater turmoil than ever.
Singling out property, a matter close to the hearts of the landowners who
were steering the Revolution: the Assembly's own measures had if anything increased disruption on the land. Further, one issue which had
helped trigger the revolution, taxation and the national debt – that of
who had the right to levy taxes and to maintain or repudiate the national
debt – still had to be confronted.[63] This was an appropriate time, or
rather, there was an urgent need, to step up the campaign for the security
of property and the rights of citizens in general. By coupling citizen rights
with human rights, by formulating a set of universal principles underlying
a Declaration of Rights and a new Constitution, the reformers hoped to
give their creations an air of sacrosanctity and make them the more
impregnable.

For this, a contribution from philosophy was required. Some deputies
would have nothing to do with philosophy. Mirabeau was at best lukewarm, as we saw. Dominique Garat, a deputy from the Basque country,
was expounding a theoretical distinction between the rights of individuals
and of corporations such as the clergy, when he was interrupted by cries
of 'We don't need philosophy.' Others encouraged the speaker with shouts
of: 'Go on! Go on!'[64] Adrien-Cyprien Duquesnoy of Lorraine noted in his
journal under 18 August that the task of arriving at a formula of rights
'lends itself too readily to vague and metaphysical musings'. He went on:
'There is not a single point, not a single word, that is not open to dispute
and wrangling, not one on which one could not write volumes. Yet the
rights of man are quite transparent, they are engraved on every heart.'[65]

The philosophical background to the French Revolution is a dense fog.
The influence of the Physiocrats, Rousseau, Locke, among others, is well
established. Blandine Kriegel believes that the contribution of the natural
law tradition was significant and has been underrated.[66] There are documents that support her case. It was an issue among Assembly members
whether a Declaration of Rights should take the form of a reasoned

---

[63] See Sonenscher (1997) for an exhaustive study.   [64] *AP* 8, 394.
[65] Quoted in Rials (1988), 210.
[66] See Kriegel (1994); (1995a, b); cf. Gauchet (1989). See the account of the vigorous debate among
contemporary French thinkers in Souillac (2006), with reference to Kriegel, Gauchet, Ferry and
Balibar. Ferry and Renaut (1984) provide a useful account of political philosophy at the time of the
Revolution and its aftermath.

exposition of principles or simply a list of articles. In the end they opted for the latter. However, several examples of the former were produced, and they are of exceptional interest. The edited Proceedings of the Assembly contain a statement by Jean-Paul Rabaut de Saint-Etienne, a Protestant pastor from Nimes, entitled 'Idées sur les bases de toute constitution'. Under the heading of 'The Rights of Men', he writes:

In order to understand the rights of man, it is necessary to understand the end for which he was created and of which he never loses sight: his preservation. Everything conducive to his destruction he flees, everything that works to maintain him, he seeks out. This sentiment comes to him from the right that he has to existence: to live, to live well, to live as long as he can, this is his primitive and inalienable right. All the rest simply follow.

It follows therefore that no other man may prevent him from procuring the means by which he can stay alive; that he himself retains the right to stand against the wrongs that others might inflict on him in this regard; that he has therefore the right to preserve himself, and to do whatever he judges necessary to achieve that end. This is called the right to liberty.

But every man has this right, as much as and as completely as his fellows. This linking right is called equality, that is equality of rights. Finally, man may possess such things as are appropriate to preserve himself and satisfy his needs; it is over these things that his right to liberty is exercised in all its fullness. This is called property. The end of communal association is to put all these rights, as they apply to individuals, under the protection of everyone. That is called security. One may conclude from all that has just been stated, that the rights that men bring into society revolve around these three: liberty, equality, property; and from this it follows that the end of guardian laws should be to guarantee the security of these rights.

A bad constitution is one which violates rights; a good constitution is one which renders them secure; an excellent constitution is one which allows them the opportunity to develop to the greatest possible extent.[67]

This statement draws on a long and continuous tradition of natural law theory. Jurists, philosophers and theologians from the Middle Ages to the eighteenth century had advanced self-preservation as the first and basic natural right, from which any others were derived, of higher or lower station. John Locke comes towards the end of this line of succession, and his influence is conspicuous in the document before us. The appearance of property as one of a chain of interlocking rights, in conjunction with life, liberty and security, was above all his doing.

---

[67] *AP* 8, 403–4.

Briefer contributions along the same lines are recorded in the Proceedings.[68] A particularly arresting document (not in the Proceedings) comes from the pen of Sieyès and belongs to July 1789. When the deputies resumed their discussion of Rights after the Mirabeau débâcle, they turned to earlier statements such as those of Lafayette, Mounier and Sieyès. In the judgement of Marcel Gauchet, the influence of Sieyès on the final document was paramount.[69] His 'projet de déclaration' consists of an introduction of 'Observations', an extended 'Reconnoissance et exposition raisonnée' and finally a catalogue of thirty-two articles. The 'Reconnoissance' includes the following paragraphs on property:

Ownership of one's person is the first of one's rights. From this primitive right is derived the ownership of one's actions and one's labour; for labour is simply the constructive use of one's faculties; it clearly emanates from the ownership of one's person and one's actions.

Ownership of external objects, or real property, is likewise a consequence and as it were an extension of personal property. The air we breathe, the water we drink, the fruit we eat, are transformed into our own substance, through the work of our body, involuntary or voluntary.

Through analogous operations, though this time more dependent on our will, I appropriate to myself an object which belongs to nobody, and which I need, by a labour which modifies it, which prepares it for my use. My labour was mine, and it still is. The object on which I fixed it, which I invested it in, belonged to me as it belonged to everyone. Indeed it belonged to me more than to others, since I had in it, more than others did, the right of first occupant. These conditions suffice to make of this object my exclusive property. Civil society then gives it by means of a general convention a kind of legal consecration; and one must include this last act in one's reconstruction in order for the word property to embrace the full extent of the meanings that we are accustomed to attach to it in our orderly societies.

There was much in Locke's political philosophy to attract the French Revolutionaries: his opposition to authoritarianism, his insistence on contract and consent as the basis of government, his assertion of the rights of individual citizens, and the formula of rights that he came up with. His highly individual account of the manner in which a natural property right is acquired (see Chapter 7) was surely an optional extra. However, it appealed to Sieyès, and through his mediation – for his exposition is clearer and more compelling than Locke's own – may well have secured other admirers among the more influential deputies of the National

---

[68] Ibid., 431–2; 457; etc.
[69] Gauchet (1988). For Sieyès, see e.g. Bastid (1939); Bredin (1988); Sonenscher (1997).

Assembly. One group that might fruitfully be followed up in this connection (but not here) are the lawyers. Jean-Etienne-Marie Portalis, the
Father of the *Code Civil*, was not a Constituent, but like Sieyès (whose
political career had taken a downturn from 1790) was influential under
Napoleon. Following in the track of lawyers such as Germain Garnier
(who was a Constituent), Portalis argued vigorously for a natural right to
property, and in doing so took over Locke's argument and his central
image: 'The principle of the right [to property] is in us', he wrote. 'It is
not at all the result of human convention or positive law; it is in the
constitution of our being and in different relationships with the objects
around us.' Humans in the state of nature 'mixed' their labour with the
resources of the earth and made them theirs, inasmuch as they contained
'quantities of labour'.[70]

CONCLUSION

It is understandable that historians should herald the Revolutions in
America and France as the beginning of the modern age. I see the
revolutionary era as Janus-faced, looking both ways. If one follows the
historical development of human rights as I have been doing, one is
struck by how firmly the discourse of human rights in the revolutionary
age was rooted in the past. Natural rights theory evolved out of natural
law theory, which arose in antiquity, reached its apogee in the Middle
Ages and was still going strong in the early Enlightenment. It had a
following among men of influence in France in the Revolutionary Age.
However, the Terror proved that no Declaration of Rights, however
carefully tuned, could protect the persons and property of individual
citizens in the face of a ruthless government. The 'Human Rights
Movement' fell into disrepute, from which it did not really recover until
the middle of the twentieth century in consequence of the experience and
the defeat of Fascism.[71] Modern human rights theory is a different
creature altogether. This is not because the rights in question are for the
first time subjective, in the sense of being attached to the individual as
subject in virtue of his or her intrinsic nature and capacity as a human

---

[70] Portalis (1844), 211. The citation comes from an edition of Portalis' papers produced by his
grandson, Etienne-Frédéric-Auguste Portalis. See also Garnier, *De la propriété* (1792), 87, with
Kelley (1984), 207–8. Portalis' allegiance to natural law theory is stressed by D'Onorio (2005),
201–13.

[71] On the domestic critics see Jennings (1992). For Burke, Bentham and Marx, see Waldron (1987).
On nineteenth-century liberalism and human rights, see Ferry and Renaut (1984), 130–8.

being, for this idea had already been arrived at in the medieval period. The essential difference lies in the degree of emphasis given to rights as distinct from duties. Rights and duties are correlative terms.[72] As long as Natural Law Theory reigned, and as long as Christianity acted as incubator for the emerging theory of natural rights, there was (at the least) ambiguity as to where the priority lay as between rights and duties. Modern Rights Theory is unequivocally rights-based.[73]

---

[72] As noted by Burlamaqui (1748), 1.7.6.
[73] The difference between a rights-based and a duty-based theory is set out clearly in e.g. Dworkin (1977), 171.

Conclusion

It may not be a natural or human right to own property, but it is no accident that humans in complex societies strive assiduously to acquire, possess and attach the label 'mine' to external objects that are felt to be needed or seen to be of value. Aristotle was reflecting the *communis opinio*, then as now, when he claimed that a private property regime was preferable to one of communal ownership. His specific arguments, too, have struck a chord with theorists and politicians down the ages. They are primarily utilitarian: private property makes good social and economic as well as moral sense. It is important however not to overlook two other aspects of his intervention: first, the fact that he spoke out at all, and second, the fact that he misrepresented Plato in the course of doing so.

On the first of these points: Aristotle was provoked by the arrangements that Plato prescribed for his ideal state. It was the same with slavery (though in this case Plato was not the provocateur). There is no reason to suppose that Aristotle would ever have produced his theory of natural slavery, had not its basis been queried by certain (unnamed) individuals. Private property was an even more firmly established institution in Greek society than was slavery.

As to Aristotle's misrepresentation of Plato: Plato's message was that only if the governing class – any governing class – were denied access to wealth and to the family (the main social institution by which private wealth was passed down) could civic unity and harmony, the prime desideratum, be achieved. Aristotle took this doctrine and twisted it, with the astonishing result that for centuries afterwards it has been believed that Plato prescribed a communistic regime involving the sharing of property and families throughout the polis. Aristotle may not have intended to have represented Plato's prescriptions as (even) more shocking than they actually were, but this was certainly a consequence of his intervention. The end that he had in view, which in his mind justified his manipulation and transformation of Plato, was not so much to distance himself from Plato's doctrines in the *Republic* as to attack the whole principle of common ownership.

Over the historical period I have been studying, apologists for private property have tended to be, after the manner of Aristotle, reactive, even on the defensive. The running has been made on the whole by critics and doubters of private property. After Plato, Jesus of Nazareth: 'No salvation without renunciation!' This was a bitter pill to swallow for people with property. Christian spokesmen like Augustine and Thomas Aquinas, coming to the rescue of the wealthier members of their flock and the institutional Church itself, offered palatable interpretations of the crucial phrases, and found various ways of arguing against their literal meaning. The issue was never resolved (how could it be, given that there were always some Christians who rejected wealth and power and others who embraced it?), it surfaced from time to time, and in spectacular fashion in the Franciscan poverty dispute. The Franciscans were deemed to pose a challenge not just to institutional Christianity, but also to conventional monasticism. Periodic reformist movements within the Church had in the past invoked as their model the *ecclesia primitiva*, the community of the first Christians at Jerusalem of the Acts of the Apostles. This was not good enough for the Franciscans. They, and in particular the radical wing of the Order, claimed to have renounced not only private but also common ownership, and to be following in this St Francis, who was modelling himself on Christ. The literature that poured out for and against their case is a happy hunting ground for political theorists interested in property theory. Protagonists on both sides made it their business to improve on existing definitions of the concepts of right (*ius*) and ownership (*dominium*) in order to clinch their case.

The myth of primeval communality (itself of primordial and obscure origin) cast a shadow over private ownership by associating it with the moral decline of societies and individuals. The myth became something of a topos among poets and philosophers in classical Greece and Rome, but it was also used, and probably invented, in order to criticize the attitudes and behaviour of the contemporary rich. Christians gave it teeth by grafting it on to their own (Judaeo/Christian) myth of the Fall, so that private property along with other human institutions became a product of sin. If the authority of the Old and New Testaments were not enough, the medieval monk Gratian in his digest of Canon Law found private property and the legal system that propped it up wanting in comparison with communality and natural law. He rubbed salt into the wound by drawing a parallel between the communal property regime of the first Christians at Jerusalem and the sharing of everything, including wives and children, in Plato.

Gratian's intervention brought new urgency to an old debate about the origins of private property. For centuries to come, theologians, jurists and philosophers working within or influenced by the natural law tradition put their minds to defending or elevating the status and reputation of private property. Medieval canonists produced a reading of natural law out of which a correlative idea of natural rights could be derived. And by ingenious and involved argument they were able to award the right to property the status of a natural right, albeit at a lower level, as one of the 'adventitious' rights created by humans themselves through the application of their (God-given) reason, rather than as a primary right such as the right to life, a direct gift of God to humanity. Philosophers of the seventeenth and eighteenth centuries were much exercised over the problem of *occupatio*, or first acquisition, in the state of nature. This was a particularly sensitive matter, because *occupatio* patently disrupted God's original dispensation for humanity, according to which everything was to be accessible to and shared by all. (That the creator had had a regime of communality in mind was universally accepted by thinkers operating within the natural law tradition.) Grotius and Pufendorf proposed that the community had consented, tacitly or explicitly, to private ownership, and Pufendorf that the state of nature was in the first instance a negative community wherein there were no rights or claims to be challenged or set aside. The same thinkers advanced, albeit tentatively, a progressivist account of the evolution of society. This idea, which came to fruition in the four-stage theory of Adam Smith, offered a more favourable context for *occupatio*. John Locke's doctrine that labour conferred a natural entitlement to property sidelined *occupatio* altogether, or so he imagined. Around four decades earlier Hobbes' *Leviathan* was added to the ranks of great works with the power to shock and scandalize, to be joined in this around a century later by Rousseau's *Second Discourse* and *Social Contract*. Kant, against his will and better judgement, was drawn by Hobbes and Rousseau into the quagmire that was the state of nature debate. While conceding that 'conclusive' property rights could only be conferred by civil society, Kant nevertheless wanted to classify first acquisition in the state of nature as 'true', even if only 'provisional'. It was important for him to show that the transition from natural to civil society could be controlled and orderly.

Property's status as a natural right remained suspect and uncertain in the minds of many throughout our period. John Locke was breaking new ground when he argued that the primary rights of life and liberty *entailed* a natural right to property. Locke's baton passed not to the American

Revolutionaries of 1776, but rather to the French Revolutionaries of 1789. Jefferson rejected, whereas Sieyès and his colleagues accepted, that there was an inalienable, natural right to property. In each case both politics and philosophy influenced the decision. With regard to philosophy, the formative influence of the long-evolving tradition of Natural Law Theory should not be discounted. There is a case for saying that historians of the American and French Revolutions make too much of their modernity and too little of their early modernity.

My last words go to Proudhon, like Rousseau an autodidact who authored a book that sent shock waves through the establishment – and through Proudhon to the 'forgotten men' of the ancient world, the emperor Justinian and his jurists. Proudhon saw that the argument over first acquisition was going nowhere and that there could be no resolution. He also noted in passing that the definition of property in the French Civil Code was from Roman law. Justinian and the team of codifying jurists are the 'forgotten men' in the sense that no modern political or legal philosopher is likely to include them in their book about property theory. This is because they are of the opinion that the Romans had no property theory. I am in two minds as to whether Justinian (and company) were villains or heroes: villains because they threw away a huge quantity of juristic material from the classical Roman period in the process of producing the centrepiece of their codification project, the *Digest*; heroes because in the *Digest* Justinian and his team created the most important law book in the history of Western Europe. If the process of compilation of that work is taken into consideration, if certain key texts in the *Digest* are read accurately, and if supporting material is brought into play from other Roman literature and from epigraphy, then the case for the Romans having had the concept of a property right becomes compelling. It becomes clear that the Romans created over time a system of legal rights, including the right to property, which were held to accrue to their citizens and were available to be exercised within the framework of the Roman civil law. As for the *Digest* and the other works that made up Justinian's *Corpus* of Civil Law, the medieval jurists who descended on these books as a treasure trove once they had been rediscovered in the late eleventh century knew how to winkle out of the texts the raw material of a concept of property (and also how to twist the texts to fit their own local legal systems). Bartolus' definition of property, derived from Justinian's texts, passed through many hands before it reached the jurists who framed the *Code Napoléon*. It would not have occurred to jurists working in the Romanist tradition from the twelfth to the early nineteenth century, to

Accursius and Bartolus, Donellus and Grotius, Pothier and Portalis, that the classical Roman lawyers who constructed a highly complex and sophisticated system of property law lacked the concept of property or the idea of a right to property. If I have done something to encourage a reconsideration of the contribution of Roman law to Rights Theory, then this enterprise will have been worthwhile.

Bibliography

EDITIONS OF TEXTS

Abelard, Peter, *Opera Theologica II: Theologia Christiana*, ed. E. M. Buytaert, *Corp. Chr. Con. Med.* 12, Turnhout 1969.

Adams, John, *Works*, ed. C. F. Adams, Boston 1851–6.

Alcinous, *Enseignement des doctrines de Platon (Didaskalikos)*, ed. J. Whittaker, French trans. P. Louis, Paris 1990; Engl. trans. J. Dillon, Oxford 1993.

Ambrose, *De Fuga Saeculi*, ed. G. Banterle, *Sant' Ambroglio: Opere Esegetiche* IV: *La Fuga dal Mondo*. Latin and Italian. Milan and Rome 1980.

De Officiis, ed. I. J. Davidson, 2 vols. Oxford 2001.

Hexaemeron, ed. G. Banterle, *Sant' Ambriglio: Opere Esegetiche* I: *I sei giorni della creazione*. Latin and Italian. Milan and Rome 1979.

Anonymus, *Prolégomènes à la philosophie de Platon*, ed. L. Westerink, French trans. J. Trouillard and A. Segonds, Paris 1990; ed. and Engl. trans. L. Westerink, Amsterdam 1962.

Anonymus, *[Tractatus] De Divitiis (On Wealth)*, PL Suppl. **1**, 1380–1418.

Aquinas, Thomas, *In Libros Politicorum Aristotelis Expositio*, ed. R. M. Spiazzi, Turin 1951.

Opuscula Philosophica, ed. R. M. Spiazzi, Turin 1954.

Summa Theologiae. Latin and English, ed. T. Gilby, 61 vols. London 1964–81.

Political Writings, ed. and Engl. trans. R. W. Dyson, Cambridge 2002.

Aratus, *Phaenomena*, ed. D. Kidd, Cambridge 1997.

Archives Parlementaires de 1787 à 1860. Recueil Complet des débats législatifs et politiques des chambres françaises, ed. J. Mavidal, E. Laurent and E. Clavel; *première série (1789 à 1799), vol. VIII: du 5 mai 1789 au 15 septembre 1783.* Paris 1873.

Aristotle, *Politics. Books I and II*, ed. & Engl. trans. T. J. Saunders, Oxford 1995. *The Politics and the Constitution of Athens*, Engl. trans. S. Everson, Cambridge 1996.

Augustine, *Confessions*, ed. J. J. O'Donnell, Oxford 1992.

De Opere Monachorum, ed. J. Saint-Martin, *Oeuvres de Saint Augustin 3: L'ascéticisme Chrétien*. Paris, 1949.

Enarratio in Psalmos vol. 3, ed. E. Dekkers and J. Fraipont, *Corpus Christianorum Series Latina* **40**. Brepols, 1956.

Augustine, *Epistulae*, pars III *CSEL* 44, ed. Al. Goldbacher. Vienna/Leipzig, 1904.
In Iohannis Evangelium Tractatus XXXIV, ed. R. Willems, *Corpus Christianorum Series Latina 31*. Brepols, 1954.
Letters, vol. III, Engl. transl. W. Parsons. New York, 1953.
The Lord's Sermon on the Mount (De Sermone Domini in Monte). Engl. transl. D. J. Kavanagh, *The Fathers of the Church* 11. Washington, DC, 1951.
Sermones Selecti Duodeviginti, ed. C. Lambot. Utrecht 1950.
Sermones III/10 (341–400) On Various Subjects. The Works of S. Augustine, A Translation for the 21st Century, trans. E. Hill. New York 1994.
Averroes, *On Plato's Republic*, ed. & Engl. trans. E. I. J. Rosenthal, Cambridge 1956; ed. & Engl. trans. R. Lerner, Ithaca and London 1974.
Bartolus of Sassoferrato, *Bartoli Interpretum Iuris Civilis Coryphaei, In Ius Universum Civile, Commentaria*, ed. J. Concenatius, Basel 1562.
Basil of Caesarea, *The Ascetic Works of Saint Basil*. Engl. trans. W. K. L. Clarke. London 1925.
Bede, *Historia Ecclesiastica Gentis Anglorum*, ed. B. Colgrave and R. A. B. Mynors. Oxford, 1969.
Vita Sancti Cuthberti, ed. B. Colgrave, *The Lives of Saint Cuthbert*. Cambridge, 1940.
Benedict, *Rule*, ed./transl. T. Fry *et al*. Collegeville, 1981.
Bernard of Chartres, *Glosae super Platonem*, ed. P. E. Dutton, Toronto 1991.
Bernard of Clairvaux, *Letters*, transl. B. S. James. Chicago, 1953.
Bessarion, *In Calumniatorem Platonis, Libri IV*, ed. L. Mohler, Paderborn 1927.
Letters. Aus Bessarions Gelehrtenkreis: Abhandlungen, Reden, Briefen von Bessarion et al., ed. L. Mohler, Paderborn 1942.
Bonagratia of Bergamo, *Tractatus de Paupertate Christi et Apostolorum*, ed. L. Oliger, *Archivum Franciscanum Historicum* 22 (1929): 292–335 and 487–511.
Bonaventura, *In Apologia Pauperum*, in *Opera Omnia* vols. VII–VIII, Quaracchi 1889.
Burlamaqui, Jean-Jacques, *The Principles of Natural Law and Political Law*, trans. T. Nugent, 2nd ed. London 1763. (Reprint of 5th ed., corrected, of 1807, as *The Principles of Natural and Politic Law*. 2 vols. New York, 1972).
Cassian, John, *Collationes Patrum*, ed./transl. E. Pickery, *Conférences. SC* 42, 54, 64, Paris, 1955–9.
De Institutionibus Coenobiorum, ed./transl. J.-CI. Guy, *Institutions Cénobitiques. SC* 109. Paris, 1965.
Cicero, *On Duties*, ed. and Engl. trans. M. T. Griffin and E. M. Atkins, Cambridge 1991.
Clareno, Angelo, *Liber Chronicarum sive Historiae septem tribulationum ordinis minorum*, ed. G. Rossini, Rome 1999.
Clement of Alexandria, *Quis Dives Salvetur? (Who is the Rich Man Who Can Be Saved?)* vol. 3, *GCS*, ed. O. Stählin. Leipzig, 1909.
Codex Theodosianus: Theodosiani Libri XVI cum Constitutionibus Sirmondianis et Leges Novellae ad Theodosianum Pertinentes, eds. T. Mommsen, P. M. Meyer and P. Krueger, 2 vols. Berlin 1905.

Consultationes Zacchei Christiani et Apollonii Philosophi, ed. & French trans. J. L. Feiertag and W. Steinmann, *SC* 401–2, Paris 1994.

Corpus Glossatorum Iuris Civilis, Univ. di Torino, Centro di Studi di Storia del Diritto Italiano, 11 vols. Turin 1966–73.

Corpus Iuris Canonici, ed. E. Friedberg, 2 vols. Leipzig, 1879–81.

Corpus Iuris Civilis, eds. T. Mommsen and P. Krueger, 2 vols. Berlin 1959.

Donellus, Hugo, *De Iure Civili*, 12 vols. Florence 1840.

Extravagantes Iohannis XXII, ed. J. Tarrant. Vatican City 1983.

Ferguson, Adam, *Essay on the History of Civil Society*. Edinburgh, 1767.

Ficino, Marsilio, *Divini Platonis Opera Omnia*, Venice 1581.

    Platonic Theology, vol. 1, ed. and Engl. trans. M. J. B. Allen and J. Hankins, Cambridge, Mass. 2001.

Filmer, Robert, *Patriarcha and Other Writings*, ed. J. P. Sommerville, Cambridge 1991.

Fontes Iuris Romani Antejustiniani, ed. S. Riccobono *et al.*, 3 vols. Florence 1941–3.

Francis of Assisi, *Early Documents*, ed. R. J. Armstrong, J. A. W. Hillman and W. J. Short, 3 vols. New York, London and Manila 2001.

Frontinus, Sextus Iulius, *De Aquaeductibus Urbis Romae*, ed. P. Grimal, *Les aqueducs de la ville de Rome*. Latin and French. Paris 1944.

Gaius, *Institutes*, in ed. F. de Zulueta, *The Institutes of Gaius*, 2 vols. Oxford 1946.

Garnier, Germain, Marquis, *De la propriété considérée dans ses rapports avec le droit politique*, Paris 1792.

Germanicus, *Aratus*, ed. D. B. Gain, London 1976.

Gerson, Jean, *Oeuvres complètes*, Paris 1960–73.

Godfrey of Fontaines, *Le Huitième Quodlibet*, ed. J. Hoffmanns, *Les Philosophes Belges, Textes et Etudes*, vol. 4. Louvain 1924.

Grotius, Hugo, *De Iure Praedae Commentarius*, ed. H. G. Hanaker, The Hague 1868; Engl. trans. G. Williams and W. H. Zeydel, Oxford 1950.

    De Iure Belli ac Pacis. Libri Tres, reproduction of the edition of 1646, Washington, DC 1913; *On the Law of War and Peace*, Engl. transl. F. W. Kelsey *et al.* Oxford 1925.

    The Jurisprudence of Holland (1620), trans. R. W. Lee, Oxford 1926.

Guyot, Pierre-Jean-Jacques-Guillaume, *Répertoire universel et raisonné de jurisprudence civile, criminelle, canonique et bénéficiale*, Paris 1775–83.

Harrington, James, *The Commonwealth of Oceana; and A System of Politics*, ed. J. G. A. Pocock, Cambridge 1992.

Hegel, Georg Wilhelm Friedrich, *Elements of the Philosophy of Right*, ed. A. W. Wood, Engl. transl. H. B. Nisbet, Cambridge 1991.

    Political Writings, ed. L. Dickey and H. B. Nisbet. Cambridge 1999.

Hervaeus Natalis, *De Paupertate Christi et Apostolorum*, ed. J. G. Sikes, *Archives d'histoire doctrinale et littéraire du moyen âge*, 2/13 (1937–8): 209–97; Engl. trans. J. D. Jones, Toronto 1999.

Hesiod, *Works and Days*, ed. M. L. West, Oxford 1978.

Hobbes, Thomas, *On the Citizen*, ed. R. Tuck and M. Silverthorne, Cambridge 1998.

    Leviathan, ed. R. Tuck, Cambridge 1991.

Hume, David, *Enquiries Concerning Human Understanding and Concerning the Principles of Morals*, ed. L. A. Selby-Bigge, 3rd edn. revised by P. H. Nidditch, Oxford 1975.

Political Essays, ed. K. Haakonssen, Cambridge 1994.

A Treatise of Human Nature, ed. L. A. Selby-Bigge, 2nd edn. revised by P. H. Nidditch, Oxford 1978.

Hutcheson, Francis, *A Short Introduction to Moral Philosophy*, London 1747.

Iamblichus, *De Vita Pythagorica Liber*, ed. L. Deubner, Leipzig, 1937; Engl. trans. G. Clark, Liverpool 1989; ed. and Engl. trans. J. Dillon and J. Hershbell, Atlanta 1991.

Ibn at-Tayyib, *Proclus' Commentary on the Pythagorean Golden Verses*, ed. and Engl. trans. N. Linley, Buffalo 1984.

Jefferson, Thomas, *The Papers*, ed. J. P. Boyd *et al*. Princeton 1950–.

Works, 12 vols. ed. P. L. Ford, New York 1904–5.

Jerome, *De Viris Inlustribus Liber*, ed. G. Herdingius, Leipzig 1879.

Joachim of Fiore, *Il libro delle figure dell'abate Gioachino da Fiore*, eds. L. Tondelli, M. Reeves and B. Hirsch-Reich, Turin 1953.

John of Paris, *De Potestate Regia et Papali*, ed. F. Bleienstein. Latin and German. Stuttgart 1969.

On Royal and Papal Power, Engl trans. J. A. Watt. Toronto 1971.

John of Salisbury, *Letters, vol. 1: The Early Letters (1153–71)*. ed. W. J. Millor and H. E. Butler, rev. C. N. L. Brooke. Oxford, 1955.

Kant, Immanuel, *Grounding for the Metaphysics of Morals*, Engl. trans. J. W. Ellington, 3rd edn., Indianapolis and Cambridge 1993.

The Metaphysics of Morals, ed. M. Gregor, introduction by R. J. Sullivan, Cambridge 1996.

Political Writings, ed. H. Reiss, Engl. trans. H. B. Nisbet, 2nd edn. Cambridge 1991.

Lactantius, *Divine Institutes*, ed. and Engl. trans. A. Bowen and P. Garnsey, Liverpool 2003.

Opera Omnia, ed. S. Brandt and G. Laubmann, *CSEL* 19 and 27, Prague, Vienna and Leipzig 1890–3.

Institutions divines: Livre V, 2 vols. ed. and French trans. P. Monat, *SC* 204–5, Paris 1973.

Liber Graduum, ed. M. Kmosko, *Patrologia Syriaca* 3, Paris 1926.

Lincoln, Abraham, *The Collected Works*, ed. R. P. Basler, 9 vols. New Brunswick, N.J., 1953–5.

Locke, John, *Second Treatise of Government*, ed. C. B. McPherson, Indianapolis 1980.

Two Treatises of Government, ed. P. Laslett, Cambridge 1967.

Lucretius, *De Rerum Natura Book Five Lines 772–1104*, ed. G. Campbell, Oxford 2003.

Marx, Karl, *Pre-Capitalist Economic Formations*, ed. E. Hobsbawm, London 1964.

Marx, Karl and Engels, Friedrich, *The Communist Manifesto*, ed. G. Stedman Jones, London 2002.

Mill, John Stuart, *Principles of Political Economy: With Some of their Applications to Social Philosophy*, in *Collected Works of John Stuart Mill*, ed. J. M. Robson, Toronto 1965.

Mommsen, Theodor, *Die Grundrechte des deutschen Volkes*, Leipzig and Frankfurt 1969.

Olivi, Petrus Ioannis, *Das Heil der Armen und das Verderben der Reichen*, ed. J. Schlageter, *Franziskanische Forschungen* 34, Werl/Westfalen 1989.

    De Usu Paupere: The Quaestio and the Tractatus, ed. D. Burr, Firenze, Olschki, Perth 1992.

    Lectura super Actus Apostolorum (On the Acts of the Apostles), ed. D. Flood. New York, 2001.

    On Poor Use, transl. D. Burr. Retrieved 25 February 2007 from www.history. vt.edu/Burr/heresy/beguins/olivi/Olivi_Usus.html.

Origen, *Contra Celsum*. Greek and French, M. Borret, *SC* 5 vols. 132, 136, 147, 150, 227, Paris 1967–76; Engl. trans. H. Chadwick, corr. ed. Cambridge 1965.

Pachomius, *Life of Pachomius and his Disciples*, trans. A. Veilleux, vol. 1, Kalamazoo 1980.

Pecham, John, *Tractatus Tres de Paupertate*, eds. C. L. Kingsford, A. G. Little and F. Tocco, Aberdeen 1910.

Plato, *The Republic*, ed. G. R. F. Ferrari, Engl. trans. T. Griffith, Cambridge 2000.

    Statesman, Engl. trans. J. Annas and R. Waterfield, Cambridge 1995; ed. and Engl. trans. C. Rowe, Indianapolis 1999.

    Timaeus a Calcidio Translatus Commentarioque Instructus, ed. J. H. Waszink, *Plato Latinus IV*, London and Leiden 1962.

Plethon, G. Gemistus *Ad Principem Theodorum de Rebus Peloponnesiacis*, *PG* 160, 841–56.

    Ad Regem Emmanuelem de Rebus Peloponnesiacis, *PG* 160, 821–40.

    Nomôn Syngraphê (*Traité des Lois*), ed. C. Alexandre, Paris 1858 (reprinted Amsterdam 1966).

Porphyry, *De L'Abstinentia*, ed. and French trans. J. Bouffartigue, Paris 1977; *On Abstinence*, ed. and Engl. trans. G. Clark, London 2000.

    De Vita Plotini et Ordine Librorum eius, ed. L. Brisson, Paris 1982–92.

    Vie de Pythagore; Lettre à Marcella, ed. and French trans. E. des Places, Paris 1982.

Portalis, Etienne-Frédéric-Auguste, *Discours, rapports et travaux inédits sur le Code Civil*, Paris 1844.

Pothier, Robert-Joseph, *Traité du droit de domaine de propriété*, Paris 1772.

Proclus, *In Platonis Rempublicam Commentarii*, ed. W. Kroll, Leipzig 1899–1901 (reprinted Amsterdam 1965); ed. and French trans. A. J. Festugière, Paris 1970.

Proudhon, Pierre-Joseph, *Qu'est-ce que la propriété? Ou recherches sur le principe du droit et du gouvernement*, ed. E. James, Paris 1966; ed. and Engl. trans. D. R. Kelley and B. G. Smith, Cambridge 1994.

Pufendorf, Samuel von, *De Iure Naturae et Gentium Libri Octo*, photographic reproduction of the edition of 1688, ed. J. B. Scott. *On the Law of Nature and of Nations*, Engl. trans. C. H. and W. A. Oldfather, Oxford 1934.

Rerum Novarum: Encyclical Letter of Pope Leo XIII on the Condition of the Working Classes, ed. and Engl. trans. J. Kirwan, London 1983.

Rousseau, Jean-Jacques, *Oeuvres complètes*, eds. B. Gagnebin, M. Raymond *et al.* Paris 1959.

The Discourses and Other Early Political Writings, ed. and Engl. trans. V. Gourevitch, Cambridge 1997.

The Social Contract and Other Later Political Writings, ed. and Engl. trans. V. Gourevitch, Cambridge 1997.

Rutherforth, Thomas, *Institutes of Natural Law; Being the Substance of a Course of Lectures on Grotius' De Iure Belli et Pacis*, 2 vols. Cambridge 1754–6.

Scholarius, G. Gennadius, *Epistula ad Josephum Exarchum*, PG 160, 631–48.

Suarez, Francisco, *Tractatus de Legibus ac Deo Legislatore*, eds. L. Pereña *et al.* 8 vols. Madrid 1971.

The Summa Parisiensis on the Decretum Gratiani, ed. T. P. McLaughlin, Toronto 1952.

Virgil, *Eclogues*, ed. W. Clausen, Oxford 1994.

Vitoria, Francisco de, *Commentarios a la Secunda Secundae de Santo Tomás*, 6 vols., ed. V. Beltrán de Heredia, Salamanca.

De Indis et de Iure Belli Reflectiones, ed. E. Nys, Washington 1917.

William of Conches, *Glosae super Platonem*, ed. E. Jeauneau, Paris 1965.

William of Ockham, *'A Letter to the Friars Minor' and Other Writings*, ed. and Engl. trans. A. S. McGrade and J. Kilcullen, Cambridge 1995.

Opus Nonaginta Dierum, in *Guillelmi de Ockham Opera Politica* vols. 1–2, eds. H. S. Offler and J. G. Sikes, Manchester 1963–74.

Wilson, James, *Works*, ed. R. G. McCloskey, 2 vols. Cambridge, Mass. 1967.

Zasius, Ulrich, *Operum Tomus Tertius Commentaria seu Lecturas eiusdem in Titulos Tertiae Partis Pandectarum (quod vulgo Digestum novum vocant) Complectens*, Lyon 1550 (repr. ed. J. U. Zasius and J. Münsinger von Frundeck. Aalen 1964–6).

SECONDARY LITERATURE

Abbate, M. (1999) 'Gli aspetti etico-politici della Repubblica nel commento di Proclo (Dissertazioni VII/VIII e XI)', in Vegetti and Abbate (1999): 207–18.

Adams, R. M. (ed.) (1992) *Sir Thomas More: Utopia. A Revised Translation; Backgrounds; Criticism*, 2nd edn. New York and London.

Albanese, B. (1949) *La successione ereditaria in diritto romano, Annali del seminario giuridico di Palermo* 20, Palermo.

Angle, S. C. (2000) 'Should we all be more English? Liang Qichao, Rudolf von Jhering, and rights', in *Jl. Hist. Ideas* **61**(2): 241–61.

Annas, J. (1989) 'Cicero on Stoic moral philosophy and private property', in *Philosophia Togata: Essays on Philosophy and Roman Society*, eds. M. Griffin and J. Barnes, Oxford: 151–73.

Arnaud, A.-J. (1973) *Essai d'analyse structurale du code civil français*, Paris.

Athanassiadi, P. (2002) 'Byzantine commentators on the *Chaldaean Oracles*: Psellos and Plethon', in Ierodiakonou (2002): 237–52.

Atkins, E. M. (2000) 'Cicero', in Rowe and Schofield (2000): 477–516.

Aubert, J.-M. (1955) *Le droit romain dans l'oeuvre de saint Thomas*, Paris.

Baker, K. M. (1990) *Inventing the French Revolution: Essays on French Political Culture in the Eighteenth Century*, Cambridge.

Baldry, H. C. (1952) 'Who invented the Golden Age?', *CQ* **2**: 83–92.

Baloglou, Ch. (2001) *Plethôneia Oikonomika Meletemata*, Athens.

Barker, E. (1957) *Social and Political Thought in Byzantium: From Justinian I to the Last Palaeologus; Passages from Byzantine Writers and Documents*, Oxford.

Barnes, T. D. (1981) *Constantine and Eusebius*, Cambridge, Mass.

Bassani, L. M. (2004) 'Life, liberty and . . . : Jefferson on property rights', *Jl. Libertarian Studies* **18**: 31–87.

Bastid, P. (1939) *Sieyès et sa pensée*, Paris.

Becker, C. (1922) *The Declaration of Independence: A Study in the History of Political Ideas*, New York.

Behrends, O. *et al.* (1978) *Festschrift für Franz Wieacker*, Göttingen.

Benson, R. L. (1982) 'Consciousness of self and perceptions of individuality', in *Renaissance and Renewal in the Twelfth Century*, eds. R. L. Benson and G. Constable, Oxford: 263–95.

Berger, A. (1953) *Encyclopaedic Dictionary of Roman Law*, Philadelphia.

Bertram, C. (2004) *Rousseau and the Social Contract*, London and New York.

Betti, E. (1953) 'Falsa impostazione della questione storica, dipendente da erronea diagnosi giuridica', in *Studi Arangio-Ruiz* **4**: 83–9.

Betz, O. (1999) 'The Essenes', in *Cambridge History of Judaism* vol. 3, eds. W. Horbury, W. D. Davies and J. Sturdy, Cambridge: 440–70.

Birks, P. (1985) 'The Roman law concept of *dominium* and the idea of absolute ownership', *Acta Juridica* (1985): 1–37.

  (ed.) (1989) *New Perspectives in the Roman Law of Property: Essays for Barry Nicholas*, Oxford.

Blum, W. (1988) *Georgios Gemistos Plethon: Politik, Philosophie und Rhetorik im spätbyzantinischen Reich (1355–1452)*, Stuttgart.

Blundell, S. (1986) *The Origins of Civilization in Greek and Roman Thought*, London.

Bobbio, N. (1996) *The Age of Rights*, trans. A. Cameron, Cambridge.

Bobonich, C. (2002) *Plato's Utopia Recast: His Later Ethics and Politics*, Oxford.

Bock, G., Skinner, Q. and Viroli, M. (eds.) (1990) *Machiavelli and Republicanism*, Cambridge.

Bori, P. C. (1974) *Chiesa primitiva: L'immagine della comunità delle origini – Atti, 3,42–47; 4,32–37 – nella storia della chiesa antica*, Brescia.

Bornemann, E. (1923–4) 'Aristoteles' Urteil über Platons politische Theorie', *Philologus* **79**: 70–158, 234–56.

Boyancé, P. (1937) *Le culte des muses chez les philosophes grecs: études d'histoire et de psychologie religieuses*, Paris.

Boys-Stones, G. R. (2001) *Post-Hellenistic Philosophy: A Study of its Development from the Stoics to Origen*, Oxford.

Bredin, J. D. (1988) *Sieyès: la clé de la révolution française*, Paris.

Bretone, M. (1999) *I fondamenti del diritto romano: le cose e la natura*, Bari.

Brett, A. S. (1997) *Liberty, Right and Nature: Individual Rights in Later Scholastic Thought*, Cambridge.

   (2003) 'The development of the idea of citizens' rights', in *States and Citizens: History, Theory, Prospects*, eds. Q. Skinner and B. Strath, Cambridge: 97–114.

Brito, G. (2003) 'Historia de la denominacion del derecho-faculdad como subjectivo', *Revista de Estudios Historico-Juridicos* **25**: 407–43.

Brooke, C. N. L. (1984) 'John of Salisbury and his world', in ed. M. Wilks, *The World of John of Salisbury*, Oxford: 1–20.

Brown, L. (1998) 'How totalitarian is Plato's *Republic*?', in *Essays on Plato's Republic*, ed. E. N. Ostenfeld, Aarhus: 13–27.

Brown, P. (1972) *Religion and Society in the Age of St Augustine*, London.

   (2002) *Poverty and Leadership in the Later Roman Empire*, Hanover, N.H.

Brundage, J. A. (1995) *Medieval Canon Law*, London and New York.

Brunt, P. A. (1993) 'The model city in Plato's *Laws*', in *Studies in Greek History and Thought*, Oxford: 245–81.

Buckland, W. W. (1963) *A Text-Book of Roman Law from Augustus to Justinian*, 3rd edn. ed. P. Stein, Cambridge.

Buckle, S. (1991) *Natural Law and the Theory of Property: Grotius to Hume*, Oxford.

Burkert, W. (1972) *Lore and Science in Ancient Pythagoreanism*, trans. E. L. Minar, Cambridge, Mass.

   (1982) 'Craft versus sect: The problem of Orphics and Pythagoreans', in *Jewish and Christian Self-Definition*, eds. E. P. Sanders *et al.* Philadelphia: 1–22.

Burnett, C. (1999) 'The "sons of Averroes with the emperor Frederick" and the transmission of the philosophical works by Ibn Rushd', in Endress and Aertsen (1999): 259–76.

Burnyeat, M. F. (1994) 'Did the ancient Greeks have the concept of human rights?', *Polis* **13**: 1–11.

   (1998) 'The past in the present: Plato as educator of nineteenth-century Britain', in *Philosophers on Education: Historical Perspectives*, ed. A. O. Rorty, London and New York: 353–73.

   (1999) 'Utopia and fantasy: The practicability of Plato's ideally just city', in *Plato 2: Ethics, Politics, Religion and the Soul*, ed. G. Fine, Oxford: 297–308.

   (2000) 'Plato on why mathematics is good for the soul', in *Mathematics and Necessity: Essays in the History of Philosophy*, ed. T. J. Smiley, Oxford: 1–82.

Burr, D. (1989) *Olivi and Franciscan Poverty: The Origins of the Usus Pauper Controversy*, Philadelphia.

   (1993) *Olivi's Peaceable Kingdom: A Reading of the Apocalypse Commentary*, Philadelphia.

   (2001) *The Spiritual Franciscans: From Protest to Persecution in the Century After Saint Francis*, University Park, Pennsylvania.

Butterworth, C. E. (1975) 'New light on the political philosophy of Averroes', in Hourani (1975b): 118–27.

(1985) 'Ethics and classical Islamic philosophy: A study of Averroes' *Commentary on Plato's Republic*', in *Ethics in Islam*, ed. R. G. Havannisian, Malibu, Calif.: 17–45.

Buzzacchi, C. (2002) *L'abuso del processo nel diritto romano*, Bari.

Caner, D. (2002) *Wandering, Begging Monks: Spiritual Authority and the Promotion of Monasticism in Late Antiquity*, Berkeley.

Canning, J. (1987) *The Political Thought of Baldus de Ubaldis*, Cambridge.

Capogrossi Colognesi, L. (1969) *La struttura della proprietà e la formazione dei "iura praediorum" nell' età repubblicana*, Milan.

(1999) *Proprietà e diritti reali: Usi e tutela della proprietà fondiaria nel diritto romano*, Rome.

(2000) *Cittadini e territorio: Consolidamento e trasformazione della 'civitas Romana'*, Rome.

(2002) *Persistenza e innovazione nelle strutture territoriali dell'Italia Romana: L'ambiguità di una interpretazione storiografica e dei suoi modelli*, Naples.

Capper, B. J. (1995a) 'Community of goods in the early Jerusalem Church', in *ANRW II* XXVI.2: 1730–74.

(1995b) 'The Palestinian cultural context of earliest Christian community of goods', in *The Book of Acts in its First Century Setting vol. 4: The Book of Acts in its Palestinian Setting*, ed. R. Bauckham, Grand Rapids, Mich.: 323–56.

(1998) 'With the oldest monks . . . : Light from Essene history on the career of the beloved disciple?', *JTS* **49**: 1–55.

(2001) 'Two types of discipleship in early Christianity: Review article of K.-J. Kim, *Stewardship and Almsgiving in Luke's Theology*', *JTS* **52**: 105–23.

(2002) 'The Church as the new covenant of effective economics: The social origins of mutually supportive Christian community', *Int. Jl. St. Chr. Ch.* **2**: 83–102.

Carlyle, R. W. and Carlyle, A. (1950) *A History of Medieval Political Theory in the West*, Edinburgh and London.

Chadwick, H. (1966) *Early Christian Thought and the Classical Tradition: Studies in Justin, Clement and Origen*, Oxford.

(1976) *Priscillian of Avila: The Occult and the Charismatic in the Early Church*, Oxford.

Chadwick, O. (1968) *John Cassian*, 2nd edn. Cambridge.

(1998) *A History of the Popes 1830–1914*, Oxford.

Chinard, G. (ed.) (1926) *The Commonplace Book of Thomas Jefferson: A Repertory of his Ideas on Government*, Baltimore.

Chodorow, S. (1972) *Christian Political Theory and Church Politics in the Mid-Twelfth Century: The Ecclesiology of Gratian's Decretum*, Berkeley and London.

Clark, E. A. (1999) *Reading Renunciation: Asceticism and Scripture in Early Christianity*, Princeton.

Clark, G. (2000) 'Philosophic lives and the philosophic life: Porphyry and Iamblichus', in *Greek Biography and Panegyric in Late Antiquity*, eds. T. Hägg and Ph. Rousseau, Berkeley, Los Angeles and London: 29–51.

Clarke, A. and Kohler, P. (2005) *Property Law: Commentary and Materials*, Cambridge.

Coffinières, A. S. G. (1805) *Analyse des nouvelles de Justinien conferées avec l'ancien droit français et le code napoléon*, Paris.

Cohen, G. A. (1995) *Self-Ownership, Freedom and Equality*, Oxford.

Cohn, N. (1957) *The Pursuit of the Millennium*, London.

Coing, H. (1953) 'Zur Eigentumslehre des Bartolus', *ZSS* **70**: 349–71.

(1959) 'Zur Geschichte des Begriffs *subjektives Recht*', in *Das subjektive Recht und der Rechtsschutz der Persönlichkeit*, eds. H. Coing, F. H. Lawson and K. Gronfors, Frankfurt: 7–23.

Cole, T. (1967) *Democritus and the Sources of Greek Anthropology*, Cleveland, Ohio.

Coleman, J. (1988) 'Property and poverty', in *The Cambridge History of Medieval Political Thought*, ed. J. H. Burns, Cambridge: 607–49.

(1996) 'The individual and the medieval state', in *The Individual in Political Theory and Practice*, Oxford: 1–34.

(2000) *A History of Political Thought from the Middle Ages to the Renaissance*, Oxford.

(2006a) 'Pre-modern property and self-ownership before and after Locke', *Eur. Jl. Pol. Theory* **4**: 125–45.

(2006b) 'Are there any individual rights or any duties?', in Mäkinen and Korkman (2006): 3–36.

Colish, M. L. (1990) *The Stoic Tradition from Antiquity to the Early Middle Ages vol. 2: Stoicism in Christian Latin Thought through the Sixth Century*, Leiden.

Congar, Y. M.-J. (1961–2) 'Aspects ecclésiologiques de la querelle entre mendiants et séculiers dans la seconde moitié de XIIIe siècle et le début de XIVe siècle', *Archives d'histoire doctrinale et littéraire du moyen âge* 36: 35–151.

Constable, G. (1995) *Three Studies in Medieval Religious and Social Thought*, Cambridge.

Countryman, L. W. (1980) *The Rich Christian in the Church of the Early Empire: Contradictions and Accommodations*, New York and Toronto.

Courtonne, Y. (ed.) (1935) *Sainte Basile: homélies sur la richesse*, Paris.

Couvreur, G. (1961) *Les pauvres: ont-ils des droits?*, Paris.

Cox, P. (1983) *Biography in Late Antiquity: A Quest for the Holy Man*, Berkeley.

Crawford, M. H. (ed.) (1996) *Roman Statutes*, 2 vols. London.

Crone, P. (1991) 'Kavad's Heresy and Mazdak's Revolt', *Iran* **29**: 21–42.

(1994) 'Zoroastrian Communism', *Comp. Stud. Soc. Hist.* **36**: 447–62.

(2004) *Medieval Islamic Political Thought*, Edinburgh.

Crook, J. A. (1967) *Law and Life of Rome*, London.

Curran, J. R. (2002) *Pagan City and Christian Capital*, Oxford.

Cusato, M. F. (2002) 'Whence "the Community"?', *Franciscan Studies* **60**: 39–92.

Dagger, R. (1988) 'Rights', in *Political Innovation and Conceptual Change*, eds. T. Ball, J. Farr and R. L. Hanson, Cambridge: 292–308.

Daube, D. (1991a) 'Doves and bees', in *David Daube: Collected Studies in Roman Law* vol. 2, eds. D. Cohen and D. Simon, Frankfurt: 899–914.

(1991b) 'The self-understood in legal history', in *David Daube: Collected Studies in Roman Law* eds. D. Cohen and D. Simon, Frankfurt: 1277–85.

Davis, D. B. (1966) *The Problem of Slavery in Western Culture*, Cornell.

Dawson, D. (1988) 'Primitive Church, concept of', in *Dictionary of the Middle Ages*, ed. J. R. Strayer, vol. 10, New York: 121–3.

(1992a) *Cities of the Gods: Communist Utopias in Greek Thought*, Oxford.

(1992b) *Allegorical Readers and Cultural Revision in Ancient Alexandria*, Berkeley and Oxford.

Derrett, J. D. M. (1965) 'Plethon, the Essenes and More's *Utopia*', *Bibl. d'Hum. et de Renaiss.* **27**: 579–603.

(1971) 'Ananias, Sapphira, and the right of property', *Downside Review* **89**: 225–32.

De Ste. Croix, G. E. M. (1975) 'Early Christian attitudes to property and slavery', in *Church, Society and Politics*, ed. D. Baker, Oxford: 1–38.

De Vogel, C. J. (1966) *Pythagoras and Early Pythagoreanism: An Interpretation of Neglected Evidence on the Philosopher Pythagoras*, Assen.

Dillon, J. (1977) *The Middle Platonists*, London.

(1997) 'Plato and the Golden Age', in *The Great Tradition: Further Studies in the Development of Platonism and Early Christianity*, Aldershot, Hampshire, 1997: 21–36.

(2001) 'The Neoplatonic reception of Plato's *Laws*', in Lisi (2001): 243–54.

D'Onorio, J.-B. (2005) *Portalis, l'esprit des siècles*, Paris.

Dunn, J. (1969) *The Political Thought of John Locke: An Historical Account of the Argument of the 'Two Treatises of Government'*, Cambridge.

(1996) *The History of Political Theory and Other Essays*, Cambridge.

DuQuesnay, I. Le M. (1976) 'Virgil's fourth *Eclogue*', in *Papers of the Liverpool Latin Seminar*, ed. F. Cairns, Liverpool: 25–99.

Dutton, P. E. (1983) '*Illustre civitatis et populi exemplum*: Plato's *Timaeus* and the transmission from Calcidius to the end of the twelfth century of a tripartite scheme of society', *Medieval Studies* **45**: 79–119.

Dworkin, R. (1977) *Taking Rights Seriously*, Cambridge, Mass.

Edelstein, L. (1967) *The Idea of Progress in Classical Antiquity*, Baltimore.

Endress, G. (1999) 'Le projet d'Averroes: constitution, réception et édition du corpus des oeuvres d'Ibn Rushd', in Endress and Aertsen (1999): 3–31.

Endress, G. and Aertsen, J. A. (eds.) (1999) *Averroes and the Aristotelian Tradition: Sources, Constitution and Reception of the Philosophy of Ibn Rushd (1126–1198), Proceedings of the Fourth Symposium Averroicum* (Cologne, 1996), Leiden.

Evans, R. F. (1962) 'Pelagius, Fastidius, and the Pseudo-Augustinian *De Vita Christiana*', *JTS* **13**: 72–98.

Fakhry, M. (1983) *A History of Islamic Philosophy*, 2nd edn. London.

Feenstra, R. (1974) 'Les origines du *dominium utile* chez les glossateurs', in *Fata Iuris Romani*, Leiden: 215–59.

(1978) 'Der Eigentumsbegriff bei Hugo Grotius im Licht einiger mittelalterlicher und spätscholastischer Quellen', in Behrends *et al.* (1978): 209–34.

(1989) '*Dominium* and *ius in re aliena*: The origins of a civil law distinction', in Birks (1989): 111–22.

Ferlito, S. (2003) *Diritto soggettivo e libertà religiosa: Riflessioni per uno studio storico e concettuale*, Naples.

Ferry, L. and Renaut, A. (1984) *Philosophie politique 3: des droits de l'homme à l'idée républicaine*, Paris.

Festugière, A. J. (1937) 'Sur une nouvelle édition du *De Vita Pythagorica* de Jamblique', *REG* **50**: 470–94.

Finn, R. (2006) *Almsgiving in the Later Roman Empire: Christian Promotion and Practice: 313–450*, Oxford.

Finnis, J. (1980) *Natural Law and Natural Rights*, Oxford.

(1998) *Aquinas: Moral, Political and Legal Theory*, Oxford.

Flood, D. (2004) Review of Nold (2003), *Franciscan Studies* **62**: 225–35.

Forbes, D. (1975) *Hume's Philosophical Politics*, Cambridge.

Fortenbaugh, W. W. and Schütrumpf, E. (2002) *Dicaearchus of Messana: Text, Translation and Discussion*, New Brunswick and London 2002.

Frede, M. (forthcoming) 'A notion of a person in Epictetus', in *The Philosophy of Epictetus*, eds. T. Scaltsas and A. S. Mason, Oxford.

Fubini, R. (1966) 'Tra umanesimo e concilio', *Studi Medievali* ser. **3**, 7: 322–70.

Furley, D. (1989) *Cosmic Problems*, Cambridge.

Gagnebin, B. (1944) *Burlamaqui et le droit naturel*, Geneva.

Ganz, D. (1995) 'The ideology of sharing: Apostolic community and ecclesiastical property in the early middle ages', in *Property and Power in the Middle Ages*, eds. W. Davies and P. Fouracre, Cambridge: 17–30.

Garnsey, P. (1996) *Ideas of Slavery from Aristotle to Augustine*, Cambridge.

(2005) 'Pythagoras, Plato and communality: A note', *Hermathena* **179**: 77–87.

Garnsey, P. and Humfress, C. (2001) *The Evolution of the Late Antique World*, Cambridge.

Garrison, R. (1993) *Redemptive Almsgiving in Early Christianity*, Sheffield.

Gatz, B. (1967) *Weltalter, goldene Zeit und sinnverwandte Vorstellungen*, Hildesheim.

Gauchet, M. (1988) '*Droits de l'homme*', in *Dictionnaire critique de la Révolution française*, eds. F. Furet and M. Ozouf, Paris: 685–95.

(1989) *La révolution des droits de l'homme*, Paris.

Geltner, G. (2001) 'Eden regained: William of Ockham and the Franciscan return to terrestrial paradise', *Franciscan Studies* **59**: 63–89.

Geuss, R. (2001) *History and Illusion in Politics*, Cambridge.

(2005) *Outside Ethics*, Princeton and Oxford.

Gewirth, A. (1978) *Reason and Morality*, Chicago.

(1982) *Human Rights*, Chicago.

Giannantoni, G. (1986) 'Socrate e i socratici in Diogene Laerzio', *Elenchos* **7**: 185–217.

Giet, S. (1941) *Les idées et l'action sociales de Saint Basile*, Paris.

(1948) 'La doctrine de l'appropriation des biens chez quelques-uns des pères: peut-on parler de communisme?', *Rech. Sc. Rel.* **35**: 35–91.

Giglioni, G. B. (1986) 'Dicearco e la riflessione sul passato', *Riv. Stor. It.* **98**: 629–52.

Goldie, M. (1999) *The Reception of Locke's Politics vol. 6: Wealth, Property and Commerce, 1696–1832*, London.

Gonzales, J. L. (1990) *Faith and Wealth: A History of Early Christian Ideas on the Origin, Significance, and Use of Money*, New York.

Gray, J. (1986) *Liberalism*, Minneapolis.

Grossi, P. (1972) 'Usus facti: La nozione di proprietà nell'inaugurazione dell'età nuova', *Quaderni fiorentini* **1**: 287–355.

(1985) 'Gradus in dominio: Zasius e la teoria del dominio diviso', in *Satura Roberto Feenstra*, eds. J. A. Ankum, J. E. Spruit and F. B. J. Wubbe, Fribourg, Switzerland: 505–22.

(1992) *Il dominio e le cose*, Milan.

Guichard, P. (1977) *Structures sociales 'orientales' et 'occidentales' dans l'Espagne musulmane*, Paris.

Gutas, D. (1988) *Avicenna and the Aristotelian Tradition: Introduction to Reading Avicenna's Philosophical Works*, Leiden.

(1998) *Greek Thought, Arabic Culture: The Graeco–Arabic Translation Movement in Baghdad and Early 'Abbāsid Society (2nd–4th/8th–10th centuries)*, London and New York.

Guyer, P. (2006) *Kant*, London and New York.

Haakonssen, K. (2002) 'The moral conservatism of natural rights', in *Natural Law and Civil Society*, eds. I. Hunter and D. Saunders, Basingstoke, Hampshire and New York: 27–42.

Hamowy, R. (1979) 'Jefferson and the Scottish Enlightenment: A critique of Garry Wills' *Inventing America: Jefferson's Declaration of Independence,*' *The William and Mary Quarterly* **36**: 503–23.

Hankins, J. (1990) *Plato in the Italian Renaissance*, 2 vols. Leiden.

Hanson, R. P. C. (1959) *Allegory and Event: A Study of the Sources and Significance of Origen's Interpretation of Scripture*, London.

Harris, I. (1994) *The Mind of John Locke: A Study of Political Theory in its Intellectual Setting*, Cambridge.

Harris, J. W. (1996) *Property and Justice*, Oxford.

Hart, H. L. A. (1984) 'Are there any natural rights?,' in Waldron (1984): 77–90.

Harvey, R. F. (1937) *J. J. Burlamaqui: A Liberal Tradition in English Constitutionalism*, Chapel Hill, N.C.

Harvey, S. (1999) 'Conspicuous by his absence: Averroes' place today as an interpreter of Aristotle', in Endress and Aertsen (1999): 32–49.

Hines, H. (1995) 'Seneca, Stoicism, and the problem of moral evil', in *Ethics and Rhetoric: Classical Essays for Donald Russell on his Seventy-Fifth Birthday*, eds. D. Innes, H. Hine and C. Pelling, Oxford: 93–106.

Hochstrasser, T. J. (2000) *Natural Law Theories in the Early Enlightenment*, Cambridge.

Hoffmann, D. and Rowe, J. (2006) *Human Rights in the UK: An Introduction to the Human Rights Act 1998*, London.

Hohfeld, W. N. (1913) *Fundamental Legal Conceptions*, New Haven, Conn. and London.

Honoré, T. (2002) *Ulpian: Pioneer of Human Rights*, 2nd edn. Oxford.

Hont, I. (2005a) 'Jealousy of trade: An introduction', in *Jealousy of Trade: International Competition and the Nation-State in Historical Perspective*, Cambridge, Mass. and London: 1–156.

  (2005b) 'The language of sociability and commerce: Samuel Pufendorf and the theoretical foundations of the "four-stages" theory', in *Jealousy of Trade: International Competition and the Nation-State in Historical Perspective*, Cambridge, Mass. and London: 159–84.

Hont, I. and Ignatieff, M. (2005) 'Needs and Justice in the Wealth of Nations', in *Jealousy of Trade: International Competition and the Nation-State in Historical Perspective*, ed. I. Hont, Cambridge, Mass. and London: 389–446.

Hourani, G. F. (1961) *Averroes on the Harmony of Religion and Philosophy*, London.

  (1975a) 'Ethics in medieval Islam: A conspectus', in *Hourani* (1975b): 128–35.

  (ed.) (1975b) *Essays on Islamic Philosophy and Science*, Albany, N.Y.

Humfress, C. (2000) 'Roman law and the formation of Christian Orthodoxy', in *Orthodoxy, Christianity, History*, eds. S. Elm, E. Rebillard and A. Romano, Rome: 125–47.

  (2007) *Orthodoxy and the Courts in Late Antiquity*, Oxford.

Huyler, J. (1995) *Locke in America: The Moral Philosophy of the Founding Era*, Kansas.

Hyman, A. (1999) 'Averroes' theory of the intellect and the ancient commentators', in Endress and Aertsen (1999): 188–98.

Ierodiakonou, K. (ed.) (2002) *Byzantine Philosophy and its Ancient Sources*, Oxford.

Ilting, K.-H. (1978) 'The structure of Hegel's *Philosophy of Right*', in *Hegel's Political Philosophy: Problems and Perspectives*, ed. Z. A. Pelczynski, Cambridge: 90–110.

Irwin, T. H. (1991) 'Aristotle's defense of private property', in Keyt and Miller (1991): 200–25.

Jennings, J. (1992) The '*Déclaration des droits de l'homme et du citoyen* and its critics in France: Reaction and *idéologie*', *The Historical Journal* **35**: 939–59.

Johnston, D. (1989) 'Justininian's *Digest*: The interpretation of interpolation', *Oxford Jl. of Legal Studies* **9**: 149–66.

  (1999) *Roman Law in Context*, Cambridge.

  (2000) 'The Jurists', in Rowe and Schofield (2000): 616–34.

Jugie, M. (1935) 'La polémique de Georges Scholarios contre Pléthon: nouvelle édition de sa *Correspondance*', *Byzantion* **10**: 517–30.

Kagan, R. (2006) *Dangerous Nation: America and the World*, 1600–1898, London.

Kaiser, T. E. (1994) 'Property, sovereignty, the Declaration of the Rights of Man, and the tradition of French jurisprudence', in *The French Idea of Freedom: The Old Regime and the Declaration of Rights of 1789*, ed. D. van Kley, Stanford: 300–39, 418–24.

Karamanolis, G. (2002) 'Plethon and Scholarios on Aristotle', in Ierodiakonou (2002): 253–82.

Kelley, D. R. (1984) *Historians and the Law in Postrevolutionary France*, Princeton.

Kelley, D. R. and Smith, B. G. (1984) 'What was property? Legal dimensions of the social question in France (1789–1848)', *Proc. Am. Phil. Soc.* **128**: 200–30.

Kelly, J. M. (1992) *A Short History of Western Legal Theory*, Oxford.

Kennedy, H. (1996) *Muslim Spain and Portugal: A Political History of al-Andalus*, London and New York.

Kerr, P. (1993) 'Adam Smith's theory of growth and technological change revisited', *Contrib. Pol. Econ.* **12**: 1–27.

Kersting, W. (1992) 'Politics, freedom and order: Kant's political philosophy', in *The Cambridge Companion to Kant*, ed. P. Guyer, Cambridge: 342–66.

Keyt, D. and Miller, F. D., Jr. (eds.) (1991) *A Companion to Aristotle's Politics*, Oxford and Cambridge, Mass.

Kirk, G. S., Raven, J. E. and Schofield, M. (1983) *The Presocratic Philosophers: A Critical History with a Selection of Texts*, 2nd edn. Cambridge.

Knowles, D. (1983) 'Hegel on property and personality', *Philosophical Quarterly* **33**: 45–62.

Kolakowski, L. (1990) *Modernity on Endless Trial*, Chicago and London.

Korkman, P. (2006) 'Life, liberty and the pursuit of happiness: Human rights in Barbeyrac and Burlamaqui', in Mäkinen and Korkman (2006): 257–83.

Kramer, M. H. (1997) *John Locke and the Origins of Private Property: Philosophical Explorations of Individualism, Community, and Equality*, Cambridge.

Kraut, R. (2002) *Aristotle: Political Philosophy*, Oxford.

Kriegel, B. (1994) *La politique de la raison*, Paris.

(1995a) 'Rights and natural law', in *New French Thought: Political Philosophy*, ed. M. Lilla, Princeton: 155–63.

(1995b) *The State and the Rule of Law*, trans. M. A. LePain and J. C. Cohen, Princeton.

Kuttner, S. (1976a) 'A forgotten definition of justice', in *Studia Gratiana* 20, eds. I. Forchielli and A. M. Stickler, Rome: 73–110.

(1976b) 'Gratian and Plato', in *Church and Government in the Middle Ages: Essays presented to C. R. Cheney on his 70th Birthday*, eds. C. N. L. Brooke *et al.* Cambridge: 93–118.

(1982) 'The revival of jurisprudence', in *Renaissance and Renewal in the Twelfth Century*, eds. R. L. Benson and G. Constable, Oxford: 299–323.

Ladner, G. B. (1967) *The Idea of Reform: Its Impact on Christian Thought and Action in the Age of the Fathers*, Cambridge, Mass.

Laks, A. (1990) 'Legislation and demiurgy: On the relationship between Plato's *Republic* and *Laws*', *ClAnt* **9**: 209–29.

(2000) 'The *Laws*', in Rowe and Schofield (2000): 258–92.

(2001) 'In what sense is the city of the *Laws* a second best one?', in Lisi (2001): 107–114.

Lambert, M. D. (1961) *Franciscan Poverty: The Doctrine of Absolute Poverty of Christ and the Apostles in the Franciscan Order 1210–1323*, London.

Landsberg, E. (1883) *Die Glosse des Accursius und ihre Lehre vom Eigenthum*, Leipzig.

Lane, M. (2001) *Plato's Progeny: How Socrates and Plato Still Captivate the Modern Mind*, London.

(2006) 'The evolution of *eironeia* in classical Greek texts: Why Socratic *eironeia* is not Socratic irony', *OSAP* **31**: 49–83.

Lange, M. (1997) *Römisches Recht im Mittelalter*, 2 vols. Munich.

Lawless, G. (1987) *Augustine of Hippo and his Monastic Rule*, Oxford.

Leaman, O. (1998) *Averroes and his Philosophy*, Richmond, Surrey.

Le Bras, G. (1968) 'Accurse et le droit canon', in Rossi (1968): 219–31.

Lefebvre, Ch. (1968) 'La Glose d'Accurse, le décret et les décrétales (vers *le ius commune)*', in Rossi (1968): 249–84.

Lefebvre, G. (2001) *The French Revolution from its Origins to 1793*, trans. E. M. Evanson, London and New York.

Legendre, P. (1968) 'Accurse chez les canonistes', in Rossi (1968): 235–45.

Lemay, E. N. (1991) *Dictionnaire des constituants 1789–1791*, 2 vols. Oxford and Paris.

Lerner, R. and Mahdi, M. (eds.) (1963) *Medieval Political Philosophy: A Sourcebook*, New York.

Levin, H. (1970) *Myth of the Golden Age in the Renaissance*, London.

Levy, E. (1949) 'Natural law in Roman thought', *SDHI* **15**: 1–23.

(1951) *West Roman Vulgar Law: The Law of Property*, Philadelphia.

Leyser, C. (2000) *Authority and Asceticism from Augustine to Gregory the Great*, Oxford.

Lisi, F. L. (ed.) (2001) *Plato's* Laws *and its Historical Significance: Selected Papers of the First International Congress on Ancient Thought, Salamanca, 1998*, Sankt Augustin.

Long, A. A. (1997) 'Stoic philosophers on persons, property-ownership and community', in *Aristotle and After*, ed. R. Sorabji, London: 13–31.

Long, A. A. and Sedley, D. N. (1987) *The Hellenistic Philosophers*, 2 vols. Cambridge.

Lopata, B. B. (1973) 'Property theory in Hobbes', *Political Theory* **1**: 203–19.

Lovejoy, A. O. (1948) *Essays in the History of Ideas*, Baltimore.

Lovejoy, A. O. and Boas, G. (1935) *Primitivism and Related Ideas in Antiquity*, Baltimore.

MacQueen, D. J. (1972) 'St Augustine's concept of property ownership', *Rech. Aug.* **8**: 187–229.

Mäkinen, V. (2006) 'Rights and duties in late scholastic discussion on extreme necessity', in Mäkinen and Korkman (2006): 37–62.

Mäkinen, V. and Korkman, P. (eds.) (2006) *Transformations in Medieval and Early-Modern Rights Discourse*, Dordrecht.

Maleville, J. (1805) *Analyse raisonnée de la discussion du Code civil*, Paris.

Maraval, P. (2003) Review of Caner (2002), *AnTard* **11**: 363–64.

Marenbon, J. (1983) *Early Medieval Philosophy (480–1150)*, London.

(1987) *Later Medieval Philosophy (1150–1350)*, London.

(1997) *The Philosophy of Peter Abelard*, Cambridge.

(2000) 'The Platonisms of Peter Abelard', in *Aristotelian Logic, Platonism, and the Context of Early Medieval Philosophy in the West*, Aldershot.

(forthcoming) 'Peter Abelard and Platonic politics'.

Markus, R. (1990) *The End of Ancient Christianity*, Cambridge.

Masai, F. (1956) *Pléthon et le platonisme de Mistra*, Paris.

Maxwell, J. F. (1975) *Slavery and the Catholic Church: The History of Catholic Teaching Concerning the Moral Legitimacy of the Institution of Slavery*, Chichester and London.

Mayhew, R. (1993a) 'Aristotle on property', *Review of Metaphysics* **46**: 803–31.

(1993b) 'Aristotle on the extent of the communism in Plato's *Republic*', *Anc Phil.* **13**: 313–21.

(1995) 'Aristotle on the self-sufficiency of the city', *Hist. Pol. Th.* **16**: 488–502.

(1996) 'Aristotle's criticism of Plato's communism of women and children', *Apeiron* **29**: 231–48.

(1997) *Aristotle's Criticism of Plato's Republic*, Lanham, Md.

McGinn, B. (1980) *Apocalyptic Spirituality: Treatises and Letters of Lactantius, Adso of Montier-en-Der, Joachim of Fiore, the Franciscan Spirituals, Savonarola*, London.

McGrade, A. S. (1996) 'Aristotle's place in the history of natural rights', *Rev. of Metaphysics* **49**: 803–29.

McIntyre, A. (1982) *After Virtue: A Study in Moral Theory*, 2nd edn. London.

(1998) *A Short History of Ethics*, 2nd edn. London and New York.

Mealand, D. L. (1975) 'Community of goods at Qumran', *Theol. Zeitschr.* **31**: 129–39.

(1977) 'Community of goods and utopian allusions in Acts II–IV', *JTS* **28**: 96–9.

Mesbahi, M. (1999) 'Ibn Rushd critique d'Ibn Sina ou le retour à Aristote', in Endress and Aertsen (1999): 73–80.

Metzger, E. (ed.) (1998) *A Companion to Justinian's Institutes*, London.

Michel, A. (1996) 'Du *De Officiis* de Cicéron à Saint Ambroise: la théorie des devoirs', *St. Eph. Aug.* **53**: 39–46.

Miller, F. D. (1995) *Nature, Justice and Rights in Aristotle's Politics*, Oxford.

Minar, E. L., Jr. (1942) *Early Pythagorean Politics in Practice and in Theory*, Baltimore.

(1944) 'Pythagorean communism', *TAPA* **75**: 34–46.

Mitsis, Ph. (1999) 'The Stoic origin of natural rights', in *Topics in Stoic Philosophy*, ed. K. Ierodiakonou, Oxford: 153–77.

Monfasani, J. (1976) *George of Trebizond: A Biography and A Study of his Rhetoric and Logic*, Leiden.

(1991) 'The Fraticelli and clerical wealth in quattrocento Rome', in *Renaissance Society and Culture: Essays in Honor of Eugene F. Rice Jr.*, eds. J. Monfasani and R. G. Musto, New York: 177–95.

(1994) 'Pseudo-Dionysius the Areopagite in mid-quattrocento Rome', in *Language and Learning in Renaissance Italy: Selected Articles*, Aldershot: IX 189–214.

(1995) 'Bessarion Latinus', in *Byzantine Scholars in Renaissance Italy: Cardinal Bessarion and Other Emigrés: Selected Essays*, Aldershot: II 165–209.

Moore, J. (1976) 'Hume's theory of justice and property', *Pol. Stud.* **24**: 103–19.

Moran, Francis III (1993) 'Between primates and primitives: Natural man as the missing link in Rousseau's *Second Discourse*', *Jl. Hist. Ideas* **54**(1): 37–58.

Morris, J. (1965) 'Pelagian literature', *JTS* **16**: 26–60.

Morrison, J. S. (1956) 'Pythagoras of Samos', *CQ* **6**: 135–56.

Nelson, E. (2004) *The Greek Tradition in Republican Thought*, Cambridge.

Nikolaou, Th. St. (1974) *Hai peri Politeias kai Dikaiou Ideai tou G. Plethônos Gemistou*, Thessaloniki.

Nold, P. (2003) *Pope John XXII and his Franciscan Cardinal: Bertrand de la Tour and the Apostolic Poverty Controversy*, Oxford.

Ober, J. (1998) *Political Dissent in Democratic Athens: Intellectual Critics of Popular Rule*, Princeton.

Offler, H. S. (1977) 'The three modes of natural law in Ockham: A revision of the text', *Franciscan Studies* **37**: 208–17.

Olsen, G. W. (1969) 'The idea of the *ecclesia primitiva* in the twelfth-century canonists', *Traditio* **25**: 61–86.

(1980) 'St. Boniface and the *Vita Apostolica*', *Am. Ben. Rev.* **31**: 6–19.

(1982a) 'Reform after the pattern of the primitive church in the thought of Salvian of Marseilles,' *Cath. Hist. Rev.* **68**: 1–12.

(1982b) 'Bede as historian: The evidence from his observations on the life of the first Christian community at Jerusalem', *Jl. Eccl. Hist.* **33**: 519–30.

(1984) 'The image of the first community of Christians at Jerusalem in the time of Lanfranc and Anselm', in *Les mutations socio-culturelles au tournant des XIe–XIIe siècles: études anselmiennes (IVe session). Abbaye Notre-Dame du Bec, Le Bec-Hellouin 11–16 Juillet 1982*, ed. R. Foreville, Paris: 341–53.

(1985) 'Reference to the *ecclesia primitiva* in the *decretum* of Burchard of Worms', in *Proceedings of the Sixth International Congress of Medieval Canon Law, Berkeley 28 July–2 August 1980*, eds. S. Kuttner and K. Pennington, Vatican City: 289–307.

(1998) 'John of Salisbury's humanism', in *Gli umanesimi medievali*, ed. C. Leonardi, Florence: 447–68.

O'Meara, D. J. (1999) 'Plato's *Republic* in the school of Iamblichus', in Vegetti and Abbate (1999): 193–205.

(2003) *Platonopolis: Platonic Political Philosophy in Late Antiquity*, Oxford.

Orabona, L. (1958) 'I passi neotestamentari sulla comunione dei beni nel commento dei Padri della Chiesa', *AFLN* **8**: 77–100.

Osiek, C. (1982) 'Wealth and poverty in the Shepherd of Hermas', *SP* **17**(2): 725–30.

Pagden, A. (1982) *The Fall of Natural Man: The American Indian and the Origins of Comparative Ethnology*, Cambridge.

(1987) 'Dispossessing the barbarian: The language of Spanish Thomism and the debate over the property rights of the American Indians', in *The Languages of Political Theory in Early-Modern Europe*, ed. A. Pagden, Cambridge: 79–98.

Palmer, R. R. (1959–64) *The Age of the Democratic Revolution: A Political History of Europe and America, 1760–1800*, 2 vols. Princeton.

Parel, A. (1979) 'Aquinas' theory of property', in *Theories of Property: Aristotle to the Present*, eds. A. Parel and T. Flanagan, Calgary: 89–111.

Paton, H. J. (1947) *The Categorical Imperative: A Study in Kant's Moral Philosophy*, London.

Patten, A. (1995) 'Hegel's Justification of Private Property', *Hist. Pol. Th.* **16**: 576–600.

Pembroke, S. G. (1971) 'Oikeiosis', in *Problems in Stoicism*, ed. A. A. Long, London: 114–49.

Perrin, M. (1978) 'Le Platon de Lactance', in *Lactance et son temps: recherches actuelles. Actes du IVe Colloque d'Etudes Historiques et Patristiques, Chantilly 21–23 Sept.*, eds. J. Fontaine and M. Perrin, Paris: 203–34.

Pertusi, A. (1967) 'In margine alla questione dell'umanesimo bizantino: il pensiero politico del cardinal Bessarione e i suoi rapporti con il pensiero di Giorgio Gemisto Pletone', *Riv. St. Biz. Neoellen.* **14**: 95–104.

Philip, J. A. (1966) *Pythagoras and Early Pythagoreanism*, Toronto.

Piccaluga, G. (1974) *Terminus: I segni di confine nella religione romana*, Rome.

(1996) '*Ius e vera iustitia* (Lact. *Div. Inst.* VI 9, 7): Rielaborazione cristiana di un valore assoluto della religione romana arcaica', *St. Eph. Aug.* **53**: 257–69.

Plinval, G. de (1939) 'Le problème de Pélage sous son dernier état', *Rev. Hist. Eccl.* **35**: 5–21.

(1943) *Pélage, ses écrits, sa vie, et sa réforme*, Paris.

Pocock, J. G. A. (1975) *The Machiavellian Moment: Florentine Political Thought and the Atlantic Republican Tradition*, Princeton.

Pugliese, G. (1951) 'Res corporales, res incorporales e il problema del diritto soggettivo', *RISG* **5**: 237–74.

Quiroz, M. (2003) 'El derecho subjectivo en el derecho romano (un estado de la custion)', *Revista de Estudios Historico-Juridicos* **25**: 35–54.

Rankin, H. D. (1983) *Sophists, Socratics and Cynics*, London.

Rathbone, D. W. (1998) 'Early Rome: A peasant republic?', in *Collection of the Second International Conference on Ancient World History in China* (*Journal of Ancient Civilizations*, suppl. 3), Changchun: 209–15.

(2003) 'The control and exploitation of *Ager Publicus* in Italy under the Roman Republic', in *Tâches publiques et entreprise privée dans le monde romain*, ed. J.-J. Aubert, Geneva: 135–78.

Rebenich, S. (2002) *Theodor Mommsen: Eine Biographie*, Munich.

Rees, B. R. (1998) *Pelagius: Life and Letters*, Woodbridge.

Reilly, B. F. (1993) *The Medieval Spains*, Cambridge.

Reisman, D. C. (2004) 'Plato's *Republic* in Arabic: A newly discovered passage', *Arabic Sciences and Philosophy* **14**: 265–300.

Reyburn, H. A. (1921) *The Ethical Theory of Hegel: A Study of the Philosophy of Right*, Oxford.

Rials, S. (1988) *La déclaration des droits de l'homme et du citoyen*, Paris.

Riedweg, Chr. (2002) *Pythagoras: Leben, Lehre, Nachwirkung*, Munich.

Rodger, A. (1970) *Owners and Neighbours in Roman Law*, Oxford.

Rosenblatt, H. (1997) *Rousseau and Geneva: From the* First Discourse *to the* Social Contract, *1749–1762*, Cambridge.

Rossi, G. (ed.) (1968) *Atti del Convegno internazionale di studi Accursiani, Bologna, 21–26 Ott. 1963*, Milan.

Rousseau, Ph. (1978) *Ascetics, Authority and the Church in the Age of Jerome and Cassian*, Oxford.

(1985) *Pachomius: The Making of a Community in Fourth Century Egypt*, Berkeley.

(1994) *Basil of Caesarea*, Berkeley.

Rowe, C. and Schofield, M. (eds.) (2000) *The Cambridge History of Greek and Roman Political Thought*, Cambridge.

Ryan, A. (1987) *Property*, Milton Keynes.

(1989) 'Property', in *Political Innovation and Conceptual Change*, eds. T. Ball, J. Farr and R. L. Hanson, Cambridge: 309–32.

Ryan, M. (2000) 'Bartolus of Sassoferrato and free cities', *Trans. Royal Hist. Soc.* **10**: 65–90.

Sanchis, D. (1962) 'Pauvreté monastique et charité fraternelle chez saint Augustin: le commentaire augustinien des Actes 4 32–35 entre 393 et 403', *St. Mon.* **4**: 7–33.

Sargent L. T. (1998) 'Communism', in *Routledge Encyclopedia of Philosophy*, ed. E. Craig, London and New York: 462–4.

Saunders, T. (2002) 'Dicaearchus' historical anthropology', in Fortenbaugh and Schütrumpf (2002): 237–54.

Schneewind, J. B. (1998) *The Invention of Autonomy: A History of Modern Moral Philosophy*, Cambridge.

Schofield, M. (1991) *The Stoic Idea of the City*, Cambridge.

(1999) *Saving the City: Philosopher-Kings and other Classical Paradigms*, London and New York.

(2006) *Plato: Political Philosophy*, Oxford.

Schütrumpf, E. (2002) 'Dikaiarchs *Bios Hellados* und die Philosophie des vierten Jahrhunderts', in Fortenbaugh and Schütrumpf (2002): 255–77.

Seelmann, K. (1979) *Die Lehre des Fernando Vazquez de Menchaca vom Dominium*, Cologne.

Sheehan, B. W. (1973) *Seeds of Extinction: Jeffersonian Philanthropy and the American Indian*, Chapel Hill, N.C.

Shinners, J. (ed.) (1997) *Medieval Popular Religion, 1000–1500: A Reader*, Peterborough, Ont.

Simpson, P. L. Ph. (1998) *A Philosophical Commentary on the Politics of Aristotle*, Chapel Hill, N.C. and London.

Siola, R. B. (1993) 'Proprietà secolare e proprietà ecclesiale nel pensiero di S. Ambrogio', *AARC* **9**: 139–85.

Siorvanes, L. (1996) *Proclus: Neo-Platonic Philosophy and Science*, Edinburgh.

Skinner, Q. (1998) *Liberty before Liberalism*, Cambridge.

    (2002a) *Visions of Politics, vol. 3: Hobbes and Civil Science*, Cambridge.

    (2002b) 'Thomas More's *Utopia* and the virtue of true nobility', in *Visions of Politics, vol. 2: Renaissance Virtues*, Cambridge: 213–44.

Smith, J. Z. (1986) 'Golden Age', in *Encyclopaedia of Religion*, ed. M. Eliade, vol. 6, New York: 69–73.

Smith, M. (1973) *Clement of Alexandria and a Secret Gospel of Mark*, Cambridge, Mass.

Sonenscher, M. (1997) 'The nation's debt and the birth of the modern republic: The French fiscal deficit and the politics of the revolution of 1789', *Hist. Pol. Th.* **18**: 64–103, 267–325.

Sorabji, R. (1993) *Animal Minds and Human Morals*, Ithaca, N.Y.

Sordi, M. (1990) 'La concezione politica di Ambrogio', in *I Cristiani e l'Impero nel IV Secolo: Colloquio sul Cristianesimo nel mondo antico. Atti del Convegno (Macerata 17–18 Dicembre 1987)*, eds. G. Bonamente and A. Nestori, Macerata: 143–54.

Souillac, G. (2006) *Human Rights in Crisis: The Sacred and the Secular in French Thought*, Landam, Md.

Southern, R. W. (1966) *Saint Anselm and his Biographer*, Cambridge.

Spentzas, S. (1987) *G. Gemistos-Plethôn, ho philosophos tou Mustra: Hoi Oikonomikes, koinônikes kai Demosionomikes tou Apopseis*, Athens.

Sreenivasan, G. (1995) *The Limits of Lockean Rights in Property*, New York.

Stalley, R. F. (1991) 'Aristotle's criticism of Plato's *Republic*', in Keyt and Miller (1991): 182–99.

    (1995) 'The unity of the state: Plato, Aristotle and Proclus', *Polis* **14**: 129–50.

    (1999) 'Plato and Aristotle on political unity', in Vegetti and Abbate (1999): 29–48.

Stein, P. (1966) *Regulae Iuris: From Juristic Rules to Legal Maxims*, Edinburgh.

    (1968) 'The formation of the gloss *de regulis iuris* and the Glossators' concept of *regula*', in Rossi (1968): 699–722.

    (1978) 'The place of Servius Sulpicius Rufus in the development of Roman legal science', in Behrends *et. al.* (1978): 177–84.

    (1988) 'The four stage theory of the development of societies', in *The Characters and Influence of the Roman Civil Law: Historical Essays*, London: 395–409.

    (1993) 'Donellus and the origins of modern civil law', *Mélanges Felix Wubbe*, ed. J. A. Ankum *et al.* Fribourg, Switzerland: 439–52.

    (1997) 'The medieval rediscovery of the Roman civil law', in *The Civilian Tradition and Scots Law: Aberdeen Quincentenary Essays*, eds. D. L. Carey Miller and R. Zimmermann, Berlin: 75–86.

    (1999) *Roman Law and European History*, Cambridge.

Stewart, C. (1998) *Cassian the Monk*, New York.

Strauss, L. (1964) *The City and Man*, Chicago and London.

(1987) 'Plato', in *History of Political Philosophy*, eds. L. Strauss and J. Cropsey, 3rd edn. Chicago and London: 33–89.

Surtz, E. (1957) *The Praise of Pleasure: Philosophy, Education and Communism in More's Utopia*, Cambridge, Mass.

Swanson, S. G. (1997) 'The medieval foundations of John Locke's theory of natural rights: Rights of subsistence and the principle of extreme necessity', *Hist. Pol. Th.* **18**: 399–459.

Swift, L. J. (1968) 'Lactantius and the Golden Age', *AJPh* **89**: 144–56.

(1979) '*Iustitia* and *ius privatum*: Ambrose on private property', *AJPh* **100**: 176–87.

Tackett, T. (1996) *Becoming a Revolutionary: The Deputies of the French National Assembly and the Emergence of a Revolutionary Culture*, Princeton.

Thomas, P. (2003) 'Property's Properties: From Hegel to Locke', *Representations* **84**: 30–43.

Tierney, B. (1959) *Medieval Poor Law: A Sketch of Canonical Theory and its Application in England*, Berkeley and Los Angeles.

(1997) *The Idea of Natural Rights: Studies on Natural Rights, Natural Law and Church Law 1150–1625*, Emory.

(2006) 'Dominion of self and natural rights before Locke and after', in Mäkinen and Korkman (2006): 173–203.

Tocco, F. (1910) *La quistione della povertà nel secolo XIV, secondo nuovi documenti*, Naples.

Tuck, R. (1979) *Natural Rights Theories: Their Origin and Development*, Cambridge.

(1999) *The Rights of War and Peace: Political Thought and the International Order from Grotius to Kant*, Oxford.

(2002) *Hobbes: A Very Short Introduction*, Oxford.

Tully, J. (1980) *A Discourse on Property: John Locke and his Adversaries*, Cambridge.

(1993) *An Approach to Political Philosophy: Locke in Context*, Cambridge.

Turner, C. J. G. (1970) 'The career of George-Gennadius Scholarius', *Byzantion* **39**: 420–55.

Urvoy, D. (1991) *Ibn Rushd (Averroes)*, trans. O. Stewart, London and New York.

van Engen, J. (1986) 'The "crisis of cenobitism" reconsidered: Benedictine monasticism in the years 1050–1150', *Speculum* **61**: 269–304.

Vasey, V. R. (1982) *The Social Ideas in the Works of St. Ambrose: A Study on De Nabuthe*, Rome.

Vegetti, M. (1999) 'L'autocritica di Platone: il *Timeo* e le *Leggi*', in Vegetti and Abbate (1999): 13–27.

Vegetti, M. and Abbate, M. (eds.) (1999) *La Repubblica di Platone nella Tradizione Antica*, Naples.

Verheijen, L. (1979) *Saint Augustine's Monasticism in the Light of Acts* **4**: 32–35, Villanova.

(1980) *Nouvelle approche de la Règle de St Augustin*, Bellefontaine.

Vickers, M. (2004) 'Aspasia on stage: Aristophanes' *Ecclesiazusae*', *Athenaeum* **92**: 431–50.

Villey, M. (1946–7) 'L'idée du droit subjectif et les systèmes juridiques romains', *RHD* **4**(24–5): 201–28.

(1949) 'Du sens de l'expression *jus in re* en droit romain classique', *RIDA* **2**(2): 417–36.

(1950) 'Le *jus in re* du droit romain classique au droit moderne', *Conférences faites à l'Institut de Droit Romain en 1947*, Paris: 187–225.

(1956) 'Suum jus cuique tribuens', in *Studi in onore di P. di Francisci*, 4 vols. Milan, 2: 361–71.

(1962) *Leçons d'histoire de la philosophie du droit*, 2nd edn. Paris.

(1969) 'La genèse du droit subectif chez Guillaume d'Occam' in *Seize essais de philosophie du droit*, Paris: 140–78.

(1975) *La formation de la pensée juridique moderne*, 4th edn. Paris.

Von Jhering, R. (1872) *Der Kampf um's Recht*, Vienna.

Wacht, M. (1982) 'Privateigentum bei Cicero und Ambrosius', *JbAC* **25**: 28–64.

Waldron, J. (ed.) (1984) *Theories of Rights*, Oxford.

(1987) *Nonsense upon Stilts: Bentham, Burke and Marx on the Rights of Man*, London.

(1988) *The Right to Private Property*, Oxford.

(2002) *God, Locke and Equality: Christian Foundations in Locke's Political Thought*, Cambridge.

Wallace, A. F. C. (1999) *Jefferson and the Indians: The Tragic Fate of the First Americans*, Cambridge, Mass.

Watson, A. (1971) *The Law of Succession in the Later Roman Republic*, Oxford.

Watts, E. J. (2004) 'Justinian, Malalas, and the end of Athenian philosophical teaching in A. D. 529', *JRS* **94**: 168–82.

(2006) *City and School in Late Antique Athens and Alexandria*, Berkeley and London.

Weigand, R. (1967) *Die Naturrechtslehre der Legisten und Dekretisten von Irnerius bis Accursius und von Gratian bis Johannes Teutonicus*, Munich.

Wessley, S. E. (1990) *Joachim of Fiore and Monastic Reform*, New York.

White, M. (1978) *The Philosophy of the American Revolution*, New York.

Whitman, J. Q. (1990) *The Legacy of Roman Law in the German Romantic Era: Historical Vision and Legal Change*, Princeton.

Wickert, L. (1959–80) *Theodor Mommsen: Eine Biographie*, 4 vols. Frankfurt.

Wiggins, D. (2006) *Ethics: Twelve Lectures on the Philosophy of Morality*, London.

Wilks, M. J. (1962) 'The problem of private ownership in patristic thought and an Augustinian solution of the fourteenth century', *SP* **6**: 533–42.

Williams, B. (1993) *Shame and Necessity*, Berkeley and Oxford.

Wills, G. (1978) *Inventing America: Jefferson's Declaration of Independence*, New York.

Winroth, A. (2000) *The Making of Gratian's Decretum*, Cambridge.

Winslow, D. F. (1983) 'Poverty and riches: an embarrassment for the early church', *SP* **18**(2): 317–27.

Wokler, R. (1978) 'Perfectible apes in decadent cultures: Rousseau's anthropology revisited', *Daedalus* **107**: 107–34.

(1994) 'Rousseau's Pufendorf: natural law and the foundations of commercial society', *Hist. Pol. Th.* **15**: 373–402.

(2001) *Rousseau: A Very Short Introduction*, Oxford.

Wolff, J. (1996) *An Introduction to Political Philosophy*, Oxford.

Woodhouse, C. M. (1986) *Gemistos Plethon: The Last of the Hellenes*, Oxford.

Zaccaria, V. (1959) 'Pier Candido Decembrio traduttore della *Repubblica* di Platone: (Notizie dall'epistolario del Decembrio)', *Italia Medioevale e umanistica* **2**: 179–206.

(1974–5) 'Pier Candido Decembrio, Michele Pizolpasso, e Ugulino Pisano', *Atti dell'Istituto Veneto di Scienze, lettere ed arti* **133**: 187–212.

Zhmud, L. (1997) *Wissenschaft, Philosophie und Religion im frühen Pythagoreismus*, Berlin.

Zuckert, M. (1997) 'Do natural rights derive from natural law?' *Harvard Journal of Law and Public Policy* **3**: 695–731.

Index

Abbasids 36
Abelard, Peter 32, 34, 35
Abraham 96
Accursius 195, 202, 212, 237
Acts of the Apostles *see* Christians, first
    community at Jerusalem
Adam 141, 143
Adams, John 223
ager publicus 193–4
agrarian laws 114, 194
agreement 136–43, 146, 157–8, 175, 206; *see also*
    Pufendorf: consent/agreement
agriculture 122, 123, 139–40, 164, 172, 174, 193;
    see also farmers; stages theory
Alanus Angelicus 207, 217
Alcinous 28
Alcuin 80
Alexander of Aphrodisias 37
Alexandria 32, 64, 70, 71–2
Alfarabi 36, 38, 42
allegory 89, 91, 97
All Souls College 185–6
Almohads 36–7
Almoravids 37, 41
alms, almsgiving 61, 65, 67–8, 94, 215–21
Ambrose of Milan 74, 93, 94, 109, 118, 125–8,
    129, 131, 132, 213–14
Ananias 60, 66, 73–4
Anonymous Decretalist 35
Anonymus, *On Wealth* 75–6, 94–8, 111, 130–1
Antony, St 64–5, 72
Apostolici 75
Aquinas, Thomas 36, 43, 59, 93, 94, 96, 106, 113,
    129, 131, 132–3, 209, 214, 217–18, 219, 234
Aristophanes 18, 19–20
Aristotle 2, 8, 9, 12, 15, 19, 21, 23, 24–30, 31–2, 33,
    36–9, 43–53, 80, 123, 132, 139, 142, 145, 180,
    204, 208, 209–10, 233–4
Aristoxenus of Tarentum 21
Arnaud, André-Jean 179
artisans 15, 19, 47, 55
asceticism 72, 74–6, 84–106, 116; *see also* monasticism

Athens 6, 20, 52
Augustine of Canterbury 77
Augustine of Hippo 33, 44, 72–5, 77, 79, 88,
    90–4, 95, 96, 129, 213, 234
Auxiliaries, in Plato 2, 31, 33
Avempace 36
Averroes 2, 36–43
Avicenna 36

Baghdad 36
Baldus de Ubaldis 195, 202
barbarians 24, 139
Barbeyrac, Jean 224
Bartolus of Sassoferrato 179, 195, 197–203,
    212, 237
Basil of Caesarea 69, 74, 93, 215–17
Bede 72, 79
Benedict of Nursia 73, 76, 79
Bernard of Chartres 33–4
Bernard of Clairvaux 79, 90
Bertrand de la Tour 104, 105
Bessarion, Cardinal 31, 34, 44, 47, 48–51, 53
Boethius 33
Bologna 33, 195
Bonagratia of Bergamo 102, 133–4
Bonaventura 97, 102
Brahmins 53
Bruni, Leonardo 44
Budé, Guillaume 23
Burchard of Worms 78
Burlamaqui, Jean-Jacques 207, 224–5

Calcidius 33, 34, 35, 81
Calvinism 163
Campanella, Tommaso 141
canonists, canon lawyers 111, 132, 163, 174, 206,
    207–8, 212–13, 235; *see also* Alanus
    Angelicus; Anonymous Decretalist;
    Huguccio; Johannes Monachus; Rufinus
Caracalla, emperor 119
Cassian, John 63–4, 71, 73, 79
categorical imperative 167

Cato, the Elder 193
Celsus, jurist 190, 191
Celsus, philosopher 65
charity 59, 61, 86, 106
children, in Plato 6–14, 17–20, 23–4, 29, 42
Christianity: and state of nature 111, 136, 174–5;
    and rights 213–21, 232
Christians, first community at Jerusalem 1, 3, 18,
    53, 59–83, 108, 116, 139, 234
Chrodegang of Metz 77–8
Chrysippus 113, 116, 213
Chrysoloras, Manuel 44
Cicero 33, 61, 80, 176, 193; on property 111–18,
    121, 125–7, 137–8, 174, 213–14
citizens 20, 24, 25, 26, 31, 40–2, 46, 51, 112, 119,
    165, 180, 182, 191, 193, 225–8, 230, 236
Clareno, Angelo 84–5
Clement of Alexandria 87–90, 93, 95, 96
Clement of Rome 78
Code Civil (Code Napoléon) 106, 177–9, 198, 212,
    231, 236
communality: defined 8, 12; original (primeval),
    136, 137, 174, 175, 217, 220, 221, 234;
    Platonic, in Renaissance 45–53; in Stoic
    theory, *see* Stoics; *see also* Golden
    Age myth; nature, state of
communism, communistic 3, 6–8, 12–13, 17,
    175, 233
Condorcet, Marquis de 163
Constantine, emperor 69, 90, 178, 199;
    Donations of 45
Constantinople, fall of 51
Cordoba 36
Corinth 214
Corpus iuris civilis: reception by the Glossators
    196–7; *see also Institutes*, Justinian,
    Theodosian Code
Cosimo de' Medici 51, 52
Cousin, Victor 146
Crates of Thebes 66
Cyprian, bishop 63–5, 67–8, 88

Damascius 32
Da Rho, Antonio 31, 46, 53
David, King 96, 214
Dead Sea Scrolls 22, 61
Decembrio, Pier Candido 31–2, 44–7, 49, 53
Decembrio, Uberto 44
Declaration of Independence, American 5, 205,
    222–5
Declaration of Rights: French 5, 105–6, 177, 205,
    221, 225–32; of the United Nations 211; *see
    also* Virginian Bill of Rights
democracy, at Athens 20
Democritus 109, 177

Dicaearchus 109, 123, 139–40
dignity 114, 167, 205
Diocletian, emperor 69, 129
Diodorus Siculus 109, 140
distribution, of resources 175
dog 23
Dominicans 98
dominium 93, 99, 100, 103, 105, 128–9, 141, 145–6,
    177–80, 212, 218–19, 234; *dominium
    directum/utile* 200
Donellus, Hugo 5, 201–2, 206, 237
Donatists 75
Duns Scotus, John 134
Duquesnoy, Adrien-Cyprien 228
Dutch, commercial policies of 137
duties 208, 211, 213, 215, 220, 232

ecclesia primitiva 3, 59–83, 85, 234
Eco, Umberto 101
economy, of polis 19, 27
education: in Plato 15; in Pythagorean
    community 21–2
Egypt 64–5, 69–71
Engels, Friedrich 61
Epictetus 113
Epicurus/Epicureanism 109, 112, 118, 177; *see also*
    Lucretius
equality/inequality 58, 154, 160, 166, 172, 208, 229
equestrian order 117
Erasmus 57
essenes 53, 61, 116, 139
eudaimonia see happiness
Eusebius of Caesarea 64, 69–72

family 157, 158, 233
farmers 15, 19, 26, 47, 55, 126, 193
Fascism 231
Ferguson, Adam 139
Ferrara 47, 48, 54
Fichet, Guillaume 50
Ficino, Marsilio 8, 31, 33, 44, 45, 50–3
Filmer, Robert 134–5, 138, 141, 142, 143
Florence 32, 45, 53; Academy of 51; Synod at 47,
    48, 54
Florentinus 120, 208
Francis, St 46, 82, 84–5, 98, 234
Franciscan poverty dispute 85, 98–106, 111, 133,
    218, 234
Franciscans 53, 63, 76, 82–3, 84–5, 86–7, 128, 133,
    203, 211, 218
Frederick II Hohenstaufen 37
freedom 150, 151, 166–7, 169, 172, 175, 205, 207;
    see also liberty; right, to liberty
friendship 60, 80–2
Frontinus, Sextus Julius 191

Gaius, jurist 119, 187–9
Galen 39, 52
Gallienus, emperor 9
Garat, Dominique 228
garden of Eden 128, 133
Garnier, Germain 231
Gauchet, Marcel 230
Genesis 111, 133
Genoa 194
George Gennadius Scholarius 47, 54
George of Trebizond 47, 48
Gerson, Jean 190, 215
Glossators 33, 34, 195–203
Godfrey of Fontaines 218
Goethe, Johann Wolfgang von 166
Golden Age myth 3, 108–12, 121–5, 127, 129–30,
    139, 140, 155, 162, 171, 173, 208; *see also*
    Ambrose; Dicaearchus; Hesiod; Lactantius;
    nature, state of; Plato; Posidonius; Seneca;
    Virgil
Gratian, *Decretum* of 3, 4, 18, 32–3, 35, 53, 60, 78,
    81–2, 111, 120, 131–2, 168, 174, 206, 207, 208,
    217, 234
Gregory of Nazianzus 80
Grotius, Hugo 109, 111, 113, 116, 117, 118, 123,
    136–9, 143, 154, 156–7, 171, 173, 174, 197,
    199, 203, 205–6, 207, 214, 219, 235, 237
Guards, in Plato 2, 6, 9–20, 24, 25, 29, 31, 33,
    40–2, 46, 50, 56
Guillaume de Vair 138
Gymnosophistae 53

Hadrian, emperor 196
happiness 41, 168, 175, 222–3, 226; *see also* right
    to pursue happiness
Harrington, James 9
Hegel, Georg Wilhelm Friedrich 113, 147,
    149–54, 174, 175, 176
Heineccius 178
Henry of Ghent 217
Henry of Segusio 218
Herder, Johann Gottfried 171, 166
heresy/heretics 54, 85–6, 94–5, 101, 103, 133
Hermarchus 112
Hervaeus Natalis 103
Hesiod 3, 122, 140
Hierocles, Stoic philosopher 156–7
Hilary, correspondent of Augustine 90, 91,
    93, 95
Hippodamus 18, 19, 57
Hippo Regius 72
Hobbes, Thomas 136, 138, 140, 141, 158, 174, 175,
    205, 210, 219, 235
Horace 140
Huguccio (Hugh of Pisa) 132, 217

Hume, David 147–8, 154, 155–9, 170, 174
hunter/gatherer 139–40, 174
Hutcheson, Francis 207, 225

Iamblichus 20–3
Ibn Rushd *see* Averroes
Ibn Tufail 36, 37
'Indians' 223–4
Institutes: of Gaius 182; of Justinian 190
Irnerius 195
Islam, medieval, Platonism in 36–43; *see also*
    Averroes
ius 119, 180–95, 211–12, 215, 234
ius abutendi, *see* right, to use up/misuse
ius alienandi 188
ius altius tollendi 187
ius civile see law, civil
ius commercii 192
ius conubii 192
ius disponendi 197
ius dominii 188–90
ius et potestas 188, 190–2, 211
ius fori/poli 211
ius gentium 119
ius in re 200
ius in re aliena 201–2
ius naturale see law, natural
ius non tollendi altius 187
ius provocationis 192
ius utendi see right, to use
ius vindicandi/vendicandi 197

Januarius 73–4
Javolenus 189
Jefferson, Thomas 5, 27, 205, 222–5, 236
Jerome 45, 69, 71–2
Jesus Christ 59–83, 84–106, 110, 131, 167, 214, 234
Joachim of Fiore 79–80, 82
Johannes Bassianus 200
Johannes Monachus 212
John Chrysostom 74, 93
John of Paris 145, 218
John of Salisbury 80–1
Josephus 69
Judas 86, 97
Julius Caesar 191
Jupiter 122, 130
jurists: French 178, 198; medieval 195–203, 221;
    natural, 119–21, 136–46, 155, 156, 158, 174,
    220; Roman 180, 182–4, 185, 208, 237
justice 137, 155, 157, 180, 210
Justinian, emperor 4, 32, 119, 178–9, 190, 195,
    199, 236; *Digest* of 105, 107, 108, 182–4, 192,
    196–7, 200–1, 212, 236
Justus Lipsius 138

Kant, Immanuel 145, 146, 148, 154, 165–73, 175, 197, 235
Kepler, Johannes 171

Labeo 189, 197
labour, as conferring property rights 136, 144–54, 177, 230, 235
Lactantius 18, 31, 129–30, 133, 140
Lafayette, Marquis de 222, 226, 230
Las Casas 210
law: civil 115, 119, 177–203, 206, 208, 211, 236; divine 206, 207, 211; natural 3, 4–5, 119–20, 129, 131–3, 137, 206, 207–8, 211, 212, 217–18, 221, 228–9, 231, 234–5, 236; Roman 207, 211–12
Lex Aquilia 194
Lex Falcidia 191
Lex Ursonensis 191
liberality 27
liberty 199, 205, 206, 221, 227; *see also* freedom; right to liberty
Lincoln, Abraham 225
Livy 211
Locke, John 5, 56–7, 111, 113, 118, 135, 136, 142–6, 174, 205, 220–1, 235–6; reception of 146–54, 224, 228, 229, 230–1
Lucretius 109, 111, 118, 140, 173
Luke, St 60, 61, 62, 71, 72, 80
Lupset, Thomas 23

Machiavelli 193
Magnesia 7, 9, 14, 17, 28; *see also* Plato, *Laws*
Maimonides 36
Manuel, emperor 32, 54
Mao, Chairman 56–7
Marakesh 37
Mark, St 69, 71, 72
Mason, George 222
Marx, Karl 8, 147, 175, 177, 231
Michael of Cesena 106, 133, 134
Michel Le Moine 85
Milan 45
Mill, John Stuart 144
Minuciorum sententia 194
Mirabeau, Comte de 226–7, 228, 230
Mistra 32, 54
Mommsen, Theodor 107–8, 166
monasticism 64, 69–72, 76–80, 139, 234
money 10, 12, 41, 47
More, Thomas 2, 56–8, 141
Moses 127, 214
Mounier, Jean-Joseph 226, 230–1

Naboth 126

Napoleon 178, 231
native peoples 137, 144, 148, 163, 209
nature, state of 107–35, 136–76
Nédellec, Hervé de *see* Hervaeus Natalis
Neoplatonism, Neoplatonists 28, 29, 31, 32, 36, 38, 48, 51, 54; *see also* Plotinus; Porphyry; Proclus
Nerva, the younger, jurist 120–1, 197
Newton, Isaac 155, 171

occupatio (first acquisition) 109, 114–18, 120–1, 125–8, 136–40, 142–3, 147–8, 151–4, 164, 169–70, 174–5, 175–6, 212, 235–6
Ockham, William of 90, 94, 99–100, 102, 128–9, 133, 134, 138, 176, 181, 190, 207, 209, 211, 212, 219
oikeiosis 138, 156–7, 214
Olivi, Peter 82, 97, 100–1
Origen 63–8, 95
Orléans 195
Ovid 122
ownership *see dominium*; right, to own

Pachomius 69
pain 11, 16
Panaetius 113
Papal bull: *Ad Conditorem Canonum* 103–4, 105; *Cum Inter Nonnullos* 85, 86, 103; *Exiit Qui Seminat* 86, 99, 100, 102, 103, 104; *Quia Nonnumquam*; 103; *Quia Vir Reprobus* 106, 133; *Quorundam Exigit* 84; *Rerum Novarum* 59; *see also* Pope
Papal letters 78
passions 157, 161
pastoralism 139–40, 152, 173, 174
patriarchs, of the Old Testament, 96
Paul, jurist 120, 186, 190–1, 197, 202
Paul, St 59, 63, 65, 70, 92, 96, 214
Pecham, John 97
Pelagius, Pelagians 90–1; *see also* Anonymus, *On Wealth*
Peloponnesus 32, 47, 48, 54
perfectibility 141, 161, 162, 163, 167, 172, 173
persecution 67, 68, 84
Persia 32
Peter, Abbot of Celle 80–1
Peter, St 60, 62, 66, 69, 74, 90
Petronius 124
Philo of Alexandria 69–72
Physiocrats 228
Pico della Mirandola 57
Pillius, Glossator 200
Pisa 178
Pizolpasso, archbishop of Milan 45

Plato, ideal polity of 6–30, 31–58, 233–4; *Critias*
2, 13–14, 16; and Golden Age myth 122–3;
Laws 2, 9, 13–17, 49; *Politicus* 55; *Republic* 1,
2, 3, 31, 32, 33, 34, 35, 44, 49, 51, 57, 108, 150,
233; *Timaeus* 2, 13, 16, 28, 33–6; reception
of, in Aristotle 25–7; in Proclus 28–30; in
the middle ages 32–43; in the Renaissance
43–53
Plato/Aristotle controversy 31, 32, 38, 43–53
Platonopolis 9
Plethon, George Gemistus 2, 32, 47–8, 53–8
Plotinus 9, 45
Pomponius, jurist 187
poor, poverty 3, 85, 86, 88–9, 210, 215–21
Pope: Boniface VIII 84; Celestine IV 84;
Clement I 81; Gregory I 77; Gregory VII
78; Gregory IX 86; Honorius III 98;
Innocent III 98; Innocent IV 102; John
XXII 85, 86–7, 97, 103–6, 128, 133–5,
138, 219; Leo XIII 59–61; Nicholas III 86,
99, 100, 102, 104
Porphyry 9, 20, 112
Portalis, Jean-Etienne-Marie 231, 237
Posidonius 111–12, 123–4, 125
possession 115, 117, 120, 122, 124, 126, 127, 132,
152, 169, 194; and ownership 197; *see also*
right to possess
Post-Glossators 195–203; *see also* Baldus; Bartolus
Pothier, Robert 177, 237
praetor 184, 190, 191, 196, 200
Priscillian 86
Proclus 2, 28–30, 31, 32, 45, 49–50, 51
property: as theft 107, 130, 142, 166, 175, 177;
common *see* communality; denial of 6, 44;
in the Church 59–83, 84–106; origins of
107–35, 136–76; renunciation of 67, 68, 85,
86, 87–90, 91, 93, 94, 99,
234 (*see also* Franciscans; poor) Rich Man;
right to 4–5, 136–76, 177–232, 233, 235–7
Prosper of Aquitaine 77–8
Protagoras 18
Proudhon, Pierre-Joseph 107–8, 111, 113, 126,
130, 146, 147, 175, 177, 178, 188, 198, 201, 236
Ps.-Dionysius 33
Ps.-Isidore 78, 132
Pufendorf, Samuel, 111, 113, 145–6, 154–8, 161,
174–6, 205–6, 207, 220, 235; community,
negative/positive 8, 115–18, 136, 139–41, 140–1,
143, 170, 235; consent/agreement 136, 141–2,
174–5; on slavery 210; and Stoicism 214
purse, of Jesus (or Judas) 86, 97
Pythagoras, Pythagoreans 18–24, 53

Quirites 182; *see also* citizens

Rawls, John 175

Reid, Thomas 113, 225
reciprocity 27
res corporales/incorporales 200
res nullius 115, 121, 170, 212
Rich Man, and Jesus 62, 66–7, 76, 87–90
right, rights 1, 4, 87, 99–106; abstract 150–1; in
antiquity 208–14; distinct from duties, *see*
duties; legal, of citizens 4, 182, 192–5, 205,
221–32, 236; natural/human 4, 137, 142, 182,
203, 204–32, 235; objective 180; personal
145; subjective 179–82, 185, 190, 212, 215; to
enjoy 143, 177, 186, 189, 198, 222; to
honour/reputation 206, 222, 226; to
liberty, 205, 210–11, 222, 229, 235, *see also*
liberty; to life/self-preservation 5, 94, 137,
215–21, 235; to own 177–203; to pass down
to heirs 194; to possess 194, 226; to
property, *see* property, right to; to pursue
happiness 205, 222; to resist oppression
205, 222; to security 205, 206, 221, 222,
226, 229; to sell 194, 226; to use 99, 140,
141, 143, 177, 186, 189, 198; to use up/
misuse 100, 103–6, 177, 188, 198–9; of way
(*via*) 189
Rousseau, Jean-Jacques 56, 110, 146, 147, 154,
159–65, 166, 171–3, 175, 176, 228, 235
Rufinus 132
Rutherforth, Thomas 143, 147

Saint-Etienne, Jean-Paul Rabat de, 229
Sallust 211
Samuel ben Judah, translator of Averroes 39
Sapphira *see* Ananias
Saturn 122, 130
savagery, state of 139, 173; *see also* stages
theory
Savigny, Frederick Karl von 178
schism 65; *see also* Donatists
Seneca 112, 113, 117, 123–5, 126, 127, 137
Sepulveda, Juan Ginés de 210
servitudes 186–90, 191
Servius Sulpicius Rufus 190, 192
Sieyès, Abbé, 226, 230, 236
slavery, slaves 4, 15, 20, 88, 108, 120, 129, 145, 190,
208–11, 223–4, 233
Smith, Adam 139, 220, 235
sociability 138, 141, 158, 161, 172, 214, 219
socialism 59
society, civil 141, 148, 151–76, 205, 230, 235; moral
164–8; tribal 158
Socrates 2, 8, 16, 19, 25, 31, 33, 34, 46
Solomon 96
Sparta/ Spartiates 19–20, 24
Spirituals 82, 85, 98; *see also* Franciscans; Olivi,
Peter

stages (stadial) theory 139–42, 157, 159, 160, 171, 172, 174, 235
Stoicism/Stoics: and communality 35, 126, 156; and Golden Age myth 109, 111, 123; and Natural Law Theory 4, 57, 211, 213–14; and objective standard of justice 180; and property 111–15, 208; reception of 138; wise man, 89; *see also oikeiosis*; Chrysippus; Cicero; Epictetus; Panaetius; Posidonius; Seneca; Zeno
Strauss, Leo 20
Stuart monarchs 137, 143
Suarez, Francisco 207, 219

Tacitus 211
tax 12, 55, 228
Tertullian 18
theatre exemplum 113–17, 132, 137, 216
Theodore, despot of Mistra 32, 54
Theodore of Gaza 57
Theodoret 18
Theodosian Code 201
Therapeutae 69–71
Tiberius Gracchus 194
Timaeus, historian 21, 22, 23
timocracy 20
Toullier, Charles 178
traders 47, 55
tutor/tutela 190
Twelve Tables 191, 194

Ulpian 107, 119–20, 180, 186, 188–90, 191, 192, 197–8, 208

unity 26, 27, 29, 32, 39, 40, 49, 108, 233
usucapio 115
usufruct 99, 186, 188, 189, 198
usurpatio 116, 118, 126, 147, 164, 165
usus facti, simplex 100, 101–3, 134, 203
usus pauper 100–1

Vacarius 195
Valla, Lorenzo 45
Villey, Michel 99, 179, 184, 186, 187, 188–90, 207
Virgil 110, 122, 129–30
Virginia 223–4
Virginian Bill of Rights 222, 227
virtues 155; wealth as a virtue 41
vita apostolica 3, 85, 87, 98
Vitoria, Franciscus de 209, 219
Vultejus, Hermann 201

war 138, 141, 160, 163, 164, 172
will, free 166, 169–70, 174, 175
William of Conches 34
Wilson, James 222–3, 224
women: in Plato/Platonists 6, 8, 10, 11, 14, 17, 18, 20, 23, 24, 29, 34, 38, 42, 49, 50, 54, 88; in Averroes 39–40

Xenophanes 23

Zacchaeus 68
Zasius, Ulrich 177, 198, 199
Zeno 123, 213

IDEAS IN CONTEXT

Edited by
Quentin Skinner and James Tully

1 RICHARD RORTY, J. B. SCHNEEWIND and QUENTIN SKINNER (eds.)
Philosophy in History
Essays in the Historiography of Philosophy
pb 978 0 521 27330 5

2 J. G. A. POCOCK
Virtue, Commerce and History
Essays on Political Thought and History, Chiefly in the Eighteenth Century
pb 978 0 521 27660 3

3 M. M. GOLDSMITH
Private Vices, Public Benefits
Bernard Mandeville's Social and Political Thought
hb 978 0 521 30036 0

4 ANTHONY PAGDEN (ed.)
The Languages of Political Theory in Early Modern Europe
pb 978 0 521 38666 1

5 DAVID SUMMERS
The Judgment of Sense
Renaissance Nationalism and the Rise of Aesthetics
pb 978 0 521 38631 9

6 LAURENCE DICKEY
Hegel: Religion, Economics and the Politics of Spirit, 1770–1807
pb 978 0 521 38912 9

7 MARGO TODD
Christian Humanism and the Puritan Social Order
pb 978 0 521 89228 5

8 LYNN SUMIDA JOY
Gassendi the Atomist
Advocate of History in an Age of Science
pb 978 0 521 52239 7

9 EDMUND LEITES (ed.)
Conscience and Casuistry in Early Modern Europe
pb 978 0 521 52020 1

10 WOLF LEPENIES
Between Literature and Science: The Rise of Sociology
pb 978 0 521 33810 3

11 TERENCE BALL, JAMES FARR and RUSSELL L. HANSON (eds.)
Political Innovation and Conceptual Change
pb 978 0 521 35978 8

12 GERD GIGERENZER *et al.*
The Empire of Chance
How Probability Changed Science and Everyday Life
pb 978 0 521 39838 1

13 PETER NOVICK
That Nobel Dream
The 'Objectivity Question' and the American Historical Profession
hb 978 0 521 34328 2 pb: 978 0 521 35745 6

14 DAVID LIEBERMAN
The Province of Legislation Determined
Legal Theory on Eighteenth-Century Britain
pb 978 0 521 52854 2

15 DANIEL PICK
Faces of Degeneration
A European Disorder, c.1848–c.1918
pb 978 0 521 45753 8

16 KEITH BAKER
Inventing the French Revolution
Essays on French Political Culture in the Eighteenth Century
pb 978 0 521 38578 7

17 IAN HACKING
The Taming of Chance
hb 978 0 521 38014 0 pb 978 0 521 38884 9

18 GISELA BOCK, QUENTIN SKINNER and MAURIZIO VIROLI (eds.)
Machiavelli and Republicanism
pb 978 0 521 43589 5

19 DOROTHY ROSS
The Origins of American Social Science
pb 978 0 521 42836 1

20 KLAUS CHRISTIAN KOHNKE
The Rise of Neo-Kantianism
German Academic Philosophy between Idealism and Positivism
hb 978 0 521 37336 4

21 IAN MACLEAN
Interpretation and Meaning in the Renaissance
The Case of Law
hb 978 0 521 41546 0 pb 978 0 521 02027 5

22 MAURIZIO VIROLI
From Politics to Reason of State
The Acquisition and Transformation of the Language of Politics 1250–1600
hb 978 0 521 41493 7 pb 978 0 521 67343 3

23 MARTIN VAN GELDEREN
The Political Thought of the Dutch Revolt 1555–1590
hb 978 0 521 39204 4 pb 978 0 521 89163 9

24 NICHOLAS PHILLIPSON and QUENTIN SKINNER (eds.)
Political Discourse in Early Modern Britain
hb 978 0 521 39242 6

25 JAMES TULLY
An Approach to Political Philosophy: Locke in Contexts
hb 978 0 521 43060 9 pb 978 0 521 43638 0

26 RICHARD TUCK
Philosophy and Government 1572–1651
pb 978 0 521 43885 8

27 RICHARD R. YEO
Defining Science
William Whewell, Natural Knowledge and Public Debate in Early Victorian Britain
hb 978 0 521 43182 8 pb 978 0 521 54116 9

28 MARTIN WARNKE
The Court Artist
The Ancestry of the Modern Artist
hb 978 0 521 36375 4

29 PETER N. MILLER
Defining the Common Good
Empire, Religion and Philosophy in Eighteenth-Century Britain
hb 978 0 521 44259 6 pb 978 0 521 61712 3

30 CHRISTOPHER J. BERRY
The Idea of Luxury
A Conceptual and Historical Investigation
pb 978 0 521 46691 2

31 E. J. HUNDERT
The Enlightenment's 'Fable'
Bernard Mandeville and the Discovery of Society
hb 978 0 521 46082 8 pb 978 0 521 61942 4

32 JULIA STAPLETON
Englishness and the Study of Politics
The Social and Political Thought of Ernest Barker
hb 978 0 521 46125 2 pb 978 0 521 02444 0

33 KEITH TRIBE
Strategies of Economic Order
German Economic Discourse, 1750–1950
hb 978 0 521 46291 4 pb 978 0 521 61943 1

34 SACHIKO KUSUKAWA
The Transformation of Natural Philosophy
The Case of Philip Melancthon
hb 978 0 521 47347 7 pb 978 0 521 03046 5

35 DAVID ARMITAGE, ARMAND HIMY and QUENTIN SKINNER (eds.)
Milton and Republicanism
hb 978 0 521 55178 6 pb 978 0 521 64648 2

36 MARKKU PELTONEN
Classical Humanism and Republicanism in English Political Thought 1570–1640
hb 978 0 521 49695 7 pb 978 0 521 61716 1

37 PHILIP IRONSIDE
The Social and Political Thought of Bertrand Russell
The Development of an Aristocratic Liberalism
hb 978 0 521 47383 5 pb 978 0 521 02476 1

38 NANCY CARTWRIGHT, JORDI CAT, LOLA FLECK and THOMAS E. UEBEL
Otto Neurath: Philosophy Between Science and Politics
hb 978 0 521 45174 1

39 DONALD WINCH
Riches and Poverty
An Intellectual History of Political Economy in Britain, 1750–1834
pb 978 0 521 55920 1

40 JENNIFER PLATT
A History of Sociological Research Methods in America
hb 978 0 521 44173 5 pb 978 0 521 64649 9

41 KNUD HAAKONSSEN (ed.)
Enlightenment and Religion
Rational Dissent in Eighteenth-Century Britain
hb 978 0 521 56060 3 pb 978 0 521 02987 2

42 G. E. R. LLOYD
Adversaries and Authorities
Investigations into Ancient Greek and Chinese Science
hb 978 0 521 55331 5 pb 978 0 521 55695 8

43 ROLF LINDNER
The Reportage of Urban Culture
Robert Park and the Chicago School
hb 978 0 521 44052 3 pb 978 0 521 02653 6

44 ANNABEL BRETT
Liberty, Right and Nature
Individual Rights in Later Scholastic Thought
hb 978 0 521 56239 3 pb 978 0 521 54340 8

45 STEWART J. BROWN (ed.)
William Robertson and the Expansion of Empire
hb 978 0 521 57083 1

46 HELENA ROSENBLATT
Rousseau and Geneva
From the First Discourse *to the* Social Contract, *1749–1762*
hb 978 0 521 57004 6 pb 978 0 521 03395 4

47 DAVID RUNCIMAN
Pluralism and the Personality of the State
hb 978 0 521 55191 5 pb 978 0 521 02263 7

48 ANNABEL PATTERSON
Early Modern Liberalism
hb 978 0 521 59260 4 pb 978 0 521 02631 4

49 DAVID WEINSTEIN
Equal Freedom and Utility
Herbert Spencer's Liberal Utilitarianism
hb 978 0 521 62264 6 pb 978 0 521 02686 4

50 YUN LEE TOO and NIALL LIVINGSTONE (eds.)
Pedagogy and Power
Rhetorics of Classical Learning
hb 978 0 521 59435 6

51 REVIEL NETZ
The Shaping of Deduction in Greek Mathematics
A Study in Cognitive History
hb 978 0 521 62279 0 pb 978 0 521 54120 6

52 MARY MORGAN and MARGARET MORRISON (eds.)
Models as Mediators
hb 978 0 521 65097 7 pb 978 0 521 65571 2

53 JOEL MICHELL
Measurement in Psychology
A Critical History of a Methodological Concept
hb 978 0 521 62120 5 pb 978 0 521 02151 7

54 RICHARD A. PRIMUS
   The American Language of Rights
   hb 978 0 521 65250 6 pb 978 0 521 61621 8

55 ROBERT ALUN JONES
   The Development of Durkheim's Social Realism
   hb 978 0 521 65045 8 pb 978 0 521 02210 1

56 ANNE MCLAREN
   Political culture in the Reign of Elizabeth I
   Queen and Commonwealth 1558–1585
   hb 978 0 521 65144 8 pb 978 0 521 02483 9

57 JAMES HANKINS (ed)
   Renaissance Civic Humanism
   Reappraisals and Reflections
   hb 978 0 521 78090 2 pb 978 0 521 54807 6

58 T. J. HOCHSTRASSER
   Natural Law Theories in the Early Enlightenment
   hb 978 0 521 66193 5 pb 978 0 521 02787 8

59 DAVID ARMITAGE
   The Ideological Origins of the British Empire
   hb 978 0 521 59081 5 pb 978 0 521 78978 3

60 IAN HUNTER
   Rival Enlightenments
   Civil and Metaphysical Philosophy in Early Modern Germany
   hb 978 0 521 79265 3 pb 978 0 521 02549 2

61 DARIO CASTIGLIONE and IAIN HAMPSHER-MONK (eds.)
   The History of Political Thought in National Context
   hb 978 0 521 78234 0

62 IAN MACLEAN
   Logic, Signs and Nature in the Renaissance
   The Case of Learned Medicine
   hb 978 0 521 80648 0

63 PETER MACK
   Elizabethan Rhetoric
   Theory and Practice
   hb 978 0 521 81292 4 pb 978 0 521 02099 2

64 GEOFFREY LLOYD
   The Ambitions of Curiosity
   Understanding the World in Ancient Greece and China
   hb 978 0 521 81542 0 pb 978 0 521 89461 6

65 MARKKU PELTONEN
The Duel in Early Modern England
Civility, Politeness and Honour
hb 978 0 521 82062 2 pb 978 0 521 02520 1

66 ADAM SUTCLIFFE
Judaism and Enlightenment
hb 978 0 521 82015 8 pb 978 0 521 67232 0

67 ANDREW FITZMAURICE
Humanism and America
An Intellectual History of English Colonisation, 1500–1625
hb 978 0 521 82225 1

68 PIERRE FORCE
Self-Interest before Adam Smith
A Genealogy of Economic Science
hb 978 0 521 83060 7

69 ERIC NELSON
The Greek Tradition in Republican Thought
hb 978 0 521 83545 9 pb 978 0 521 02428 0

70 HARRO HOPFL
Jesuit Political Thought
The Society of Jesus and the State, c.1540–1640
hb 978 0 521 83779 8

71 MIKAEL HORNQVIST
Machiavelli and Empire
hb 978 0 521 83945 7

72 DAVID COLCLOUGH
Freedom of Speech in Early Stuart England
hb 978 0 521 84748 3

73 JOHN ROBERTSON
The Case for the Enlightenment
Scotland and Naples 1680–1760
hb 978 0 521 84787 2

74 DANIEL CAREY
Locke, Shaftesbury, and Hutcheson
Contesting Diversity in the Enlightenment and Beyond
hb 978 0 521 84502 1

75 ALAN CROMARTIE
The Constitutionalist Revolution
An Essay on the History of England, 1450–1642
hb 978 0 521 78269 2

76 HANNAH DAWSON
Locke, Language and Early-Modern Philosophy
hb 978 0 521 85271 5

77 CONAL CONDREN, STEPHEN GAUKROGER and IAN HUNTER (eds.)
The Philosopher in Early Modern Europe
The Nature of a Contested Identity
hb 978 0 521 86646 0

78 ANGUS GOWLAND
The Worlds of Renaissance Melancholy
Robert Burton in Context
hb 978 0 521 86768 9

79 PETER STACEY
Roman Monarchy and the Renaissance Prince
hb 978 0 521 86989 8

80 RHODRI LEWIS
Language, Mind and Nature
Artificial Languages in England from Bacon to Locke
hb 978 0 521 87475 0

81 DAVID LEOPOLD
The Young Karl Marx
German Philosophy, Modern Politics, and Human Flourishing
hb 978 0 521 87477 9

82 JON PARKIN
Taming the Leviathan
*The Reception of the Political and Religious Ideas of Thomas Hobbes in England
1640–1700*
hb 978 0 521 87735 0

83 D WEINSTEIN
Utilitarianism and the New Liberalism
hb 978 0 521 87528 8

84 LUCY DELAP
The Feminist Avant-Garde
Transatlantic Encounters of the Early Twentieth Century
hb 978 0 521 87651 3

85 BORIS WISEMAN
Lévi-Strauss, Anthropology and Aesthetics
hb 978 0 521 87529 5

86 DUNCAN BELL (ed)
Victorian Visions of Global Order
Empire and International Relations in Nineteenth-Century Political Thought
hb 978 0 521 88292 7

87 IAN HUNTER
The Secularisation of the Confessional State
The Political Thought of Christian Thomasius
hb 978 0 521 88055 8

88 CHRISTIAN J EMDEN
Friedrich Nietzsche and the Politics of History
hb 978 0 521 88056 5

89 ANNELEIEN DE DIJN
French Political Thought from Montesquieu to Tocqueville
Liberty in a Levelled Society?
hb 978 0 521 87788 6

90 PETER GARNSEY
Thinking about Property
From Antiquity to the Age of Revolution
hb 978 0 521 87677 3 pb 978 0 521 70023 8